NO LONGER PROPERTY OF
SEATTLE PUBLIC LIBRARY

FROM
HANG TIME
TO
PRIME TIME

FROM HANG TIME TO PRIME TIME

BUSINESS, ENTERTAINMENT, AND THE BIRTH OF THE MODERN-DAY NBA

PETE CROATTO

ATRIA BOOKS

NEW YORK   LONDON   TORONTO   SYDNEY   NEW DELHI

ATRIA
BOOKS

An Imprint of Simon & Schuster, Inc.
1230 Avenue of the Americas
New York, NY 10020

Copyright © 2020 by Peter Croatto

All rights reserved, including the right to reproduce this book or portions thereof in any form whatsoever. For information, address Atria Books Subsidiary Rights Department, 1230 Avenue of the Americas, New York, NY 10020.

First Atria Books hardcover edition December 2020

ATRIA BOOKS and colophon are trademarks of Simon & Schuster, Inc.

For information about special discounts for bulk purchases, please contact Simon & Schuster Special Sales at 1-866-506-1949 or business@simonandschuster.com.

The Simon & Schuster Speakers Bureau can bring authors to your live event. For more information, or to book an event, contact the Simon & Schuster Speakers Bureau at 1-866-248-3049 or visit our website at www.simonspeakers.com.

Interior design by Jill Putorti

Manufactured in the United States of America

1 3 5 7 9 10 8 6 4 2

Library of Congress Cataloging-in-Publication Data has been applied for.

ISBN 978-1-9821-0395-8
ISBN 978-1-9821-0397-2 (ebook)

For Laura and Olivia,
the ultimate home court advantage

CONTENTS

CONTENTS

In most cases, cultural transition is gradual, intelligible only in retrospect, like the last days of a marriage. Revolution doesn't usually doesn't rush in, like brick through the glass. . . .

—SAM WASSON, *FOSSE*

Evolution, man. It just changed. That's just the way it is.

—NBA LEGEND GEORGE GERVIN, TO THE AUTHOR

TIMELINE OF NOTABLE EVENTS

1975—Larry O'Brien is named NBA commissioner.

1976—The American Basketball Association "merges" with the NBA.

1978—Attorney David Stern agrees to work full-time for the NBA.

1979—Larry Bird and Magic Johnson enter the NBA; ESPN debuts; "Rapper's Delight" hits airwaves.

1982—NBA Entertainment is formed; Ted Shaker starts as executive producer for *The NBA on CBS*.

February 1983—Marvin Gaye performs the national anthem at the NBA All-Star Game.

March 1983—The NBA and the Players Association agree on a salary cap.

September 1983—The NBA and the Players Association agree on a drug policy.

January 1984—The NBA hosts its first All-Star Weekend, featuring the Slam Dunk Contest and Old-Timers Game, in Denver.

February 1984—Stern succeeds O'Brien as NBA commissioner.

TIMELINE OF NOTABLE EVENTS

October 1984—Michael Jordan debuts with the Chicago Bulls.

April 1985—The first Air Jordans from Nike are released nationwide.

February 1986—All-Star Weekend introduces the Three-Point Shootout.

October 1987—The Milwaukee Bucks win the first McDonald's Open, an international basketball tournament.

1988—Spike Lee and Michael Jordan star in their first Nike commercial.

November 1989—The first wave of star European players, including Russians Alexander Volkov and Sarunas Marciulionis, make their NBA debuts; NBC acquires the rights to air the NBA.

INTRODUCTION

OUR GAME

Derek Fisher's debut performance on *Dancing with the Stars* was normal—if you weren't a basketball fan. The trim former Los Angeles Lakers point guard donned a glittery, hoops-themed costume while strutting to a whitewashed version of Kurtis Blow's old-school rap classic "Basketball." (Basketball is my favorite sport / I like the way they dribble up and down the court.) But NBA Twitter—one of the numerous cliques of the massive social media time suck—was bewildered and amused by this bite-sized piece of "entertainment," which provided a hilarious distraction from Donald Trump's alarmist blather and the daily ennui of life in America. As a sports fan, you beheld Kobe Bryant's former teammate, a five-time NBA champion, in his retirement and asked yourself, "What the hell?"

The goofy transience of Fisher's prime-time spectacle—who knew dribbling a basketball could preface a sexy, shimmying salsa routine—obscured a greater historical significance. Here was a black man, representing an overwhelmingly black sport, strutting to a rap classic on a popular network program. And this program was like *The Lawrence Welk Show* with a shorter hemline, which enthralled the portion of America that shied away from edgier fare on Netflix, Hulu, and cable

1

TV. Such a confluence of circumstances would have caused a near-riot thirty-five years ago. Unabashedly black culture thrust front and center would have made white people uncomfortable. The calls to ABC would have been ceaseless and ugly.

In 2017, Fisher's hoofing provided fodder for the bottomless trough of NBA Twitter and a way for nearly 11 million people to spend another Monday night. At the very least, it thrilled Fisher's immediate family.

"This is literally my mom's favorite show on earth," Fisher said.

Pro basketball had traveled a long way to reach this point. Between Bill Russell's trailblazing leadership (yes, a black man can coach) and Michael Jordan's status as the world's pitchman (yes, a black man can sell underwear), the NBA had an interminable and frequently painful puberty. Countless whites couldn't accept the game's changing demographics—as well as the changing demographics of the country. The sport was dominated by black men, so it was natural that their influence would spread from within, especially since sports, in its simplest definition, is entertainment. James A. Michener portrayed the frustration in his 1976 nonfiction book, *Sports in America*. One sports fan told the historical novelist that "in basketball you sit right on the playing floor and the men are almost undressed and their blackness hits you right in the face." Another suggested that since African-Americans (at the time) consisted of 12 percent of the population, that was exactly the percentage of players that should have been represented in the NBA.

"From here on out it's their game," the anonymous sports fan declared, "not mine."

The narrative of the NBA's rise to become arguably the world's second-most popular sport is frequently summed up as a rapid-fire afterthought: *BirdMagicMichaelStern*. That's Larry Bird, Magic Johnson,

Michael Jordan, and longtime NBA commissioner David Stern (for those who grew up without Brent Musburger as their Fred Rogers). That is correct, but it neglects the myriad of social, cultural, and business factors that contributed to Derek Fisher sashaying in sequins.

February 13, 1983, led to September 19, 2017. Marvin Gaye's sexy, smooth interpretation of the national anthem at the 1983 NBA All-Star Game in Los Angeles is now considered a classic, a worthy competitor to Whitney Houston's majestic performance at Super Bowl XXV, right as America entered the first Gulf War. But Gaye's version did not receive automatic approval. Lon Rosen, then the Lakers' director of promotions, and his boss, Bob Steiner, sent one thousand letters to aggrieved parties. The phones at the Great Western Forum, where the Lakers played, glowed with indignation.

Gaye's anthem lasted two minutes and thirty-five seconds. As soon as he opened his mouth, turning Francis Scott Key's stodgy jingoistic dirge into baby-making music, the forever cool crooner officially signaled the change that was taking place in the NBA. The performance was a tacit admission that pro basketball wasn't going to play to the establishment. The NBA—and popular culture—was evolving, and it was too much fun to ignore. America had to catch up, whether it wanted to or not.

But Marvin Gaye is one in the lengthy roster of men and women who helped initiate a series of changes that occurred from 1975 to 1989. Those years led to today's NBA.

This book examines how that happened. What may surprise readers is that much of the action takes place away from the court, in conference rooms and offices, in soundstages and recording booths. The NBA reached its true success once it started thinking beyond ten players on the floor—"Madison Avenue bullshit," to quote sportswriter and essayist Howard Bryant. Stern, who became commissioner in 1984, knew it needed to be cultivated, protected, and spread to any place where a ten-foot hoop could be secured. "We're Disney," Stern said once, and believed it constantly. If Stern was Walt Disney with a David Mamet character's vocabulary, then Michael Jordan was Mickey Mouse with hang time, a universally recognizable symbol who exemplified a family-friendly brand.

As David Stern worked his way from Larry O'Brien's consigliere to Godfather and Larry and Magic were sexing up fundamentals, allies aligned. Cable television, led by a twenty-four-hour cable station called ESPN, provided a perfect platform for NBA highlights with *SportsCenter*. VHS tapes helped spread the message. Rap was inching into Top 40 radio and its upbeat, pulsating rhythm gave the NBA a soundtrack—plus, later, a way to court the kids. A company known for running shoes was poised to take it to the hoop, revolutionizing sports marketing with the unlikeliest of icons—a black national spokesperson. These embryonic symbols of cool became cultural landmarks of our lives—the click of a play button, a swoosh, an adroitly edited highlight, rhyming to a prerecorded beat—that we frequently enjoyed at once.

Derek Fisher's fancy footwork was no joke; Kurtis Blow enjoyed Fisher's performance. It was the latest page in the NBA's new history, one that was part of our world, not a world apart.

THE POLITICIAN,
THE DOCTOR, AND THE BRAT

Feet on the desk in his corner office located high above Madison Square Garden, NBA commissioner Larry O'Brien exuded corporate confidence. O'Brien chatted for two hours with a reporter, smoking cigarette after cigarette, basking in the glow of a job well done. Not two years into his regime, and the former Democratic Party chairman—who had helped bring John F. Kennedy to power and sat opposite his coffin on Air Force One—was a star. And he had a seven-year, $2 million contract to prove it.

Despite having no experience working in professional sports, O'Brien had been recruited by his predecessor, the beleaguered J. Walter Kennedy. John G. Stewart, a longtime aide to Senator Hubert Humphrey, couldn't believe the news. *Larry is going to do what?* But O'Brien had provided gravitas and stability to the NBA, resolving two labor-related hassles that had become profanities—the Oscar Robertson suit and, most notably, the interminable standoff with the NBA's rival, the American Basketball Association.

The impact of the ABA's open, freestyling play was undeniable. Ten former ABAers had played in last month's All-Star Game, and what a game that was. The public had gotten to see "what the NBA is all about more than anything you could articulate," O'Brien said. The 125–124 nail-biter was "a whale of a game," he added, that highlighted the players' heart and hustle—the qualities that detractors, undoubtedly white and older, believed were lacking. Plus, it had been a showcase for the game's MVP, Julius Erving, whose otherworldly acrobatics would surely grant the NBA a place next to Major League Baseball and the National Football League in America's living room.

Larry O'Brien had much to celebrate, so he entertained a reporter's philosophical detour about sports' status in society.

He reclined in his high-back chair, lit yet another cigarette—he had wisely switched from the tar-heavy Camels of his political days—and unknowingly summarized the world of chaos the NBA had to navigate.

"Sports is not isolated from society," O'Brien began in his booming New England croak. "We are not an island unto ourselves. Sports at all levels is an integral part of American society. It's a rare young person, boy or girl, that hasn't had some exposure to participation in sports. It's a healthy situation. It adds a dimension to free society."

O'Brien thought limits were good. He didn't want basketball, or any sport, "to become so involving" that it ruled people's lives.

"There has to be a rule of normality in a healthy society," he concluded.

Larry O'Brien had orchestrated and endured a lifetime of societal change. In 1952, he had directed the senatorial campaign of an ambitious, wavy-haired congressman from Massachusetts. A little more than eight years later, JFK sat in the Oval Office, and O'Brien had cemented his reputation as a first-rate political operator.

The former bartender had begun "The O'Brien Manual" when he ran Massachusetts congressman Foster Furcolo's campaign in the late 1940s. By 1960, several pages of instructions for local workers had ballooned to a not-so-little black book of sixty-four bound pages, a complete blueprint for every Kennedy campaign.

"Its burden is that every vote counts," Theodore H. White wrote in his classic *The Making of the President 1960.* "That every citizen likes to feel he is somehow wired into the structure of power; that making a man or woman seem useful or important to himself (or herself) in the power system of American life takes advantage of one of the simplest and noblest urges of politics in the most effective way." White provided a brilliant example of that theory in action. During Kennedy's 1958 Senate campaign, 256,000 Massachusetts citizens signed nominating petitions. Some 1,800 residents wanted to volunteer for Kennedy but had little to do. O'Brien tasked those volunteers to write each petition signee a thank-you note. He did not solely traffic in Emily Post niceties. At the 1960 Democratic National Convention in Los Angeles, O'Brien established a system of walkie-talkies and telephones between each delegation's headquarters and the convention floor, allowing for instant, twenty-four-hour-a-day communication.

In the White House, O'Brien enjoyed "the all-out backing of the President himself." The understanding on Capitol Hill was that anybody who wanted to run policy by Kennedy had to speak with O'Brien first. And befitting a man of influence, he had made the cover of *Time.*

O'Brien remained influential after Kennedy's assassination, serving on Lyndon B. Johnson's staff and being named postmaster general in 1965. What was remarkable was that the two developed a steady, respectful rapport despite JFK and his staff putting the master politician "out to pasture," said Wilbur Mills, then chairman of the House Ways and Means Committee. Kennedy, like every president before or since, was content to keep his vice president from having true impact. "No good politician," Doris Kearns Goodwin wrote, "willingly cedes power to another politician he cannot control." Johnson "detested every minute" of the ceremonial role.

As Johnson focused on the Vietnam War, O'Brien landed the authority to negotiate substantial changes in the administration's stalled legislation. In 1965, he won approval of 84 of the 87 major bills proposed by the White House, and in 1966, 97 of 113 measures proposed got approved. Among the bills passed in O'Brien's White House career: those creating the Peace Corps and the Alliance for Progress, Medicare, the model cities program, the Civil Rights Act of 1964, related voting rights legislation, a nuclear test ban treaty, and increased aid to education.

The gentle ethos of Camelot soured: the morass of the Vietnam War, the growing influence of young protestors, and the rise of Richard Nixon. O'Brien, who knew that his boss equated honesty with disloyalty, told Johnson his chances to win the presidency in 1968 were slim. O'Brien then resigned as postmaster general. Johnson, battered and exhausted, decided not to seek reelection. Opportunities awaited. The ink was barely dry on O'Brien's resignation letter when he was invited to helm Robert Kennedy's presidential run—and to have another front-row view of incomprehensible tragedy. He then joined Hubert Humphrey's campaign, which was plagued by several issues, notably divisiveness in the party. Some liberals saw little difference between the former vice president and Nixon, who won in a rout.

Four years later, O'Brien was a late addition to George McGovern's campaign. This was after McGovern had asked O'Brien to stay on for a third term as Democratic National Committee chairman—until he suddenly named Jean Westwood to the post. The "three worst months of [O'Brien's] life" culminated in McGovern coldly rebuffing O'Brien as his vice president on the ticket: "You're identified as a politician, and we feel we should stay away from a political image." McGovern was doomed to defeat. He didn't have the support of moderates and big labor. The loathing on the floor of the Democratic National Convention was palpable, political insider Joseph Califano recalled.

Gary Hart, the future Colorado senator and presidential hopeful, was a young lawyer working for the McGovern campaign. He believed the tumultuous, protest-heavy 1968 Democratic National Convention caused a division within the Democratic Party. No longer were "the

regulars of the party establishment"—state chairs and county chairs—
in charge. It was people whose *instincts* were Democratic. Party loy-
alists hadn't gotten McGovern nominated, but, rather, newcomers
who "were cause-oriented, not party-oriented," Hart said. In explor-
ing White's dwindling influence as a chronicler of modern-day politics
as younger, tradition-smashing New Journalists like Timothy Crouse
(*The Boys on the Bus*) and Joe McGinniss (*The Selling of the President*)
took over, *Esquire*'s Nora Ephron deftly summarized O'Brien's status:
"Larry O'Brien used to be important; now it was these kids." He turned
fifty-five in 1972, a Beltway fossil. The party he had dedicated his heart
and soul to since he passed out fliers and organized car pools to the
polls in Springfield as a teenager had no use for him.

"We were all sort of out in the wilderness," said John G. Stewart.
"Unless you're obviously wired in to where the power is, people very
quickly don't give a damn what you think."

O'Brien kept busy. He ran a consulting firm. He reentered the public eye when burglars broke into his office at the Watergate Hotel. Nixon
considered O'Brien the "Democrats' most professional political operator." That notorious event was preceded by three separate audits by the
Internal Revenue Service, part of "an extensive program of surveillance
and harassment" that flattened him emotionally. After his 1974 autobiography, *No Final Victories*, was released, O'Brien had no specific plans.
Politics was different than other vocations. "You are left with memories
and scrapbooks, but little provision for your later life," he wrote.

Then J. Walter Kennedy called.

O'Brien grew up in the literal birthplace of basketball: Springfield,
Massachusetts. The YMCA stood at the corner of Mattoon Street, an
outlet pass from O'Brien's parents' house. Though he was not a great
player, shooting baskets in the gym turned into "a ritual." The Celtics,

of course, were his team. Before Washington beckoned, O'Brien regularly drove through Massachusetts's brutal winters to see Bob Cousy and Bill Russell build the Celtics mystique at the Boston Garden. His love of the sport made him an anomaly with the Kennedys, a football family, who joked of O'Brien's love of "roundball."

These were swell anecdotes, but they didn't qualify O'Brien to become the National Basketball Association's next commissioner, right?

Kennedy, the league's second commissioner, yearned for retirement. And he wanted O'Brien, whom he knew only through brief exchanges at Madison Square Garden—where O'Brien had season tickets to the Knicks—to succeed him. Kennedy was serious; O'Brien was incredulous. "I had really no knowledge of the operation of the league office," he wrote years later in an unpublished history of his time in the NBA. "I didn't know any of the owners of the NBA teams; I paid no attention to the business operation of the sport. Needless to say, I never envisioned having a direct relationship with sports at any level in any formal sense."

Regardless of O'Brien's interest, J. Walter Kennedy's days were numbered. Basketball was no longer a time-killer for arenas between hockey games. The NBA had a national television contract, something it had lacked as recently as 1964. Spurred by the arrival of the American Basketball Association, it had expanded into the South (Atlanta, New Orleans), Midwest (Milwaukee, Cleveland), and the Pacific Northwest (Portland, Seattle). The Knicks' fabled championship teams of 1970 and 1973—plus the team's location in the media capital of the world—had pushed the NBA into the national spotlight, a feat those great Celtics teams hadn't accomplished. Jay Rosenstein covered sports for *Time* before a lengthy career at CBS Sports. In his five years at the magazine, he can't recall the NBA being discussed for editorial coverage. The Knicks, already the subject of innumerable books, mattered. At one point, the team's star point guard, Walt "Clyde" Frazier, was slated for a cover before he was traded to the Cleveland Cavaliers, said Rosenstein.

He was less a great player but more of "an interesting New York character" with a cool-cat image.

The NBA was proclaimed the sport of the 1970s by more than a few publications. That had happened on Kennedy's watch, but like O'Brien, the ravages of time had turned him into an irrelevancy. He was in his sixties, and he was tired. As the league rounded into a legitimate business, Kennedy—who had handled public relations for both the Basketball Association of America, a precursor to the NBA, and the Harlem Globetrotters when the team was *the* draw for NBA games—was weak, said Paul Snyder, who owned the Buffalo Braves. Michael Burns, Kennedy's assistant from 1970 to 1973, saw an honest, smart man with a crippling lack of imagination. Burns once approached Kennedy with a can't-miss idea: teams should sell basketballs in their colors—that is, orange and blue for the Knicks; white and green for the Celtics. It would be a great way to fill those empty seats—"No team sold out," Burns recalled—and to get vendors for promotions.

"Oh, we can't even touch this!" Kennedy told a stunned Burns. "It's too close to the ABA red, white, and blue basketball."

Burns couldn't understand Kennedy's reluctance. The NBA wasn't yet thirty years old and was writing its history. It lagged behind baseball and football, so it should take risks to differentiate itself. The owners had ideas about some topic, like the league's logo. Inevitably, Kennedy would look up and say, "What has football done?"

"Walter was a plugger," said Pat Williams, the longtime general manager of the Chicago Bulls and Philadelphia 76ers. "He kept at it, did his very best . . . I think everybody realized Walter had a difficult job."

Kennedy's desk featured a little figure of an iron fist. Few were scared off. He possessed, recalled Howard Cosell, a friend, not "a mean bone in his body." Nick Curran, the NBA's public relations director from 1969 to 1976, said that Kennedy was clearly in charge; Williams said the owners respected him. But Cosell felt for his neighbor in tony Stamford, Connecticut, where Kennedy also served as mayor from 1959 to 1963. The famed announcer thought Kennedy had done well given the circumstances. "In perfect honesty—and this has hurt him deep inside—some of the owners have betrayed him and undercut him," he wrote in *Cosell*, one of his many books. "I can recall a lot of dissension," Kennedy's daughter-in-law Bartan Kennedy recalled years later.

Keeping the owners in line was a "huge job" for Kennedy, Pat Williams said, and he wasn't always equal to the task. ABC Sports' Jim Spence believed Kennedy "let himself be controlled and manipulated by the owners who made the most noise." The NBA's contract with ABC was up in 1973. Renewal was thought to be a certainty. ABC Sports president Roone Arledge had turned *Monday Night Football* and Cosell into cultural phenomena and later ran ABC News. Kennedy had worked with ABC for years; the two sides enjoyed a close relationship.

Renewal seemed inevitable until Franklin Mieuli, the Golden State Warriors' irreverent owner, objected at an owners' meeting, Burns recalled: Why are we sticking with ABC? Why aren't we negotiating with other networks? We're selling ourselves too short. Kennedy was agog. "This was heresy," Burns recalled. It was, he said, like saying God was dead.

The commissioner tried to steer the meeting toward decorum, but other owners agreed with Mieuli, notably the Los Angeles Lakers' Jack Kent Cooke and the New York Knicks' Ned Irish. The owners had every right to get the best television deal, and "ABC was not giving us any deal that was worthwhile," Burns said. (In the 1990s, David Stern would transform Turner Sports and NBC into gears in the NBA's relentless cross-promotional machine.)* The vocal opponents outlined

---

*Gil Kerr, NBA Entertainment's director of broadcasting in the mid-1990s, attended the meeting when Stern said Turner Sports would promote games on NBC and vice versa. A Turner executive objected. Stern, in a scene Kerr described as "chilling and brilliant," made it clear there'd be no discussion. "You saw the force of his personality and vision playing out in front of you," Kerr said. "It felt like an historic moment."

their concerns. For the league to gain interest from viewers, a network had to air NBA games when the season started, not months later. And by blacking out local games, viewers would be more inclined to pay for their team's home games when they came to cable television. ABC declined to do either. The network had an agreement to air college football on Saturdays, and to put the NBA against Sunday's NFL games was a notion Spence deemed "crazy." Mieuli seethed.

"We had established ourselves as a clear leader in television sports in America, and here's this owner of a basketball team kind of screaming at Roone Arledge," said Spence, then ABC Sports' vice president of program planning. *This* was heresy.

As part of its agreement with ABC, the NBA had to make a "good faith effort" to negotiate with the network, which also had the right of first refusal. The owners and the NBA's representative, Barry Frank, a former ABC Sports employee, didn't want to be bothered with such formalities. Plus, according to Arledge, Cooke already had a commitment from CBS without the restrictions. In February 1973, Frank, Cooke, and his associates met in the bar at the Barbizon-Plaza Hotel on Central Park South.* The purpose of the get-together, according to Los Angeles Lakers attorney Alan Rothenberg, Frank later testified, was to "find as many ways as we can . . . [to] fuck ABC."

"My memory is so friggin' vague of that," Frank said years later. "I should remember it better, but I just don't."

One clause was particularly ingenious, Arledge thought: the network that got the NBA rights had to air that week's game every Saturday between 2 p.m. and 3 p.m. from October to December. That time frame, not coincidentally, was when ABC aired college football. The network had no choice but to reject the deal.

The NBA went to CBS, but Arledge was a vengeful god. He had no

---

*In his memoir, Arledge wrote that it was at the Plaza hotel.

intention to quietly concede. Not to Lakers owner Jack Kent Cooke, whom he deemed a collector of teams—he also owned the NFL's Washington Redskins—and a cheapskate. Not to Franklin Mieuli, who questioned his instincts on sports television. Arledge unleashed irresistible programming opposite the NBA's games: a second edition of the immensely popular *Wide World of Sports* and *Superstars*. The latter was, to quote Arledge, "an unapologetic ratings grabber" where pro athletes competed against each other in other sports. The idea came from Barry Frank, the erstwhile ABC Sports employee turned NBA ally.

"Roone's Revenge" summarized the NBA's second-class-citizen status in the early 1970s and beyond. After all the contract chicanery that led to a desired deal, NBA games were getting slaughtered by Rod Laver and Joe Frazier running the 100-yard dash. Franchises eked out a living. In 1970, three out of the league's fourteen teams—the Milwaukee Bucks, the New York Knicks, and the Los Angeles Lakers—made nearly 50 percent of the league's gate receipts. Few teams felt secure in their current digs, shacks compared to today's gigantic odes to commerce. Even the storied Boston Celtics considered a move to Long Island, New York. If Kennedy possessed the composed brilliance of the NFL's Pete Rozelle or the sober authority of baseball's Bowie Kuhn, maybe pro basketball might have been taken more seriously. But Kennedy lacked the proper gravitas. He'd host owners, his employers, in his hotel suite barefoot and in pajamas, recalled Paul Snyder, the Braves owner, embarrassed at the memory nearly fifty years later. Kennedy was a notorious spendthrift who once questioned why two days' worth of ice was ordered for an NBA event: "Why couldn't you save it? Why did you have to order it twice?" Kennedy clearly favored established franchises—after all, they held the power—a stance that didn't sit well with the newer franchises.

"With Walter as commissioner, I didn't feel like I was part of a first-class organization," Snyder said. "I thought it was ridiculous." Near the end of his term, Snyder practically ceased talking to Kennedy. "It was utter chaos," said Sam Shulman, the Seattle Supersonics' owner, in 1983. The NBA didn't just need a stronger leader; it needed someone who could *play* the part. O'Brien had helped push through the Great Society, so he could get the ABA to merge with the NBA. He carried the aroma of John F. Kennedy, so the NBA would have instant credibility.

"He was a *big deal*," Williams said. "Big deal."

The league had to get him first. Through January and February of 1975, Kennedy courted a reluctant O'Brien with lunches, dinners, and phone calls, stopping short of serenading him outside his bedroom window. "I recognized that he was most anxious to have a successor," O'Brien recalled, "so he could at long last finalize his retirement. He was extremely anxious to accomplish that." Perhaps too anxious—Kennedy had wanted to leave since late 1973, O'Brien later learned.

On March 3, Kennedy and a small group of NBA owners met O'Brien for a pleasant breakfast at the Plaza hotel. As the meal wrapped up, Bob Schmertz of the Boston Celtics asked O'Brien why he felt he was suited to serve as NBA commissioner. O'Brien stopped Schmertz and his tablemates cold.

I am not a candidate for commissioner of the NBA, he told the group.

The misunderstanding festered as the day progressed. Back in his apartment, O'Brien got a phone call from Sam Goldaper, the *New York Times'* basketball writer. You're scheduled to be elected NBA commissioner today. Would you care to comment in advance? O'Brien wondered if he'd said anything construed as acceptance. Hadn't he detailed his intentions? After setting Goldaper straight, O'Brien called Kennedy to explain, once again, that he 1) was not a candidate for commissioner and 2) would not give permission to have his name introduced for election at today's board of governors' meeting.

"Oh God," Kennedy said.

The NBA launched into damage control. Mike Burke, president of the New York Knicks, called O'Brien that afternoon. The board was not screwing around; Burke urged him to reconsider taking the position. Every time O'Brien backed away from the idea of being commissioner, someone from the league tried to pull him back in. Shelly Beychok, an old friend from Louisiana politics and an owner of the New Orleans Jazz, visited O'Brien in his Washington, D.C., apartment. The Atlanta Hawks' John Wilcox, a member of the committee selecting the commissioner, kept appearing at O'Brien's door. Alan Rothenberg, a member of Jack Kent Cooke's inner circle and a candidate for commissioner, offered to throw any support O'Brien's way to ensure a smooth transition.

Wilcox then said the magic words: read the league's bylaws and constitution. O'Brien came away impressed with the authority he'd have to run the league. He could be a strong commissioner. O'Brien's reluctance stemmed from a miserable few months working in a brokerage firm after the Humphrey campaign. But this wasn't counting widgets in some anonymous midtown office. This wasn't just sports, it was pro basketball, the game that he loved. Besides, every job he'd ever had had involved risk.

It was time to bite the bullet.

Nick Curran arrived at his Dobbs Ferry, New York, home exhausted, his sport jacket and shirt soaked in sweat. He smelled terrible. Hours before, Wayne Embry, the general manager of the Milwaukee Bucks, had called requesting a conference call immediately. This was routine. Back then, trades were completed via a conference call between the teams and an NBA official, usually the commissioner or Simon Gourdine, the respected deputy commissioner. Neither was available, so Curran, the league's director of public relations, stepped in.

"Okay," Curran said. "Who are the players involved?" It was June 16, 1975.

That day Curran helped bring Kareem Abdul-Jabbar, the league's premier player, to the Los Angeles Lakers. The historic trade, which featured six players total, set up the Lakers' championship run of the 1980s.

"No league executive had a job description," Curran wrote years later. "We just did what had to be done." That's why Curran lugged the NBA's championship trophy—packed in a crate—from city to city. He checked it at baggage claim with his suitcase.

O'Brien discovered that the staff of sixteen was one of many issues that plagued the NBA. What had driven Kennedy nuts—shaky franchises, an indifferent television audience, owners who had more passion than business savvy—persisted. There was an adjustment period. O'Brien used to ask Curran to stick around after-hours so he could decide on something before holding a press conference. Curran had to remind his new boss that newspapers were being put to bed. Announcements had to be timed for deadlines and to make the evening news. O'Brien's style was based on his experience at the White House, but there was no NBA press corps next door ready to drop everything to hear what O'Brien had to say.

His one professional foray outside politics had been at McDonnell and Company, an arrangement he deemed "disastrous." At first, O'Brien thought the NBA was a replay of that unfortunate time. But he had faced challenges before. He figured the owners had hired him to turn things around. He had a three-year contract. O'Brien got to work. The move that earned O'Brien's respect among the owners, thought Pat Williams, came in June 1975. The Knicks had signed George McGinnis, a former star with the ABA's Indiana Pacers, whose NBA rights were owned by the Philadelphia 76ers, to a six-year, $2.4 million deal. "They just signed him," said Williams, the 76ers general manager at the time. "It was an absolute pirate move." O'Brien ordered the Knicks to rescind the signing, relinquish a first-round pick, and reimburse the 76ers any reasonable expenses.

"He spanked the Knicks real hard for what seemed like just a ridiculous move, in which they thought the new commissioner would not react or wouldn't do anything," Williams said. "Well, he did. I think that got him off to a good start. The other teams were just waiting for O'Brien to deal out major punishment to the Knicks, who thought that they could do anything. If it was good for New York, it was good for the league." No longer would the NBA commissioner be a target. Afterward, Williams noted, "everybody was on their best behavior."

O'Brien's defining triumph happened a year later. The "merger" with the ABA had been blocked by the Oscar Robertson suit, which the Hall of Fame guard had filed in 1970. O'Brien settled that in February 1976. If the league had lost that lawsuit, "they would have been faced with extinction," said agent Richie Phillips, who represented the NBA's referees in its labor disputes. The Oscar Robertson Rule eliminated the "option" or "reserve" clause in the NBA's uniform player contract (which bound a player to one team for life at the team's option) and was the first step toward unrestricted free agency. That cleared the path for an agreement with the ABA, a deal that unfolded with remarkable ease given the animus-filled years of antitrust lawsuits and vying for players. Many would benefit from the deal, but not Robertson, whom Washington Bullets All-Star Phil Chenier considered "the Michael Jordan of his time." Robertson retired in 1974 as an all-time great—he averaged a triple-double in the 1961–62 season—but a man apart. He felt the owners took him off TV for speaking out. No NBA team asked him to coach or work in a front office, positions offered to his lofty brethren with little hesitation. Robertson was okay with the consequences. The rules had to change. He was happy to have made those sacrifices, even if it meant not being embraced by the NBA family.

The ABA's big-money courting of college players and NBA play-ers forced the senior league to pay more to keep its current and fu-ture stars. Players had leverage, an unimaginable perk. As the money increased, agents, the scourge of every traditionalist general manager and owner, entered the picture. The NBA hated the competition, said Peter Gruenberger, who served as counsel for the National Basketball Players Association, because the league always owned the players. The ABA's talent exceeded its reputation as a cash-strapped bush league of gimmicks. Before its 1970–71 championship season, the Milwau-kee Bucks played four preseason games against ABA teams. Bob Dan-dridge, the Bucks' star guard, considered those the toughest games he played all season. Dandridge was relieved not to see ABA stars such as Zelmo Beaty and Willie Wise in games that counted.

"They were playing to prove that they were as good as we were and that they belonged, and we were playing to let them know we were the NBA," Dandridge said. "That we were the top dog. That we were the best. It was pride."

"To me, I wasn't worried about a confidence builder," said James "Jimmy" Jones, a perennial ABA All-Star. "I was confident that we could play with anybody."

The ABA was ultimately defeated by itself. For starters, it wasn't the NBA. When the Kentucky Colonels drafted Dandridge, he turned them down. He had never dreamed of playing in the ABA, he told the club, but he had dreamed of playing in the NBA. The fourth-round NBA draft pick from Norfolk State was content to take his chances. The ABA never had a national television contract. It never trademarked that famous red, white, and blue ball, a surefire moneymaker, you know, for kids. It struggled to maintain fan interest beyond a few cities; franchises folded, moved, and generally struggled to make ends meet like any family wait-ing for the next paycheck. The ABA was "bush league" and not "even reasonably close" to the NBA, said Rick Barry, a star in both leagues. At one game, he remembered, more people sat at the scoring table and the benches than in the stands. Wheezing out an existence was a triumph. In his second stint with the Virginia Squires in 1976, center Swen Nater learned to skip the shower after practice on payday. Instead, he raced to Bank of America. "The first one to the bank gets the cash," he said. "The rest? Maybe not. That's why I got a fast car, man."

"When the ABA first came into existence, there was a lot of papering of the house," said Dan Issel, the Hall of Fame center–power forward for the Kentucky Colonels and Denver Nuggets, two of the ABA's more stable franchises. "A lot of giveaways. A lot of tree tickets. A lot of very cheap tickets. I think kids in Kentucky could come to a Colonels game for fifty cents. As the league got better, obviously salaries went up and they couldn't raise the ticket prices fast enough to make up for all of the good, young players they were getting." Without a national TV contract and with stagnant ticket prices, Issel said, the ABA was doomed. The ABA's founder, Dennis Murphy, wanted to merge with the NBA within three years. Nine years after its first jump ball, the ABA had to face reality. The league was down to seven teams. The Squires were basically penniless, and the Spirits of St. Louis were lucky to draw two thousand fans to a game.

The ABA made the first move on April 16, 1976: Dave DeBusschere, the former Knicks star and the league's seventh commissioner in nine years, and two owners came to O'Brien with a proposal: six ABA teams join the NBA. O'Brien listened and deemed what he heard unrealistic: "We had no guarantee that any ABA clubs coming into the NBA, other than possibly Denver and New York, would attract any fans." O'Brien felt that DeBusschere was being pushed by the ABA owners. The effort, he observed, featured "some elements of near hysteria."

The NBA had incentive to pursue a merger. CBS had promised to pay an additional $5 million in its new television contract if that happened. Explosive ABA arrivals such as Julius Erving and David Thompson could affect viewing habits. "I think the problem with our ratings were that the superstars weren't super enough and the super teams didn't play up to expectations," Bob Wussler, president of CBS Sports, said in May 1976. The year before, the Golden State Warriors won the championship over the heavily favored Washington Bullets. The New York Knicks, beset by key retirements, failed to make the playoffs. "I think the NBA needs new faces," Wussler added, "but the ABA in itself is not that strong to warrant a TV contract."

In mid-June, the ABA and NBA contingents headed to Hyannis, Massachusetts, to make a deal. Six teams went down to four: the San Antonio Spurs, the Denver Nuggets, the Indiana Pacers, and the New York Nets. Their owners would pay $3.2 million each for the honor of joining the NBA. The Nets, soon to become the New Jersey Nets, paid another $4.8 million to atone for encroaching on the Knicks' territory. Players not on those four teams' rosters would enter an NBA dispersal draft. That "never could happen if the four ABA survivors insisted on keeping Kentucky, Virginia, and St. Louis' players," O'Brien wrote. "If that were the case, then all bets were off."

On Thursday, June 17, an agreement was close to being in place, though both sides had reservations. O'Brien went to bed at midnight, but sleep proved elusive. He wanted the agreement done. At 4:30 a.m., O'Brien called a meeting with the ABA delegation. At 8 a.m. he summoned the NBA's advisory group on the merger—a half hour before the board of governors, or fancy-speak for owners, joined the proceedings.

"I told them [the ABA] the deal of yesterday was the deal of now, and I had to ask my board to vote on it by 9 a.m.," O'Brien told Bob Logan of the *Chicago Tribune*.

Or, as O'Brien clarified when he was far away from a reporter's open notebook: "I had tried to put across some of the facts of life and convince the ABA representatives that they were on the verge of going home losers if they didn't face reality."

"The difference between a good negotiator and a bad negotiator is that the good one knows when someone has him by the proverbial balls," San Antonio Spurs owner Angelo Drossos said years later. "Well, at our final merger talks in Hyannis, that was how the NBA had us, and we knew it."

Before O'Brien spoke, Mike Burke of the Knicks and Washington Bullets owner Abe Pollin offered a few brief comments on the merits of the deal—again, pretty much the same one from Wednesday—to the owners. O'Brien's most persuasive argument wasn't Julius Erving's marquee value or the acquisition of three markets away from the Interstate 95 corridor, but the desire to get the hell out of Dunfey's Resort. Thursday was the last day of meetings. Everyone had a flight to catch, so as *Sports Illustrated*'s Frank Deford observed with his characteristic wit, the owners "didn't have time to be selfish."

"Up or down?" O'Brien said.

The meeting lasted forty-four minutes. By the end, the NBA had four new franchises and eighteen owners walked away with $700,000. They also got to keep their share of the TV money, as the four new expansion franchises relinquished that money for four years. "Soon everybody rushed for planes, the ABA guys going first," Deford quipped, "presumably to get to the banks back home before 3 p.m. closing."

"Larry made it work," said the Kansas City Kings' general manager Joe Axelson. "Whenever there was a problem, he seemed to have a solution."

Harvey Benjamin, an attorney working for the NBA, directed anyone talking to the press not to describe the deal as a "merger." Under the technical definition of a merger, Benjamin said, "whatever company survives the merger becomes liable for any debts and obligations and the [other company] then disappears." The four teams were applying for *expansion franchises* because Benjamin didn't want the NBA responsible for any unseen liabilities.

Bobby "Slick" Leonard, the Indiana Pacers' head coach, put it best.

"They pulled a massacre on us," he said. "What we did," clarified then NBA attorney David Stern, a key player in the deal, "was save the business."

For now.

Flash, the ABA's defining trait, had gradually found its way into a physical, ground-bound game. It hadn't been that long ago when a player leaving his feet ended up flat on his back or shoved into the crowd. The jump shot was considered exotic in the early 1950s. When Bill Russell attended high school, coaches deemed it "a hot dog move" that belonged in the playgrounds. "Some coaches would bench a player automatically for taking a jump shot," Russell remembered. "And I witnessed a couple of strict disciplinarians who actually threw players off their teams for this offense."

Bob Cousy's behind-the-back passes and fancy dribbling, now the go-to move for any eleven-year-old who considers And-1 mixtapes nostalgia, were a dazzling outlier. The Minneapolis Lakers' Elgin Baylor arrived and essentially created the concept of hang time in 1959. "He did stuff nobody had thought of yet," said Warren Williams, a friend and high school rival of Baylor's in Washington, D.C. Later, Connie Hawkins arrived with swooping, looping drives, perfected on Bed-Stuy's courts; Earl "the Pearl" Monroe's yo-yo dribbling, honed on the Philadelphia playgrounds and derived from the jazz and R&B he heard in his head, drew the appreciation of deep thinkers. Woody Allen ranked Pearl among the rare athletes "who went beyond the level of sports as sport to the realm of sports as art." Noted writer John Edgar Wideman, a University of Pennsylvania hoops star in the 1960s, credited Monroe for the "paradigm shift in the pro game of basketball" toward the playground style. Pete Maravich's ball handling, the result of ceaseless drilling by his coach father, Press, dazzles in the YouTube era.

But these players did not peak at the same time. Their style came saddled with qualifiers. Cousy told author Gary M. Pomerantz that 90 percent of what he did on the court was normal. "It's kind of a misnomer that I'm associated to the degree that I am with that," Cousy said. "Anytime I could do it the orthodox way, that's what I would choose." Hawkins's college and pro careers were derailed by an imaginary betting scandal, an overzealous New York DA's office, knee surgery, and partying. NBA fans caught only four decreasingly transcendent seasons from "the Hawk," who was twenty-seven when he took the floor for the Phoenix Suns. By the early 1960s, the pain in Baylor's knees was so bad he was chauffeured to home games. Maravich, the great white hope, was an enigmatic loner who couldn't win in the playoffs. Wali Jones, a veteran NBA guard, thought Maravich parroted what black players had done. Pistol's results appeared labored and studied. Allen's prose aside, Monroe tamped down his flamboyance to win a championship with the team-oriented Knicks in 1973. Want to see "Black Jesus" in action? Wait for summer and head to the Baker League in Philly for the resurrection.

The slam dunk's arrival as the NBA's signature play also took a long route. In 1967, the National Collegiate Athletic Association (NCAA) banned the move. It didn't take a sociologist to find the context. "The white establishment has an uncomfortable feeling that blacks are dominating too many areas of sports," Hunter College assistant coach Robert Bownes said. "So they're setting up all kinds of restrictions and barriers. Everybody knows that dunking is a trademark of great playground black athletes. And so they took it away. It's as simple as that."

Julius Erving's career at the University of Massachusetts coincided with the dunk ban, so the *Boston Globe*'s Bob Ryan raved about Erving's prowess as a rebounder. He was Julius Erving there. "Doctor J" was bestowed upon Erving in the Rucker League, said Ryan, referring to the vaunted outdoor basketball league in New York City. Peter Vecsey, the longtime *New York Post* NBA columnist, had seen guys dunk before. But at Rucker, where Vecsey was Erving's coach and teammate, "it was like, '*What the fuck was that?*'"

Erving grew up on Long Island and played basketball throughout New York City's playgrounds, a narrative in line with basketball's status as a city game. Jews flocked to the sport from the 1920s to the 1940s. "It was absolutely a way to get out of the ghetto," said Dave Dabrow, a guard with the South Philadelphia Hebrew Association team (SPHAs), which barnstormed throughout the East and Midwest. "It was where the young Jewish boy would never have been able to go to college if it wasn't for the amount of basketball playing and for the scholarship."

Basketball provided an introduction for immigrants' distinctly American education, wrote Elliott J. Gorn and Warren Goldstein in *A Brief History of American Sports*.

> Basketball served as the foundation on which social workers and re-formers built huge intellectual and bureaucratic structures. Without a game so suitable for the cities where the largest number of immigrant children were concentrated, and where settlement-house workers saw the greatest need for social work, the movement for organized play might very well have sputtered out soon after its birth. . . . Basketball became part of the Progressive, professional, middle-class effort to channel, guide, and Americanize immigrant youth through elementary and secondary extracurricular activities.
>
> This history helps explain why, through much of [the twentieth century], basketball has been the preferred sport of working-class ethnic communities. That is where it was first played, where it was promulgated, where local institutions took the game to heart.

Then in the 1940s, as blacks continued to enter southern and northern cities, the blacktop became a laboratory where players like Baylor could experiment and not be restrained by coaches who envisioned basketball as chess in short pants.

The NBA's absorption of the ABA, said Nathaniel Bellamy Jr., a playground veteran, was when blacktop style reached the masses. With Erving serving as its kindly, reassuring doctor, the ABA injected the dunk right into the NBA's veins. More high-profile white players drafted were dunkers, Howard Bryant thought: Tom Chambers, Danny Vranes, Rex Chapman. The frills-free great white player—Bill Walton, Dave Cowens, John Havlicek—increasingly became an outlier. A big reason for the change, thought Baylor, who spent forty years as an NBA coach and front-office executive after his playing days, was financial. The more entertaining style of play brought more fans to the games. That meant more money for the owners. Coaches had to adjust if they wanted to stay employed. There wasn't much to object to if the team won. That's how Baylor, who was responding to the defense he encountered, could play his way back in the 1960s.

The NBA pre-1976 was workmanlike, dominated by large, skilled men like Kareem Abdul-Jabbar, Wilt Chamberlain, and Bob Lanier who pounded the opposition like a chicken cutlet on their way to the basket. The ABA had a shortage of high-quality big men. The three-point line spaced the floor, allowing players a chance to drive to the hoop. The court became a stage. Erving knew this way back with the Virginia Squires, when he teamed up with another dazzling scorer, George Gervin. "Before we went out of the locker room it was like, 'Let's put on a good show tonight,'" Erving said. "We didn't know whether we were going to win or lose the game, but we were definitely going to put on a good show. People were going to walk away seeing something maybe they never saw before." It made sense to Gervin: "Our marketing was pretty much word-of-mouth."

Thanks to the "merger," the NBA was poised to receive an unprecedented infusion of razzle-dazzle. Erving was the draw. "Buy the whole league to get Julius," said Charley Rosen, the author and basketball coach. First, he needed a team. Philadelphia 76ers general manager Pat Williams had to convince new team owner Fitz Dickson to spend a whopping $6 million—half to the financially depleted Nets; the other half in salary—to get Erving, who was sitting out. He traveled to Dickson's farm in Lafayette Hill, Pennsylvania.

"Tell me, Pat," said Dickson. "Who is Julius Erving?"

"Well, Fitz, he is the Babe Ruth of basketball," Williams said.

"What's it going to take to get him?"

Williams muffled the staggering financials, endorsed the signing, and got his Babe.

Erving knew his value. Before a 2018 interview, he discussed a recent episode of ESPN's sprawling documentary series *Basketball: A Love Story*. "I was thrown for a little bit of a loop, because the episode was basically saying that the NBA wanted David Thompson," Erving said. "And I was like, 'Really?' All these years everybody's been saying they wanted me." In previews to the 1976–77 NBA season, the first after the ABA's absorption, Erving's NBA arrival came with a level of hyperbole that would have made a tabloid editor blush. It was understandable. Very few people had seen Erving play in the ABA. Those who saw Erving in flight described an otherworldly experience, a forever rising epiphany with a monstrous Afro and hands the size of catcher's mitts. Erving, Bill Russell thought, was beautiful in the same way a painting or an ice skater's leap was. Now this supernova was headed to a league that televised its games nationwide and projected an air of stability.

"Writers aren't supposed to idolize, only report," sportswriter Woody Paige gushed in a feature for the 1977 edition of *The Complete Handbook of Pro Basketball*. "But it's difficult to distinguish between the two when describing Erving. He is the greatest I've ever seen." Over five seasons, Paige had witnessed Erving top himself again and again. Those moments were stashed away, "dredged up for another day of memories."

Erving's skills were that extraordinary. The attention didn't bother the other ABA stars. He earned it, said one of them, Artis Gilmore. "I realized very quickly if Julius took off from twelve feet out and dunked the basketball and I picked a loose ball up off the floor and laid it in off the backboard they both count as two points," Dan Issel said. It was no secret that the ABA's talent pool ran deep. The ABA and NBA played dozens and dozens of hard-fought exhibition games; the ABA won most of them. Smart basketball writers like Vecsey and Ryan recognized the talent. Before working for the NBA, Arlene Weltman occasionally provided color commentary for the Spirits of St. Louis with an impish twenty-two-year-old play-by-play announcer named Bob Costas. (Weltman had a pretty good connection. Her then husband, Harry, was the Spirits' team president.) More than forty years later, she remembered a St. Louis sportswriter proclaiming on a radio show that if the ABA and NBA merged, two ABA players would succeed in the NBA: Erving and ex-Celtic Don Chaney, an aging defensive specialist who was injured that year.

"Think of who he didn't name," Weltman said. "They didn't know shit about basketball."

Gervin, Issel, Thompson, Larry Kenon, Artis Gilmore, Bobby Jones, Maurice Lucas, Moses Malone. On and on. The ABA had stars in their prime. The key, thought Hall of Fame coach and ABA veteran Larry Brown, was that young ABA players saw game action right away, while NBA youngsters sat on the bench and learned. "The ABA would take an eighth grader if they thought he could play," Issel half-joked. The NBA kept losing their headliners. From 1971 to 1974, Oscar Robertson, Jerry West, Wilt Chamberlain, and Elgin Baylor, a basketball Mount Rushmore, retired. Someone had to fill the gap—and provide some competition. "I look around and see a bunch of guys who shouldn't be playing in this league," Dave Cowens, the Celtics star, told *Sports Illustrated*. "Year after year they don't improve. Just pick up the checks. It's no motivation to play against these dogs. Now the best in the world are in one league. The best against the best at their best."*

The effect of the ABA on the NBA was empirical, thought Costas. The All-NBA team for 1977 featured four ABA alumni. Another four made the All-Defensive team, deflating the former league's soft-defense reputation. The league leaders teemed with refugees; Indiana's Don Buse topped the NBA in assists and steals. "Don Buse!" Vecsey said. "Who the fuck ever heard of Don Buse in the NBA? What the hell is that?" Scoring was well represented: Buse's teammate Billy Knight and Thompson finished in the top five in points per game. Years later, Howard Bryant spotted the impact watching Game 5 of the 1976 Finals online. The guards—including Hall of Famers Jo Jo White and Charlie Scott—in that classic contest didn't dribble between their legs. Guards turned their *bodies* to evade defenders, like foosball players. That was considered solid, fundamental basketball. Erving obliterated that concept, Bryant said, and style stopped being problematic. Today, Gervin said, the NBA "is the ABA with a lot of money."

The NBA would reap the benefits of flashy play. The endeavor irked the traditionalists, but, Baylor said, it was great for teams that wanted to make money. Ron Thomas, the future NBA editor at *USA Today*, watched the 76ers play the Bulls in Chicago. Two extraordinary moments from an otherwise ordinary game were burned into Thomas's brain decades later. Erving raced to the basket, where the Bulls' 6'10" Mickey Johnson waited. Erving could have stopped or gone around Johnson. Instead, he chose a third scoring option. "I still have this memory of Mickey looking up as Doc flew *over* him," Thomas said.

---

*Decades later, when asked about these comments by the author, Cowens denied saying anything like this.

With ninety seconds left, Erving left the game. Thousands of fans followed suit, including Thomas and another nearby patron.

"Doc be gone," the man said, "I be gone."

Success bred success. When Phil Jackson scouted teams as an assistant coach with the Chicago Bulls in the late 1980s, teams based their playbooks on "power basketball." The big man getting the ball remained an option, but if he was double-teamed, he'd pass to a player on the wing, who had more space. That player would shoot, drive, or set up a screen-and-roll play, that is, a teammate would block out the defender so the man with the ball could freelance.

That style of play, Jackson observed, was a staple of playground basketball. Erving and his talented ilk turned it into NBA normalcy. "It misleads everyone into thinking that basketball is nothing more than a sophisticated slam dunk competition," Jackson wrote.

The NBA lacked the public capital to have a status quo, let alone maintain one. That made the fury over the three-point shot, introduced in 1979, a puzzlement. For one thing, the idea had a long precedent. Basketball coach Howard Hobson, who coached the University of Oregon to the first NCAA championship in 1939, had endorsed a three-point shot for years. In 1945, Fordham and Columbia played in "an experimental game," cosponsored by Hobson, featuring the three-point line. Two hundred fifty-three attendees completed surveys about the new rule; a majority liked it. Pro leagues, notably the American Basketball Association, used it to great effect. Oddly enough, when the NBA leaned toward the staid—shooting the ball, but from farther away—the NBA's guardians of the good old days headed to their fainting couches. Warriors owner Franklin Mieuli called the new shot "a panic move" destined to "destroy the team concept." In protest, he resigned from the NBA's board of governors and was rumored to have left one league meeting in tears.

Sure, Mieuli had flouted tradition by drafting a woman, Iowa high school basketball phenom Denise Long, to a pro contract in 1969, but this was different.*

Eddie Gottlieb, whose involvement in organized basketball dated back to 1918, wrote a three-page objection to the shot, calling it "a major step backward." It had been a gimmick back in the ABA days— "in no other game is distance given extra points"—and it was a gimmick now. Points closer to the basket are difficult and more exciting than the three-pointer, he reasoned, so it's a slap in the face to a spectacular Julius Erving dunk.

Sure, the dunk horrified basketball purists ten years earlier, but this was different.

The most powerful opponent was Red Auerbach, the great Celtics coach who was now the team's president "and controlled the league to a great degree," said former Detroit Pistons executive Tom Wilson. He remembered an owners' meeting where Auerbach's opposition was unceasing, logical, and passionate. "You're going to ruin the game," Wilson recalled Auerbach saying. "You're ruining the purity of the game."

There's no way they'll vote against Red, Wilson thought. *He has such influence in the league.* When the three-point shot passed, Wilson thought a new day had arrived.

Nobody looked to Auerbach or Gottlieb as paragons of the future-forward businessman. Auerbach was a firm believer that the team was the selling point—the Celtics wouldn't feature cheerleaders until after Auerbach's 2006 death. As the NBA's schedule maker, Gottlieb wrote them out with a pencil and ruler on manila folders—one for every team—like a Brooklyn drugstore bookie taking action on the Dodgers. Washington Bullets president Jerry Sachs would take the train with owner Abe Pollin to Philadelphia, where they would beseech Gottlieb to give the Bullets Friday, Saturday, and Sunday games. "Goddamnit,"

---

*Mieuli drafted Long in the hopes of building a women's basketball league.

Gottlieb would say. "You're going to mess up the whole schedule! If I have to do this for you, that means I've got to do it for four other teams."

The great irony is that the NBA embraced change—and thrived on it: the twenty-four-second shot clock; wider lanes; the elimination of a jump ball after every made basket. Those rules weren't handed down by Dr. James Naismith after he put up that first peach basket. In the early 1950s, all kinds of amendments were discussed, including lowering the baskets and raising the baskets, as remedies to revive the NBA. "Everybody knew there was something wrong with the game, and everyone had some sort of remedy in mind," wrote Leonard Koppett in his classic early history of the NBA, *24 Seconds to Shoot*. Innovation was always part of the NBA's corporate culture, even if nobody cared to admit it.

The three-point shot in the NBA began as a seldom-used curiosity, then a well-timed weapon in the late 1980s—Larry Bird loved using it to break the opposition's spirit late in games. Time was the three-point shot's greatest ally. Now, said Rick Barry, one of the best shooters in basketball history, the benefits are too obvious to ignore. All the analytics fans now: *shooting 33 percent from three-point territory is equivalent to shooting 50 percent in twos.* In 2016–17, the top 100 in three-point percentage shot at least 36 percent, Barry said. "How do you not want to use it?" he asked. In the 1979–80 season, the three's first season, according to Basketball Reference, teams shot around three three-pointers a game.* In 2017, the era of the Splash Brothers, the number had ballooned to twenty-seven. San Antonio Spurs head coach Gregg Popovich, one of the NBA's best coaches of all time, hates the three-point shot, but he relied on it heavily to win the 2014 Finals. "It makes it tougher to cover that much room defensively on the court," he said. ". . . To me, it's not basketball, but you've got to use it. If you don't, you're in big trouble."

---

*The first player to hit a three-point shot wasn't Larry Bird, but his Celtics teammate Chris Ford.

Joey Crawford, the longtime NBA referee, loved the shot. It made for an easier game to call because there wasn't as much of two guys beating the ever-loving shit out of each other. For the first five years of his career, Crawford had a recurring thought on the floor. *How the hell do I call this here?* Plus, the three-point shot appealed to the fans. They want to see more scoring, as did Crawford.

The idea, back in the day, was to get closer to the basket, said Dave Cowens, the Boston Celtics' Hall of Fame center. A twenty-three-foot jump shot was the same number of points as a layup. As time went on, the center's role as an inside force changed. They became more versatile athletes. Then the NBA permitted the zone defense. It was harder for a center to go one-on-one. He had to find new ways to score; the outside shot was an option. Today, a center who isn't comfortable from three-point range is a rarity and, increasingly, a relic. And it's not that hard for a player to learn, Cowens said.

"Why do you think a 6'10" guy is a decent three-point shooter?" he said. "Do you think he has a special athletic talent that allows him to do that, that a 6'10" guy in 1969 wouldn't be able to do? It's about practice. It's just about repetition and getting confidence." During his later years in Milwaukee, Jack Sikma made the adjustment. Coaches Don Nelson and Del Harris opened the three-point competitions to the big men. Sikma, who once led the league in free-throw percentage, excelled. The spacing on the floor was changed, so Sikma got comfortable looks outside. "It was pretty natural," he said.

During the 1976–77 season, Erving had to set aside his usual statistical dominance to fit in with his talented, but undisciplined, Philadelphia 76ers teammates. He had a glorious NBA career, but he never reached his ABA peak. "He allowed himself to be coached," Vecsey said. Erving said he was asked to do less by his coaches in Philadelphia. He had no regrets. "It paid off with a championship," he said. That meant the 7'2" Abdul-Jabbar remained the NBA's most dominant player, possessor of arguably the deadliest move in basketball history: the sky-hook. Using his body as a barrier and concluding with a release point that left Abdul-Jabbar high-fiving angels and as the NBA's all-time points leader, the shot was "virtually unstoppable," said 7'4" Mark Eaton, the Utah Jazz's towering defensive standout. "Fucking unstoppable," clarified Jeff Ruland, the Washington Bullets' bruising All-Star center. "Unselfish, skilled. Fuck, I got him in his late to mid-thirties. I can't imagine what he was like when he was twenty-one."

Gervin says Abdul-Jabbar is the greatest player in NBA history, not the greatest entertainer. That distinction, he believes, belongs to Michael Jordan and Magic Johnson. The lack of showmanship, along with his prickly demeanor with fans and the media and his devotion to Islam (forever an unfamiliar religion to white America,) isolated the public from a thoughtful, intelligent man. Away from the game, Abdul-Jabbar was great, said Lesley Visser, a reporter with CBS Sports. He loved jazz and would expound on *Bitches Brew* and Thelonious Monk's technique. He gave Visser notes to help with her reporting. When the cameras rolled, that man vanished. Visser once asked Abdul-Jabbar how the Lakers came back to beat an opponent. Abdul-Jabbar looked down at the 5'8" Visser, waited at least five seconds—an eternity for live television—and unleashed his answer.

"What?"

"I wanted to die," Visser said.

Jon McGlocklin, the Milwaukee Bucks guard and the team's long-time announcer, loved Abdul-Jabbar as a teammate and has kept in touch. Yet, at his most engaging, McGlocklin noticed that it was a real effort for his old friend. "If he was more like Magic, the world probably would have embraced him more," he said.

The churlishness, regardless of its source—shyness, publicity fatigue, or the burden of being an intelligent black man in America—contributed to some rocky years after basketball. Well after his retirement, Abdul-Jabbar met with his former Lakers teammate, the perpetually effervescent Magic Johnson. Johnson had become a massively successful businessman who owned Starbucks franchises, movie theaters, and, later, the Los Angeles Dodgers. More important, the public loved him. Abdul-Jabbar wanted the same. Johnson, who cringed at how Abdul-Jabbar treated people during their playing days, tried to dissuade Abdul-Jabbar: You've got to be on all the time—hugging people, shaking hands, making small talk, Johnson advised. You've got to be cordial. There's no other way to do it.

Johnson then told Abdul-Jabbar a story from twenty years before, when Johnson was a young star and Abdul-Jabbar was deep into his brilliant career. A father and his seven-year-old son gingerly approached Kareem as the pregame shoot-around wrapped.

"Kareem," the man asked, "can we please get a picture?"

"No," said Kareem, who didn't break stride. The boy was crushed. Magic went up to the father and volunteered to take a photo. Hey, he joked, maybe I'll be in the Hall of Fame someday, too. Years later, Johnson was meeting with a prospective client. Afterward, the CEO of the company Johnson had just pitched—and the father of that snubbed little boy—approached Johnson. That kid was now twenty-nine, and the photo from that day hung on his wall.

Magic landed the account. *See, Kareem?* Magic thought as he chipped away at his life's work. *It could have been you.*

Center Moses Malone was another indisputable talent. His arrival to the Philadelphia 76ers in 1982 turned Erving's team from a perennial runner-up to fabled world champions. Whereas Kareem's game was defined by a graceful finish, Moses's was one of relentless pursuit. He was an insatiable rebounder, especially on the offensive end. "Every time the ball was shot, you had to look for Moses," said

Wayne Cooper, the veteran center. "He was going after *every rebound*." Not only was he incredibly strong, Cooper said, but his second jump was astounding. No one got off the ground faster after coming back down. If Malone faced trouble under his own basket, said his long-time coach Del Harris, he could throw the ball off the backboard and put it back in. Malone's quick feet allowed him to pull off the "Moses Move," an explosive, modified drop step, on stymied opponents for a good decade.

Malone's skill set was not sexy. He also was not a self-promoter. A rough, impoverished childhood and going straight to the ABA from high school made Malone reticent, Harris said. "He was a little hard to understand the first couple of years," Harris recalled. "He got considerably better over the years at communicating. I've got to tell you, our first few weeks together, I didn't want to ask him to repeat anything." Until he understood Malone's cadence, Harris simply nodded or shook his head depending on how the words sounded. "You just had to spend time with him," Harris said. Those who did discovered a kind man who was forthright and respected those who reciprocated. Early on, Dale Ellis, a teammate during Malone's brief stint in Milwaukee, politely asked Moses to repeat himself. That honesty, Ellis felt, endeared him to Malone. The two's friendship lasted until Malone's 2015 death.

"He would answer the phone," Ellis said. "I have teammates, it might take them a week or two for them to return a phone call." Malone possessed a great sense of humor. Spud Webb, Malone's teammate for three seasons with the Atlanta Hawks, would sit by Malone on the team plane and savor the hilarious (and unpublishable) stories from his long career. But unless you played with Malone, Webb said, you never saw that side.

The camera-ready tasks that Malone and Abdul-Jabbar disdained, Erving embraced, contributing to his classy aura. Timing helped. The controversies that plagued Erving—the affairs and illegitimate children, including a daughter with Samantha Stevenson,* the sportswriter who ghostwrote his wife Turquoise's article for the *New York Times*; the death of his troubled nineteen-year-old son, Cory; financial misjudgments—came well after his playing days. The notion of Erving as an NBA ambassador is "a bunch of bullshit," said Vecsey. People tend to overlook some not so great behavior from Erving the player, such as forcing a trade from the Nets that nearly capsized the new NBA franchise. Class mixed with fame and athletic brilliance proved a powerful deceiver. "I would have eaten his shit," said Turquoise, who ignored Erving's infidelities, years later. The player who existed to the world in a limited realm—a 94' x 50' stage; a television screen; a press scrum—was a god. The flawed man in the larger world emerged later, said John Lucas, the former NBA star and drug counselor. Stately and eloquent, Erving thoughtfully answered every reporter's question, even the ones not about basketball, from the opposing team's beat writer to the high school reporter who hid his fandom behind a press credential. The combative Vecsey liked him: Erving served as best man at his wedding.

Nobody in the NBA told Erving that he was now the guy, but Erving recognized the new reality he inhabited. If he put the time and effort in at practice to round his game into form, then he had to do the same when a reporter shoved a microphone in his face. There was an upside to being available to everyone, though Erving admitted it grated on his family and friends: he controlled the narrative. If Erving let someone else talk about him, it would be opinion or subject to misinterpretation. It would not be the truth.

Erving was a mensch, thought Paul Gilbert, the league's director of production. You *always* had a positive experience with him. That made Erving a perfect spokesperson for the league. If the NBA asked him to

---

*Alexandra Stevenson became a world-class tennis player, reaching Wimbledon's semifinals in 1999. The tournament is when the news broke.

do something, Erving never said no, said Adrian De Groot, the head of NBA Properties. "We used him a lot, because we knew we could count on him." He was not a superstar for black or white fans. *Everyone* loved Julius Erving, Gilbert said. "Doctor J was always my measuring stick," said Bernard King, the Knicks' superlative small forward. Not *everyone* knew him. During an Erving poster shoot in Philadelphia at a fancy-pants medical health club for Converse, copywriter Theodore Duquette passed two "very old, blue-blood surgeon types" sheathed in towels. "Doctor Who?" one said to the other.

The NBA had a superstar with crossover appeal. Now it had to get people to see him.

O'Brien considered the ABA's absorption into the NBA a top-ten career highlight. It reminded him of Kennedy winning the presidency in 1960. That took place just a mile and a half down the road from Dunfey's Resort. He and the rest of the Irish Mafia, JFK's inner circle, stayed up late, tracking the election results. The next day, he greeted Jack Kennedy with "Good morning, Mr. President."

The NBA was no match for working in the White House for a young, war-hero president whose charisma captivated the nation, whose numerous, sordid transgressions remained overlooked. Really, what could? Wheeling and dealing with Congress to initiate social change so the less fortunate and oppressed could grab a piece of the American dream. Hobnobbing with the political elite at his Washington, D.C., home. O'Brien had observed, and shaped, American history as it happened.

All that remained were memories of the good old days. Ed Desser, the league's director of broadcasting, would occasionally get a call.

"Ed?"

"Yeah."

"Commissioner O'Brien. Got a minute?"

Desser, like everyone else around the office, knew "Got a minute?" was code. He'd walk over to O'Brien's dark office, where he was pummeled with secondhand smoke. After he answered one or two league-related questions, the commissioner whisked Desser back to 1600 Pennsylvania Avenue. For hours, O'Brien smoked and unfurled story after story—about JFK and Jackie and Robert. "It was just *fascinating*," Desser said. "It was like an out-of-body experience." Frequently, said Barbara Ward, then an administrative assistant in the NBA office, would knock on O'Brien's door to retrieve two young executives, David Stern and Russ Granik, so they could answer an important phone call.

"I think the NBA job really was it for Larry," said Ted Van Dyk, a friend and colleague of O'Brien's from the Democratic Party. He dropped by to visit O'Brien early in his reign. The office was quiet. He breezed past two secretaries and found the new commissioner leaning back in his chair, feet propped on his empty desk.

"How is it here, Larry?"

"Well, I'll tell ya. It's the easiest job I've ever had," O'Brien told Van Dyk, "but I'll you this: the owners are the biggest bunch of assholes you'll ever want to meet."

The first day on the job, recalled former NBA Properties head Howard Berk, O'Brien confidently strode down the hall to his office. Each day after, he'd take the same path and never leave. The move had a clear meaning to Berk: if you wanted to talk to O'Brien, you saw him, not the other way around. "I figured you couldn't even talk to *him*," Larry Bird recalled, "that it was like getting through to the president of the United States or something."

Ward compared O'Brien to the Wizard of Oz. Jan Akerhielm, his longtime assistant, added to the aura. Immaculately dressed and coiffed, she was a model of 1960s secretarial propriety. "She was demanding," Ward said. "Maybe I like to please people, or I liked to do a good job, but you always felt that Jan had her eye out. . . . You couldn't get to behind who she was, because she was this perfect, chipper, organized, heel-wearing, well-dressed presence."

O'Brien—he was always addressed as "Mr. O'Brien" or "Commissioner O'Brien"—tended not to answer phones or doorbells or get his own coffee. He wasn't very subtle about showing who was the boss, Howard Berk thought. Berk, a politics fan, thought O'Brien was trying to emulate John F. Kennedy. Over the summer, O'Brien took Thursdays and Fridays off to spend long weekends at his beach house in Cape Cod, just like Kennedy. Berk knew O'Brien was allergic to the sun, so what did the commissioner do for half the week in an area fabled for its beaches? "I stay inside and watch TV," O'Brien told Berk. He may have been kidding. The fair-skinned O'Brien enjoyed setting up on the back porch—well shaded, of course—with a history book or an autobiography.

Today, the term "politician" clings to O'Brien like cigarette smoke on one of his suits. Back then, the NBA required exactly that. "I think all of us had a sense that there was more show to Larry than there was substance," said Harvey Benjamin, an attorney who worked for the NBA. "But that doesn't mean that the show wasn't important in that context." Few could detail what O'Brien did day-to-day to propel the league. Simon Gourdine, the league's deputy commissioner, worked with O'Brien for six years. The most positive thing Gourdine's widow, Patricia, remembered her husband saying about O'Brien was that he ran the best meetings. For a league where meetings got contentious, that was an integral skill.

Akerhielm said O'Brien trusted his employees to do their jobs and to fill him in. The person in charge of "a company or the NBA, cannot do everything," she said. "He always knew what was going on because of the people he delegated." Or, as Patricia Gourdine said, her husband did the work; O'Brien was the face.

Alex Sachare, the former Associated Press basketball writer and the league's director of information, believed O'Brien's mandate from the owners was to end the war with the American Basketball Association. Now that he had done that, it was time to build the NBA staff for a new era, and O'Brien wasn't a businessman, attorney Peter Gruenberger said. The author of "The O'Brien Manual" did know how to organize his assets—both on the campaign trail and in Washington. During his days as postmaster general and as the Democratic National Committee's head, O'Brien's right-hand-man was former journalist Ira Kapenstein, who died at age thirty-five in 1971. "He was the perfect complement to Larry," Van Dyk said. "He was the guy who went in behind him and made sure everything happened. He was a dedicated Democrat, but also was dedicated to Larry. So if you thought of one you always thought of the other." Betty Myers, Kapenstein's widow, said her late husband and O'Brien were a team. "Ira always felt that he was listened to, and that he was honored," she said.

On the recommendation of his son, Larry III, O'Brien interviewed Larry's law school classmate Russ Granik, a jack-of-all-trades whom he deemed indispensable. But O'Brien knew whom he wanted to step up: the man who really ran the NBA.

"David was absolutely the puppeteer," Desser said, "pulling the strings behind the scenes."

When David Stern joined the law firm Proskauer, Rose, Goetz & Mendelsohn in 1966, his relationship with basketball ripened into a force that changed his life and the course of sports history.

The son of a Chelsea delicatessen owner, Stern grew up a rabid Knicks fan who played ball well into adulthood—his tender left knee was a memento of New York Lawyers League games. He could get good seats at Madison Square Garden with a fifty-cent student card and a tip to the usher. The NBA was in its infancy back then. Stern's hero was Harry "the Horse" Gallatin, a great center before Bill Russell and Wilt Chamberlain transformed that line of nondynamic, crafty big men into well-paid spectators. The nostalgia lingered. Adrian De Groot, the longtime NBA executive, occasionally grabbed a ride home with Stern. Both men lived in Scarsdale, New York. The trips predictably featured their commentary on the Knicks' current shabby condition and what could be done to get them back to glory.

"First love is sentimental," an old saying goes. "Second, voluptuous." Stern's early duties at Proskauer included working on Connie Hawkins's lawsuit against the league. A flimsy charge of fixing games led to the Brooklyn dynamo's dismissal from the University of Iowa and wiped away his prime after the district attorney told the NBA commissioner that Hawkins's reputation was now radioactive. Hawkins's biggest crime was knowing shady attorney Jack Molinas, a New York hoops legend tossed from the NBA for shaving points. (Later, Molinas became a pornographer. He was murdered in 1975 in an apparent mob hit.) Though Stern knew the NBA had faulted—Hawkins was ultimately vindicated—he loved taking the depositions of early NBA influencers like Red Auerbach and Eddie Gottlieb. It was, Stern recalled decades later, like conducting an oral history of the game's early days. When the Oscar Robertson case contributed to the firm's billable hours, Stern interviewed players. Their qualities as intelligent, decent men radiated from them, he thought.

"If there was one lesson he was learning," David Halberstam wrote of Stern years later, "it was that the league was its players, nothing more, nothing less, and that the best of these players, white and black, were uncommon men."

The 1970s were a litigious time in the NBA—the Robertson case; various squabbles stemming from the American Basketball Association; the rise of player agents. Running a team grew more complicated almost by the day, Michael Burns said, so "you couldn't do anything without checking with Proskauer." George Gallantz, the NBA's main attorney at the firm, ceded more responsibilities to his young protégé. Stern became a key contact for teams, and a regular presence in the NBA office, playing a significant role in the ABA deal—he talked to the NBA owners, said Harvey Benjamin—and the Oscar Robertson suit. His intelligence was undeniable and impossible to holster. If something was on his mind, he *had* to say it.

"Around the office we called him 'the Brat,'" Burns said.

Peter Gruenberger, who opposed Stern on numerous occasions as counsel for the Players Association, liked Stern. He helped his adversary find a home in Scarsdale. They were at each other's throats all the time professionally, but Gruenberger respected Stern and enjoyed his company. He would not be the last person to land in this paradox.

In 1978, O'Brien hired Stern as the league's executive vice president of legal affairs, a title Stern insisted on having. Gallantz was less than thrilled at the move. "Well, you schmuck," Gallantz said, "how can you put your life in the hands of one client?" Stern's duties under O'Brien were clear, according to Sachare: "rebuild the office as you see fit." O'Brien deemed the hire a necessity.

Not everyone shared O'Brien's enthusiasm. A wary respect existed between him and deputy commissioner Simon Gourdine, a proud, intelligent man, said Michael Burns, Walter Kennedy's assistant. Gourdine's appointment in 1974, according to the NBA, marked the highest position an African-American had reached in professional sports. Based on his title, Gourdine was next in line as commissioner. He knew the league and its issues. He had lobbied the owners hard to succeed Kennedy, then saw them court O'Brien for a position he resisted for months. After O'Brien's election, Gourdine abandoned his campaign. O'Brien noticed resentment when he first met Gourdine, who told him that if any of the other active candidates—chiefly Henry Steinman or Alan Rothenberg—had been elected, he would have continued to push for the job.

"I loved the man," Burns said of Gourdine, who died in August 2012. "I really did. That's the proper term. . . . He was a very special man. But he was tone-deaf on assessing the politics of the league as far as whether he was going to be the next commissioner. And the reason he was tone-deaf was the makeup of the owners." NBA teams—as well as every major sports league—lacked a black owner until 1989, when Bertram M. Lee and Peter C. B. Boyne bought the Denver Nuggets for $65 million.

"Si Gourdine is very efficient, he follows through, he's informed, and he's experienced," Houston Rockets general manager and president Ray Patterson told New Jersey's *Bergen Record* in 1977. "Will he make a good commissioner? Call me in eight years and ask me again."

Two immutable forces stood in Gourdine's way: the color of his skin and David Stern, who made more money than the veteran NBA executive. Peter Gourdine said his father had great respect for Stern and felt the feeling was reciprocated; Patricia Gourdine said the two men had a good relationship. Years later, Stern endorsed Gourdine for enshrinement in the Basketball Hall of Fame, an honor Patricia Gourdine felt had been withheld far too long. Patricia had a hefty binder as evidence indexed with photocopied newspaper articles, a biography, and Stern's Hall of Fame recommendation letter for her late husband.

"I think it's a testament to my father's abilities and capabilities that he had no doubt that he both could have been, and perhaps should have been, fairly considered to be the commissioner," said Peter Gourdine, who later worked for the NBA. "I think that his reality suggested that simply wasn't going to happen to him."

Mike Suscavage, Gourdine's coworker and friend, saw Stern grow more emboldened. "When he became executive vice president," he recalled, "there was no open door to Larry's office unless it was some kind of life-and-death situation." Suscavage had held meetings with executives from Anheuser-Busch and Wilson to discuss potential league sponsorships. Both times, Stern burst in and declared those deals dead without explanation. Afterward, Suscavage tried to save face. "They could see it was a complete surprise to me. And, in essence, I said, 'The guy is a prick.'" It was very clear, Suscavage recalled years later: NBA employees knew it was in their best interest to align themselves with Stern. "There's no way I was kissing his ass," Suscavage said, "which is what he wanted." O'Brien shifted from a politician to, in the words of Phoenix Suns general manager and future owner Jerry Colangelo, "a placeholder."

"Si, you have no shot," Suscavage would tell Gourdine when they hung out. "No shot." Being overlooked twice for the commissioner position was why he left the NBA in 1981. "There were never any barriers against me," Gourdine said. "It's just, how long do you want to stay after being passed over."

The start of Stern's rise to power coincided with a period he later called the "dark ages." The NBA's violent reputation culminated in December 1977 when Kermit Washington decked Rudy Tomjanovich, nearly killing him, during a scuffle between the Houston Rockets and the Los Angeles Lakers. The haunting incident was caught on videotape, leading Walter Cronkite, the nation's journalist grandfather, to voice grave concern.

"The league had a number of players who were regarded as enforcers, which in itself was disturbing to me," O'Brien recalled.

Advertisers were leery. Suscavage took a marketing executive from Campbell's Soup to Game 2 of the 1977 Finals in Philadelphia. The center-court seats were phenomenal. Then Blazers enforcer Maurice Lucas clocked the mammoth Darryl Dawkins, who had thrown Lucas's teammate, Bobby Gross, to the floor. Both players were ejected. Dawkins's temper didn't cool down. The 6'11", 251-pound Dawkins stomped to the 76ers locker room and embarked on a rage-fueled renovation that turned toilets and urinals into rubble. As a perk, Suscavage brought his guest down there. The client loved what he saw—as a fan. "Mike, this is one of the problems we have: We are a family-oriented brand. Young kids and families are important to us. When I saw that kind of behavior by these guys, it's tough for me to justify spending money against this." Suscavage found it hard to retort.

Drugs in the NBA became front-page news, though cocaine use took off in any profession where employees had money to burn. As Robin Williams famously quipped, "Cocaine is God's way of telling you you're making too much money." The NBA's culture didn't help, thought David DuPree, the longtime NBA reporter for the *Washington Post* and *USA Today*. "It's a fast life," he said. "It's a glamorous-type life where things don't happen until after the game. So that plays into a certain clientele. So, the game is over at ten, and by the time people are ready to act like normal people, it's midnight"—the time of day when people get into trouble.

Robert Stutman, a retired Drug Enforcement Administration special agent, used to talk to the Celtics about drug use when he worked in Boston. Afterward, a player approached Stutman with an admission: "We really fucked up." It wasn't just basketball players. Major League Baseball's drug issues were exposed in the infamous 1985 Pittsburgh cocaine trial. New York Mets star Keith Hernandez testified that nearly 250 players used cocaine in "the romance years" between America's pastime and America's party drug. Users were ignorant of the damage cocaine could inflict. "They compared it to heroin and they thought it was a lot safer drug," Stutman said. "As we know, cocaine doesn't kill as many people as heroin, but it's actually far faster addicting than heroin."

In 1980, Chris Cobbs of the *Los Angeles Times* reported that up to 75 percent of NBA players used cocaine. Cobbs stood by his work. Ditto Michael Granberry, then his colleague at the *Times*. "That story was sourced very carefully," said Granberry, who recalled Cobbs making dozens of phone calls. "Chris is a person of impeccable integrity. We underwent rigorous editing at the *LA Times*." Of course, the NBA went on the defensive, minimizing and disputing the story's credibility. "I remember thinking at the time, *You really want to go there?*" Granberry said. "As the years went by, Chris was totally vindicated by that story." The death of Len Bias was sad proof of Cobbs's prescience.

Years later, Spencer Haywood, whose own battles with the drug derailed a Hall of Fame career, estimated that 80 percent of the league used cocaine in the 1979–80 season, a claim seconded by Haywood's old drug dealer. "Oh yeah," he said. "It was everywhere."

"So much coke is snorted in the NBA that if 10 players sneezed at once you could bet that one or two of them was losing money," Bill Russell wrote in 1979.

The NBA's preponderance of black players fed the accusation. "If someone chose to, they could have concluded that 100 percent of the black players were involved with drugs," Gourdine told the *New York Times* in 1981. "Any time there are social problems like drugs and alcohol, the perception is that it's black players involved. That concerns me. Sometimes perception becomes reality. You have to go out aggressively and fight those perceptions."

What bothered Alvan Adams, the Phoenix Suns' white All-Star, who was not implicated in the team's tangled 1987 drug scandal, was the guilt by association. If your teammate got caught, the public assumed you were using as well. Allan Bristow, the future Charlotte Hornets coach, was a reserve for most of his ten-year career in the ABA and NBA. Drugs were a luxury he couldn't afford. "It was usually always the star—or would-be stars—because the team [had] invested a whole lot of money into those players." Teams, he added, had no room for a marginal talent as a known drug user on the roster. It wasn't worth the risk. "The talk among the players was that if a guy was being promoted as part of the NBA's marketing program," said Dawkins, "the league couldn't afford to have him disgraced."

The rise of cocaine in the 1970s started with young, white professionals who mimicked the behavior of rock singers and entertainers. That skewed the numbers. Journalist Lewis Cole pointed out that cocaine's statistical record featured a "built-in class bias." A wealthy user could enter a private hospital, their ordeal likely kept away from the rigid public record. When the user population expanded to include teenagers, blacks, and the poor—all of whom could not afford private doctors—the cocaine stats exploded. The rise of crack, a cheaper form of cocaine, did little to focus perspective.

The irony of the perceptions and the unreliable data contained some truth. As more blacks entered the league, Kareem Abdul-Jabbar wrote, some brought along social drugs beyond alcohol. "Professional basketball players almost all come out of college," he explained, "and the campus at the time was the new cultural breeding ground, so almost everyone who was coming into the NBA had at least been exposed to the idea of recreational drugs."

The problem, Abdul-Jabbar thought, came down to excess. "Most guys," he wrote, "can take it, having developed the ability to withstand and even channel the pressure to their benefit, the same way they developed their inside moves." DuPree agreed. Many players were good enough to endure a few toots. George Gervin, the four-time scoring champion in San Antonio, was one of them. "The coke, it only derailed him a little bit," he said. "The kid could play hot." Gervin told *Sports Illustrated* that his cocaine addiction accelerated after his NBA career ended. "I didn't feel I was worth very much," he said. "That's when the disease took hold of me."

"With so many games, it gave you energy when your body was feeling down," said Mark Landsberger, a forward with the Chicago Bulls and Los Angeles Lakers. "A lot of guys depended on it to get us up for games. If you did it once in a while, using your judgment, you were okay. If you didn't . . ."

The ignorance regarding drug use, coupled with the intense pleasure and a lack of league policy, made just saying no a complicated act. The Knicks' Micheal Ray Richardson submarined a brilliant career because of his love of freebasing cocaine. "That first hit felt like the best thing that could ever happen to me," he said. "I was invisible and invincible." Haywood compared his first time to having sex, scoring 50 points, and winning the lottery simultaneously. Richardson spent the next seven years trying to replicate that initial high. Basketball didn't seem that important anymore. He had company: Richardson claimed that one out of every three players in the NBA was freebasing. Drug use was not a black problem, Dawkins told basketball writer Charley Rosen.* The talk among the players was that a couple of white stars would sit on the bench with towels over their heads to hide their bleeding noses.

There was an accidental advantage to cocaine use. "When you knew a guy was on cocaine, everybody on the other team wanted to guard that guy, because they knew they could," said Steve Mix, the Philadelphia 76ers forward. "You could just see their talent level deteriorating with each passing year." It's why Mix, a grinder, volunteered to guard David Thompson, a supernova gradually dimmed by years of cocaine addiction.

"It seemed so harmless, but in that way it's similar to carbon monoxide poisoning," Thompson wrote in his memoir. "It's a slow and seemingly painless death."

As players struggled with an incomprehensible reality fueled by fame and money, most NBA teams confronted the blunt despair of a spreadsheet. In 1981, sixteen of the league's twenty-three teams lost money. Four were on the block. Nobody wanted to buy them. Contraction was

---

*Rosen supplied Steve Patterson of the Cleveland Cavaliers (*not* the former general manager of the Rockets and Trailblazers) with marijuana for the Cavs from 1971 to 1975 when the team visited New York to play the Knicks. Patterson, who died in 2004, then smuggled the one-ounce baggies in the fingers of his gloves.

viewed as a real possibility. Forty percent of the teams depended on its $800,000 check from CBS to stay afloat and would call the NBA offices if it were late by a day. As soon as the check came in, "we paid off bills like it was going out of style," said David Axelson, then a front-office executive with the Kansas City Kings. Suscavage called Jazz owner Sam Battistone about the team's uniforms. The franchise was moving from New Orleans to Salt Lake City, so logic dictated a new name. "I have no money," Battistone said. "I cannot afford it."

Things barely improved in Salt Lake City, where David Allred, the Jazz's longtime PR guy, received an instruction with his first paycheck: don't cash it until Tuesday so Adrian Dantley, the team's star, got paid first. "We had is-it-going-to-stay-or-is-it-going-to-go promotion parties *a lot*," said Grant Harrison, a longtime Jazz employee. In San Diego, Clippers employees were sometimes told not to cash their check until they heard otherwise. "There were days I thought, *Wow, this may not survive,*" said Pete Babcock, an assistant coach there. When the Pacers were between owners, Bob Whitsitt recalled, nobody received a paycheck for about two months. Whitsitt, a young front-office employee, didn't feel the impact. "Slick" Leonard, the treasured longtime Pacers coach, did. "It had become such a struggle to me to keep hearing about money and all these things, it wore me down," he said. "It really wore me down."

Harvey Benjamin, the attorney for the NBA, said an "early warning system" ensured that teams avoided financial catastrophe. Occasionally, the NBA had to intervene on a team's behalf—find new lenders, negotiate with old ones to restructure a loan, lean on national sponsors to divert money to a struggling team. The good news was teams rarely reached that point.

Denver was in a state of permanent flux. By 2018, Lisa Johnson, who had been with the Nuggets since 1981 and was then its vice president of administration, had seen twelve ownerships. (Basketball columnist Peter Vecsey could have had part of one in the early 1980s, but said he didn't have the million dollars in cash required.) When she started, Johnson sold season tickets on commission; her first year, she sold the most—a whopping thirty-two. After nearly every season, there'd be a new owner, a new general manager. The questions stayed the same. *How are we going to do this? Are we going to make it? Am I going to have my job?*

But she loved working for the Nuggets. Johnson gained invaluable experience by getting thrown into projects. Everyone worked together, so it was a lot like a family. What your grandpa said was true in the NBA: if you had initiative, any job was yours. David Fredman was attending Loyola University in New Orleans when he started chatting with Jazz general manager Bill Bertka at Pat O'Brien's, the bar famous for the Hurricane.

"I'd love to work in professional sports," Fredman said. "I would do anything."

"I like your attitude," Bertka said, handing the young man his business card. "You should come and see me sometime."

The next morning, before the Jazz's office opened for business, Fredman was waiting for Bertka.

"I guess I'm going to have to find something for you to do," the GM said.

He was a gofer, not an intern. Fredman did any task asked of him—selling stock, assisting on game nights, working in the ticket office. He helped in public relations. Fredman attended practices, where he learned the game. Years later, Frank Layden, now the coach of the Utah Jazz, asked Fredman if he wanted to scout. He did advance scouting. He scouted college players. He became an assistant coach. Save for a five-year detour in Denver and a year as the general manager of the Jazz's minor-league team, Fredman has spent his entire basketball career with the Jazz and his entire working life—nearly fifty years—in professional basketball. It's never felt like a job.

In July 1977, the Indiana Pacers held a sixteen-and-a-half-hour telethon to sell eight thousand season tickets to stay solvent. A year later, the team's long-term prospects remained dire. Bob Whitsitt, then an intern from Ohio State, remembered John Jewett, a partner, banging his shoe on the conference room table to get the staff's attention. We have businesspeople downtown, pound the pavement! Burn a hole in your shoe leather! Cold call! We need season tickets! Jewett left—with his shoe on—and nothing changed. After all, there was no sales staff.

Whitsitt approached Nancy Leonard, the Pacers' general manager and coach "Slick" Leonard's wife, to ask if he could stay after his internship to sell season tickets. He'd work on commission, so the Pacers wouldn't have to pay him a salary. Whitsitt knew nothing about sales. He hated talking to people, but he wanted to work in the NBA.

"Well, let me check with Mr. Jewett," Leonard said.

He's only been asking you to do this for the past three meetings, Whitsitt thought. He spent sixteen-hour days working throughout the Pacers front office, getting paid to learn. He visited successful franchises to see how they sold tickets. He'd arrive for work at 7 a.m. eager to get started. "I never felt like tomorrow could be the end," Whitsitt said.

You had to have enthusiasm for this life, for the game. That enthusiasm was quarantined. During one summer early in his 76ers career, Julius Erving golfed with his former New York Nets teammate Bill Melchionni. Erving started to talk about the upcoming season when Melchionni said, "I don't even like watching it anymore." The statement struck Erving, who couldn't fathom a life without enjoying or watching basketball. Melchionni wasn't a relic from the set-shot era. He had retired in 1976 after winning championships in the NBA and the ABA; he later worked in the Nets' front office. "I thought that was a bold statement, and a reflection of someone being an insider who didn't like what they were seeing," Erving said.

O'Brien's defense at an April 1979 talk with the Associated Press

Sports Editors of New England and Upstate New York provided a good guess as to what the outsiders thought:

"This is not a dying sport," he said.

Back in the NBA office, Stern turned to Matt Winick, the league's schedule maker. The Brat's brashness broke.

"Matt, what are we going to do?"

Well, he said, Bird and Magic will be playing in the NBA a lot longer than in college.

"That kind of summed up where we were," Winick said.

A popular subplot of Larry Bird and Magic Johnson's narrative is that they possessed transcendent team-first abilities. They also came with a huge built-in audience, a trick even Julius Erving couldn't conjure. Bird and Johnson were the stars of March's 1979 NCAA championship between Big 10 powerhouse Michigan State and small Indiana State. These young men, the two best players in the nation, were unicorns. Johnson was a 6'9" point guard, Godzilla in a position full of jockeys, whose ebullient personality matched his play. Bird was a 6'9" forward who, like Johnson, was a sparkling playmaker. "What I remember most about Larry's early years was his beautiful passing," said his former teammate and future coach, Chris Ford. "The way we moved the ball." The difference is that Bird could shoot a basketball like Michelangelo painted or Fred Astaire danced. If you knew nothing about the game, you knew Bird and Johnson were special.

Another reason lay in what was absent. ESPN was months away from premiering. Sports fans were not overfed daily with scouting reports and hot takes and soft-focus features. As college basketball writer Seth Davis observed, never again would two wonderful college basketball players be "introduced to a rapt nation at the very moment they [were] taking the court for the national championship." (When NBC put together its college basketball schedule for that season, Indiana State wasn't on it.) A media frenzy accompanied that game, remembered John A. Walsh, who was then editing the test issue of *Inside Sports.* It felt special. The game itself was forgettable. Michigan State won easily, 75–64, with Bird shooting an ice-cold 7-for-21. The ratings—more than 30 million people watched—were stupendous. It still ranks as the highest-rated college basketball game of all time. The *New York Times'* longtime sports columnist Robert Lipsyte believed the NBA survived because of college basketball's scandals in the early 1950s and early 1960s. "The NBA, above suspicion, stepped forward into its contemporary era of stabilization and expansion and black superstars," he wrote.

Erving stretched the imagination of what could be done on a basketball court, thought Dave Hollander, a lifelong hoops fan and marketing professor at New York University. That narrative went only so far. Sports is all about storytelling, said ESPN veteran Steve Bornstein. With Bird and Magic, the NBA had a built-in rivalry to attract casual and new fans. Any sentient adult who had seen a movie or read a book recognized the foundation of a killer narrative. Magic was black; Larry was white. Their future teams, the Los Angeles Lakers and the Boston Celtics, had a bitter rivalry. Their cities featured vastly different cultural attitudes. Boston and Los Angeles also promised coast-to-coast viewership whenever these men met. And these kids were guileless. Bird was twenty-two; Magic turned twenty in August. The summer after his senior year, Bird was student-teaching at West Vigo High School in West Terre Haute, Indiana. He also mowed the ballfield grass. The school's manager joked he had the world's only millionaire lawn mower. When CBS producer Bob Stenner asked Johnson what he was going to do with the money from his pro contract, he replied, "I'm going to fill up my gas tank." The rivalry could last a decade if these kids were as good as they looked.

That meant nothing without decent television coverage.

THE PLAYERS GET
THEIR CLOSE-UP

"You can't do this to the NBA!"

David Stern was begging for a loved one's life. There was little justi-fication for CBS Sports to show mercy.

Since its deal with CBS Sports, the NBA had not fulfilled its prom-ise as the sport of the 1970s. President Bob Wussler and O'Brien had shaken hands on an extension, but "we agreed somewhat reluctantly," said Neal Pilson, then director of business affairs for CBS Sports. "It was not a substantial deal." The NBA's ratings were not great, but there was a history. On the heels of improperly paying tennis players money at "winner-takes-all" events, Wussler resigned in April 1978. New pres-ident Frank Smith wanted the NBA excised from the network's sched-ule. Here's how Pilson remembered hearing the news:

Smith: "I want to cancel the NBA. I want to do more golf."

Pilson: "Frank, we have a handshake [deal] with Larry O'Brien."

Smith: "I don't give a damn. It's a handshake. It doesn't bind me. I want to drop the NBA. Get Larry O'Brien over here."

Pilson: "Jesus, Frank. We've had the NBA for years. It's a good prod-uct. We don't have a substitute for it."

Smith: "I don't care."

O'Brien was stunned. The CBS and NBA had a good relationship, he explained, plus the NBA had a deal with Wussler. Stern asked Pilson if they could talk outside. There, Stern got right in Pilson's face and put a finger in his chest. "You can't do this to Larry. You can't do this to the NBA. You had a deal. You have to stay with it. We need to continue on CBS!"

Pilson knew Stern was desperate. Without CBS, he thought, the NBA would disappear from network television. Jack Kent Cooke, unhappy with CBS Sports, had already crawled back to ABC, but the network harbored resentment over the league's shifty defection to CBS. Pilson promised to talk to Smith. Stern and Pilson ended their sidebar. Everyone agreed to defer the decision. Pilson then did his best to convince Smith: The network had nothing to replace the NBA. It's profitable. It's a good deal. Let's stay with it. The four-year deal was renewed. O'Brien later said Smith, who died in 1998, initially couldn't honor Wussler's deal, because it hadn't been approved upstairs.

The $74 million contract failed to resolve every issue. "We were never given the opportunity to determine whether we were ready for prime time," O'Brien recalled later. At one league meeting, O'Brien announced that its cocktail reception with CBS was scheduled for 5:30 p.m. After a beat, Jim Foley, then the Houston Rockets' PR guy, responded, "Is that 5:30 p.m. real-time or tape-delayed, Commissioner?" The league's championship series coincided with May's networks sweeps. The ratings for that period dictated what advertisers would pay for the next season. There was no conceivable way the NBA Finals would draw as many viewers as *The Dukes of Hazzard* or *Dallas*—two of the 1980s most popular shows, for better or for worse. That meant some Finals games were tape-delayed. It was an easy decision to make. David DuPree covered the Golden State Warriors–Washington Bullets 1975 Finals for the *Washington Post*, one of five publications reporting on the series. The NBA, he said, barely had a national presence.*

The irony was the level of play was increasingly watchable to a general audience. Erving launched a generation of aspiring basketball players, who had a role model widely available for adulation and imitation. Larry Nance, the future All-Star and Slam Dunk Contest champion, spent hours confronting his backyard hoop—reinforced with double planks of wood by his father—trying to dunk. When he finally did, his first thought was, *I'm Doctor J.* The television coverage did not match the product, though basketball fit the medium perfectly. It was self-contained. There were no home runs or shanks. "The game is in front of you" and allowed for a wider variety of camera angles, said Don Ellis, a longtime television executive, who worked on NBA games in the 1950s for NBC. The court served as a perfect stage. The players, ostensibly dressed in their underwear, were always visible. They didn't wear helmets; they didn't retreat into dugouts. CBS devoted little energy and few resources to the NBA, and it showed. The NFL and television had come of age together, leading to Howard Cosell and the innovative coverage of *Monday Night Football*. Major League Baseball had grown up with America, burrowing into metropolitan areas, creating a bond with each Mel Allen "How 'bout that?" or rapturous Vin Scully sentence. The NBA had no identifiable hook, no bouncy theme song, no memorable broadcast duo. CBS's ubiquitous play-by-play man Brent Musburger was a star, but the color analysts through the 1970s and 1980s left little to be desired.

When the NBA's contract was renewed in 1982, Pilson was CBS Sports' president. He asked Ted Shaker to helm the NBA's coverage; it wasn't because Shaker was a major talent. "It was, 'No one else wants it, do you want to give it a whirl?'" said Shaker, who previously worked on

---

*According to basketball historian Todd Spehr, seven Finals games were shown on tape delay. And of those seven, three aired live somewhere in the nation.

The NFL Today, CBS's pregame studio show. Shaker's lawyer, Todd Musburger, Brent's brother, advised him to turn it down. Todd Musburger's verdict: "This is where people's careers end." Shaker decided to give it a try, though he knew the NBA's reputation: the players didn't play hard, there was no structure or strategy, everybody freelanced. "You could check off the clichés, and that's what the general perception was," Shaker recalled. "And people didn't watch."

As the *Boston Globe*'s Jack Craig pointed out, the NBA's $88 million contract in 1982 was hardly good news. First, there was inflation. Second, the NBA's deal was nightstand change compared to the NFL's $2.4 *billion*, five-year contract from the three networks—an increase of more than $1.7 *billion* from the previous four-year deal. CBS aired fewer regular season games—seven in the 1982–83 season, down from nineteen the previous season—in addition to the All-Star Game and the postseason.

Shaker had one big advantage in what the NBA billed as a "less is more" approach: he could work with limited interference from higher-ups. CBS held little interest in the NBA, Brent Musburger recalled, because it was more concerned with profitable prime-time programming, including the NFL, which made *60 Minutes*. The NBA was in the sports division's hands. Shaker and his allies' "tiny brains" concocted a two-part plan to generate relevancy. First, the NBA had four bona fide stars: Abdul-Jabbar, Erving, Bird, and Magic. Free of regional restrictions, a game would feature at least two of those players. The network focused on players and rivalries. That was easy to do, Pilson said, because the NBA wasn't as deep as it is today. Some teams never aired.

The second aspect: to further turn NBA games into events, not afterthoughts. Fortunately, the network had a ton of sports showcases as a foundation. Shaker managed to get the NBA on after the Daytona 500, the Super Bowl of NASCAR, and before the actual Super Bowl. Unlike today, the hours before the NFL's final game cum advertising extravaganza lay barren. "If there's this early part of the day and people are going to build their day around the Super Bowl, there will be some percentage of audience that will be looking for something else to watch before the game came on," Shaker said. "We would do one of those match-ups at 1 p.m. on Super Bowl Sunday and have that until 3:30 p.m. It was a big success. These games got a lot of viewers, against all odds." By the start of the postseason, Shaker felt something was happening aside from hours being swallowed.

"It wasn't an overnight success," said Mike Burks, a lead producer for *The NBA on CBS*. "It was kind of slow and go. I think we had an underlying feeling—I can remember saying this any number of times—that if we treat the league like it matters, the public will perceive that it matters."

That included halftime. The affable, precocious Pat O'Brien, formerly from KNXT in Los Angeles, hosted an irreverent halftime report. O'Brien had a glint in his eye, thought John Kosner, then manager of sports programming at CBS. "He was clever and different," Kosner said. "He wasn't another blow-dried announcer on at halftime."

Time-killers such as H-O-R-S-E contests shuffled off to the glue factory. Now O'Brien revealed that Buck Williams, the bruising Nets forward, developed his blue-collar game by playing against his sister when they were kids. (Williams also showed his chops on the piano.) The player-centric pieces got viewers to know these young men, whose personalities and backstories that were obscured in concerned editorials. "I think our group coming in, in being fresh faces and also being able to articulate a point in front of the camera, let America know you were all right, so to speak," said star Detroit Pistons guard Isiah Thomas, who entered the league in 1981. At the time, TV was largely bereft of positive black images. "The self-depreciating role of blacks as comic relief in television is not unlike those that were once so pervasive in films," journalist Knolly Moses observed in 1979. Portrayals tended to stick. Media experts George Gerbner and Larry Gross suggested to Moses that television was used to test reality. Eventually, the stereotyped portrayal became real and behavior in real life was guided by the expectations derived from the stereotypes.

Pat O'Brien encountered some resistance. When the mustachioed newsman called the NBA to request access to players for halftime pieces, the voice on the other end asked, "Why?"

CBS's coverage grew more refined. Rick Barry, a transcendent talent, had a lifelong knack for irritating people. Bob Bestor, the Golden State Warriors' director of public relations and marketing, said Barry was a smart, stand-up guy who couldn't keep quiet. He'd offer advice to flight attendants on how to do their jobs on flights. Little changed during his time at CBS, which dropped him. "He was brutally honest," said Bob Stenner, lead producer for *The NBA on CBS* and a friend of Barry's. "Some people have a tone in their voice that sounds condescending. What they're saying is accurate; it just sounds nasty. That's who Rick was and is. That's held him back." Russell owned a keen, curious mind but his thoughtful, meditative approach wasn't a good fit for the broadcast table, Stenner thought. But another Celtics legend, the excitable Tommy Heinsohn, could keep up. In his interview with CBS Sports, Heinsohn offered some advice. Stop with the Basketball 101 approach. "Every game is different; every game can be a murder mystery," he said. The broadcast can provide clues as to who was murdered and how. The picture creates an idea of how to win the game.

Director Sandy Grossman obliged. Broadcaster Dick Stockton, an on-air staple of CBS's NBA coverage during the 1980s, said the beauty behind Grossman's approach was that he captured players' reactions. Shots of a frenzied crowd served no purpose. But Larry Bird whipping a towel from the bench, turning the Boston Garden into a rock concert, did. Michael Cooper lying on the floor in astonishment after Ralph Sampson's improbable buzzer-beater sent the upstart Houston Rockets to the 1986 Finals told a story. Reporter Lesley Visser, who went from the *Boston Globe*'s heralded sports department to CBS Sports in the early 1980s, was floored at the behind-the-camera talent. "They were all giants," she said. The emerging talent in the NBA, she thought, mirrored the *NBA on CBS*'s crew. Two supporting members—Artie Kempner and Suzanne Smith—went on to brilliant careers directing NFL games for Fox and CBS, respectively. It wasn't about showing up and putting on another game, Smith said. Burks would arrive with a yellow pad filled with forty things to do. He made sure, Smith recalled, to have a player's head shot and some personal information accompany their stat line. It put a face to the players *and* familiarized them to the viewers. *Hey, this guy also likes chocolate ice cream.*

What also helped, Stockton thought, was that viewers were no longer plopped into a game. There was now context. *Here's how the two teams are performing going into today's game. Here's what's at stake. Here's what to look for.* The elements were presented like a feature story: facts accented with color. Heinsohn, a former head coach, got scouting reports for both teams, and fed that information to help the crew set up shots. Visser felt her role didn't change on television. Instead of writing on deadline, she spoke on deadline.*

Added to that mix was an introduction to excite viewers. Husband-and-wife production team Bill and Joyce Feigenbaum, with help from the New York Institute of Technology's computer animation laboratory, created an animated basketball court complete with a bouncing ball and a crowd. It was a grind. Video, said Joyce Feigenbaum, is thirty frames a second; some details-crammed frames took as long as an hour to produce. "We didn't expect it to be that great," Joyce said. Larry O'Brien, she said, couldn't determine whether what he saw on CBS was concocted in a studio or belonged to the material world. Ken Wesley, who went on to do animation and video effects for *Star Trek* and *Pirates of the Caribbean*, took the Feigenbaums' ideas and put them on the screen. In 2019, he laughed when he watched the now-primitive

---

*Visser and Stockton were married in 1983. They have since divorced.

introduction, which could be done now in two days as opposed to two months. But in the heyday of Donkey Kong, it was groundbreaking.

Then Shaker and Doug Towey, CBS Sports' creative director, developed a strategy to work elements of the tease—the "setup" for the game—with what the Feigenbaums and Wesley had concocted. Nothing like this, Shaker said, had been attempted. Brevity was key. The breakdown, he recalled, went like this:

* 12 seconds of computer animation with that peppy, instrumental theme song,* a horn and guitar-fueled mini-rock anthem. That dropped into . . .
* 15 seconds of footage of the teams, voiced by whoever did the play-by-play that day. Then up came . . .
* 5 seconds of animation and music. That dropped into . . .
* 15 seconds of additional follow-up into the day's game. Then up with . . .
* 5 seconds of music and graphics, which led into . . .
* 7 seconds of final setup to pump you up. Then . . .
* The music begins again as the camera cuts to live coverage of the game.

Much had changed since NBC's Don Ellis waved a white towel to signal NBA commissioner Maurice Podoloff to stop the game for a commercial break.

Individuals were important—to a point. "It's not tennis," Dick Stockton said. "It's a team game." An announcer who talked about one

---

*The song's author remains a mystery. CBS Sports has no record; neither did BMI or ASCAP. High-profile TV composers Bob Christianson, Allyson Bellink, and John Tesh (via a spokesperson) said they didn't write the original version. Most composers are "very blasé when it comes to appreciating or documenting the music—whether it be the theme, highlight[s], or bumpers," Bellink explained via email.

player found themselves without a hook—and presumably viewers—if that player struggled or left the game. The discussion went beyond Larry Bird's greatness to the critical roles Kevin McHale and Robert Parish played on the Celtics or how speedy Lakers forward James Worthy was the key to Magic Johnson's magnificent fast breaks. Finally, the NBA's TV coverage featured storytelling, led by the play-by-play of Musburger, a former newspaperman. And the personalities were there. It was very much from *The NFL Today* playbook, manna for a sports fan in the 1970s. If TV viewers wanted sports, said John A. Walsh, there was the nightly news. And that was it. "You got three and a half minutes. And if there was any stormy weather, it was taken out of sports. Sports was disenfranchised."

Musburger is loath to credit CBS, or television in general, for the NBA's improved status. "The changes were within the league itself," he explained. "Television did nothing except they showed the games live more in the 1980s. TV was a carrier. The product sold itself. The NBA is largely a league built around a handful of major cities and franchises that capture the public's imagination. It has obviously gone beyond that, but if you ask anyone, and they want to be honest about it, you want the Lakers, the Celtics, the Knicks, and the Bulls. And now [2018] certainly the Warriors have played themselves into that practical role. It's a major market sport and it will always be that way. Once the Lakers and the Celtics became must-see TV, that's what propelled the league."

Shaker's response: "I'm sorry he feels that way."*

---

*Shaker said CBS wanted Musburger to scale back his workload as the 1980s concluded to accommodate a new wave of talent, including Visser, Jim Nantz, and Greg Gumbel. "I remember sitting next to him as we were flying to Detroit, and that's when I first broached the idea of maybe doing fewer things, not being the number-one guy on everything. He was on the inside seat, I was on the aisle. To me, it was like that scene with Linda Blair in *The Exorcist*. His head didn't do a 360, but it felt that way to me. He gave me a look—it could have made me shrink into the size of a mouse. That's where our relationship started to go apart. It was not even something he would consider." Musburger's contract wasn't renewed in 1990. At the time, he claimed that Shaker and Neal Pilson, the president of CBS Sports, "conspired" to remove him from CBS.

Musburger's comments held some truth; the players' abilities determined whether a viewer stayed or trudged to the knob. But 1981 marked the start of MTV and of a culture where image became an increasingly critical component of content. CBS Sports got that style and substance were partners. More important, so did David Stern, who understood the NBA could do only so much to influence the product on the court. Nothing could be done about the steadily increasing number of black players. America had to come around. Some already had. Donald Pitt, one of the Phoenix Suns' owners, recalled Knicks owner Ned Irish's logic: "It doesn't matter who I put on the court in a Knick uniform. When they make the point spread, the fans are going to get up and cheer." In the meantime, how the league could enhance its attractiveness and expand its audience via marketing—which cost little and involved limited risk—were essentially limitless for TV and beyond.

This was not cocktail party pontification. Stern caught crucial details that professionals overlooked. And he was unafraid to share his thoughts. One postseason, Shaker left a Saturday afternoon playoff game at Madison Square Garden early and headed to his empty office to do some work. The game ended. The music and end credits rolled. The phone rang. *Who the fuck knows I'm here?*

"Did you just see that?!" David Stern bellowed. "Did you just see that?!"

"What?"

"You guys just did the credits," Stern said. "The picture behind the credits was an empty Madison Square Garden. What image are you projecting for the game?"

"You mean empty seats?"

"You're killing me!"

CBS began to conclude its broadcast with a montage of stills from the game above each credit, a concept developed by Mike Burks. "We never showed an empty stadium again," Shaker said. "He was such a detail-oriented guy," said Don Sperling, executive producer and senior vice president at NBA Entertainment, the league's video and highlights juggernaut. "*You* needed to issue spot *everything*, which is the most important thing you can do in your business: make sure if you're giving something to somebody, follow up." Stern's belief was very simple: if anyone wasn't in step with the NBA's "relentless pursuit of perfection," he made sure *everyone* knew that.

Gregg Winik, a longtime executive at NBA Entertainment, deemed Stern a "street fighter." He never lost the litigator's attitude: the NBA was always his client, thought Bill Daugherty, who worked for the league in the 1990s.

"Pilson!" Stern would bark at Neal Pilson before demanding why the network ignored Houston at Kansas City or Cleveland at Utah or any of the NBA's fine franchises bereft of sexy, easily identifiable stars.

"Nobody cares about that game."

"What do you mean 'nobody cares'? I care!"

Pilson didn't mind. If he were in Stern's position, he would have done the same thing. Besides, the NBA and CBS were deep collaborators. "Nobody had the be-all and end-all answers," Ted Shaker said, "because everything was fucked up."

Stern recognized the value of individuals to sell the game. A huge component was that Bird and Johnson were great so soon. In Bird's second season, the Celtics dispatched the Houston Rockets in six games to win the championship. Johnson got a head start. He led the Lakers to a world championship in 1980. The rookie won the deciding Game 6 in Philadelphia filling in for Abdul-Jabbar at center and showing the world how special he was, putting up an iconic stat line of 42 points, 15 rebounds, and 7 assists. Harvey Araton savored the performance twice. After he filed his game story for the *New York Post*, Araton drove home to Brooklyn Heights and caught the second half of the game he had covered hours ago on CBS. The start of Magic

Johnson's legend was tape-delayed in favor of *reruns* of *Dallas* and *The Dukes of Hazzard*. "That's how little power the NBA as an industry had," Araton said.

When the Lakers and Celtics first met in 1984, the first of three (live) meetings that decade, the NBA took its first steps into the spotlight. What stood out about the Bird-Johnson story line, said Jack Sikma, the Seattle SuperSonics' star center, was there was nothing manufactured or fake about it. "It was an antagonistic rivalry," Brent Musburger said. "You took sides." The pair didn't change the league, Dave Cowens thought. Television did. The bulk of his Hall of Fame career occurred in the 1970s, a beige decade for the NBA on TV. "Instead of talking about the team, they started talking about the individual first and the team second," Cowens said. "It was *Larry Bird* and the Celtics as opposed to the Celtics with Larry Bird."

The 1984 Finals was a classic seven-game brawl won by Bird's Celtics that marked a tipping point, Sperling said: personalities drove the sport. He thought Bird and Magic were superstars who shared a competitive drive. They were two different leading men. In the locker room, Bird was initially a reluctant and stoic interview, a tone that didn't improve after *Inside Sports* ran a profile revealing a two-year-old daughter and a failed marriage in Bird's not-so-distant past. "Larry is a very nice person but sometimes he just forgets about other people," his ex-wife, Jan Condra, told writer Diane K. Shah. "He sort of forgot about us." He was a prankster whose humor surfaced in private. Theodore Duquette, who wrote many basketball commercials for Converse, was on set at Harvard with Bird and Julius Erving for one shoot. Erving was to show off the latest basketball shoe and say, "They call me the Doctor because of how I operate. So, if you want to improve your game . . ." The spot ended with Bird sneaking from behind, grabbing the shoes, and saying, "Take two of these and call me in the morning." Bird kept flubbing the moment. His moves were off. The expression wasn't right. Around take sixty, Bird blurted, "Take two of these and stick 'em up your ass!" That take was played at board meetings for years, Duquette said.

The superstar's rapport with the media improved dramatically as his career progressed. During Bird's last hurrah with the Dream Team in 1992's Summer Olympics, *Sports Illustrated*'s Jack McCallum and *USA Today*'s David DuPree looked to take a photo with the storied super team as a memento. McCallum was uncomfortable with Du-Pree's idea, and begrudgingly posed with the confused superstars. As the camera clicked, Bird chirped, "Hey, Jack. Later on, you wanna blow us?"

The charismatic, perpetually smiling Johnson was a reporter's dream from the start. "Magic did every interview like it was the only one he was doing that day," Pat O'Brien said. Johnson was an ambassador. When the Lakers first visited the Dallas Mavericks, an expansion team, Magic found a television crew. He started gushing about the city and how great the game would be, recalled Doug Adkins, the Mavericks' general counsel and secretary. After talking to the media, Magic was informed the game had sold out. "He rubbed his hands together and said, 'Okay, then,' like it was mission accomplished," said Kevin Sullivan, the Mavericks' longtime public relations man.

Like Erving, Bird and Magic belonged to everybody. Their games reinforced and contradicted common stereotypes. Bird's stardom certainly quenched the NBA's need for a great white hope, but his game found an audience beyond the armchair traditionalist—read: old white guys—enamored with grit, hustle, and every play-the-game-the-right-way cliché. Johnson visited his barbershop and found "the elders" reveling in Bird's memorable offensive rebound against the Rockets in the 1981 Finals. Bird clanked a seventeen-foot jump shot on the wing and instantly raced to the carom. He leaped, securing the ball on its way down. In midair, heading toward the sideline, he switched the ball from his right hand to his left hand to finish the play underneath the backboard with a graceful finger roll. Hall of Famer Dominique Wilkins put it best: Bird played a white man's game "with a black head."

Bird and Johnson made fundamentals and teamwork into entertainment, writer Charles P. Pierce observed. For all the no-look dishes and full-court bounce passes, Magic Johnson's game was rooted in the basics. It started as a child watching Detroit Pistons games on television with his father, Earvin Sr. "Dad pointed out everything down to the smallest detail," Johnson recalled. "The footwork, the head fakes, the defensive stances, blocking out underneath the boards, all the things that separated the great players from the good players." What made him so special, his college coach Jud Heathcote said, was evident in summer pickup games. Johnson deliberately picked three or four clearly inferior teammates. His teams always won not because Magic made every basket, but because he made those other players better.

Bird and Magic, along with Michael Jordan, were "the most diabolical, psychotically competitive, tear-your-mother's-heart-out-motherfucker competitive competitors ever," said Stephen Koontz, a producer with NBA Entertainment.

Sidney Moncrief, the Milwaukee Bucks' superlative guard, played with Johnson and Bird in college as part of a postseason tournament team. He saw the glow of those intangibles early. Johnson was in his teens, but he directed players (correctly) on the court with the confidence of a thirty-year-old. Bird's physical gifts and basketball IQ were evident, but what stood out about Bird to Moncrief was he had the toughness and aggressiveness to be a great player. When a fight broke out at one game, most of the white boys dove for cover. Not Bird. "He was throwing down," he said. "He's going *at it* with somebody."

As Bird and Magic's rivalry and skills ripened, a country was being wired to catch more than what CBS captured.

* * *

It was the funniest thing. Bill Rasmussen's sports report for the NBC affiliate in Western Massachusetts lasted three and a half minutes, but there'd always be calls by viewers provoked by something as simple as the Red Sox–Yankees score. Or they were upset a local game got the shaft. People were passionate—and they hungered for more sports. Years later, that observation propelled Rasmussen to found Entertainment and Sports Programming Network, a national cable station broadcasting sports twenty-four hours a day, seven days a week.

Leigh Montville, the *Boston Globe* sports columnist, got exposed to the network, better known as ESPN, when his Florida motel room carried it. Nonstop sunshine was no match for nonstop sports.

"I began to feel physically ill," he wrote in 1981. "If too much is not good for you, as mother always said, this definitely was too much. The set controls you. There is no time, nor inclination, to watch the rest of television anymore. Not even the news. There is no inclination to read books, newspapers, anything. Turn the knob. Watch the games. No need to talk."

The illness had become an outbreak. In 1975, a young channel called Home Box Office broadcast Muhammad Ali and Joe Frazier's "Thrilla in Manila" live. Kay Koplovitz, the founder of USA Network, knows the exact date of "the night that changed the course of television history": September 30, 1975. Cable, she said, finally had the infrastructure to send programming to households immediately. Koplovitz explained the setup years later: in anticipation of receiving a live satellite feed from Manila, Bob Rosencrans, president of UA-Columbia Cable Systems, installed a ten-meter satellite dish at his Vero Beach Florida Cable System. Monte Rifkin, president of ATC Systems, also installed a dish in Jackson, Mississippi. The fight came in on time and clear to a group of VIPs assembled in Vero Beach to watch cable's version of the moon landing. The success of that historic title bout prompted HBO to file a lawsuit against the Federal Communications Commission to give cable operators greater access to current programming.

Before then, Koplovitz said, HBO was "sending tapes around the United States of movies, and the tapes would arrive, they'd be worn out, they'd be torn, they wouldn't arrive on time—there were a lot of problems with it." The cable industry, she said, was nascent, rural, and barely organized.

In 1977, the federal district court in Washington, D.C., ruled that the Federal Communications Commission (FCC) was not justified in restricting cable TV to protect the broadcast networks. That prompted other courts to quash more of the FCC's cable restrictions. Notably, cable operators could now offer current sporting events in the nation's top television markets. In addition, the cable industry no longer had to provide communities with special channels to air their own programming. Satellites allowed channels to spread their programming throughout North America instead of hopping across microwave points.

Like most great creations, ESPN was built upon smaller precedents. New York–based MSG Network was the nation's first regional sports network, launching in 1969. That spun off into the USA Network, which was originally named Madison Square Garden Sports, in 1977. Long before it became a sanctuary for horny teenage boys shackled by basic cable (*Up All Night, Silk Stalkings*) or aired acclaimed original series such as *Monk* and *Mr. Robot*, the national network carried games from the National Hockey League, Major League Baseball, and the NBA. ESPN launched on September 7, 1979.

USA Network carried other sports, too—tennis, college football. Eddie Doucette, the treasured Milwaukee Bucks announcer who worked there for nine years, joked that he called every sport short of nude celebrity bowling. Koplovitz knew that after movies, sports provided the most popular programming on television. She knew cable operators would clamor for it. "You wouldn't have a hard sell," she said. "They needed original programming in order to build out their systems and get more subscribers. They had to have something original to present. Live sports drive live viewership on television today."

USA, said analyst Hubie Brown, a breakout star there, said the network was ESPN before ESPN. Koplovitz's strategy was to get all the major sports, because why not? It fit into her business strategy of "seek and get in trouble when you can scramble out of it."

Koplovitz started (inadvertently) with Major League Baseball. She scored an agreement with Yankees owner George Steinbrenner to televise a portion of the team's games on USA. In 1978, the Yankees were fresh off a world championship and had a national presence stoked by years of Ruth-DiMaggio-Mantle pinstriped mythology. The first game the network televised was between the Yankees and the Boston Red Sox, a classic division rivalry that would conclude with a memorable one-game playoff after the Red Sox blew a seemingly insurmountable eight-game lead on August 8. The game in late June wasn't too bad. Graig Nettles hit a two-run homer in the bottom of the fourteenth inning to beat the Red Sox, 6–4.

The next morning, she received a phone call from Bowie Kuhn, baseball's commissioner.

"I see you televised the Yankee game last night, Ms. Koplovitz," Kuhn said.

Koplovitz, high on last night's drama, gushed to Kuhn about how great the game had been. Kuhn didn't share her enthusiasm: Koplovitz, he ordered, was to "cease and desist" future broadcasts. A restraining order was imminent.

Kuhn insisted that Steinbrenner didn't have the right to sign that deal. *What am I going to do?* Koplovitz thought. She talked to her husband, a lawyer. There were no good legal options. She didn't have the money to fight Major League Baseball in court, and there was a good chance USA might have committed an FCC violation.

Koplovitz called Kuhn back, and tried to convince the somber commissioner about how strong the Yankees deal was. Kuhn was unmoved.

She stopped, and went all in.

"Okay, I'll trade you," Koplovitz said.

The silence went on forever. Koplovitz thought Kuhn was going to hang up on her.

"Trade what?"

"I'll trade you this Yankee deal for a deal with Major League Baseball."

More silence. What was she doing?

"I'll see you in my office tomorrow morning, Ms. Koplovitz."

"Kay Koplovitz, of all the people I've met in my career, is one of the brightest creative people that I have ever known," Doucette said. "She has a way of expressing herself which is totally engaging."

The NBA was next. USA paid $400,000 for the first year in a three-year deal, which proved advantageous to both parties. Stern knew the value of signing with USA, said Joe Cohen, who helped launch MSG Network and was a longtime Stern associate and friend. The deal gave the NBA national exposure beyond then-disinterested CBS. One of the NBA's conditions—Stern negotiated the contract—was that all the teams had to have network exposure. It helped, Doucette said, that USA promoted the league constantly.

"It was a less competitive entertainment landscape then, so even though the NBA was smaller, it may have been a relatively more recognizable fish in a smaller pond," Cohen said. USA Network got a boost, too. So many pro sports in one place was "a fresh concept," Koplovitz said. "It was trying to get people to have a habit to know that Thursday night, they could watch an NBA doubleheader if that's what they wanted to see." Or baseball. Or hockey. Or tennis.

What ESPN provided back then was leverage. Stern said ESPN was interested in NBA games, and made Koplovitz aware of that. Koplovitz, then a cable industry veteran, didn't flinch. "ESPN wasn't the ESPN that you think of, it was 'Connecticut Sports Network,' and it had no major sports," she said. "It had third-rate college sports out of Connecticut."

"Before the NBA would make a deal with USA, something had to come into existence to create a marketplace so that they could place a value on the rights," Cohen said. "They didn't want just one buyer, they wanted a competitive situation." That also allowed Stern to change the copyrights of the game telecasts. The league now owned the copyright to the games, not the home arena, and would sublicense the copyright back to the team for local broadcast. That proved beneficial in a few short years.

The NBA's embrace of cable began a corporate viewpoint that persists to this day. "It's no accident that the NBA is at the forefront of sports gambling, was at the forefront of all new media as it came online," Cohen said. "Every league has its own character, and the character of the NBA is to run to the cutting edge, to run to over the top."

Doucette credits Stern and Koplovitz with the NBA's growth. "The NBA Thursday night package was a chance for the country to be exposed to live, professional basketball," said Jim Zrake, vice president and executive producer of USA Sports from 1981 to 1987. "If you didn't have an NBA team in your city, you weren't seeing a lot of live national coverage. There might have been something on a Sunday, but the live Thursday night package was something people looked forward to. It was a great property for us."

Zrake made sure to invest money—whatever was available—into covering the games like USA was a Big 3 network. That meant upgraded trucks with more cameras and better announcers. "The position I wanted us to take was we are going to be for the true basketball fan, because that's who's watching us," he said. "We want to be able to give you the ins and outs. We want to give you the x's and o's and be maybe a little more technical than the broad-based network coverage would be, which was covering a lot more people obviously."

The late 1970s to early 1980s was an era of experimentation for cable, sometimes when it was most inconvenient. In the early days of USA Sports, Zrake lugged a little metal box with wires coming out of it—yes, it looked like a bomb; yes, he lugged it through airport security and explained what it was to the guards—to locales. That piece of equipment interfaced with the telecast's audio and opened the network's temporary satellite, which ensured the game went to homes nationwide. Seconds before going live, the telecast's audio guy hit a button on the box. The box with no name opened with a *bloop bloop*. And the satellite connection was a go. Maybe. Not until Zrake got a phone call—*okay, I see you*—was everything all right.

The minute before going to air was nerve-racking. There was no backup should the signal falter. But it was live TV with no net. Zrake loved it.

Meanwhile in Atlanta, erstwhile billboard salesman Ted Turner, founder of local channel WTCG and owner of the Atlanta Hawks and baseball's Atlanta Braves, coordinated with HBO head Jerry Levin to split the cost of a satellite-receiving antenna, and built an uplink to send up the signal. It was an exorbitant proposition for the cash-strapped Turner—to lease the satellite cost $100,000 a month—but the potential subscriber base was enormous.

Like many NBA owners at the time, Turner had more than a little fan in him. At one Hawks game, Turner felt the team's public address announcer failed to get the crowd sufficiently pumped. He rose from his seat, raced to the other side of the court, and pried the microphone from the PA guy's hands. Turner then led the fans in cheers, much to the referees' chagrin, said Bob Sieber, a longtime Turner employee. When Sieber interviewed at WTCG, Turner's office featured a giant map on the wall covered with stick pins. Each pin represented a station carrying WTCG. Turner asked Sieber to point to the closest NBA franchises. He obliged: Washington, D.C., New Orleans, Houston. Besides the Hawks, none of the franchises Sieber located was close to the southern states, let alone located in one.

"We bought these teams as TV programming," Turner told Sieber. "We have limited sports competition in these areas."

WTCG, rebranded as "SuperStation TBS"—a nod to its new corporate name, Turner Broadcasting System Inc.—showed the value of a sports team being identified with a region, something Chicago-based WGN would capitalize on during Michael Jordan's glory days. The NBA, during the 1978–79 NBA season, had 22 teams in 21 television markets, recalled Sieber, who became vice president of research at Turner Sports. That meant 189 television markets lacked a home team. Most lacked an independent station and got their sports programming from the national networks. Turner would air as many Hawks and Braves games as possible on TBS, Sieber said. Any financial losses were viewed as the cost of programming.

Not everyone understood the value of cable television. It was deemed a major deterrent to attendance: Why televise the games, when fans can pay to watch them at the arena? When you approached team owners about airing their home games, almost all of them chased you out of the room, said Tony Acone, a longtime cable executive. It didn't help that some of the stations lacked the gravitas of the networks. Before Ted Turner became a mass-media megastar, WTCG's station on West Peachtree Street in Atlanta had one studio. Large blocks of ice would form over the winter, causing the roof to leak. Occasionally, Sieber remembered, that ice would rocket off the top of the 1,100-foot TV tower and plummet toward the unprotected parking lot. The conference room doubled as a dressing room for the station's wrestlers, who taped their show on Saturday. On Monday, it reeked of aftershave and baby lotion.

These networks had nothing to lose. In the early 1980s, Acone ran a regional sports network in Southern California as part of cable pioneer's Bill Daniels's empire. He had spent months trying to secure the TV rights for the NBA's San Diego Clippers. That meant endless talks with the team's exasperating and racist owner, Donald Sterling, an experience Acone compared to "pinning Jell-O to the wall." Now, in yet another meeting, Sterling was babbling about moving a young franchise with no history and zero championship pedigree to Los Angeles. It was a crazy idea, Acone told Sterling. The Lakers owned LA.

An inspired Acone raced back to the office. Forget about spreading gradually; the station needed to be the affiliate for Lakers games. Daniels agreed. Acone grabbed his secretary and another employee, and issued an order: "Go to the library and find every piece you can on Jerry Buss." Acone read up on the Lakers owner. He was a real estate magnate—his purchase of the Lakers involved the Chrysler Building—who loved the University of Southern California's sports teams. He had a Ph.D. in physical chemistry, a relief to Acone, as "working with dummies is a pain in the ass." Buss agreed to meet with Acone for ninety minutes at the Polo Lounge in the Beverly Hills Hilton; they talked for five hours. After two or three more meetings, Buss and Acone agreed to a handshake deal to start a regional sports network once the Lakers' current TV deal expired. Lakers games would serve as the centerpiece of what became Prime Ticket Television Sports Network.

"Here's our deal," Acone said Buss told him. "You're going to teach me as much as you can teach me about the cable business. I'm going to teach you as much as I can teach you about the sports business."

Buss knew that the product on the court—the world champion Lakers of Magic, Worthy, and Abdul-Jabbar—would entice viewers to attend a game in person. Or a Duran Duran concert. Or Ice Capades. After all, the Forum, the Lakers' home court, hosted events 250 to 275 days a year. Buss, Acone said, used those events as a marketing tool. NBA owners were wary of cable, but Bob Thompson, who started as general manager and vice president of Denver's Prime Sports Network in 1989, saw the surveys: televising a team's games locally didn't harm the gate. Home games were a better advertisement: when the team was winning, the crowd was raucous. "It can come off as a two-and-a-half-hour commercial for your local NBA team," he said. Sieber saw the results at the Atlanta airport, where buses assembled to pick up scattered Hawks fans enticed by promotions and airline packages.

There were more benefits. Regional sports networks (RSNs) could offer a guaranteed rights fee. Prior to that, an independent TV station would offer a barter arrangement, Thompson explained. The team handled advertiser sales and production; the station broadcast the games. Steve Patterson, the general manager of the Houston Rockets, thought the couple of million bucks from Home Sports Entertainment (HSE) far exceeded what the team would lose if fans stayed home.

Independent stations, which later attached to Fox—and in the 1990s, the WB and UPN—grew less enamored with the NBA in prime-time, Thompson said. Teams got tired of heavy lifting. The arrangement could get messy. In 1966, Bill Rasmussen's NBC affiliate suddenly aired Boston Celtics playoff games. Another contractor had the gig, but a cameraman made a stupid move: he told off Red Auerbach. The Celtics' head coach and NBA power broker tossed the cameraman—and the independent TV company hired to produce the gig—from the Boston Garden the day of the game. Auerbach called his backup, so Rasmussen and the station's vice president drove ninety miles to get started. The pair sat in Auerbach's tiny office to hash out a per-game payment schedule per town. Once that was agreed upon, Auerbach added a request: "Make those checks payable to Arnold E. Auerbach."*

RSNs provided an ideal solution, Thompson said: RSNs got programming; NBA teams got a nice check for being there. And by working together constantly, instead of a handful of times a year, the production teams that covered the games got better. The quality of the telecasts improved, and that increased interest, said Jack Stanfield, HSE's first

---

*Auerbach's middle name was Jacob.

program director. The game was easy to sell. Regional sports networks could promote a game with the 76ers (Erving) or the Celtics (Bird) as an introduction to the local players, he said. After all, teams did the same thing. The Jazz gave away posters of *other teams'* stars, but TV's constant slate of games incited, Stanfield said, viewers to root for their hometown players.

The NFL, said Frank Vuono, the league's former vice president of retail licensing, ruled the national airwaves. The NBA could claim local territories with relatively little interference. They replaced radio stations as the way for fans to develop a relationship with announcers. Tommy Heinsohn and Mike Gorman became institutions in Boston. Marv Albert and rambling hook-shot enthusiast John Andriesse covered Knicks games for years on MSG. Chick Hearn and Stu Lantz owned Los Angeles. New franchises got in on the act. A young announcer named Kevin Harlan called games on radio and television for the expansion Minnesota Timberwolves.

Bob Stein, the Wolves' president and CEO, had to gently remind Harlan that he was selling a product. "Kevin, I know you get excited, that's part of what makes you so great, but can you please get a little more excited when *our* guys do something?"

To the superstations and regional cable stations, ESPN was a complementary piece. What ESPN did, Thompson thought, was make sports relevant beyond the weekend. Despite its explosive growth and 24/7 pace, ESPN couldn't cover every game. The network craved highlights, so it could be the record of sports, said Steve Bornstein, ESPN's former chairman and CEO. All the network needed, he explained, was *access* to every sport.

ESPN's mission did not clash with the regional sports networks' agendas. "Sports and politics are local," Thompson said. "You get beyond the hard-core sports fan." Regional sports networks allowed for a squadron of "mini-ESPNs" so you wouldn't miss out on the next day's water cooler chatter. Jody Shapiro worked at Washington, D.C.–based Home Team Sports for sixteen years. The teams the network carried— including the perpetually mediocre Washington Bullets—weren't big winners. But the network enjoyed a great following. Viewers felt they were part of the team, Shapiro said: they didn't get caught up in wins and losses.

Since every network had its own territory, there was no competition, said Shapiro, who in 1984 started as the head of programming and production for Home Team Sports. "We had 24/7 programming," he said. "We're all trying to figure out what worked, what didn't work, how do we fill 24 hours/365 days a year?" The RSNs worked together, sharing fill-in content that could be nationally distributed. "It made our channels better," said Ed Frazier, CEO of Liberty Sports. "Because we could pick and choose from a wide array of content" geared for their audiences.

With the increased use of satellites, Stanfield observed, the volume of highlights available to national networks and broadcast networks— and the quality of those clips—increased exponentially. That was where ESPN came in. Showing the best parts of various NBA games every night on *SportsCenter*, the network's signature news program, provided free advertising. The highlights were really a teaser to the game. As *SportsCenter* grew more sophisticated in its writing and anchors, it elevated all sports into events worthy of a narrative. The games we enjoyed were no longer boiled down to drab recaps to kill the few remaining minutes of a newscast, like John A. Walsh and countless dissatisfied sports fans had to endure. They were now an acceptable part of television journalism.

"The theory was: tell a story, do a lead-in to a game and establish a story line, do a game, and hold the result out for a dramatic revelation of who wins the game, and then tell who wins the game," said Walsh, who revitalized *SportsCenter* in the late 1980s after working at the fabled *In-*

side Sports. "The humor, the vocabulary, the linguistics—everything else was great. They helped tell the story in a better way."

When it came to cable networks airing NBA games, Stern was intimately involved. Dealing with Major League Baseball, Frazier said, was an aggravation. "Their strategy was to extract every possible asset and revenue that you could generate," he said. "They wanted to capture it." Teams knew someone would pay for the games. Stern grasped a simple concept, Frazier thought: if he killed the goose, there'd be no golden eggs. Stern was not a pushover—in fact, he drove Frazier nuts a lot—but the cable executive said he left the RSNs, his clients, with "enough on the table" to make it work. Stern saw television as an ally. After every Thursday night doubleheader on USA, there'd be a Friday conference call with the NBA, led by Stern, that served as half pep talk, half strategy session. Stern wanted the USA crew to inform the viewers, to tell it like it is, but to get people excited. "How do you do that when not every team has a star player?" said Eddie Doucette, who took part in those calls. "You sell players on other teams."

When the NBA moved to TBS in the mid-1980s, Stern would sometimes duck into the production truck on game day. It was like having another producer or director there, said Rex Lardner, Turner Sports' vice president. The attention to detail was staggering. After the games, he'd call Lardner and his boss, Bob Wussler, with a critique.

The game's presence on television was nowhere near its zenith in the early 1980s. Yet the NBA had no control over its image. That could not last much longer—and it would not.

The Brat was about to come of age.

SETTING UP THE BUSINESS PLAN

March 1982, Boston to New York City

Before Rob Millman boarded his flight to New York, he grabbed that day's copy of the *Boston Globe*. He turned to the sports section and was greeted with nothing short of a warning to get off the plane, head home, and forget about the NBA.

The article was the second part of the *Globe*'s weeklong series, "The National Basketball Affliction—The NBA: A Major League with Major Problems."

Millman, a divisional sales manager and buyer at the established New England department store chain Jordan Marsh, was an NBA fan. He kept his job interview with David Stern. At the NBA office, Millman asked Stern if anyone had called the NBA to comment on the *Boston Globe*'s series. No one had. "It seemed like either most people didn't care enough at the time to bother to call and follow up about it or it didn't matter," Millman said. "As a person thinking about joining the organization, in some ways I was comforted, I guess. In some ways, I wasn't."

It took Stern ten minutes to allay Millman's fears. Stern outlined his vision for the league. Marketing, sponsorships, publishing, and the players would work together to build a brand. Millman was transfixed and inspired. "That was the spirit and culture he created," he said. "It was right from that first interview that I felt it." Rick Welts, a future star in the league office, and Adrian De Groot also heard the sermon. The NBA needed to be a better partner. It had to embrace and showcase its history. It needed to work with the players so both sides shared in the success. Teams had to unite for the common good, working together and with the league. Stern weaved such a hopeful vision for anyone who loved the NBA and knew its potential. He talked only about what the NBA would become. Followers flocked.

"There was never a doubt that it wasn't going to happen," said De Groot, who became president of NBA Properties.

"He just kept working at it, and we kept banging away at it every day," Millman said.

The *Boston Globe*'s series, featuring contributions from ace staff writers such as Bob Ryan and Dan Shaughnessy, was not a hit piece. The NBA's myriad problems had not disappeared because of Magic and Bird and Doctor J or television's promise.

Something had to be done about the owners.

Mike Suscavage couldn't comprehend what he was watching. It was June 24, 1980, and it was raining softballs in Cleveland.

The head of NBA Properties was there on league business. He decided to visit a promotion that Cavaliers owner Ted Stepien had organized for his professional softball team, the creatively named Cleveland Stepien's Competitors. Stepien stood out among the owners, the least of the reasons being that he was a terrible businessman, an observation made by Dr. Jerry Buss, the flashy, brilliant owner of the Los Angeles Lakers before the start of a Suscavage-led meeting.

"Shut up, son," Buss said. "I want to know why this asshole"—Buss pointed at Stepien—"is paying Scott Wedman $750,000 a year. If he's worth $750,000 a year, I'm going to offer Magic Johnson a million dollars a year for life." (Instead, Buss signed Johnson to a twenty-five-year, $25 million contract.)

Wedman, an All-Star with the Kansas City Kings, wasn't the most egregious free agent acquisition to occur under Stepien's watch. That distinction belonged to center James Edwards.

The Indiana Pacers, then Edwards's team, offered around $200,000 a year. Stepien countered with $500,000, a fortune for a seven-foot center with an aversion to rebounding who wasn't an All-Star. Bob Whitsitt, who then worked in Indiana's front office, said Edwards's agent called Stepien a week later: We've got an offer for $500,000. It's now $700,000.

The agent didn't disclose a minor detail: the $500,000 offer was Stepien's original offer.

Edwards got $700,000 a year from Cleveland plus an incentive for bonuses. He didn't last two full seasons before he was traded to Phoenix.

Shockingly, Stepien's lack of savvy extended to promotions. That was why Suscavage witnessed Stepien toss softballs from the Terminal Tower, as his players braced for the 140-mph death spheres seven hundred feet below. The first throw belted the hood of a passing car on Superior Avenue. The second found twenty-four-year-old Gayle Falinski, who was *not* participating. She broke her wrist. "It could easily have been her head," Falinski's husband, Regis, fumed to the Associated Press. The third toss grazed a man on the shoulder. Luckily, no additional property or people were damaged in the stunt.

"It was a total disaster," Suscavage said. "It was just indicative of the kind of ownership that you had." Stepien was a special kind of terrible, but Suscavage was unimpressed by most of the owners. They were, he thought, men with lots of money and little knowledge of how to run a sports team. "Everybody was George Steinbrenner," said David Du-Pree, the veteran sportswriter for the *Washington Post* and *USA Today.*

The owners, David Stern observed, needed to be protected from themselves.

Stern said that two years after the landmark 1983 collective bargain agreement between the NBA and its Players Association served as a major renovation of the league's image by enforcing fiscal responsibility on the owners. The salary cap prevented Ted Stepien from being Ted Stepien—at least to a lesser degree. It also gave teams in smaller markets equal footing to compete. Forget about the San Diego Chicken or Bill Cosby performing after the buzzer. Winning was the biggest attraction. No longer could the Lakers, the Knicks, and the big-market teams use money to establish or maintain dominance, as Buss had in signing Johnson to that controversial quarter-century deal.

The other critical component of the deal was revenue sharing. The players got 53 percent of the league's gross; the owners took the rest. The Oscar Robertson rule may have granted players the freedom to go where they wanted, but it also contributed to skyrocketing salaries, said Jim Quinn, Robertson's attorney, who also represented the National Basketball Players Association. That was great for such players as Moses Malone and his league-high $2 million yearly salary. But teams could not keep up with the increased figures. The Jazz and Nuggets merging was reported as a possibility. The New Jersey Nets were a perpetual mess.

The players had their pride. So did the owners, said Eric Fleisher, a longtime agent. Their identities were locked into the fate of their franchises. They had invested money and endured terrible times. The breakthrough came when the NBA got vulnerable. Quinn hated how the NBA team owners cried poor. The Players Association's pleas to see the books were never met until fall 1982. "Holy shit," Quinn said to Larry Fleisher, the head of the Players Association. "This is not good." The data were reported in booklets going back several years, one for each team. It was all quite dramatic, remembered Quinn, whose fear proved correct: five or six teams teetered toward bankruptcy. That was when the NBA floated the idea of a salary cap and the Players Association offered revenue sharing, contributing to the NBA's Era of Good Feelings.

A work stoppage spelled doom for the NBA, said the Milwaukee Bucks' Junior Bridgeman, the Players Association's treasurer. The association voted to strike on April 2 if a deal hadn't been reached. Many owners, O'Brien recalled later, dreaded a strike. If the strike had lasted into the 1983–84 season, replacement players would have filled teams' rosters. Both sides, Bridgeman said, knew they had to get a deal done: the NBA lacked the popularity to keep fans from wandering to college or even to high school basketball. The goal of the Players Association was enormous, said Steve Mix, the association's secretary: How do we protect the owners from financial self-harm and save the jobs of the players and the franchises themselves? Both sides *had* to find a solution. "I never doubted," O'Brien wrote years later, "that, eventually, somehow, somewhere, common sense would prevail."

"It was just amazing to me how you had to not think about the current issue, but you had to think two or three issues down the line," said Bridgeman. Something you said or did, he added, might affect the whole process.

Some key decisions got made outside the bargaining table. Late in the negotiations, Quinn and Larry Fleisher were walking up Manhattan's Sixth Avenue with Milwaukee Bucks center Bob Lanier, the association's dedicated president. Years before, the Loyola Opera House, the New Orleans Jazz's temporary home, had installed Louisiana fishnet around its raised court to protect the players. The Players Association wanted to ensure its soundness. Lanier, on an off day, flew to New Orleans. He grabbed a cab to the arena, got out, ran from one end of the court into the netting, and repeated the process. "This works fine," Lanier told Barry Mendelson, the Jazz's twenty-nine-year-old executive. Mission accomplished, he left the arena and returned to the parked cab. Now the massive Lanier looked down at Quinn and Fleisher and said, "You know, fucking Moses is going to have to learn to live on the $2 million." The $3.6 million cap was a soft cap—there were loopholes, including the "Larry Bird exception" allowing teams to exceed the cap to re-sign one of their own players. Larry Fleisher thought that if the superstars were happy, the money would trickle down to the Marc Iavaronis of the world. But what if the owners didn't want to spend the money? asked Celtics guard Quinn Buckner, who was active in union matters. The owners can't help themselves, Fleisher told Buckner. They will spend the money. That's who they are. They just need parameters.

The cap's complicated reputation was overblown, said Bill Jemas, an NBA attorney who helped teams interpret the cap. Jemas was working late as his future wife, Jane, tried to get him to get the hell out of there. A junior lawyer came in to ask Jemas a question about the cap's bonus rule. He explained it once. Then twice. After a third visit, Jane, who lacked a financial background, grabbed the colleague by the elbow and pulled him into the hallway to explain it. If you weren't afraid of math and "let your brain to be plastic and intake it," a general manager could master the salary cap. Really, there was no choice. Those who learned the ins and outs of the cap—such as Jerry West of the Los Angeles Lakers—gave their teams a competitive advantage. And when any element of the collective bargain agreement (CBA) was murky, said the Lakers' Lon Rosen, NBA attorney Gary Bettman improvised a solution.

Irwin Mandel of the Chicago Bulls was another salary cap maestro. It added a fun, creative wrinkle to the job and got his competitive juices racing. How could he take advantage of the rules—which changed every year—and legally work around them to improve his team? "It's like the difference," Mandel half-joked, "between tax avoidance and tax evasion." Here, it was "cap avoidance."*

---

*FYI: Mandel knew when to skimp and save. "Michael Jordan was a bargain at any amount," he said.

The salary cap was meant as a stopgap, said Charles Grantham, the Players Association's executive vice president. Today, "there's no need for a salary cap," Quinn said. "There may have been back then. Part of it was optics as much as anything else."

Good public relations gave the NBA a boost as the 1980s continued, Quinn said: Stern, now at the forefront, could sell previously unsellable teams and enjoy the success of league-wide stability. As *BusinessWeek* reported in its 1985 cover story on the NBA, "the prospect of profitability means that basketball franchises are beginning to attract buyers who are both stronger financially and more astute managerially." In the 1970s, agent Barry Frank said, the owners "were businessmen who were basketball junkies. They all, I think at one time, hoped they could be in their workout clothes out on the floor with these huge guys playing ball."

Today a sports franchise adds a splash of color in a black-and-white business portfolio. Herb Simon and his late brother, Mel, bought the Indiana Pacers in 1983, mostly as a favor to the Indianapolis mayor and the powers-that-be. But as time passed and Herb Simon got more involved, the Pacers grew on him. When the team finally got good, owning a team became intoxicating. Nearly forty years later, Simon hasn't lost the feeling of anticipation that accompanies a new season.

"If I had bought a factory or a shopping center or even T-bills, it wouldn't have been any fun," Houston promoter and Denver Nuggets owner Sidney L. Schlenker said. "And besides, who would have known or cared? Everyone in Denver knew about me when I bought the Nuggets and then a condominium [in town] and promised to keep the team in Denver."

The franchises' value appreciated, said Rick Sund, the front-office executive for the Dallas Mavericks. But the prevailing thought among the owners, he said, was "'I bought the franchise for $3 million, now it's worth $40 [million]. The appreciation is carrying my losses.' You got to the point where people didn't care." Owners would sign players, borrow money, and sell the team to pay off the debt—and get a nice profit. That's why so many teams, Sund said, were sold from the 1970s to the 1990s. "That's kind of how teams were managed back in those days until it got to the point where we said, 'This is crazy. We're spending all this money, we should have the right to make a profit.'"

Schlenker got a good return on his investment. Four years later, he sold the Nuggets for $65 million. According to *BusinessWeek*, Schlenker reportedly paid $20 million.

Optics meant everything, especially when it came to the NBA's revolutionary drug policy. The league wasn't trying to be crusaders or form a policing unit, O'Brien said.* "We're trying to be responsible to the people who, in turn, enjoy our sport, attend our sport, and view our sport," he told Lesley Stahl on *Face the Nation*. "There's a credibility factor." Lanier hated how the public thought the players were perpetually coked up because Micheal Ray Richardson or John Drew made headlines for the wrong reasons. Players pushed for the policy, said Quinn. In fact, Russ Granik, the NBA's executive vice president, said the players initially wanted a lifetime ban for caught players, until Stern and the NBA pushed for compassion. Under the arrangement, any player who initially came forward received no penalty, and the club paid for his rehabilitation without a reduction in salary. It was a firm but reasonable plan. As Grantham noted, the policy treated drug use as an addiction, not a character flaw or a component of race. It wasn't until the player

---

*In Jonathan Abrams's wonderful oral history of the 1986 Houston Rockets for *Grantland*, Robert Reid said his teammates Mitchell Wiggins and Lewis Lloyd, who were suspended for drug use, were set up by the NBA. Darryl Dawkins said Micheal Ray Richardson was tailed by a shadowy security force. In *Sugar*, Rosen reported that Phoenix Suns star Walter Davis was busted for cocaine use by an undercover cop hired by the NBA. Davis, through his current employer, the Denver Nuggets, declined to be interviewed.

committed a third offense that he was dismissed from the league, but he could apply for reinstatement after two years. That fate befell Richardson. The decision, which Stern (then NBA commissioner) hated to enact, served as a warning to the players and a motivation for the troubled young man. (The fatal drug overdose of college star Len Bias in June 1986, two days after he was drafted by the Boston Celtics, provided another moral and legal deterrent.) At the McDonald's Open in 1997, Richardson grabbed a seat next to Stern and told him that he saved his life. Getting exiled opened his eyes and set him straight. Stern's reputation also got a boost. It was clear that Stern was in charge, and that he wasn't going to allow unruly behavior, NBA Entertainment's Don Sperling said. There were now consequences to actions.

Norm Sonju, the general manager of the Dallas Mavericks, thought the drug policy gave players hope. But, he added, it wasn't as strong as the Mavericks' 24/7 policy, a requirement in every contract. Granik and Stern told Sonju that when they asked him to drop the clause. "It won't be as good and defined as well as yours, but there will be twenty-two other teams now having what they don't have now."* Doug Adkins, the Mavs' general counsel, said the NBA's policy prevented teams from testing players who needed it—or who wanted it. Freshly drafted Mavs forward Roy Tarpley, Adkins said, admitted to smoking marijuana and requested to be tested by the team every day. The Players Association nixed the arrangement. "We did everything we could to salvage that kid," Adkins said. Tarpley, who died in 2015 at age fifty, missed three whole seasons due to substance abuse–related suspensions. The league blanched at an independent drug clause, because it looked as if the owners were against the players, but Adkins said the team wanted to help its players, not look for an excuse to void a contract.

---

*Sonju can't remember whether Stern or Granik made the request but said they were on the phone call. Granik declined interview requests.

Players were not keen on taking away another man's livelihood, Grantham said, but the new reality demanded it. Money was on the line. Grantham thought the CBA, along with the drug policy, provided security for buyers—they had a way to control labor costs. Plus, a guaranteed percentage of the revenue tied both parties together. The more money the players made, the more money the owners made. Owners abhor flat revenue; a percentage of the gross promised steady growth and an incentive to improve the product.

Though O'Brien hailed the deal to the media, Bridgeman always dealt with Stern. He could be forceful and abrasive, but he knew the players serving as partners was a critical concept and never jeopardized that, Grantham said. Gary Way, who worked for the NBA and Nike, said the salary cap enabled the NBA's marketing push. "Both David and the Players Association realized that for the league to grow and to prosper, the players were more important than just being the employees who played the game," he said. "They were a big part of your product."

What also worked in Stern's favor was that he spoke the owners' language, Suscavage said. Their trust carried enormous value, as did his long relationship with Larry Fleisher, who had led the Players Association since its creation in the early 1960s. They were evenly matched adversaries, attorney Peter Gruenberger said: vipers who ultimately believed you got more with honey than with "the opposite end of a broom handle." CBA negotiations were always contentious, Fleisher's son Eric said. Stern and a pack of lawyers arrived at Fleisher's small, comfortable office in the Gulf + Western building on Columbus Circle. The elder Fleisher pulled chairs from everywhere, invited everyone to sit, and closed the office door. Then he would take on the NBA's legal team; sometimes with Jim Quinn. Screaming and shouting would commence, Eric Fleisher remembered. Eventually, the door opened. Larry Fleisher would emerge with a smile and a wink to his son. He'd head to the bathroom and then resume combat.

Substance existed behind the bluster. Fleisher realized that fighting for the players' rights required a trip to the courts, as happened with the Oscar Robertson suit. "When we won all of those motions, he could have held out for a much larger per-player payment of cash," Gruenberger said. It was more important for Fleisher to give the players their freedom and to change the dynamics at the bargaining table.

Fleisher was "a genuinely honest man," Oscar Robertson said. Howard Cosell, a man not known for gooey testimonials, called Fleisher "a warm and loving and loved human being." When Fleisher died suddenly of a heart attack at fifty-eight in 1989, Stern spoke at the funeral and bawled at the cemetery.

He never took a salary from the Players Association—though it did pay for office space. Fleisher served as an agent to many NBA players, which rankled some of his colleagues. "I used to tell the other agents, 'If he's able, because of his skill and stature and trust that players put in him, to create rules that enable everyone else to make a lot of money representing players, you should thank him,'" said agent David Falk, a power broker. The game and the players—he took only 2.5 percent for services rendered, compared to an agent's typical 20 percent cut—were his life. Eric Fleisher reaped the benefits, shooting baskets with a young Bill Bradley in his backyard and playing the Bullets' Archie Clark one-on-one. While other kids in his travel league scouted the crowd for their parents, ten-year-old Eric spotted the Captain, Willis Reed, his dad's client.

Marc Fleisher, Larry's other agent son, thought Stern grasped that the value of the league lay in its players. Stern was in perfect position to turn his belief into an incomprehensibly profitable fact. And he had a massive amount of goodwill to expend. He helped pull the NBA through a potentially disastrous squall and into a safe clearing. He had the owners' trust while saving them from financial ruin. Larry O'Brien signed off on what Stern did. Years later, Robertson said that when Stern took over as commissioner, he had fallen into an ideal situation because of all the great players who blossomed in his era. But Stern steered the NBA's appeal of its players beyond zealots and beat writers. Throughout the early 1980s, he assembled his army, including Rick Welts, who worked for sports agent and promoter Bob Walsh in Seattle after serving as media relations director for the SuperSonics and Brian McIntyre, the league's universally adored public relations director. Rob Millman's old boss, Bill Marshall, capitalized on rookie Larry Bird's popularity by designing a Bird-themed T-shirt for Jordan Marsh. His boss didn't care—until a thousand boys' shirts were sold in two hours. Celtics shirts soon sprang up in fifteen Jordan Marsh shops. David Stern liked what he saw.

"You can do this in Boston; can you do it in Utah?" Stern asked Marshall.

"Well, all I know [is,] if nothing has ever been done in Boston, then probably nothing's ever been done in Philadelphia, Seattle, Chicago, L.A.," Marshall replied. "I was right."

Barbara Ward noticed a change in the office as Stern and Granik continued their ascent. A new breed, divorced of any two-martini lunch tendencies, had arrived. Most secretaries hated to have lunch with their bosses. Ward had no such issues with Stern and Granik. They were, she said, "the type of person I thought I'd grow up to be" and why Ward became a lawyer. When she left for Harvard Law School, the staff gave her a hard-side briefcase with her initials on it. Granik thought Ward would consider a soft-side one sexist.

She was also the secretary for Gary Bettman, who previously worked with Stern at Proskauer. He felt a twinge of jealousy when Stern left for the NBA. He's got the greatest job in the world, he told a colleague. I'd love to work with him. Ward marveled at Bettman's intelligence. Early on, Bettman had to review a binder teeming with documents. It would have taken Ward, who later became a United States attorney, a day to navigate. Bettman finished it in maybe a half day. She thought he was joking. He wasn't. Same when he incorporated NBA Entertainment, the league's film and video arm, in less than an afternoon. Do you know what you're doing? Ward asked. Sure, Bettman said, this gets done all the time. A binder. Some papers to fill out. A notary stamp. *Voilà.* "It's done!"

"He's brilliant," said Lon Rosen, Magic Johnson's longtime agent, who credits Bettman as the architect of the collective bargain agreement.

Focused, pugnacious, and slyly funny, Bettman was almost a carbon copy of Stern, thought Adrian De Groot, the president of NBA Properties. "He wanted to be David Jr.," said John Gaffney, director of sports marketing of CBS/Fox Video. The company handled distribution, sales, and marketing for NBA Entertainment's videos, which fell under Bettman's purview. That was far from an ideal scenario for Gaffney. *This guy is a shark,* he thought, *he doesn't close his eyes.* Bob Stein, the Minnesota Timberwolves' president, dealt with Bettman as the expansion franchise navigated parking issues and the various headaches of building a massive new arena smack-dab in then-cozy downtown Minneapolis. Finesse was required with Bettman. "The harder you pushed, the harder he pushed back," Stein said, but when you asked for help it was like talking to a different person.*

Welts joked that there were three criteria to work in the NBA. You had to be madly in love with the NBA, be young, and work cheap. Welts's first break came at age sixteen. A classmate at Queen Anne High School, Earl Woodson, glumly announced that his family was leaving Seattle. The Sonics needed a new ball boy. Welts, trying to contain his enthusiasm, asked Woodson to introduce him to the Sonics' trainer, who hired Welts. Sports served as a treasured currency between Welts

---

*Bettman is arguably the most successful alumnus of the NBA's executive ranks: he has served as commissioner of the National Hockey League since 1993. Through an NHL spokesperson, Bettman declined to be interviewed for this book.

and his father, Keith, plus a source of civic pride. Welts was fascinated that a city could rally around a basketball team. Paul Gilbert, the director of production for the NBA, was another die-hard hoops fan in a corporate commune. If Knicks tickets were available in the office, Gilbert snapped them up. Even after a day of dealing with NBA minutiae, he hopped in a cab to see his cherished Knicks play.

"There weren't a lot of us," said Gilbert, who was NBA employee number 32. "The hires were hard-core basketball fans. We had a real passion for the game." That included Stern, who Gilbert believed made many of his decisions from that perspective. If Stern thought a person was sharp and could help the NBA, said Alex Sachare, the league's director of information, he'd hire them "and then worry how to best use them."

Stern was in the office at 7:30 a.m., gone by 8 p.m., and he was always on. "David was intense, but a good kind of intense," Gilbert added. What the game could become, Stern said years later, drove the staff. "It comes down to this," said Rich Dorfman, the league's director of broadcasting in the late 1970s and early 1980s. "David loved basketball. He *loved* basketball. He was just so bright. You couldn't tell him, 'No, we can't do this.'"

David Stern was determined to make everyone see how wonderful the NBA was. Damage control would soon give way to Madison Avenue polish—and no one was going to tell Stern what couldn't be done.

GETTING READY FOR STAR TIME

All it took was an office tour for David Stern to see the future. That is the theory of Geoff Belinfante, who played accidental gatekeeper.

In 1977, Major League Baseball Productions debuted *This Week in Baseball*, the popular weekly roundup of baseball's news and highlights narrated by honey-throated Mel Allen. The NBA took notice. The proper phone calls were made. One of Larry O'Brien's top lieutenants arrived at MLB Productions' facilities at 1212 Sixth Avenue in midtown Manhattan.

Belinfante, then senior producer of MLB Productions, hosted Stern in 1979 or 1980.

"He was far more attentive as a basketball executive than any of the baseball executives," Belinfante said.* Stern scribbled notes and asked good questions. A few years later, NBA Entertainment came along, creating segments for halftime shows and home videos. Belinfante noticed the system was very similar to MLB's: videotapes of the games were shipped in, loggers would look for the highlights, and they'd be cataloged for *This Week in Baseball* and for in-stadium entertainment.

---

*Stern confirmed his visit in an interview with journalist Shawn Fury. Stern, both individually and through his longtime assistant, Linda Tossi, declined to be interviewed for this book.

But there was a huge difference. NBA Entertainment, Belinfante observed, marketed personalities, not the game. The videos and features appealed to "the marginal side of their fan base." Plus, NBA Entertainment was part of the NBA, so it had the cooperation of players, the union, and management, a situation MLB Productions "could only dream about," Belinfante said. He and his colleagues watched with envy the money the NBA invested in production and travel as Major League Baseball closed its wallet and their mind. The guardians of the game balked at making players the stars, Belinfante said: they'd get too much power and want more money. "Baseball was battling its players," said Rick White, the former president and CEO of Major League Baseball Properties. "They despised its product and at every public turn made that clear" because of its long-standing clash with the Major League Baseball Players Association. Anything MLB Productions accomplished, Belinfante said, was done in spite of baseball's powers-that-be, not because of them.

Stern thanked Belinfante for his help whenever the two crossed paths. The NBA offered Belinfante the chance to run NBA Entertainment early on. But he made more money at MLB Productions, and baseball was always the bigger sport.

"I didn't think enough of basketball to make the switch," Belinfante said. "And, boy, was I wrong."

Stern may have looked like a kindly English teacher—a baby face hidden by glasses and a middle-management mustache—but passion and volatility came out with fire-hose force. The notion of "we've always done it that way" invited an outburst. Stern understood that the NBA was not handcuffed to tradition like football or baseball. J. Walter Kennedy was scared. Larry O'Brien lacked the imagination or the inclination, so David Stern steered the NBA toward his vision.

The creation of NBA Entertainment was inspired by the NBA's thirty-fifth anniversary in the 1980–81 season. Ed Desser, then the Lakers' director of broadcasting, thought the NBA needed to utilize television to sell and promote the NBA à la *The NFL Today* with its highlights and colorful, intelligent personalities. NBA halftime programming consisted of "what can we put on the air to fill fifteen minutes that won't cost us anything." The highlight, if one could call it that, was an interview with Sam Goldaper, the *New York Times*' NBA columnist. "I'll put it gently," Desser said. "Sam Goldaper had a great face for radio."

Desser said he urged Stern to have the NBA create and provide halftime programming for various telecasts. Thirty-five halftime segments were produced to commemorate the thirty-fifth anniversary. "That was sort of the first time the NBA got involved in having TV programming produced that was anything other than 'Here, CBS, take this license and go produce a game,'" Desser said.

If a network needed material for a feature, a lead-in, whatever, the NBA had them covered. "We asserted that we could do it whether we could or couldn't and we did," Stern said. "So that's how it grew."

Stern wanted more. There was no video library. In addition to securing old games from ABC, he sent a memo to O'Brien: Have the league buy each team a three-quarter-inch VCR—total cost: $135,000—to record the game feed and then ship the tapes via Federal Express. Years later, Stern admitted the plan was far from original. That material—which could be archived or used for programming—was one of the "things that any normal sports league should do" and the ethos behind NBA Entertainment. (The cinematic, sweeping NFL Films—an aspirational model for the NBA—perfected this principle.) It also highlighted a self-reliance that defined the Stern era. The NBA would control the content and its message, said Don Sperling, the executive producer and senior vice president of NBA Entertainment, and keep related revenue streams in-house.

NBA Entertainment later had its own facility in Secaucus, New Jersey—about eighty miles northeast from NFL Films' anonymous headquarters in Mount Laurel, New Jersey—complete with a studio where shows such as the kid-friendly hit *NBA Inside Stuff* were filmed. NBA Entertainment sprang from W & W Films, housed at a dumpy office on 1650 Broadway, where five or six rooms got divvied up into workstations and edit rooms.

Working at NBA Entertainment was very much a "wax-on, wax-off" situation, said longtime employee David Gavant, referring to Daniel LaRusso's unusual apprenticeship in *The Karate Kid*. You'd start as an intern or as a logger. You'd move on to a production assistant, where you'd learn how to edit small pieces. As an associate producer, you'd tell small stories. Finally, you were a producer. And so on.

Loggers unearthed the footage. A young NBA Entertainment staffer reviewed the game footage and hunted for amazing plays, fan reactions, whatever was funny or unusual.

"We would watch every game on three-quarter-inch tape with a little analog number that clicked over and over; it was like a tape counter," said acclaimed sports documentarian Jonathan Hock, who started as a logger in 1985. "You would zero at the head of the tape and watch the games and write on a mimeographed sheet of paper with a pencil, longhand, the mark on the tape where the play occurred, the play that occurred, who did it, what it was." For example: *Moncrief driving layup over Tree Rollins. Low-angle replay.*

Heidi Palarz began her lengthy career in television at NBA Entertainment. The more she logged, the more she recognized the qualities—angles, framing—that made a good play or reaction shot; she started to notice what the producers wanted. When she became a producer, Palarz knew what to ask the loggers, because she had been in their situation. The system was so effective that Gavant used it when he moved over to Major League Baseball Productions.

Watching the local broadcast of every basketball game—the blow-outs, the lethargic post–All-Star Game grinds—may sound tedious if you are not a basketball fan. "Can you imagine being twenty-one years old and coming out of college, and getting paid to watch basketball games every day?" Hock said. "It was awesome." Staffers chose their favorites. Jim Podhoretz dug certain announcers. Hock went for Sonics games, because he loved high-flying Tom Chambers. Stephen Koontz grabbed Spurs games, because he was an Alvin Robertson fan. Plus, you could go to any NBA game and the staff made room for you *no questions asked.*

Don Sperling set the tone. "He couldn't have been that much older than we were," Hock said. "He certainly, in his sort of jokey way, really did inspire us to work hard and care. He had a sense of people who were very young, very unskilled, or inexperienced, and put us together and in an environment that didn't offer a lot but fostered a camaraderie that was based around the game and wanting to do great things for it." There was a communal feeling in the office, like being in a college dorm, said David Check, who started as a production assistant in 1987. Staff members played Nerf basketball at 2 a.m. Koontz would announce Thorough Bread's daily soup specials over the intercom. ("Chick Suck Dump" for chicken succotash dumpling was a favorite.) Palarz, who loved to bake, brought in brownies regularly. "It was like a fraternity there, but I say that in the best possible way," she said. "I felt nothing but respect and inclusion from the first day." Coworkers, Palarz recalled, looked out for each other. NBA Entertainment, Hock said, was *Lord of The Flies* but with good guys.

The pay was lousy. The hours stretched into double digits. When a deadline loomed, staffers slept on their desks to avoid the rats that roamed, said Stephen Koontz, a producer there. The young employees did not care. Sperling reined in his staffers, Check thought, yet allowed them to push creative boundaries that reflected what was happening on the court. In those early years, Check said, NBA Entertainment felt like a fun-loving film school or graduate program where the projects made it onto TV or home video. Sperling was the professor everyone loved. "You wanted him to be proud," Hock said.

Sperling's hiring process was inexact but effective: he looked into the applicants' eyes and trusted his instincts. He wanted a good work ethic, a spark of creativity, and most important, passion. "The rest was easy," he said. "You could teach them the business." At some point, Sperling's hires held top positions at the entertainment arms of the other three major sports. Was he right 100 percent of the time? "No," Sperling said, "but I was right most of the time."

The young employees felt they were part of something special. "I remember Scott [Messick] and I getting on his bicycle—me sitting on the handlebars—and him pedaling from the postproduction office on the East Side over to our office on Fifty-first and Broadway at 2:30 in the morning to get a couple of tapes that were left back for a shot we needed to replace," Hock said. "We were kings of our little kingdom. We were making the world champion Lakers' year-end video. The one. We were in charge of this really important thing." Making it great was a source of pride, not a pain in the ass.

"Listen, those guys got the ultimate coverage," said Koontz. "There wasn't a cameraman or a production crew on the planet in any genre that covered anything better than we covered the NBA." Players, when they saw the final product, breathed easy, Koontz added. They looked good. The story was correct. They benefited. "We were directly responsible for popularizing the game, romanticizing the game."

Donna Orender had her own production company before heading to the PGA Tour, where she developed and led its global production, programming, and digital businesses. For her, NBA Entertainment was a client and "an aspirational high bar" because it presented "a way in which to build content, to build assets, and really build out a way for fans to connect with your players more than just on the court."

There was one rule, said Messick, another longtime employee: make the league look good. Everything else was open to discussion. "It was a nonstarter to do a story about Larry Bird and Julius Erving fighting at half-court," he said. "That's not the messaging. Anything about the players and the competition and helping kids or being role models, all that stuff was part of the marketing message. None of it was wrong. There were few things that sort of went the other way." The idea, said Stern, was to give the NBA "the dignity I thought it deserved."

The youthful energy of NBA Entertainment needed to be nurtured. Sperling had help. With his cousin Dick, Barry Winik had run W & W Films, a sports production company that counted the NBA as a client. Barry Winik stayed on at NBA Entertainment as director of photography, though the Oscar-nominated, pioneering sports cameraman was vastly overqualified. Winik legitimized the outfit: the players, Koontz said, saw an older guy with presence who clearly wasn't there to fuck around.

Winik knew how to put a story together, David Gavant said. A player who hit a buzzer-beater became a two-minute story, complete with highlights and interviews. "You could make a story out of anything," Gavant said, "but it was his years of experience in the field in seeing thousands of interviews of athletes, he could recognize a great story probably in a nanosecond." Gavant was interviewing Michael Jordan for the documentary *Come Fly with Me* when Jordan mentioned being cut from his high school varsity team. Gavant finished the interview but felt a tap on his shoulder. "Ask Michael about being cut from the varsity team again," Winik whispered. Gavant did. Jordan answered. More tapping. "ASK. HIM. AGAIN." Jordan finally provided an in-depth answer that satisfied Winick. "Michael Jordan got cut from his high school team" is a central part of his all-American narrative.

Winik didn't take plays off. Gavant and another young colleague were in Charlotte working on the expansion Hornets' year-in-review video. They were sitting at the Hornets media desk, feeling smug as they watched the game. "All of a sudden, we find ourselves on the floor," Gavant said. "Someone had come behind us both and pulled our chairs down."

It was Winik. "If I'm *working*, you're *working*," he barked. "Go find me shots to shoot."

Winik, deep into middle age and lugging a camera through a giant arena to cover a lousy team, was justified, Gavant thought. It provided a valuable lesson: working for the NBA was a privilege—you better work. "He did it with all of us," Koontz said. He was on the Boston Garden floor, watching Bird and Magic create history in real time until Winik turned him away from the court. "You're here to do a fuckin' job. You're not here to watch the fuckin' game."

"He was the grumpy old man, and we loved him for that, because he respected the job more than anyone else—and he worked his *ass* off," Messick said. "I loved Barry."

When NBA Entertainment moved to the nicer, rat-infested digs on East Thirty-Second Street, Winik got a corner office. Employees sought excuses to visit the elder statesman and soak up stories. Then there were what Gavant called "Obi-Wan lessons." Don't try to do too much. Slow down. Have your five most important questions ready. He was everybody's favorite teacher in a thinly veiled educational environment, Palarz said. "He would sometimes very quietly walk into the back of my editing room, and he'd sit and give you encouragement about why something worked, and he'd give you suggestions about where something could be improved," she said. "He was really the glue for everything."

The third giant influence was a young woman named Leah Wilcox. Tall, pretty, and brimming with positive energy, Wilcox was one part den mother, one part athlete whisperer, and entirely indispensable.

"She created a role that was unique to her," Palarz said, "but it was five people rolled into one." As Jim Podhoretz, a mainstay at NBA Entertainment, said: she was the NBA's secret weapon. Wilcox, said Gavant, was "just another girl from the Bronx." Everyone who entered her sphere—agents, players and their families, musicians—got treated exactly the same. And everyone trusted her immediately.

"She's like a warm blanket the moment you meet her," Gavant said.

When he started at the NBA in October 1986, Gavant, a young Georgia transplant, knew no one in New York. Home was an old fraternity brother's spare bedroom in Elmont, Long Island; the city intimidated him. Wilcox knew her coworker was overwhelmed. She took Gavant, a self-described very naïve Jewish white kid, to a rap concert in the Bronx featuring Heavy D and Salt-N-Pepa. "It was a transformative experience," he said. "She took me under her wing, and she made sure I was okay for the first couple of months I was in New York."

"Leah is and was a force of nature," Palarz said.

"Guys couldn't say no to Leah," Podhoretz said.

"The NBA players loved her," said Gil Kerr, director of production at NBA Entertainment. "Leah Wilcox could get an NBA player to do *anything*."

Kerr was working on a halftime feature for CBS featuring Isiah Thomas. Kerr had to change the location, and no one bothered to tell Thomas, who arrived late and irritable. The superstar guard continued to mope. Then Wilcox stepped in.

"Isiah, shut up and sit down!"

Kerr got his interview.

Part of Wilcox's influence stemmed from her background. The NBA was overwhelmingly African American "and she is an African American from the neighborhood," said Gary Way, the former NBA executive, who is black. "She got it," he said.

That kind of personal touch was an integral skill. NBA players in the 1980s were not as media-tolerant as today's crop, who grew up with reality television, said Gavant. During his twelve-year stint at NBA Entertainment, "you had to earn the trust of the players." Wilcox, Messick said, became "our backdoor dog whistle to the players, because she could ask them things that we couldn't as producers." A team's PR person might not secure Messick an interview with James Worthy or Mark Aguirre, "but if they saw me talking to Leah, then my credibility was elevated 50 percent." Her rapport with the players also allowed Wilcox to steer Messick away from disaster. She knew when a player took his pregame nap or when he talked to his wife and kids. She knew what musicians the players liked, a huge help when it came to assembling highlights, said Jon Miller, who started as an NBA Entertainment employee in 1987 and later served as chairman and CEO of America Online.

Wilcox was connected in a way that eluded the usual crop of Masters of the Universe, Way said. Wilcox didn't know a musician, but she went to school with his cousin. She knew a player from the Rucker Tournament. Way considered Wilcox one of the NBA's most valuable employees because she delivered "the up-close and personal opportunities that the NBA leveraged so well."

The intimate approach started with advertising. All that footage reviewed by the loggers was used for NBA promos. What sport did this? But it was an ingenious move. "The best promotion for us," Stern would tell colleagues, "is the slo-mo footage of our very beautiful and graceful game." The spots, created by Paul Gilbert, the first employee of NBA Entertainment, did much more. They showed all the fun—the dunks, the flashy dribbling, the smiles on the players' faces—set to bouncy tunes from the Pointer Sisters and other artists absent from Grandma's record collection. Ruth Pointer, an original member of the R&B hitmakers, thought the commercials were great; she loved how the most exciting plays happened at the song's peak, a maneuver NBA Entertainment mastered. The spots were also a promise to the viewer that they'd have a good time, one complete with high fives and other revelry.

"You think of the NFL programming, it was game action with studio music, studio musicians, and/or music from the public domain or
John Phillip Sousa marching kind of music," Way said. "Nobody was
exposing pop artists or emerging artists to that audience and combin-
ing it with sports. That was a convention that Don Sperling and Paul
Gilbert pioneered." It increased with time. "There was just this coming
together, because the music fit our game and our game fit the music,"
said Don Stirling, director of sponsorship at NBA Properties.

"We were more loose, more in touch with music, entertainment, our
players," Sperling said. "We were really the first league to sort of marry
the pop culture, music, entertainment, with NBA players and its lifestyle." And that tagline, delivered with such polished confidence. *NBA
action . . . It's fantastic!* That came from Stern, said Barbara Ward, the administrative assistant. Around the office, Stern had a joke. A man keeps
replying "I'm fantastic" when someone asked how he was. Finally, he
delivers the punch line: "That's what I say when I'm bullshitting you."

The promos started running after Ward left the NBA to attend Harvard Law School. When she returned to New York, Ward saw Stern and
mentioned the commercials.

"David, pretty funny."

Stern winked.

Later, Stern added "America's game" before his cherished catch-
phrase. "I was becoming obsessed with the fact that America's pastime
was baseball, America's passion was the NFL, but America's game was
basketball," Stern said. "Very sophisticated analysis." If something
seemed like a good idea, a staffer could pursue it. Every time Gilbert
went to Madison Square Garden, he'd spot celebrities. He came to
Stern with an idea: Why don't I go down to MSG with a camera and
get them to say, "It's Fantastic!"?

The first celebrity to agree was Lieutenant Columbo himself, Peter
Falk. Gilbert approached the actor at a Knicks game and asked him to

say the line. Falk agreed, and it ballooned. The process was surprisingly free of red tape. Gilbert would venture to the Garden—later expanding into the Great Western Forum in Los Angeles or wherever that year's All-Star Game was played—and "go fishing and see who we could snag." He didn't have to joust with reluctant publicists or negotiate fees. All Gilbert did was ask, shoot, and let the star return to the game. Time was extremely limited, but most celebrities—aside from the too-cool-for-anything Jack Nicholson and the publicity-averse Woody Allen—were eager to cooperate. If they did something that tied into their public persona, that was great. Lakers fan Chevy Chase went slightly off script with his trademark sarcasm: "NBA action . . . It's not bad." (That was used for a blooper-ridden spot.) If Gilbert could find an address, he'd send the participant a thank-you note. That was the compensation.

For Stern, the commercials, game telecasts, and halftime features served a greater purpose, Don Sperling said. "He had long-term vision," he said. The idea, said Sperling, went beyond entertaining the public. "That's why we did all those public service announcements with our players," Sperling said. "David always said it wasn't what they *thought* about you, it's how they *felt* about you."

Promoting the players, not the teams, drove that notion. As Sperling said, the NFL sold laundry. You rooted for a team. The NBA relied on personalities and marketing much more than the NFL. There was a good reason. The players weren't hidden under helmets, so you could root for Charles Barkley, but feel indifference toward the Philadelphia 76ers. You could watch a Nets game to see Larry Bird turn the Meadowlands into his home court. "David's vision was the NBA players are the NBA, so put all your focus on them," said Bill Marshall, who helped make league apparel relevant.

Reaching that goal was a continuous task. Sunday night, after the day's broadcasts on CBS, Sperling got a phone call from Stern to review the day's action and look ahead. But every so often, Stern's voice started low and soft, the calm before the thunder raged. "You'd go, 'Uh-oh, I'm waiting,'" Sperling said. He didn't come to that anger lightly. Like a prosecutor, Stern built a case before unleashing his wrath, said Steve Mills, who started his lengthy basketball career at NBA Properties. You had no idea if you were the first or fifth call, Mills said, but "you just hoped you weren't the last call." That meant Stern had spoken to ten people beforehand and was now "waiting to see what you're going to say."

Stern admitted that he could be unpleasant when disappointed, but it was "in pursuit of a greater good." Underneath the anger was love. "We each enjoyed each other's company," he said. Like many of his colleagues, Sperling saw the tirades as Stern's way of communicating a teachable moment. Everyone, to borrow longtime NBA employee Rod Thorn's phrase, "got read"—as in "read the riot act"—from time to time and knew exactly what that meant. Little things mattered. Stern hated if the phone wasn't picked up promptly. Before you left, no matter how late it was, you returned every phone call. "Quite frankly, it's the right way to run a business," said Marshall. The NBA had to try hardest, because it had no choice. There was no goodwill to fritter.

"I used to say to people all the time, because I think it made the NBA unique: It's the only place I ever really knew of where everybody's boss worked harder than they did," said Ski Austin, a longtime NBA employee. The relationship Austin had with his superiors was like parents and children. "There are different ways to push buttons and different ways to incentivize people and ways to set the expectation level," he said. "Underneath it all, there's a love of your brand and your product. And you understand that's where it's coming from: it's all about the game. As an individual, I didn't want to disappoint Steve Mills, when I worked for him. I didn't want Russ Granik or Rick Welts or Adam Silver or David Stern ever to be in a position where they didn't know what was going on. Even if it was bad."

"I don't recall having any sort of trepidation about the future," said Michele Brown, the former brand director at NBA Properties, who started in 1982. "I think we were so grounded in the vision, and so inspired and motivated by what we were doing. That's where our focus was: We're in the beginning stages. Let's just believe that this is a possibility." What buoyed Brown's confidence was the strategic growth. She saw how inventive Adrian De Groot and Bill Marshall were in packaging the NBA. She knew she was part of something big.

Stern's genius came with that fiery disposition. "I think he fired me three times over the years," said Austin. One longtime NBA employee thought that since Stern was smarter than everyone else and worked harder than everyone else, he was perpetually disappointed because nobody lived up to his standards. Brown said if you left the office at 5:30 p.m. or 6 p.m., and ran into Stern by the elevators, you'd hear about it. *Oh, so half a day?* Staying late, she said, became a cultural expectation and "we worked our asses off." John Kosner, formerly of CBS Sports, joined the NBA in 1987. He loved the job, but "felt like a piker over there." Once, Stern came down to Kosner's office at 6:30 with his half-a-day line, and asked Kosner about this day.

"I'm buried," Kosner said. "I've never worked so hard."

"Maybe if you do that—and do it even better for another eighteen years—you'll feel the way I do," Stern said.

During Steve Mills's last interview with Stern before he joined the NBA, Stern warned the young applicant of the world he was about to enter. "You know, there are going to be nights where—and I want you to go home and talk to your wife about this—you're going to be spending the night at the hotel here in the city because it's going to be so late that it's not going to make sense for you to go home."

Stern's work ethic remained tireless, fed by his passion for the product and a break room treat of coffee and Saltines. He didn't treat a vacation like enervated mortals did. He'd return with legal pads crammed with notes and ideas. "He'd go away on vacation, but he was always calling you," Mills said. "It was nonstop." One Saturday, Mills and colleague Joel Litvin were confined to the office, toiling away on the new collective bargaining agreement. Stern called and lit into the two men. *Shouldn't this guy be lounging by a pool in Aspen?* Mills thought.

Stern loved to walk around the office at 7 p.m. and take note of who was there. "There wasn't a lot of talk about work-life balance, because he probably wasn't the best example of that either," Rick Welts said. What stood out, he thought, was Stern approached tasks each day as if he were learning them for the first time, ready to venture from the norm. It was a rare skill to possess, and one Stern mastered.

Employees had leeway to do their jobs. The NBA was a vertical organization, attorney Bill Jemas said: You got an entire area to run, but a safety net of superiors. There really wasn't a low-level position. "You'd get a vertical slice, so you could see in your area the top-level work and the lower-level work," Jemas said, "and then you'd work next to another person who had his own vertical slice." That arrangement bred collaboration. In the 1990s, John Kosner converted the graphics on TNT and NBC broadcasts into graphics for trading cards, which Jemas ran.

Stern joked that if he wrote a memoir, it'd be titled *Episodic Micromanagement Is Underrated.* "He wanted to be told the truth, and you better be prepared when you're going in to meet him," said David Gavant, the longtime NBA Entertainment employee. "He was always five steps ahead of you." When Sandy Brown started to get NBA programming into foreign markets in the late 1980s, Stern would pop his head into Brown's office for a pop quiz. "Brown, how many households are there in Uzbekistan?" Talking to Stern was like "taking the witness stand," said Jon Miller. "You had to be ready for your cross-examination."

"If he yelled at you for something, it was because he felt you had missed an opportunity or you hadn't seen something clearly," Arlene Weltman of NBA Properties said. "It wasn't because he was in a bad mood that day. He wanted things to be as perfect as they could be, and he wanted things to be as right as they could be. And he wanted you to have a plan."

One day, Weltman and her colleague, Don Stirling, director of sponsorship at NBA Properties, were called into Stern's office to discuss some long-forgotten topic. Stern, as was his wont, fired a series of questions. Then the fatal, unanswerable one arrived. The duo tried to bluff their way with less-than-solid information. Stern caught them and unloaded into both with such vitriol that Stirling equated the haranguing to an out-of-body experience "To this day, I can see it clearly and hear it clearly," said Stirling, who felt there was nothing personal about the outburst. Stern considered Weltman and Stirling his teammates. They best come prepared. After all, information was currency. The more you had, the better a business ran. And Stern had an "insatiable passion" to turn the NBA into the greatest sports league on the planet.

Stern did whatever it took to get there. When Mike Antinoro, a young NBA Entertainment employee, defended his boss, Don Sperling, from "getting read" at a meeting, Stern's warning could have doubled as his business philosophy: "Mike, don't put your balls on this table unless you're willing to get them cut off."

"You'll hear negative, because lawyers are big, ethnic families," said Jemas. "You kind of yell at each other, you make fun of each other. You crack jokes at each other's expense. It was a really nongenteel management technique, but it was also very efficient and very honest and a wonderful place to learn a lot. We certainly didn't molly-coddle each other, but we treated each other like grown-ups up and down." That ethos, he added, "permeated the organization."

The eruptions came with fealty. The league office was so small in the early 1980s, Rick Welts thought, that Stern did more than hire every employee—he was personally invested in them. "He was the constant presence and the constant leader for us," Rob Millman said. Most employees tolerated the outbursts and sarcastic rejoinders. If he busted your chops, that was a sign of affection. Marshall once entered his office to find a note from Stern. *Stopped by at 8:30 p.m. You weren't here.* The next morning, Marshall came in at 7:30. He left a note at Stern's desk. *Came by to say hi. You weren't here.* "He had that Godfather mentality," Sperling said. "He could criticize you, knock you down, but he would always be there to pick you up." Stern was tough and exacting and knew more than everybody else and let you know it, said Jon Miller, the eventual co–general manager and vice president of NBA Entertainment. But years later, Miller knew that if he had a problem he could call his old boss. Stern once spent the day at the office before he was picked up for a 9 p.m. business flight to Los Angeles. In the car, Stern immediately picked up the phone and called doctors from a list, determined to find the best care for an NBA Entertainment employee diagnosed with a serious illness. "It just was so moving," said Stirling, who was in the car. "He didn't need to do that." In 1989, Kosner's then wife had a miscarriage in Rome, where he was working the NBA's McDonald's Open. Stern and Granik made sure she had the best hospital care and flew them back to the United States first-class.

The NBA, said Paula Hanson, who ran NBA's team services, got into your blood. Every day was different. "I could feel the energy just walking in there," said Nancy Fitzpatrick, a veteran at NBA Properties, who started in 1988. She didn't love basketball, but she loved the people. It was exciting, said Weltman, an NBA employee from 1983 to 1990. There was always a new challenge—a new player, a new award to create, new sponsors to court.

When Rick Welts arrived in 1982, he was tasked with wrangling corporate sponsorships for the league. He knocked on door after door to sell a product many companies held in outright disdain. "It was very, very hard to get sponsors, because of the reputation of the league," said Weltman, who worked for NBA Properties during that time. She couldn't get anyone to return her phone calls. When Weltman did reach a potential client, she'd hear "terrible, derogatory things about our players." There was a total misconception about who the NBA player was, Weltman said, "and you could not convince people that they were wrong." Sponsors rejected the idea that the NBA's audience would buy their products. As Michael Jordan's sensational rookie year of 1984–85 unfolded, Weltman approached the manufacturer of an African-American grooming product—she doesn't remember the company's name—to see if it wanted to sponsor the Rookie of the Year Award. Jordan was certain to win, and he had movie star allure without a basketball uniform. The price of the sponsorship was "painfully small," maybe thirty thousand dollars. Weltman was turned down cold.

Every day, Steve Mills grabbed a giant red book with the marketing and advertising contacts for various companies and embarked on a desperate day of cold-calling.

"We were trying to think about any designation we could come to," he recalled. "Edge was the official shave gel and we'd get it put in the locker rooms. Haggar was the official clothing line of the coaches and we got them to sponsor [the Coach of the Month Award]. Fujifilm, we made them the official film manufacturer of the NBA." The clothing was a boon to the coaches, who needed suits. Some were a little too eager to sample the gear. A female Haggar representative presented a rack of suits to Milwaukee Bucks head coach Don Nelson, who preceded to strip in front of her. Chris Riley, Pat Riley's husband, believed her stylish husband got snubbed for the award because the Lakers coach eschewed Haggar for Armani and other high-end duds.

As he made these soul-deflating phone calls, Mills ran into the same problem as Weltman. "We had a vision of what we wanted the league to be and David had a vision of what he thought we could be and what we aspired to be, but the advertising world didn't look at us that way," he said. Stirling knew he was in trouble when a potential client wanted its agency to "look at the numbers." The NBA didn't have numbers. "We were at the front end," he said. "We were selling hope. We were selling pixie dust. The business proposition had not caught up yet with our vision and how we were imagining this league would become."

"We were always sort of chasing, or fighting against that concept, that we were second-class citizens," Mills said. "That's what drove us to keep doing it."

Selling the Sonics in Seattle had been a breeze for Welts. It was the city's first modern-day major sports franchise and for years its most successful, winning the NBA championship in 1979. "Ultimately, we were really proud of the team that was on the floor," said Welts's sister and former coworker, Nancy Welts Schulte, as she fought back tears. "They weren't perfect people, but they were really good people." Now, Rick Welts, three thousand miles from home, was embarking on a career of "running into brick walls" before coming home. At 10:30 p.m., the phone rang. "Uncle Dave" wanted to talk about Welts's day, to assure him everything would work out great, to ask how he could help. Every morning, Welts visited Stern's office. It was filled with tiny skyscrapers of magazine stories and newspaper articles. "Let's go try to find these guys," Stern would say, handing him clips.

Welts worried about his employment status, but Stern knew the long-term value. A commitment today could lead tomorrow to spending money on the NBA's television partner or to a promotion or a company hiring an NBA athlete as a spokesperson.

Stern watched games differently. The discussion the next morning after *Monday Night Football* or the Knicks game wasn't about how many points Bernard King scored but the advertisers. Stirling got the message: he had to cease watching games as a sports fan. Any company that had a commercial on during a broadcast was a potential sponsor.

"Don and I would sit and watch any kind of sporting event on TV," Mills said. "We'd watch NFL games, we'd watch baseball games, we'd watch college basketball games, and write down every advertiser that was in the game." Stern got the staff to think about sports marketing and to take the initiative, Stirling said. People in the office started reading *Advertising Age*. When he saw a Master Lock commercial during the Super Bowl, Stirling got the company to sponsor the NBA's Defensive Player of the Year award. The arrangement lasted for several years.

The NBA was where the inventive could hopscotch the red tape and make an impact. The creation of NBA Photos, headlined by the up-close, sumptuous style of Andrew D. Bernstein and Nathaniel S. Butler, was a day at the beach. That's where Bernstein and NBA PR guy Terry Lyons chatted during a break in the 1985 Finals. There were more licensees and publications that wanted photos. Why not bring photography in-house? Soon Bernstein put the contents of his four-drawer file cabinet into bankers' boxes and shipped them from Pasadena, California, to New York City.

Apparel would become a giant part of the NBA's business, but first Bill Marshall had to get "our act together." That meant uniforms were made by one manufacturer—and not whomever the teams could find—and procuring a game ball that didn't generate rage. Wilson had handled the latter function for close to forty years but sold two options at retail: a game ball for sixty-five dollars and a nine-dollar rubber ball that went sideways if anyone had the gall to bounce it. Marshall and Stern turned to Spalding, which provided nine options to sell in stores. And the price was right. Marshall recalled Wilson initially paid a piddling $35,000 a year for the game ball rights; Spalding countered with "hundreds of thousands" beginning in the 1984–85 season to get a distinction it would hold for nearly forty years.

Spalding also made a better ball. Near the end of its deal, Marshall said, Wilson stopped skiving the balls; the leather no longer fit snugly on the ball's bladder. As a result, panels of leather started to curl back. Coaches complained that the balls did not bounce properly. Wilson also wanted to have its name bigger on the front of the ball. The NBA agreed, but found that Wilson put its name on *both* sides of the ball and at twice the agreed-upon size, a development that distracted Moses Malone.

The NBA logo, a dribbling silhouette based on Lakers great Jerry West, is now ubiquitous, to the point that West rues its existence. "It's just not who I am, period," he said. Back in the early 1980s, "Logo Man" remained a novelty. Huffy Sports put the logo on the lower left-hand corner of the baskets it sold in stores. Marshall urged Stern to have the league follow suit with its backboards, because it would authenticate the Huffy product at retail. After all, kids wanted to buy what they saw in the game. Don Stirling said the league first placed the logo on the backboard during the preseason 1984 Hall of Fame Game in Springfield, Massachusetts, between the Utah Jazz and the Boston Celtics. The logo's placement got the benediction of Larry Bird. It didn't distract the game's most heavenly shooter, Stirling said. The controversy thus defused, sales of the Huffy backboards increased. And when Huffy made adjustable hoops, at Marshall's suggestion, that "exploded the business."

Marshall also reviewed the NBA's licensees, and was appalled. Few pieces of clothing were made for fans. "The only product in Boston before I designed stuff was counterfeit merchandise," Marshall said. As a kid, he played ball and rooted for the Celtics, but could never find a Celtics shirt. Ever. "That always had an impact on me," Marshall said.

Starter made everything from team hats to shirts to jackets. Founder David Beckerman got a licensing agreement with the NBA in the late 1970s. "Licensing wasn't really a priority at the time," he said. "We were a 'comes with.' When you go buy a steak, the potato 'comes with' the steak." Leagues didn't understand the power of licensing, Beckerman said. Marshall and Stern did. When Mike Suscavage joined NBA Properties in late 1976, "they had nothing. Zero." The only real marketing came from the league's partnership with the Licensing Corporation of America. "This is," Suscavage explained, "literally if someone knocked on their door and said, 'Listen, I'd like to get a license for the New York Knicks.'" Some teams, he recalled, lacked the proper trademarks.

Clothes were like billboard advertising, Marshall thought, yet the NBA did little to take advantage of the real estate. Instead, there were ladies' rabbit fur jackets; a company called Action Sports had a green Celtics logo on a tan shirt. But what if you didn't live in New England? Marshall divided up the league's teams among its four T-shirt licensees; that way a retailer in San Antonio could see a real, live Spurs T-shirt instead of imagining the team's logo on a Celtics shirt. A product catalog shot over seven days from a garage in Fort Lauderdale, Florida, was produced.

"We understood the principles of licensing, which is you reach out to various manufacturers in various product categories, and you look to incent them on how they can broaden their product line through professional sports, or through the NBA," said Michele Brown, who worked alongside Marshall. "It was a hard sell—it was a very hard sell."

Marshall and Millman, with Stern's and the teams' backing, visited the eighteen leading retailers in eighteen NBA cities. Catalogs in hand, they convinced them to feature an in-store team shop à la Jordan Marsh's Celtics stores or the NFL Pro Shops that Mike Suscavage had worked on years before. The duo threw in an irresistible hook: customers could enter to become a "fan of the month," a package that included free tickets and a midcourt introduction with their favorite player at halftime.

If that didn't convince the store's management team, Marshall had an effective retort: if you say no, we'll talk to your competitor. Millman and Marshall finished eighteen for eighteen. The NFL and Major League Baseball, Millman said, had followed this Marketing 101 game plan for years—the league simply followed suit. In the 1980s, Stern said later, sports marketing was a four-letter-word. "We kind of looked at them, going, 'Who the *fuck* are these guys?'" said NBA Entertainment's Rich Dorfman. "Retail, this, that. Clothing." And the teams expressed reluctance. According to John Nash, a longtime executive with the Philadelphia 76ers, three teams made money selling team products: the Sixers, the Celtics, and the Lakers. The teams made their own deals and kept the money. When the terms changed, the Sixers were apoplectic. Now that a select group of licensees were dealing with the NBA, the Sixers would lose money. But there was logic. "We wanted to make sure that there was parity and somehow, even with some of the top-tier teams generating the majority of the royalties, it would be somewhat evenly dispersed amongst the bottom-tier teams," Brown said.

Stern's focus on stars and hot new teams allowed Marshall, Millman, and their colleagues to perfect an apparel pick-and-roll. The strategy was simple, but it worked—and doubled back on itself. Nearly twenty years later, NBA nostalgia provided the fashion for a musical genre that doubled as a cultural trendsetter and a soundtrack for cool kids.

As is the case today, said Tom Shine, the founder of Logo 7, the NFL ruled merchandising. Its season was bookended by two huge buying periods: back-to-school and Christmas. The NBA's long season doesn't really heat up until spring, when the playoffs loom.

The NFL was not a benevolent ruler. Marty Jacobson, the cofounder and president of Nutmeg Mills, got yelled at by the NFL's Frank Vuono because someone once wore a Nutmeg Mills product on the sidelines at a Dallas Cowboys game. "That's how sensitive the NFL was," said Jacobson, who had no idea this had happened. "He wanted nothing that would confuse the category of authentic." Stern was an active participant in the NBA's annual licensees' meeting. The commissioners in the other leagues were not, Jacobson said, nor did they discuss how your company could go into international markets.

"Stern set a commercial atmosphere," Shine said. He understood that if people wore a team's merchandise, it was exposure for the league in places you couldn't get exposure—like a school. "We would bring them colorizations with variations," Shine explained. "They would try to work through how we can do this: 'What are the issues? How can we help them bring this idea forward?' In other leagues it was, 'Oh, we can't do this, we can't do this. It's impossible.' The NBA always gave you the feeling they were partners with you." Other leagues took the money and walked away, Beckerman said. The NBA cast aside conventions and rigidity, he added. It was eager to be marketing-oriented and creative for the retailer and the consumer. Getting an idea through sometimes took a phone call to Marshall.

"It really came down to making a stance to understand our business, and our how business can be interwoven with their business to have mutual objectives," Beckerman said.

The NFL allowed fewer on-field opportunities to market stars. Superstars were on the field half the time, one of twenty-two helmeted behemoths locked in a series of scrums. At conferences, Frank Vuono, the NFL's vice president of retail licensing, always boasted of his league's assets: it had been in licensing longer; the season ran from back-to-school to the holidays, a natural buying and gift-giving time; the NFL jersey made for a more natural piece of wardrobe as opposed to the NBA's tank-top-style jersey.

Marshall would laugh. "Here's the one thing I have you on, Frank," he'd say. "I have the popularity of the athletes themselves."

Vuono looked at the Q ratings, which evaluated a person's familiarity and their popularity with the public. Joe Montana, a living legend, didn't crack the top ten. The NBA had Jordan, Bird, Magic. Vuono tried convincing the teams' owners to focus more marketing on the players; he got nowhere. If the players got more attention, the owners thought, they would want more money. As the 1980s progressed, the dynamics of fans were changing. Younger fans followed players, not teams, Vuono said.

The players-first attitude regarding merchandise got a huge assist when the NBA assumed the Players Association's licensing rights in marketing matters. The two-page agreement that seemingly came from nowhere—"It was almost done on a napkin," remembered Gary Way—coordinated player marketing and league marketing. The NBA's logic at the time, explained Way, was:

> We think we can do a better job than any other agent out there, be-
> cause of our investment and our care about the game. In return for you
> giving us these licensing rights to market on your behalf, we'll pay you
> a royalty guarantee every year, which is probably well north of what
> the Players Association have ever been able to do on their own. When
> the NBA became the licensing agent for the PA, the league actually
> had a business in marketing the players on behalf of their principal, the
> PA. You had this anomaly that doesn't exist in any other sport where
> actually you get your marketing rights for players directly through li-
> censing with the league.
>
> So truly then, on the marketing side, the NBA were genuine partners
> with the Players Association, and the cooperation that came with play-
> ers understanding that every dollar that NBA Properties makes out of
> marketing us, is some percentage directly into our pocket. You had a
> level of cooperation and care about the players as a distinct brand.
>
> That created a dynamic where the NBA was able to go out and
> [offer] sponsors one-stop shopping: if you do business with us, you
> get all of these assets that we manage.

The group license, Way said, opened the door for posters—including John and Tock Costacos's cartoonish and creative works—and Salem Sportswear's famed caricature shirts of players. The appeal of those items extended well beyond the 1980s. Shawn Kemp credited the Costacos Brothers' "Reign Man" poster with creating his image, "because that stuff was big; there was no Internet, no YouTube," said the high-flying star with the SuperSonics in the mid-1990s. "That stuff was very important back then, to do those little things to get your name out there." "The poster made you cool," said Charles Barkley, the irrepressible Philadelphia 76ers legend. "You didn't make the poster cool."

Barkley, the first NBA player to pose for the Costacos Brothers, was photographed in their garage. Keith Kennelly and Kyle Nagel, two lifelong friends from Salem, New Hampshire, started a T-shirt company with three hundred dollars. A lot of their friends and family thought not much would come of it.

Nagel's mom's back porch was soon covered in globs of ink. The founders of Salem Screen Printers were not the best at production, but they compensated by making T-shirts for any event or business that came their way. It wasn't a sophisticated outfit. Kevin Kennelly, Keith's brother and a production manager, learned screen printing from Kyle, whose body of knowledge came from a two-day class. "Everything he taught me was all wrong because he didn't know what he was doing," Kevin recalled years later.

The duo improved, hired friends and family, and kept at it. Then, in 1985, Bill Fickett paid a visit. The electrician had put caricatures of athletes on T-shirts such as his Larry Bird–inspired shirt, "The Massachusetts State Bird." Fickett's love of casual apparel went beyond athletic aesthetics or his almost childlike love of Bird. His customer base—plumbers and guys on the job—were happy to pay $10 for a shirt he bought for $5.

"I'm a capitalist at heart," Fickett said, "and I'm not afraid to admit it." Everybody, he observed, owned more than one T-shirt.

And the NBA had many more stars beyond Bird. That inspired Fickett to head to the Players Association for a license. "They gave me a premium license, which meant I couldn't go to Dick's and Sports Authority, your national retailers," Fickett said. "I had to tie it to a promotion. So, I went to Burger King. I'm a little shaky on the details, but they wanted to do five Celtics, and they were going to give away a shirt every two weeks. When I got that premium—and Burger King was talking some pretty significant numbers—that's when I went to Salem."

When he first saw Kennelly and Nagel, they were covered in ink.

"They were kind of cut from the same mold that I am, so I just became real comfortable with those guys," Fickett said. "They were aggressive, younger than me. And I just saw the motivation that these two guys had."

The motivation arose from necessity. "We didn't grow up with a whole lot of stuff," Nagel recalled. "We did what we had to do." The friends lived near a racetrack called Rockingham Park, a hustler's paradise. Kyle, Keith, and Kyle's brother Jim had a lemonade stand and sold sandwiches to people coming in and out. But the real money came from an inventive form of recycling. Jim, an eight-year-old front man, would ask departing customers for their programs. Kyle and Keith then sold them to people coming in. "Back then we'd sell them for twenty-five cents," Jim Nagel said. "But we could make twenty, thirty bucks a day. That was in the sixties." It was more than his dad made in a day.

Kyle, known in the Salem offices as "Hurricane Kyle," was a born salesman. In high school, Jim said Kyle bought candy at wholesale prices and resold it at inflated prices. "I'll tell you a small story I heard from Keith, but I never validated it with Kyle," said Doug Vennard, Salem's original art director. "He joined the navy right out of high school, and they did a Mediterranean cruise. His was in the middle of summer. He took whatever money he had—which wasn't much—and he bought freezers and Popsicles, brought them on the ship, and sold them. He came home with enough money to buy a car."

The inventiveness came with tenacity. One time, Kyle and a co-worker sold T-shirts in a parking garage, Kevin Kennelly recalled, near a group of guys who were partying. One of them grabbed a shirt from Kyle, who asked for it back. The response: "What are you going to do about it?" The culprit was flanked by about ten friends. Kyle stood his ground—over a two-dollar T-shirt.

"The next thing you know the fucking ten of them beat the shit out of Kyle," Kevin Kennelly said. "His girlfriend took pictures of him in the hospital. You could barely recognize his face."

Kyle saw an opportunity to expand Fickett's business. He and Keith scraped together funds to buy out Fickett's two partners; Nagel said it was "maybe" $200,000. Fickett joined the new company, Salem Sportswear.

Salem's lack of a retail license soon became an issue. *Boston Globe* cartoonist Larry Johnson drew more caricatures for the Burger King shirts, but the promotion left the Home of the Whopper in disarray. "They're not in the T-shirt business," Fickett said. "It was taking time from their work to find the right size, the right shirt. I realized we had to get the retail license."

Nagel was confident that if Salem got the right license from the NBA, the company would nail it. The opportunity arose thanks to NBA Properties' Bill Marshall, who saw the Bird shirt in a shop at Boston's Logan International Airport. It was a simple design, Bird as a caricature, but it grabbed Marshall. *What the heck is this?*

The NBA soon called.

"How come you don't have our logos on your shirt?" Nagel was asked.

"We don't have the rights," he said.

"Would you like them?"

The T-shirts worked perfectly under Stern's edict to promote the players. Plus, it filled an opportunity, Marshall said: the NBA had a dearth of player-specific apparel. "Everybody was doing the same stupid stuff, right?" Nagel said. "Just taking a logo, slapping it on a shirt." The image of your favorite player on a shirt, Kennelly said, clicked with people.

The NBA, said Steve White, Salem's national sales manager, "took the initial risks. Baseball came afterwards. The face recognition and the way they were drawn up, and some of the elements around it, made basketball an absolute natural."

Kyle and Keith were strictly jeans and T-shirts guys who hired friends and family. If the company had to travel with merchandise, Nagel would tip a skycap thirty dollars to put thirty boxes of shirts on the plane. Sure, the crew would have to pick up the boxes and lug them to the site. And, yes, those boxes would spill on Interstate 89, forcing employees to retrieve shirts as they dodged traffic. And, of course, David Stern would drive by as this scene—and the T-shirts—unfolded.

Stern did not care. Salem was good for the NBA brand, said Matt Mirchin, director and group manager of consumer products for NBA Properties. Stern and the Salem guys were an odd pair linked by business acumen and entrepreneurial flair, but Stern "absolutely loved and respected their entrepreneurialism, their flexibility, and their ability to drive revenues and be creative," Mirchin said. The NBA was a family business and so was Salem, said Nancy Fitzpatrick, a licensing manager at NBA Properties. "That's why we gravitated toward them," she said. Plus, the product popped. "I can't remember anything close to that in those days," said Atlanta Hawks star Dominique Wilkins, who saw people wearing his caricature shirt decades later. "The shirts were the first of a kind. They were nice. They were fun. They were different."

The impact would be felt for years. "Salem had such an incredible influence on creating the aesthetic of sports clothing in the eighties and nineties," said Philadelphia-based designer and artist Danny Finocchio. When he worked at Mitchell & Ness, the sports nostalgia apparel powerhouse, every caricature piece was "inspired in some way by the look and feel of caricature illustration from that era."

Sondra Murphy, design director of apparel at Mitchell & Ness, grew up with Salem Sportswear. She owns a dead-stock Salem shirt with caricatures of players from the 1992 Dream Team that she never wears for fear of ruining it, a sound business decision. (A quick trip on eBay shows that "Mom bagged up my Salem T-shirts for Goodwill" is the updated version of "Mom threw out my baseball cards.")

"Caricature shirts brought lightheartedness and a sense of humor to sports and licensed product at the time," she said. "You were able to accentuate a player's features—if a player had a giant smile, crazy-long legs, if he wore his uniform a certain way, if he had a special move or stance, you were able to capture these characteristics in a playful manner." The hand-drawn work, Murphy thought, humanized the players, making them more relatable and more loved by fans. It's a trend she wishes would return. "Everything now is so robotic and computerized that sometimes it makes me nuts."

Salem's shirts, Murphy said, paved the way for more player-specific licensed products, including photo real graphics and "shirtseys"—name and number T-shirts. "That was really the first launch into player-identified imaging, if you will," Marshall said. "It was caricature format, but at least it was players and images and stuff to help round out our apparel."

It was a vindication of Stern's value in names and faces. "Back in those days, we had Michael Jordan," said Jon Sherwood, the company's onetime art director. "We had Larry Bird. We had Magic Johnson. We had guys that we would set up a design and we'd run these designs on press for *days*." Jordan sold at an explosive rate. The NBA soon came back with a rule: Salem had to print at least three individual player shirts per team.

"How many Kiki VanDeWeghe shirts are we going to sell?" said Kennelly, referring to the Portland Trailblazers star.

Somehow people found what they wanted. Most sports fans owned at least one Salem shirt at some point, Murphy said, though "you probably didn't even realize it." But look at photos from the early 1990s. There's a cousin in a family photo or some kid in your yearbook wearing a Salem Chicago Bulls shirt.

Two factors propelled Salem to enter the sports fan's 1980s wardrobe and to endure as a style piece for trendy celebrities such as Adam Levine. The artwork improved significantly after Nagel forced out lead artist Larry Johnson. Key players, including Johnson, admit the early shirts were rough. "And to be honest with you, it was a brilliant move," Johnson said, "because he managed to find some other artists who were excellent. Bruce Stark was very, very good. He managed to get the job done with him, and I'm sure he worked out an agreement with him that was far more to his liking."

Stark, a former ditch digger, earned a dazzling reputation at the New York *Daily News*, where he caricatured sports and showbiz personalities from 1960 to 1982. After retiring from the *News* he became a high-profile freelance artist. On a whim, Vennard called Stark's agent to deliver his pitch. The bad news: Stark had retired to Fort Myers, Florida. The good news: Stark was a huge baseball fan and had moved there to be close to spring training. The agent followed up with his client: Stark was game. Salem contracted him for as many shirts as it could.

"He brought a whole new style to the ballgame," said Allen Mudgett, a graphic designer and freelance artist for Salem. "Instead of working with pen and ink—and having the lines and the cross-hatching—he brought brush and ink with India ink washes and made it look like beautiful watercolor paintings."

Looking good went so far. Like the players, television benefited Salem and any piece of NBA licensed apparel. Every part of an NBA game offered an opportunity—directly or indirectly—for players and employees to promote the merchandise. "You have to put exposure on it," Marshall said. "You have to market it." Some efforts were obvious, such as the commercials featuring stars like Julius Erving and Isiah Thomas for NBA Authentics. Those spots ran on TBS, then the league's cable partner. Having TV crews film practices with players in the gear provided more free advertising. If you looked at the scorer's table, a team's staff donned those cozy, sweet Nutmeg Mills sweaters. During the NBA Draft, Len Bias or Brad Daugherty was handed a colorful cap with their new team's name on it in crisp cursive from Sports Specialties.

"Bill Marshall, he was really smart at this," said Lon Rosen, director of promotions for the Los Angeles Lakers. "He kind of had a vision about, 'Wow, if the players wear it and people see it on TV, they're going to buy it at retail.' So it all worked."

The event didn't have to be hosted by the NBA. The organizers at Live Aid asked Denver Nuggets star Alex English to appear at the Philadelphia concert alongside other high-profile athletes. Don Stirling, English's escort, spotted host Chevy Chase. He handed the devoted Lakers fan a 1985 Finals hat. Chase put it on and exposed the NBA to an estimated 100,000 music fans and 1.9 billion television viewers.

Licensed NBA products—jerseys, warm-up jackets, socks—were available for sale. A fan could wear what the players wore, and Logo Man was the ubiquitous seal of approval, a mark of authenticity and a leitmotif for commerce driven by the increasingly acceptable notion of sports marketing. Salem's involvement evolved into an iconic part of any post-championship celebration. The locker room T-shirt ranks with giving thanks to God and champagne-anointed celebrations. Whatever team won the NBA Finals, its players wore a championship shirt from the plucky New England company—the whole team captured in a vivid caricature—after the game. That was when the sales exploded, Marshall said.

Years later, there was another championship shirt, designed by Salem, that players wore during the parade a few days later. Who came up with the original idea, which began after the 1987 Finals, is up for some debate. Nagel said he proposed it. "In the beginning, nobody saw the value of that locker room," he said. "Now, it's untouchable. Nike and Adidas have it all wrapped up. Back in the day, I used to do that by giving every player 144 shirts and the team a thousand. That was the trade-off to be in the locker room." Marshall can't recall the origin but said that "we knew we could do it, and somehow the players wanted it. But once that shirt went on those players, all the players absolutely loved it."

When consumers look for merchandise tied to a recent event, it is known as a "hot market." When a team wins an NBA championship, Mirchin said, a twenty-four- to forty-eight-hour window opens when people go nuts for related product. Salem excelled at this. They also created hot markets, such as its "Bad Boys" shirts to celebrate the rough-and-tumble Detroit Pistons. Something would happen on Monday. By Tuesday, Salem had artwork ready for the NBA for review, Mirchin said. The NBA tried to approve it by Wednesday. If all went well, Salem could have the shirts ready for sale by that Friday.

"We'd read the sports pages like other businesses would read the business pages," said Salem CEO Al Coburn. "We were very reactive to things that were happening in the sports world where some of our competitors, especially early on, wouldn't react to those things." After leaving Salem, Jon Weiss, the owner of New Buffalo, a T-shirt company that partnered with Salem, worked in the rock-and-roll business. Every day, he said, is a hot market. Nobody was better than Salem.

"If there were open-to-buy dollars on the table in Kyle's distribution channel, he got it all because he was willing to gamble," Weiss said.

For the championship T-shirts, Salem hedged its bets. Artists for Salem drew both outcomes; shirts were printed for both teams. For the NBA Finals, the company set up in both cities. During the 1991 Bulls-Lakers championship, the company rented out a recently closed Volvo dealership as its base of operations in Chicago.

"We probably had twenty-five people out there for a month and a half," Nagel said. "We'd be printing locally in Chicago, contract printing with other printers. We'd be printing in Alabama at our factory. We'd be printing at New Hampshire in our factory and we even used a really strong contract printer in L.A. As soon as that thing was over, the screens are all set up. If it was three–zero in the championship, we could even get a little jump on it and print ahead. We premade some shirts because we'd need them for the locker room. All those orders are already in; then we'd have all these printers start printing. The tractor-trailers would come in and they'd be gone as fast we unloaded [the presses]."

The big stores—Foot Locker, Sports Authority—needed the shirts the next day. Stores always underordered, Nagel said, because "unless your team is in the championship many times, nobody understands the scale of it." For example, when the Chicago Bulls (and Michael Jordan) won their first championship in 1991, Salem sold $10 million in shirts during the first week, an unheard-of number.

Nagel's eagerness to get ahead occasionally tormented his coworkers. In 1993, the Chicago Bulls and the Phoenix Suns played in the Finals. The Bulls pulled to a comfortable 3–1 series lead. The potential series-clinching Game 5 was in Chicago. Kyle assumed a Bulls team led by Jordan and Scottie Pippen at home was destined to win the series. He began printing most of the Bulls championship shirts.

The Bulls lost Game 5. Game 6 was in Phoenix and Coburn—"I didn't sleep the night before"—was in knots. Phoenix led most of the way, until Chicago guard John Paxson hit a three-pointer with 3.9 seconds left to win the game and save the company from financial disaster. "You had so much invested in the games," Keith Kennelly said. "It was much worse than placing a big bet on it, because some teams would do much better than other teams."

Sports licensing had become serious business in 1993, and the plucky, swashbuckling entrepreneur model ended after the big boys got in the game. Kyle and Keith knew their time was up. A bigger company, Kyle said, could take Salem to the next level. Plus, the job had become relentless. One day Kyle's son called his grandfather "Dad." What Kyle and Keith and their pals accomplished was extraordinary. Salem was now a publicly traded company that employed two thousand people in three states, boasted more than $100 million in annual sales, and had licenses from the four major sports leagues and colleges. As a bonus, Fickett met his fashion inspiration and sports hero. The entrepreneur practically skipped to the cab, he was so excited to have dinner with Larry Bird. Later, Fickett shared an intimate moment with Bird in a Chinese restaurant bathroom in Seattle. "You know what's better than taking a good piss?" Bird asked Fickett, his temporary neighbor at the urinals. "Taking a good shit!"

Fruit of the Loom bought Salem for $136.4 million. Fickett, who would go on to cofound Life is Good with Kyle, said that Fruit of Loom bought Salem at the worst time. The leagues' licensing divisions saw apparel as a cash cow, so the market grew flabby. Price wars started. Variety dried up. Those bugs got corrected. "As the leagues got bigger, better, smarter, more mature—and the revenue that started coming in from TV and sponsorships grew more dramatically than licensing revenue—they did what's right for the overall business and they started cutting back on the amount of licensees that they had to not flood the market with product," Mirchin said.

Fruit of the Loom wouldn't reap the benefits; the company filed for Chapter 11 bankruptcy in December 1999. The problem, thought

Marc Brown, Salem's production supervisor, was Fruit of the Loom kept its old business model. If a company has a 20 percent share of boys' white cotton briefs and buys its two biggest competitors, it has a dominant share of the market. By buying Salem, Fruit of the Loom got licenses for the four major sports. After the company bought Artex Manufacturing and Pro Player, it had three of everything. "You only need one to be in the business," Brown said. And a company needed to keep reinventing products to generate more sales year after year, a creativity nonexistent in a tighty-whities world.

The new corporate mind-set also grounded Salem's reputation. Flying by the seat of their pants, said Jon Weiss, allowed Kyle and Keith to create a great company. "They didn't know any better," he said.

In the early 1980s, legitimacy as a cost of doing business was absurd. The NBA was building its identity, occasionally by accident. A galling lack of knowledge regarding Top 40 radio paved the way for Marvin Gaye to make musical history and to establish the league's fate.

The NBA was about to break free of tradition and start to define itself. And it all happened in under three minutes.

OH SHIT . . . HERE WE GO

Lon Rosen, the Los Angeles Lakers' young director of promotions, felt like he was on his way to the principal's office.

Marvin Gaye's out-of-this-world version of "The Star-Spangled Banner" before the 1983 NBA All-Star Game left the players in awe and whipped the Great Western Forum crowd of 17,505—give or take a few boos—into a frenzy. Rosen knew that plenty of people might find Gaye's rendition disrespectful. Larry O'Brien was among them. During the first quarter, the commissioner unloaded on Rosen. The conversation was short and "very colorful," said Rosen, who declined to go into specifics.

"Larry was a little shocked," Ed Desser, the NBA's longtime director of broadcasting, said. "He didn't expect it. I remember having to talk him off the ledge."

Marvin Gaye had been one of Rosen's musical heroes. Now Gaye was going to get him fired. Hosting the 1983 NBA All-Star Game, televised on CBS from coast to coast, mattered to Lakers owner Dr. Jerry Buss. "When my dad bought the team, he felt there was such an East Coast bias against teams in Los Angeles, on the West Coast," said Jeanie Buss, now the Lakers' controlling owner and president, who was an intern in 1983. "I think having the All-Star Game in L.A.

just validated that Los Angeles wasn't just a blip on the screen, that it was an important part of the NBA." The staff was advised by management "not to screw up," remembered Robin Mahkorn, the Lakers' longtime official timer. That kind of directive was never given, and the Lakers were championship contenders and a cornerstone of CBS Sports' NBA coverage.

Apparently, Gaye didn't get the warning.

At the run-through the day before, Gaye ignored Rosen's request to shorten the anthem by walking away from him. Rosen had to literally chase him until Julius Erving intervened. The legendary R&B stylist had shown up five minutes before his performance this afternoon. The Lakers were *this close* to enlisting their backup: an usherette named Amanda Mayo, who was warming up in her favorite spot, a tiny broom closet, all the while hoping Gaye would show.

Gaye arrived and turned dawn's early night and rocket's red glare into bedroom music, putting Rosen's career in peril.

Halftime rolled around. Rosen had to check in with Jerry Buss. The walk to his private box was excruciatingly long.

"What's the matter?" Buss asked.

Rosen, who thought he'd be fired, told him.

"That was the greatest anthem of all time," Buss replied. "Are you *kidding*?"

Thanks to versions ranging from the iconic (Whitney Houston at Super Bowl XXV) to the unintentionally comic (Fergie's memorable portrayal as America's favorite divorced, drunken aunt at the 2018 NBA All-Star Game), the American public now expects a singer to own "The Star-Spangled Banner" and belt their patriotism to the stadium gift shop. That wasn't always the case. Gaye's rendition "opened the door for people to customize it, instead of singing a straightforward piece," said Margaret Cusack, chair of the piano and voice department at the celebrated Westminster Choir College.

It's a hard song to wrap the pipes around. "Within the first phase you have an octave and a third," said Cusack, who sang the anthem before a Cincinnati Reds game in 1981. "There's a major tenth, which is usually a big deal. But in the first phase it's a little unusual." The climax—*free*—goes higher. Finding the right spot is crucial, said Mayo, who frequently performed the anthem before Lakers games. "What's great and bad about that song is you have to be in the right key or you're screwed," she explained.

Another small issue complicates matters, according to Cusack: "Quite frankly, it's terribly written." Mayo said "The Star-Spangled Banner" is meant for marching bands. For that reason, and not to keep the fans waiting too long, when Mayo sang it, she aimed to finish in about a minute. That would have pleased Paul Zimmerman. The late *Sports Illustrated* scribe was many things: an oenophile, a revolutionary football writer, and a man obsessed with hearing the shortest possible national anthem at a ballgame. When Irvin Molotsky talked to Zimmerman for his 2001 book, *The Flag, the Poet, and the Song: The Story of the Star-Spangled Banner*, Dr. Z had clocked 1,283 performances of Francis Scott Key's peppy dirge. He longed for someone, anyone, to break the fifty-second barrier. "It's a crummy song," he told Molotsky, "and I want to get it over with as soon as possible."

A straight-ahead song deserved straight-ahead talent. The NBA played the game. The likes of "Moon River" crooner Andy Williams and opera singer Robert Merrill did the honors at All-Star Games past—safe, pleasant choices sure to please Mom and Dad America and their two and a half kids.

The time in America was ripe to keep the same treatment. Ronald Reagan's election to the White House in 1980, noted University of Southern California professor Todd Boyd, "signaled the beginning of a new America, a much more conservative and reactionary one." Under the former B-actor's conservative social agenda, it was "acceptable, even popular, to be open openly hostile toward race issues." Reagan's appreciation of the counterculture is best summed up by his love of John Rambo, Sylvester Stallone's killing machine/atonement for America's underperformance in the Vietnam War. In private, he jokingly referred to himself as "Ron-bo."

Lakers owner Jerry Buss was no one's choice to carve the turkey in a Norman Rockwell painting, but he was a true American success story. One of Buss's earliest memories was waiting in food lines in Depression-era Wyoming. His life was defined by work. He awoke at 4:30 a.m. to dig ditches for his stepfather. Then he'd go to school and work until 9 p.m. He shined shoes. He started a mail-order stamp business at age thirteen. Two years later, chafing under his stepfather's despotic, greedy hand, Buss dropped out of school to work on the railroads. Thankfully, Buss returned and found an ally in his science teacher, Walt Garrett, who put Buss up in his apartment. Garrett then peppered him with chemistry questions as they played cards and chess. Buss hated school, but education provided a ticket out of Wyoming and a life of hard labor.

Like Stern, Buss contained multitudes. He earned his Ph.D. in chemistry—"He loved being called 'Doctor'," said Mike Suscavage, the old guard at NBA Properties, "almost insisted upon it"—but his fortune came in real estate. Buss was an NBA owner, a stuffy, self-important lot, but he had a social life that rivaled his employees'. A voracious partier, Buss kept photo albums of the young stunners he dated. After he lapped the L.A. nightlife, he retreated to the White House of the west, Pickfair, a sprawling forty-two-room estate previously owned by Hollywood's original glamour couple, Douglas Fairbanks and Mary Pickford.

Beneath his California cool—dig that chest hair; dig that big, thick mustache—resided a sharp intelligence. He was a genius, said Ron Carter, the former Laker who worked for Buss in his real estate company. He learned the business in a nontraditional way. "Everything was a statistical regression," Carter said. "It was a standard deviation from the norm. If the house is this size and it has this many bedrooms—I don't care where it is—we know based on the inflation rates over the next six years, with the taxes . . . Everything was math." Buss and his partners didn't visit the property. If the land fit the formula, Carter said, they bought it. Buss was past the grandeur of owning a sports team. He was one of the first to take advantage of stadium naming rights, getting a line of credit and cash, Carter said, from Great Western Bank in December 1988.* A couple of years earlier, Buss hosted his successful head coach, Pat Riley, after a season-ending loss to the Houston Rockets in the Western Conference Finals. The conversation was convivial and loose and went on for hours. The rum and Cokes were plentiful. Buss offered Riley a new contract. More talk, more drinks. Then Buss offered a chaser of condemnation: you just cost me $3 million.

"How do you figure that?" Riley asked.

We're not playing a seventh game at the Forum, Buss said. That's $350,000 in gate revenue. With the Finals, there's TV and radio revenues, gate, concessions, licensing. That's about $3 million.

That's okay, Riley said. I've been to the Finals four times, so I'm $9 million ahead.

Buss didn't laugh.

The Forum was more than a nice place to watch a basketball game. It was where sports and entertainment converged. The downtime

---

*Corporate sponsorships for arenas were a bit of a to-do back in 1988. Here's what Steven F. Tiberi, editor of *Sports Marketing News*, a trade publication, told the *New York Times*: "Where does it end? The line has to be drawn somewhere. If they start changing the game to make it more attractive to corporate sponsors, people may well go to Little League games to avoid being bombarded by corporate names." Little League, it should be noted, is trademarked.

needed to be filled with more than a snazzy tune on the organ. "Who would you pay money to go see?" said Jeanie Buss, Jerry's daughter. "It was all part of the show." He brought in members of USC's marching band to play live music. He turned the Forum Club from a stodgy hangout where *Laugh-In* cast member Arte "Very Interesting" Johnson was the biggest celebrity to a decadent party palace that served as a worthy rival to Studio 54. "If you couldn't get laid at the Forum Club," said Jeanie Buss, "you couldn't get laid." He agreed to have USC and UCLA coeds for a cheerleading squad.

People respected Buss for his intelligence, but he knew his best attribute. "What I am better at than anyone I've ever met is being a salesman," Buss once told an aide. "The secret of all this is being able to sell. I'm a great salesman." And he was thrifty. The marketing, observed Los Angeles radio personality Joe McDonnell, was on the floor.

The Laker Girls developed into a mainstreamed sexual phenomenon on par with the Dallas Cowboys Cheerleaders, the Rockettes, or *Playboy* Playmates. This went beyond a group of curvy coeds shaking their pom-poms after every basket. "You had to be really qualified as a dancer," said Julie Ann Wasti, a Laker Girl from 1986 to 1988. Choreographers such as Donna Perkins and Paula Abdul kept everything fresh. The squad performed dance forms that Annie Yee, another Laker Girl, had studied. "It was a performance outlet for me," she said. One routine was street. Another based in musical theater. The next, jazz. These weren't layups, but "intricate, detailed, and technical routines," Yee said.

Abdul inadvertently played hit maker via Tower Records' imports section, buying "whatever got under my skin and choreograph[ing] routines to it." A day after the Laker Girls strutted their stuff to Thomas Dolby's "She Blinded Me with Science," influential Los Angeles DJ Rick Dees introduced the song with "As heard on the Lakers floor." The golden touch extended to "One Thing Leads to Another" by the

Fixx and "Freak-A-Zoid" by Midnight Star. "We took so many songs platinum," Abdul said. "It was like I was in A&R without knowing it."

Others devoted their attention elsewhere. "Oh, man, they took it to a whole other level," said actor Nathaniel Bellamy Jr. "There was one Laker Girl—man, I thought she was the finest thing I'd ever seen in life. I was like, 'Oh my God, if I could get with her, I would be in heaven.' Oh, the Laker Girls. Oh my—"

(Yes, the Laker Girls had bodyguards when they left the Forum.)

Wasti offered a more concise clarification: "We were sexy, man." It was by design, explained Donna Caravaggio, a Laker Girl from 1986 to 1988. "The minute we were walking out of our locker room, we were on," she said. Don't talk. Don't correct your hair or touch your nose. Drop something during your dance routine, too bad; keep going. There were weigh-ins. Laker Girls had to sit and get up in a ladylike way. Conservative and feminine and untouchable. "We had to be real classy gals, and we all were," Wasti said.

Buss wanted steak with his sizzle. "He relished in success," said Tony Acone, Buss's friend and cable television partner. "But it wasn't because of the notoriety and the fame that it brought—it was because he wanted to win. Winning was enough." The owner had the players necessary for style and substance. Kareem may have been a moody loner, but the charismatic showman Magic Johnson gave the Lakers a matinee idol. "Magic had—let's just call it magic. He just had this aura," said Dyan Cannon, the Oscar-nominated actress and longtime Lakers fan. "He shined. He just shined." Riley possessed dreamy good looks, gorgeous suits, and a hyperfocused, winning-is-everything attitude that embodied the 1980s corporate gladiator lifestyle. "I knew I was being packaged by CBS and everybody else in the media," Riley said years later. Magic and Riley got waylaid. Riley admitted to basketball writer Ian Thomsen that the image tripped him up. "There was no doubt that in the '80s I totally got full of myself," he said. And Magic's choirboy countenance and heavenly passes hid a voracious sexual appetite. Magic wasn't called "Buck" because of his spirited play. "During the days of slavery, the plantation owners would always use the strongest buck to impregnate all the women," Ron Carter said. "And Earvin was such a whore, we called him 'Buck.' The media never got that story right."

The Forum was intoxicating. You were surrounded by celebrities, whom Buss initially courted with tickets. The usherettes dressed in togas. The real estate magnate knew what he had and priced the experience accordingly. Courtside seats were "beachside property," said Lon Rosen. It was one hundred dollars per ticket. "The best real estate," Buss once said, "can be sold at any price." People gladly ponied up the money. "It was the event to go and be seen," Yee said. Pierce that clique, join that party, and "you were living a life that other people dream about," said Bellamy Jr., who later served as Michael Jordan's body double in commercials and on the hit 1996 movie *Space Jam*. The Forum, Bellamy concluded, was "Hollywood on steroids."

"It made you feel like you were going into a Hollywood performance," said Fred Mitchell, who covered the Chicago Bulls for the *Chicago Tribune* in the early 1980s. "It was as much an event and performance as it was an actual basketball game. The crowds were eclectic and yet they were good, knowledgeable basketball fans as well."

Buss may have been the most refined talent broker, but plenty of teams put on a show. Giveaways, after-game concerts, halftime acts, and other spectacles became a normal way of doing business in the NBA as ownership's old guard faded away. The Utah Jazz hosted dancing squads and mascots from other teams. The Dallas Cowboys Cheerleaders and their ilk had tradition. "That's what we were promoting, because we didn't have it ourselves," said Grant Harrison, the Utah Jazz's vice president of game operations and promotions director. The Detroit Pistons brought in everyone: a Simon Says champion, tumblers, a contortionist named Rubber Boy, a master hypnotist. Future Piston's president Wilson spotted a mime at SeaWorld and brought him to Michigan for a 1984 playoff game, where referee Mike Mathis advised him to "get a fucking job." Thirty years later, Wilson ran into the mime at Universal Studios, where he now played the Grinch.

The Pistons were drawing three thousand people a night to the Pontiac Silverdome, a cavernous football stadium that sat eighty thousand. For Wilson, adhering to the purity of the game was a principle he couldn't afford to follow. No rules applied. "Our job is to make this thing fun for people to come out here," Wilson said of his mind-set. "If we're not going to win, we've got to at least show them something they've haven't seen before until we have a player who will do that."

When the Pistons drafted a future superstar (Isiah Thomas) and a great white hope (Notre Dame star Kelly Tripucka), the idea was to still have fun. So, the team sold twenty thousand tickets to Marathon Gas at a buck apiece, so the gas station could give them out with a fill-up. It was a cheap, effective way to boost the attendance, Wilson said. Folks would read their newspaper and wonder why twenty-seven thousand people were at the Silverdome for a basketball game. And the people who got in for free later bought tickets to another game.

Not every promotion went according to plan. The Indiana Pacers' Sandy Knapp organized a green bagel giveaway at Market Square Arena that had a small glitch: fans got the frozen goodies before the game ended, not after. "I'm flying around the arena," Knapp said. " 'Shut down the bagels! Shut down the bagels!' Frozen green bagels were flying around the arena. It was not a good night." The Utah Jazz thought that launching fireworks inside the Salt Palace would be a wonderful way to commemorate its first playoff appearance. The team did a test run, putting the fireworks in a big metal cage—ten or fifteen square feet—and then hoisting the contraption up through the Jumbotron.

The test run, supervised by the fire marshal, was a success, Harrison, an ABA alumnus, said. Then he and the general manager had a thought: *You know, that's great, but not that impressive. Let's add more fireworks.*

Game time arrived. The national anthem was performed, and the bombs indeed burst in the air. There were too many fireworks. The metal cage started to melt and drip onto the floor. Smoke was everywhere. The game was delayed to clean the molten droppings. "That was a hell of a mess," Harrison said. But there was no rule prohibiting that. Or having a cow-milking contest on the same floor where high-priced athletes plied their trade. Teams that were not the Celtics had to justify the price of a ticket. They did whatever it took.

The Lakers were different. The cool came through when CBS aired games from The Forum. Author Jeff Pearlman saw it growing up in suburban Mahopac, New York. The Lakers represented an eighties version of Manifest Destiny.

"It was this thing that was out there that you were probably never going to touch, which is funny because I live in California now," Pearlman said. "They'd show you the wide shot of the Forum, and even though the Forum was in crappy Inglewood, you'd see some palm trees and you'd see the celebrities sliding into their seats, like Jack Nicholson and Penny Marshall. The Lakers would jog out to the court, they had their gold uniforms on, and it symbolized sunshine and palm trees and glitter. It was a life these special people had that you would never have."

Andy Williams was not going to cut it for the All-Star Game's anthem.

Pop star Lionel Richie, deep into his reign as 1980s pop royalty, got the nod. But when Rosen called the NBA to get approval, the person on the other end didn't know who Richie was. Rosen then called CBS Records, which recommended Gaye. Perfect. He was a Motown legend who had scored a recent Top 40 hit with the sultry slow jam "Sexual Healing." "He was cool," Jeanie Buss said. "He was of the moment."

Once Gaye was booked, there wasn't a lot of time to prepare. Josh Rosenfeld, the Lakers' director of public relations, said the act was locked on the Tuesday before Sunday's game. Gaye and Gordon Banks, Gaye's guitarist and former brother-in-law, worked on the song the day before the All-Star Game, with the singer rehearsing on Saturday between the East and West squads' practices.

The Saturday run-through was memorable. The reason why depended on whom you asked. Roy S. Johnson, who covered the NBA for the *New York Times*, heard no connection between that gorgeous voice and the music. The notes were long, strung together, like he was riffing, Johnson recalled. CBS Sports' Ted Shaker was stunned for the opposite reason. "When he began to sing it in this rehearsal, the whole place stopped and turned to watch," he said, because it was "so unusual and so great."

Afterward, Shaker turned to Dick Stockton, the game's announcer, producer Mike Burks, and Sandy Grossman, the director of the telecast. "We all kind of went, 'Wow.'" At that moment, Shaker didn't care how long it was, he knew CBS had to capture the anthem. "I remember that night and the following day in every conversation it was, 'Make sure you hear the national anthem.'" Roy S. Johnson left with his own highlight. He met Marvin Gaye.

Whether you loved it or hated it, Gaye's rendition was way too long. CBS had two minutes slated for the performance. Rosen tried to tell Gaye, who would have none of it. He repeatedly turned his back on the young Lakers employee. Gaye, said Banks, wasn't going to change a thing. His frustration over Saturday was probably why he waited so long to appear at the Forum.

Gaye was poised to take a huge risk. The last singer to give the anthem a stylistic, high-profile twist was José Feliciano at Game 5 of the 1968 World Series between the St. Louis Cardinals and Detroit Tigers. Gaye did the honors at Game 4, and his straight-up interpretation opened the door for Feliciano ("Light My Fire," "Feliz Navidad") to go his own way. The popular music scene of the late 1960s may have boasted its share of long-haired, talented firebrands—Joplin, Hendrix, Morrison, Jagger and Richards, McCartney and Lennon—but it occasionally sported a crew cut and a swell pair of chinos. Witness the monstrous success of army staff sergeant Barry Sadler's 1966 drab spoken-word smash "The Ballad of the Green Berets" (*Silver Wings upon their chest / These are men, America's best*).

Listening with today's ears, the blind singer's take is an acoustic guitar–driven treasure. But performed weeks before Richard Nixon was elected president, Feliciano's interpretation irked more than it inspired. The Tigers' switchboard lit up with objections. Telegrams piled up. Feliciano was told that veterans hurled their shoes at the television. No one expected this. "I picked him because he's one of the outstanding singers in America today," Tigers broadcaster Ernie Harwell, who invited Feliciano to perform, later told the *Detroit Free Press*. "I had heard from people in music whose opinion I respect that he had an interesting version of the national anthem. I feel a fellow has a right to sing any way he can sing it." All the twenty-three-year-old Feliciano wanted to do was show his patriotism. Instead, he was ostracized. He said his career stalled until he sang the theme song for the hit NBC sitcom *Chico and the Man* in 1974. Feliciano's performance of "The Star-Spangled Banner" did have an audience, landing at 50 on the *Billboard* Hot 100.

"I made history and nothing can besmirch that," Feliciano said. "Nothing can erase that. Anytime anybody talks about [making the anthem stylistic] they have to deal with the fact that I was the first one to innovate."

Nearly fifteen years later, a cram session paved the way for history. "We did a demo," Banks said. "I did a drum track, and Marvin did a keyboard track that was close enough to sing to. . . . That first draft was used to get a feel for the song and to make sure the key of the song was great for him."

Afterward, Banks made a copy of the demo and "added and sub- tracted" to complete the beat that Gaye sang over. "Overdubbing, Sat- urday rehearsal, and Sunday's performance are all the same," he said. What the sparse crowd heard at the Saturday rehearsal is what the na- tion heard on Sunday.

"We just did what we did," Banks said.

No one with the Lakers knew Gaye's plan for Sunday afternoon. The East and West All-Stars lined up along the free-throw lines. A few of the basketball writers donned mirrored sunglasses provided in gift bags from the NBA. Gaye, all Motown cool in his dark suit and manhole- size sunglasses—looking "resplendent," according to Rosen—walked to center court. "I asked God that when I sang it," Gaye said, "would He let it move men's souls."

The simple, two-part beat—created in Banks's studio, a four-by- four-feet closet—started. Panic ensued.

Ah, shit, man, thought Lawrence Tanter, the Lakers' public address announcer. *They've got the wrong tape. This is "Sexual Healing."* "I don't think anyone had a clue what was about to come," Rosenfeld said.

Jack Sikma, a reserve for the West, was perplexed: *Where is this going? This is kind of groovy, kind of funky,* Marques Johnson thought, as the performance started. *Okay, I like that.* Then Gaye opened his mouth. The players looked at each other, Johnson said, and their ex- pressions told the same story: *Oh, shit, here we go.*

"If you are listening, and if you have any ear for music at all, you heard something that should have taken precedence at that moment," said Chicago Bulls guard Reggie Theus, who played for the East team.

"It was that new, that different, that unique, and that good. And if you didn't take a moment to reflect, shame on you."

West coach Pat Riley had goose bumps. "I was so proud to be an American that day," he said. The experience was powerful and surreal, thought Isiah Thomas, the Detroit Pistons' second-year superstar. Typically, you stood still during the anthem, but everybody moved. You couldn't help yourself.

In the CBS Sports crew's truck, Shaker's expectations the day before were confirmed. "Collectively, in that truck, it was like, 'Holy shit, this is unbelievable.'" As Gaye neared the climax of the performance, the song started to seem personal; he was working through what Gaye's biographer and friend David Ritz called his "emotional shit." Roy S. Johnson's skepticism evaporated. *Okay, he found the beat.* By "rocket's red glare," he said, the crowd was all-in. By "wave," the crowd was *clapping* to the beat. After an elongated "brave," Gaye exhaled a breathy "Oh, Lord. Woo!" There was a slight pause. Not even a second, Robert Parish of the Boston Celtics said, "like nobody could believe what they just heard." And then, from the stands—an eruption, according to Parish. On the court, players high-fived each other. The players didn't want to leave, Magic Johnson recalled. They wanted more.

Whatever boos and voices of dissent existed—Mayo said she heard them—were obliterated by the Forum crowd. "It was like everybody had stuck their finger in a socket," Shaker said.

"I just never heard anything so good," said Kiki VanDeWeghe, the Denver Nuggets forward, making his first All-Star appearance. "It was just a moment in time that I don't think anybody is ever going to forget. Being so close to him when he was singing it, you could hear the voice unamplified. Wow, it was something. You get those moments in your life that you're never going to forget. I don't remember half the stuff that went on in the game, but I'll tell you what: I remember that."

Said Tanter: "When you introduce someone to do the national anthem, you expect something predicated on historical precedent. We're talking about a whole set of emotions that erupted spontaneously, that no one could anticipate."

The electricity lingered long after Gaye stepped away from the microphone. "I just remember everybody coming back to the huddle going, 'Wow,'" Riley said. The players shook their heads in amazement; Magic Johnson kept smiling. Ron Thomas covered the game as *USA Today's* basketball editor. What stood out, he said, was the spectacular play early in the game. It was as if the anthem served as a runway for the players to take off from. "The guys were just *flying* up and down the court," Sikma said. "Six minutes into the game, most of the guys were gasping. We are all on glue from the performance. It was amazing."

Isiah Thomas, who started the game, said the teams wanted to keep that energy going. "That game," he said, "was about the anthem." For a week, that's all the players, or anyone else who bumped into Reggie Theus, talked about. "I think about it to this day," Riley said.

In a way, Marvin is trying to copy something I did, Feliciano first thought when he heard the All-Star Game anthem. *Good for him.* But he wasn't enamored with Gaye's approach. "I thought it was okay," he said. "I thought singing to the track was a little bit different." Others were harsher. Legendary New York sports columnist Dick Young chided Gaye for treating the national anthem as "an entertainment song." Stan Hochman of the *Philadelphia Daily News*, confusing Gaye with Sarah Vaughan, called it an "ooh ba-ba-doo wah shambles."

"Anybody who complained about that rendition didn't know music and didn't know the national anthem," said Riley, a huge Gaye fan. "They just didn't. Anybody who would have criticized Marvin Gaye that day was simply some cynical person who wanted to take the other side." Gaye didn't care. His work won the approval of Julius Erving. It was all good.

A reworked staple of elementary school recitals provided the first push on the NBA's slow, inexorable journey toward its soul mate in commodified cool. Gaye, a basketball fan, never saw the full impact. He didn't stick around for the game, which the East won 132–123. On April 1, 1984, Gaye and his father, Marvin Gay Sr., had another in a lifetime of arguments. It got physical. Gay Sr. left. He returned to his son's bedroom with a .38-caliber revolver—the very one Gaye had given him months ago—and shot his forty-four-year-old son through the heart. Then Gay Sr. took a few steps forward and fired another shot to finish the job. Jeanne Gay, Marvin's mother, screamed for the mercy of God and found the strength to flee the room.

Nearly thirty years after her near-moment, Amanda Mayo was working at Sam's Club and as an assistant catering manager at a country club, a million miles away from Jack Nicholson's warm wishes. She hadn't sung in ages and wasn't sure what her future held.

Nowhere was the necessity of a new direction more evident than in the reaction of the NBA's two top executives. After Larry O'Brien seethed—during Gaye's performance, he instructed the NBA's respected PR director Brian McIntyre to handle the fallout—CBS hosted an after party. The soundtrack for the evening was Gaye's anthem.

As the flashy, funky version of "The Star-Spangled Banner" played, David Stern couldn't stop smiling.

FINDING A SOUNDTRACK, GAINING A CULTURE

Somewhere on your radio or, increasingly, your TV.

REPORTER STEVE FOX: Rap is likely to influence popular music for years to come. It has tremendous staying power, because it lets ordinary people express ideas they care about, in language they can relate to, set to music they can dance to.
HUGH DOWNS: That's marvelous. And it is infectious, too, isn't it? Thank you, Steve.
—FROM THE *20/20* EPISODE ON RAP, JULY 1981

Rock pretends it's still rebellious with its video posturing, but who believes it? The stars are 45-year-old zillionaires or they endorse soft drinks! The 'revolution' is a capitalist industry. Give me a break!

—BILL WATTERSON, *CALVIN & HOBBES*

After the surly sports columnists grumped out their sixteen inches and the Andy Williams fans put their complaining pencils back in their junk drawers, the legacy of Gaye's anthem emerged: he inadvertently gave the NBA an identity and shaped its embryonic mission.

"It seemed like such a nonsensical argument," said Rick Welts, then the NBA's director of national promotions, "but that anthem touched a really important spot in what the opportunity was for the NBA: to be culturally more significant to a new generation of Americans than the traditional sports of baseball and football." Journalist Roy S. Johnson, an African-American, saw black culture on center court, and it soon became ingrained in the NBA. The excitement and flair behind Gaye's performance, he added, were destined to be part of the league's success.

The desires of middle-aged white sports columnists—and middle-aged white people—were not part of the NBA's emergent agenda.

The popular music landscape was also due for an overhaul.

The difference between a eulogy and a love story is timing. It's why Marvin Gaye unleashed a stylistic triumph and José Feliciano nearly committed artistic suicide. And it's why the NBA's rise as a cultural behemoth is intertwined with rap and its culture.

Music essayist Rob Sheffield suggested 1982 as when FM radio grew more diverse, a place where new wave, pop, rock, and rap hung out. Rap was a nascent and misunderstood genre, but it already had flowed from the New York City playgrounds and rec centers into cars and poolside radios, thanks to the Sugar Hill Gang's 1979 pop-flavored classic "Rapper's Delight," which was an international hit. Two years later, Blondie's Debbie Harry got a nation grooving as she played MC in "Rapture"—"Fab 5 Freddy told me everybody's high / DJ's spinnin' are savin' my mind"—a rap-rock-disco mélange that reached number one.* "I guess for a lot of the white mainstream public, it was the first time that they heard anybody rap," said artist and hip-hop impresario Fab 5 Freddy, who is name-checked in the song and hung out with Harry and Blondie guitarist/songwriter Chris Stein. "It kind of paved the way, you could say, for what was about to come."

---

*The debate regarding whether "Rapture" is a straight-ahead rap song or not is one the author has neither the time nor the energy to pursue. Apologies.

MTV, Generation X's *American Bandstand*, kept rap at the door. Executives said they were sticking to the network's rock-and-roll format, though MTV happily aired blue-eyed R&B artists like Hall & Oates. "The people at the top had all come from radio stations," said George Bradt, a research analyst at MTV. "They were old-school, white radio guys with an AOR [album-oriented rock] mind-set, probably because in the world of eighties radio, AOR was cool." The move away from that narrow perspective started after Michael Jackson unleashed *Thriller* on the world in November 1982, but widespread acceptance was slow to occur. The video for "Billie Jean" wasn't approved for rotation until March 1983. One of MTV's early hip-hop videos was middle-aged keyboard maestro Herbie Hancock's "Rockit." The technology-run-amok video featured nary a black person, save Hancock, who was barely in it. "It's a way of programming black music to white youth without any scary black people in it," said Bill Adler, a longtime record executive. As Bradt said, MTV had yet to realize it was *the* channel for music.

The treatment was the same old song. Black music was resilient, thought Dick Griffey, the founder of SOLAR Records, home of hit singles such as "Second Time Around" and "Fantastic Voyage." It was the most widely accepted music there is—and it was not the property of blacks. The *Saturday Night Fever* soundtrack, he noted, consisted of "the Bee Gees doing black music," Griffey told *Black Enterprise Magazine* in 1982. Record companies, he added, had tried—and failed—to push other options ahead of black music: acid rock, disco, Peter Framptonesque arena rock. Black music was the only music that didn't have to be returned after being shipped. The success of the record companies hinged on "their willingness to sell black music."

Gaye had more assets on his side. Aside from being performed in— or, to be more precise, 12.5 miles from—the showbiz capital of the world, Gaye's rendition was a theme song for the contemporary NBA.

As George Carlin famously illustrated in the premiere episode of *Saturday Night Live*, football boasted sports-as-war parallels; baseball had a pastoral ethos. Basketball was a physical ballet. Gaye's rendition—blending elements of gospel, R&B, and hip-hop (the use of a prerecorded beat)—reflected who was on the floor. Marques Johnson of the Milwaukee Bucks wondered how the scene played on TV: a crowd bopping along to the national anthem was another reason to get riled up about the black-dominant NBA.

Rap connected with basketball and the NBA on a deeper level. They were young. They were stylistic. Both came from the playgrounds, so the relationship boasted an authenticity and camaraderie that rock lacked. Rap, thought Kurtis Blow, matched sports because both depended on rhythm. Here was the main thing: rap, as hip-hop impresario Russell Simmons claimed, was teenage music. Yes, it had a good beat and you could dance to it. Most important, it was *new*, like the NBA that was now varnished with a thick coat of marketing lacquer. Rock and roll was—grooaaannn—your parents' music. The rebels of the late 1960s were either dead or had become the establishment it had previously rallied against. The Who, save for Keith Moon, were far from the only active rock legends who had made the crucial mistake of not dying before they got old. Who was going to take over? Journey? Foreigner?

"I think every generation," said Doc Wynter, iHeartMedia's longtime urban and hip-hop programming executive, "deserves their own music."

Rap stars, Simmons thought, were rebellious in a way that rock stars never were. The former acted out for a real reason—personal anger, discrimination, their living conditions. Plus, they were outwardly open in their desire to make money and be successful. "The result," Simmons wrote in his 2001 memoir, "is the kind of attitude of authentic rebellion that rock was always supposed to have." Grasping

that attitude was universal and eternal. City kids heard the lyrics and found them relatable, NBA superstar Carmelo Anthony said in 2005. Suburban kids, the twenty-year-old shrewdly observed, listened to broaden their horizons, to be aware, to be down. Those desires never changed.

Simmons, like Stern, looked beyond the product itself to the *image*. When parents started to think rock and roll was okay for their kids, it became "a museum piece." It was a difficult argument to refute since key cogs in the rock-and-roll machine agreed. "There is no future in rock-and-roll," Mick Jagger told *Rolling Stone* in 1980. "It's only recycled past." The magazine's founder and publisher, Jann Wenner, shared that resignation. "The territory we're in," he said in 1981, "the thing that no one else is touching—rock, youth, drugs, a population shift, the whole consequence of a postwar baby boom, which everyone else ignored—now everyone is doing it."

In the mid-1980s, Bruce Springsteen's tales of working-class triumph and woe were co-opted by President Ronald Reagan, who evoked the blue-collar rock-and-roll king in his 1984 reelection push. If kids of America needed to look for another reason to rebel, popular conservative columnist George F. Will provided one. He attended a Springsteen concert and somehow found a solution to solve the country's manufacturing crisis in Clarence Clemons's wailing sax solos and Max Weinberg's furious drumming.

"If all Americans," Will wrote, "in labor and management, who make steel or cars or shoes or textiles—made their products with as much energy and confidence as Springsteen and his merry band make music, there would be no need for Congress to be thinking about protectionism." Apparently, Will never saw James Brown perform.

Music journalist and essayist Nelson George, then *Billboard*'s black music editor, saw music executives—specifically "the buppies and pseudo-buppies"—who were either out of touch with black urban youth or actively disdained it. They dismissed hip-hop as a fad or juvenile. It was gimmicky and unmusical and had a limited audience.

In other words, were white kids really buying this crap?

Yes, George thought. The idea that 500,000 African-Americans bought Kurtis Blow's "The Breaks"—a twelve-inch single—in 1980 was lunacy. "The numbers betray the myth," he wrote. The first national rap tour, the Swatch Watch New York City Fresh Fest, sold out ten- to twenty-thousand-seat arenas in venues across the nation. In Providence, white kids bought half the tickets. Hip-hop, Afrika Bambaataa said, was derived from an abundance of musical sources—a Nile Rodgers guitar riff here; a Kraftwerk sample there—that it was "colorless."

Getting the crossover appeal enjoyed by Springsteen required more than mimicking his live act. The *sound* of rock and roll gave rap a shove toward mainstream acceptance. Producer Rick Rubin, who originally ran Def Jam Records in his New York University dorm room, incorporated guitar licks with Run-DMC's rhymes. "Rock Box," the first rap video to land on MTV in 1984, was the start. Soon Rubin's formula would take over the mainstream. "Walk This Way," the band's reworking of the Aerosmith classic, and Beastie Boys' "(You Gotta) Fight for Your Right (to Party)" and their album, *Licensed to Ill*, hooked a legion of white kids who had previously grown up on pop or rock and roll. Both songs played on Griffey's observation regarding the Bee Gees. Rap was indisputably a black form of music. Beastie Boys were three artsy white boys from New York City who started as a punk band; Mike Horovitz's dad, Israel, was an acclaimed playwright.* The very white Aerosmith, a long way from its *Toys in the Attic* prime, collaborated with the African-American Run-DMC and appeared in

---

*In 2017, Israel Horovitz was dismissed as artistic director of the Gloucester Stage Company after the *New York Times* reported that at least nine women had been sexually assaulted or violated by Horovitz. His son did not dispute the charges.

the "Walk This Way" video. The remake, by the way, charted higher than the original single. *Licensed to Ill* became the first rap album to hit number one on the *Billboard* album charts. Some white listeners and black listeners weren't happy with what they perceived as cultural appropriation. But, as always, money had the final say. The message was clear: rap was no longer a fad.

Because Run-DMC was indifferent to the rock audience—the trio wore their "ghetto uniform" of leather suits, velour hats, and shell-toe Adidas—they *became* rock stars, Simmons said. George thought the ethos of rock translated beautifully to rap. Public Enemy might have been a "pro-black nationalist group" that praised Louis Farrakhan and called Elvis Presley "racist and plain," but it accumulated a loyal white fan base because it "rocked and rebelled literally against the status quo," an idea white teenagers had embraced since "Rock Around the Clock." (And you *could* dance to some of PE's songs. Behold Rosie Perez in the beginning of *Do the Right Thing*.) It's a superficial and frequently hypocritical form of rebellion, George observed, "but it sells a lot of records." Increasingly, noted hip-hop historian Dan Charnas, Def Jam's records were structured more like pop songs—verse, bridge, and chorus—that drew in more listeners. The formula became ubiquitous and spawned global hits that have endured. Navigate any wedding dance floor or head to a night out that involves margarita specials. *You gotta fight / for your right / to party; It takes two to make a thing go right / It takes two to make it out of sight; If you want it / you got it / if you want it, baby you got it / Stop! / Hammertime!*

Hip-hop, the culture where rap existed, became "refined like sugar," Jeff Chang wrote. The process began right after "Rapper's Delight" took off. The music that came from the streets was now brought into recording studios, where independent labels tried to make radio-friendly hits. The twelve-minute party songs and rap crews larger than families were a relic of the very recent past. The MCs took center stage, not the DJs or the dancers who shared the stage. Hip-hop, said Charlie Ahearn, the director of the hip-hop documentary *Wild Style*, was dead by 1980. Or at least the original form of it.

Russell Simmons knew rap had gone mainstream in the late 1980s, when he started vacationing in the Hamptons, the summer playground of the elite. Year after year, at the parties he attended, more rap records got played.* The jet-setters carried the message worldwide that this rap was pretty darn enjoyable, and it spread to "tastemakers in the media and the financial world." Hip-hop culture got more attention, as did urban fashion. Wall Street viewed hip-hop businesses more favorably.

It's doubtful many of these folks watched *Yo! MTV Raps*, though their kids probably did. Created by a white production assistant (the late Ted Demme, nephew of Oscar-winning director Jonathan Demme), *Yo!* debuted in 1988. It was the network's most-watched show within months, airing six days a week. As Chang pointed out, MTV went from having scant rap-related programming to twelve hours a week. MTV's power as a cultural influencer in the 1980s and early 1990s was enormous, and it meant that rap belonged to the world. Millions of subscribers—21.3 million by 1984—saw those videos and then went to Sam Goody or the Wiz to buy 45s or LPs. By 1981, the year MTV premiered, record sales had dropped more than a third from the high they had reached in 1978. Sales were up by 1983 and climbed into 1991, aided by the compact disc. In 1981, six albums had sold more than 7 million copies. By 1991, that number had nearly tripled.

Rap's emergence was aided by an acceptance of blacks in mainstream culture. Michael Jackson, Bill Cosby, and Eddie Murphy achieved massive popularity around the same time in three separate realms of popular culture. *Thriller* was a gigantic hit—it has sold more

---

*To see Simmons's statement in hilarious action, find the 2015 Vine of celebrity chef Bobby Flay strutting to Big Pun's "Still Not a Player" in a New York City bar.

than 100 million copies worldwide since its release—that turned Jackson into an international celebrity. *The Cosby Show*, a sitcom portraying Cosby as a more successful, with-it version of Ward Cleaver, debuted on NBC in 1984. It topped the Nielsen ratings for five straight seasons. The comedian parlayed that success into a family-friendly brand that included bestselling books. Murphy's *Beverly Hills Cop* made $234 million domestically and ruled the box office in late 1984 and beyond. The hilarious *Saturday Night Live* alumnus became a legitimate movie star—Sidney Poitier without the gravitas and "credit to his race" expectations—who didn't need Nick Nolte, Dan Aykroyd, or any white star to make him palatable in Peoria. The three men reached those heights without political exhortations or demands to shake up the white status quo. A white person could like all three performers and not be accused of a hostile act by their friends and neighbors. For a kid of the 1980s, they were aspirational figures and, more important, cool. (Cosby's and Jackson's abhorrent personal lives were under wraps.) The timing couldn't have been more fortuitous for Stern's desire to push the NBA into the American culture. As Russell Simmons predicted, rap's popularity came from kids, the same group that the NBA would ultimately target. They watched the videos and thought they could be like Run-DMC or LL Cool J and be part of that immediately, Fab 5 Freddy, a *Yo! MTV Raps* host, told *Time*.

DJ Jazzy Jeff, who grew up in the age of "Rapper's Delight," knew exactly what Fab 5 Freddy meant. "What was great about is, I could do it," he said. "I could sing along on the bus. I got credit if I learned all the lyrics to ['Rapper's Delight']. I know the whole 15-minute version. You hear stories of people saying, 'I did a talent show and I rapped all the lyrics to 'Parents Just Don't Understand' [DJ Jazzy Jeff and the Fresh Prince's monster 1988 hit] and I won because no one knew 'Parents Just Don't Understand.' You got credit. I can mimic what they can do." You couldn't do that with a rock song.

"If you can speak, if you can communicate, you can rap," Kurtis Blow said. "It's easy."

A dream once known to city kids was now available to any suburban kid whose parents sprang for cable, as was the lifestyle associated with it. Rap, like the NBA, was about selling ideals and aesthetics, the cornerstones of brand advertising. This was how companies started to differentiate themselves. It wasn't about the brand, Naomi Klein wrote, as much as it was the images—the marketing—behind it. *Nothing comes between me and my Calvins. Nothing. Just do it. It's fantastic!*

Marketing ideals bonded the NBA and the rap community. Bill Stephney, a founder of Public Enemy and a longtime executive at Def Jam, remembered Darryl Dawkins, a Florida native, carrying himself like a monstrous b-boy—the short hair with a part, the gold chains, the rhyming and fast talking. By the mid to late 1980s, as rap got big, that look was no longer an anomaly. A wave of New York–born ballplayers, like Kenny Smith, Rod Strickland, and Mark Jackson, entered the league and carried themselves and dressed like the guys from the neighborhood, the same ones who were rapping. "We didn't look at them as hip-hop representation in the NBA, but guys from the same 'hood where the culture was," Stephney said. The look that defined Run-DMC, the crisp Adidas shell-toes and popping sweat suits, was what the ballers at Rucker Park would wear, Kenny Smith said. The rappers popularized it.

USA Today's basketball editor Ron Thomas noticed, and loved, the league's unabashed acceptance of black culture. There were plenty of African-Americans in the NFL, but the operation felt squashed of an identity. It was so regimented. Hell, in San Francisco 49ers' practices the players couldn't sit down—and neither could the reporters. In the NBA, Thomas heard black music in the locker room. The players would hit the clubs.

"The NBA decided that it was going to make being a black league, it was going to accept it as its culture—what we could call now its brand," said Thomas, an African-American. "And the NBA was fine with that. I felt, without thinking about it, you were covering a black cultural entity called the NBA."

Christopher "Play" Martin, one half of Kid 'n Play, believed athletes, rappers, and drug dealers had much in common. They came from the streets, where they were trying to find their purpose, where they celebrated together. "We all knew our plights, our struggles, our journeys to get there," Martin said. Some members of this group, he added, wanted to trade places.

"All the dudes in the NBA loved *Yo! MTV Raps*," said John Gaffney of CBS/Fox Video, the NBA's video distributor. "They loved the look and feel and speed of that show. You have no idea. Everybody in the NBA was like, 'Did you see *Yo!* Did you see *Yo!*' That just blew through that place." The connection between rap and basketball ran deep. For Stephney, a native New Yorker, young black men played ball as a DJ worked turntables on the side. "I don't know if that distinction in this area ever expressed itself," he said. It was all part of the same experience. Baseball and stickball were also big in Stephney's day, but Major League Baseball ignored the changing cultural shifts, isolating younger Latinos and blacks. Stephney had reached out to various factions of Major League Baseball, offering to engage those groups. Nothing. In the early 2000s, Stephney asked the New York Mets if the team had any interest in using 1993's "Mo' Like Flows On," from his Tommy Boy Records tenure, for the club's new arrival, slugger Mo Vaughn. By that time, Def Jam, Tommy Boy Records, and Public Enemy were cultural touchstones. Rap was as American as baseball. Stephney's pitch was met with silence.

Rap and basketball are fueled by a sense of individual accomplishment, said DJ Jazzy Jeff. Pulling off a difficult rhyme and dunking come from the same place, and feed the other sect's fantasy. When Kris Jenkins's three-point buzzer-beater gave Villanova University the 2016 national championship, Jeff, a Philadelphia native and die-hard sports fan, expressed the hopes and dreams of frustrated gym rats from Antarctica to Zimbabwe.

"Everybody in the world wants that moment," he said.

"You had it at the Grammys," his wife, Lynette, said.

Jeff was stunned. He *did* have the music equivalent of Jenkins's heroics. He and Will Smith, the Fresh Prince before his acting career exploded, won a Grammy in 1989 *and* 1992.

"It's everybody trying to do cool stuff," Stephney said.

Rap would become a business, with an emphasis placed on showmanship and star power, not the hustle and pluck of the late 1970s and early 1980s. MC Hammer and Vanilla Ice, with their choreographed dance moves and Vegas costumes, would hawk Pepsi and rap about the Teenage Mutant Ninja Turtles. "Like anything that grows so powerful, rap lost its innocence long ago," wrote Robert Ford Jr., an early producer for Kurtis Blow.

These were the breaks, but hip-hop's popularity then and its permanence in the pop culture landscape now signified something, said MC Serch, the producer and member of 3rd Bass. The producers and artists were in positions of power and not the kids asked to sit in the corner.

"We needed time to root and time to grow," he said, "and now it's grown."

As rap videos accumulated, so did employees at NBA Entertainment entranced by quick cuts and overheated dancers. The staffers grew up on MTV, said Patrick Kelleher, who joined NBA Entertainment full-time in 1990, after serving as an intern in 1989. Rap and the NBA were soul mates in commerce. The rhythm and flow of the music matched the athleticism, NBA Entertainment producer Stephen Koontz thought.

The athletes were so dynamic, and the music was so new. It made sense to marry the two—especially on highlights. "You could dunk on the beat," NBA Entertainment's Heidi Palarz said.

Dave Zirin, the sports columnist and sports editor for *The Nation*, said the rap-NBA link goes back to at least 1984: NBA Entertainment's 1984 year-in-review video, *Pride and Passion*, where a rapper performed an original pastel-colored jam called "13 Johnsons" for a segment about the NBA players surnamed Johnson. *Thirteen men with the same last name / 13 Johnsons playing the game.* It made the "Super Bowl Shuffle" sound like "Rapper's Delight," Zirin said.

Perhaps, but the NBA was fostering a connection with rap. Zirin also recalls Kurtis Blow's rap classic "Basketball" being used in NBA promotions. Blow considered it a theme song for basketball. He performed after games "that weren't drawing people—Sacramento playing Washington or something. So, the game is half-full. They call me in. The song was so hot, we were selling out. The games would be packed. I did that for about twenty different games. It was incredible." Blow got to meet the players he rapped about: Isiah Thomas, Julius Erving, George Gervin. They all hugged him like he was part of the family.

Stern was fine with the NBA-rap relationship, Koontz said, "as long as we kept it in the bounds of sanity." That meant no "Cop Killer," no songs with outright misogyny or drug use. Into the early 1990s, most popular rap music remained benign. "There was no objection, because back then it was tamer," said Patrick Kelleher. "We were using 'Hip Hop Hooray.' It wasn't as profane as it is now." The NBA worked with Kid 'n Play but not Dr. Dre, said David Gavant. Controversy was a good way to alienate customers.

"They wanted to appeal to the youth, just plain and simple," Martin said, referring to the NBA. "That was the sound of the youth. That's what they loved. That's what appealed to them. That was the language, the style, the culture." Martin credited the NBA with recognizing rap's stamina, and to choose trustworthy brands—that is, artists—that aligned with the image the league wanted to promote.

"One of the things that David always believed was sports as entertainment," said Jon Miller, the co–general manager and vice president of NBA Entertainment. "That's probably a cliché today; it was not a cliché, it was a creation of that as a natural reality and a strategy. He was sort of the orchestra conductor for all that, and music was the easiest place for that to occur," because there was a mutual admiration between the players and hip-hop artists

But what good is music without a party?

7

MAKING A SUPER BOWL

The Los Angeles setting, and Gaye's electrifying performance, made the 1983 All-Star Game appear like a star-powered, glamorous affair. Nope. The All-Star Game, said Rick Welts, boiled down to banquet, game, and go home. The banquet's special guest in 1983 was fifty-seven-year-old comedian and *Mork & Mindy* alumnus Jonathan Winters, whose material included a bit on "Japs" that mortified most of the crowd. "I wanted to disappear," Stern said. One year, Magic Johnson snuck out during the entertainment portion. He wasn't alone. When the lights went up, the room was half-empty.

When O'Brien started as commissioner, he noticed the indifference. "There was no effort on the part of the league office to supervise, control, and promote the All-Star Game in the interests of the league as a whole," O'Brien observed. "It appeared to be something [passed] around from city to city and the league office had little or no involvement in it."

It was an honor to play in the All-Star Game, and a half-decent payday. In 1972, it was $500 for the losers; $1,000 for the winners. By comparison, when Bill Cosby performed at the All-Star Game, Howard Berk handed him $5,000 cash in an envelope. When Steve

Mix played in the 1975 All-Star Game, he got $500 for being on the winning squad. Other than that, "We got nothing," Mix said. "I got a money clip. I still have it." The game was competitive, said veteran guard Butch Beard, an All-Star for the Cleveland Cavaliers in 1972. "Shit, we wanted the money. Come on now. We weren't making millions of dollars back then. We needed the money, come on." It beat work. Beard had to cut his trip short. He deliberately lost a one-on-one competition to Jeff Mullins, so Cavs coach Bill Fitch didn't fine him for missing practice.

The All-Star Game was a trade show; the players, weary conventioneers in high-tops. Its history was not the subject of feel-good, sepia-toned documentaries. The game lacked the signature moments associated with baseball's midseason affair: Carl Hubbell striking out five Hall of Famers consecutively, Pete Rose barreling over catcher Ray Fosse to win 1970's game. The 1964 All-Star Game was considered the NBA's showcase because it needed to hook an elusive television contract. Players such as Bill Russell, Will Chamberlain, Elgin Baylor, and Jerry West and an Old-Timers' Game gave the appearance of a big deal. Then, hours before tip-off, the players—in an effort coordinated by Tommy Heinsohn—threatened to strike if they didn't get a pension. Game time neared. The players, guided by a young Larry Fleisher, held firm. The owners got testy. Bob Short of the Lakers stormed the West locker room but was stymied by an elderly security guard. "You tell Elgin Baylor if he doesn't get his ass out here fast, I'm done with him," Short screamed through the door.

Baylor's response from the other side: "Tell Bob Short to go fuck himself."

Finally, with assurances from commissioner J. Walter Kennedy that he would address their concerns, the players headed to the Boston Garden floor at 8:55 p.m.—just in time for the game's 9 p.m. start. The protest overshadowed the game, journalist Leonard Koppett thought, and was indicative of the NBA's progress. The league would get a clear path to legitimacy and somehow find the one land mine.

Aside from the talent level and snazzy uniforms, little on and off the court suggested the All-Star Game was special. "When I did the first one out in Detroit [in 1979], there was nothing else going on on the floor," said Ted Giannoulas, better known as the San Diego Chicken. "It was just me goofing with referees and fans and just doing solo gags at the Silverdome." Paul Westphal, a star guard with the Phoenix Suns in the 1970s, remembered one All-Star Game reception held in the Suns' team doctor's backyard. Eight to ten tables were placed around the pool, and that was enough for the league.

Peter Vecsey, the *New York Post*'s Zelig-like NBA columnist, also sampled the 1975 All-Star Game's lofty entertainment options with his six-year-old son, Michael. After the game, it was late. The pair ducked into a shabby diner. They had company: All-Stars Walt Frazier and Nate Archibald were eating the same shitty food. Fans expressed little interest. For the All-Star Game in 1982, held in the New Jersey Turnpike–scented glamour of the Meadowlands, the NBA gave away tickets. Administrative assistant Barbara Ward unloaded around twenty.

The drive to do more came from Denver Nuggets president Carl Scheer. Like most ABA survivors, Scheer was a shrewd marketer. Susan Hagar, the Nuggets' former marketing director, saw early that showmanship was the business plan. The mantra was drilled into the Nuggets' staff. The organization can't control how the team plays, "so we have to do everything we can to control the entertainment experience." And that started from the moment a fan parked their car.

Lisa Johnson had worked for the Nuggets for two years when Scheer approached her with an idea for a fan appreciation day to conclude the regular season. He wanted a show, a circus. Johnson quickly realized that Scheer was not talking metaphorically. She organized a real, live circus with jugglers, clowns, bagpipers, and face-painters on the concourse, outside, and during the game. And she did it in about a week.

Planning an All-Star Game was another day in Carl Scheer's fun house.

Scheer's idea for the All-Star Game came down to location and retooled nostalgia. McNichols Sports Arena hosted the 1976 ABA All-Star Game. The ABA had only seven teams left, so the Denver Nuggets played against the rest of the league's best. But halftime's Slam Dunk Contest became legend. Julius Erving won with a tomahawk dunk unleashed from a half-step *inside* the free-throw line to beat hometown favorite David Thompson. CBS had aired a Slam Dunk Contest featuring NBA players during the 1977 playoffs; interest was minimal. Scheer longed for a revival in Denver, remembered Nuggets public relations director Tom Hohensee. The Nuggets were his team. The All-Star Game was in his building. "There was a lot of ABA pride here," Hohensee said.

Scheer pitched his idea to Welts and Adrian De Groot in November 1983 at the Waldorf-Astoria in New York City. Right now, Welts said, the NBA requires two years to plan an All-Star Game. The 1984 All-Star Game was set for January 29. Welts, then the league's director of national promotions, thought of something else. The young executive was watching TV in his Manhattan apartment and came across the Cracker Jack Old-Timers Baseball Classic. It was compelling television, especially when seventy-five-year-old Luke Appling hit a home run off sixty-one-year-old Warren Spahn that sailed over a Cracker Jack sign. This, Welts thought, could work for the NBA.* Stern approached Larry O'Brien with the idea to schedule the two events a day before the All-Star Game and landed the approval. The NBA secured sponsorships

---

*In an interview with Shawn Fury, David Stern claimed credit for the idea.

from American Airlines, Gatorade, and Schick for the day. Don Stirling was among those recruited to call retired legends to see who was up for a run. He considered the task an honor.

Larry O'Brien didn't share his employees' enthusiasm for this undertaking. In 1979, Jon Spoelstra, the vice president of marketing for the Portland Trailblazers, had moved the team's radio broadcasts in-house, which gave the Blazers more flexibility to offer advertising packages— and make all the money. (The first year, the team netted $700,000, more than every NBA team combined, according to Spoelstra.)

One day, Spoelstra's phone rang. "I hear you're going to do your own radio broadcasts," Larry O'Brien said.

Yes, said Spoelstra.

"Jon, we're in the basketball business," O'Brien said in that chasm of a voice. "We're not in the entertainment business."

Nineteen eighty-four's All-Star Weekend marked O'Brien's final weekend as commissioner, with David Stern assuming a spot that he had pretty much run for years. The transition, agreed upon the previous November, was pleasantly devoid of soap opera machinations. The owners approved Stern unanimously after a brief debate over whether to make a splashy hire; Stern was an anonymous figure outside NBA circles. O'Brien pushed his right-hand man and recommendation through the process. Tom Wilson, the future Pistons president, was surprised. Stern was brilliant, but the last person the NBA needed as its leader was an attorney. But as Pat Williams said, nobody knew who Pete Rozelle and Bowie Kuhn were before they assumed the top posts in the NFL and Major League Baseball, respectively. It was obvious, said Atlanta Hawks general manager Stan Kasten, that Stern should be commissioner. "David had a much larger presence in Larry's last three, four years," he said.

"There were a number of teams that wanted to have a beauty contest," said Doug Adkins, general counsel and secretary for the Dallas Mavericks from 1980 to 1996. "They wanted to interview some big-name people around the country. That's the only way they figured they could get in on television to get coverage. Whether they made it or not, at least you'd have a splash in the press. A fair number of us said, 'Why would we waste all that money—millions of dollars—interview them, putting them in front of a television camera?'" Stern's upside, Adkins said, was tremendous. He knew every "jot and tittle" of the league. Larry O'Brien *presided* over the league, but "when it came down to grunt work and detail and working that out, that fell into David's lap."

On the night of his greatest professional triumph, November 15, 1983, David Stern came to them. With a couple of colleagues, he took the subway to Madison Square Garden. He marched through the dank underground, up the Penn Station tunnel, and to the new home of the team Stern and his father had walked a mile up Eighth Avenue in the cold to enjoy—or, more accurately, endure—some thirty years ago. In the Garden's media room, he spoke to any reporter who had the time.

"The fans want to see the players, not the commissioner," Stern said. "Unless there's a reason I should be out front, I won't be." When Stern took over, he made it clear that the owners worked for *him*; he didn't work for *them*, said Indiana Pacers owner Herb Simon. "And the league needed that," he said. "You can't get thirty cats to go in the same direction, and especially as more and more wealthy people came into the league in ownership positions—all being very successful, and, of course, all successful people think they have all the answers—you need[ed] someone at the time like David to herd us all together and go in the right direction."

Steve Patterson, the longtime Houston Rockets general manager, said Stern viewed himself as the chairman/CEO of the NBA. Everybody worked for him. Stern had an ability to convince skeptical owners that, yes, the NBA was an actual business, Adkins said. The difference between O'Brien and Stern, Stan Kasten thought, came down to approach. "David was much more operational-minded, buttoned-down in terms of doing things right, looking at how big corporations run," he said. "Larry's orientation was politics and political organizations, which as we've learned is very, very different from building a corporation, marketing a corporation. And David came in and turned the marketing vision all the way to the right."

There were more qualities Stern had that O'Brien lacked, thought Bob Whitsitt, the longtime NBA team executive: enthusiasm for the game and for being the commissioner. Whereas O'Brien had to be persuaded to do the job, Whitsitt thought Stern was "a lawyer who was probably excited not to be a lawyer anymore." When Larry O'Brien leaned back in his chair and talked to you, said NBA Properties' Adrian De Groot, he shared his memories. A conversation with David Stern focused on "business, business, business," namely the status of the NBA and how to improve it.

O'Brien's zest for the job *had* dwindled; his endorsement of All-Star Weekend was simple: Okay, but it can't cost a nickel or embarrass the league. O'Brien's health was on the wane. Though his time as commissioner was rewarding, he had no intention of dying in office. He had successors in place to operate within the parameters he had established. Stern and Russ Granik had his complete confidence. "They shared my views, they knew my mind, they had been privy to my thoughts," he wrote years later, "and . . . they had been involved in most of my actions." O'Brien had been the right commissioner in 1975, when damage control and keeping up appearances mattered. Marketing and promoting the league, he said, were the new priorities.

He would always be a politician. O'Brien's headline in his 1990 *New York Times* obituary—the doorstep tombstone of the influential—

identified him as "Democrat." The *Times* devoted four succinct paragraphs to his league work, a lengthy footnote to a life well lived. Howard Berk noticed that O'Brien's days were rarely devoid of politics. It went beyond recalling past glories. Early on, presidential candidate Jimmy Carter called for tips on how to handle his first televised debate against President Gerald Ford. (When O'Brien visited the White House with the world champion Washington Bullets in 1978, the commissioner was tickled when President Carter singled him out.) Knicks legend Bill Bradley sought O'Brien's advice on his political future. O'Brien said to start in the House; Bradley declined and served as a New Jersey senator for eighteen years.

Though politics had turned its back on him, the NBA had given O'Brien a newfound relevance. The owners had *wanted* him way back in 1975, when the Democratic Party labeled him a relic. The owners had given *him* the respect that had curdled as the nation's youth raged against the very machine he had built and run with textbook precision. Whether you considered him a stabilizing figurehead or a catalyst for change, O'Brien played a prominent role in a different kind of American history, a name associated with powerful, idolized young men identified by one word—Bird, Magic, Jordan, LeBron, Dirk, Steph. When those men reached the pinnacle of their success, they lofted the Larry O'Brien NBA Championship Trophy in triumph. The award was named after O'Brien beginning in 1984. It was a hell of a retirement gift.

O'Brien signified more than a name of a golden item these young men coveted and hugged and cried over. Larry O'Brien, the son of Irish immigrants, started these incandescent talents' long journey into the world's view by dint of his public legitimacy and his love of basketball. He planted the seed that would grow into a lithe, leaping corporate behemoth that entertained and inspired millions worldwide. That constitutes widespread impact—even if it's not the legacy he envisioned.

That June, O'Brien walked to the Boston Garden for Game 7 of the NBA Finals and basked in the greetings and warm wishes from fans. In the stifling heat of the frills-free, no-air-conditioning venue, O'Brien didn't have to worry about the referees or fans hurling insults toward him.

Finally, he could be like everyone else and enjoy a basketball game.

Tickets to the Slam Dunk Contest went for two bucks; the average cost of a movie ticket at the time was $3.36. Every time a player went up in the air, so did Welts's career prospects. *This can't embarrass the league.* The crowd loved the Slam Dunk Contest; attendees made makeshift scorecards and cheered through the perfect finale: the sentimental favorite Julius Erving, now an old man of thirty-three, versus 6'10" Larry Nance of the Phoenix Suns, a twenty-four-year-old, lanky high-flyer. The lone downside, Tom Hohensee thought, was Erving lost. "It was like being in the contest with royalty," said Dominique Wilkins, the Atlanta Hawks' sublime, high-flying forward. "I was probably more in awe than I was worried about competing." Nance had no such reservations: "I expected to win." He beat his childhood hero and left with $10,000, which the car enthusiast used to purchase his motivation: a '67 Camaro.

"There weren't any screw-ups," said Hohensee. "It was a spectacular event. Because at that time it was so fresh, there was a real element of excitement around it." Connie Hawkins, himself no stranger to aerial artistry, was impressed with the contest and the dunk's current condition. "The movements, the defiance of gravity—these guys have taken anything I did and have stretched it far beyond anything I can relate to," he told *Sports Illustrated*. It turned into one of those moments, Welts said, that 100,000 people claimed to have seen live.

The Old-Timers' Game lacked the same sizzle or narrative poetry. The NBA had done a magnificent job re-creating *Field of Dreams* on maple, though there were some snags. Stirling had difficulty securing Joe Fulks, one of basketball's first jump shooters. Stirling thought "Jumpin' Joe" had some life in his legs.

That's going to be tough, Matt Winick, the league's schedule maker, told Stirling.

"Why's that?"

"He's dead."

Ah, but the players who had survived and arrived: Bob Pettit. Jerry West. Earl Monroe. The introductions, Welts recalled, elicited goose bumps. After that, the glow of nostalgia succumbed to the high beams of reality.

"Ugh," Stirling said. "That was not pretty."

Welts's first discovery: how the players looked in their uniforms— bellies bulged, shorts stretched. The current image didn't match "the greatness that was represented in each player." Then the game started. Welts soon realized it's easier for an old-timer to look good in the languid pace of a baseball game than a basketball game's nonstop action. It pained Welts to see his heroes not display the same skill. Stirling, then a twenty-six-year-old gym rat, asked several players before tip-off the last time they had played. Each one, he recalled, hadn't picked up a ball since retirement. Once the game started, their personalities and competitiveness came out of hibernation. Some players, Stirling thought, had something to prove.

Thankfully, no major injuries occurred that day, save for a few bruised egos. "Your mind is telling you to do things, but your legs just won't do them," Celtics great John Havlicek said afterward. Such luck would not last. Injured players getting wheeled off the court—as David Thompson and Norm Nixon were in 1992's contest—wasn't exactly conducive to a good time. "That, more than anything else, caused the league to decide, that was fun, but let's move on to something else now," Welts said. Stern later said the league couldn't get insurance to cover the game, soon renamed the Legends Classic after the NBA's public relations director Brian McIntyre checked in on the players after the inaugural game.

"Do you have to call us old-timers?" a player asked. Everyone laughed.

"Do you guys have any suggestions?" McIntyre said.

Another voice: "How about 'legends'?"

By the last game in 1993, the easily identifiable legends were happy to let M. L. Carr and Dan Roundfield—good players, but hardly hardwood gods—suit up. The NBA's past is now honored with the far less injury-prone Legends Brunch.

"We were so smart," Don Stirling said. "We said, 'Okay, the marquee event won't be the slam dunk championship, it'll be the Old-Timers' Game.'" He was not alone. Ron Thomas, *USA Today*'s basketball editor, ran into Stern after the dunk contest. Stern asked Thomas for his thoughts. "You know, David, I think it was absolutely tremendous, but I don't think you can do it every year. Maybe every other year." The NBA, remembered the league's longtime director of broadcasting, Ed Desser, considered the Slam Dunk Contest gimmicky. The Legends Classic was an actual basketball game, so it was more in its wheelhouse.

The big downside was the lack of live television coverage. Desser had to beg ESPN to air the two events later. Yet the weekend was an unqualified success. The dunk contest yielded a four-page write-up in *Sports Illustrated*, then a prestige publication with a hefty circulation and influence. It was the good press the NBA craved. The significance and on-court appeal contributed to an irresistible hook. According to McIntyre, All-Star Weekend was the first day in professional sports devoted to entertainment and history. The Brown Palace, the game's host hotel in Denver, couldn't accommodate all the attendees and media that weekend. The NBA had never encountered that happy problem, Welts said.

The Nuggets and the NBA's frantic preparation—"I don't think I have ever humanly worked as hard as I did during that All-Star Game," Lisa Johnson said—continued into the festivities. PRO-Keds supplied the shoes for the Old-Timers' Game and gave the NBA a base fee of $5,000. If thirteen or more players wore the shoes, the amount rose to $7,500. Stirling was scared to death, "because I had never traded in such large dollar amounts." As Welts crashed to earth at the sight of players' atrophying bodies and abilities, Stirling counted shoes. Twelve of the twenty-four players had on PRO-Keds. At halftime, the young NBA employee entered a locker room full of grown-ass men.

"Guys, there are twelve of you wearing PRO-Keds," he announced. "I need one more of you to wear PRO-Keds in the second half. That means another twenty-five hundred bucks to us. Thank you very much."

Stirling got the extra money.

One of David Stern's missions was to better honor the game's history. The Old-Timers' Game was far from an artistic success, but it was fun. And special. An oversight had been memorably corrected. Most of the players, Stirling thought, were touched to be invited. In the Brown Palace lobby, Welts remembered, greatness was part of the décor. *Look, Oscar Robertson. Wow, Elgin Baylor.* The writers and broadcasters went nuts, Welts said, "because there were more great stories to be told just with the people who were there than they'd ever experienced in an All-Star event before."

"It was a fascinating bit of history," McIntyre said. "And to see the love these guys had for the game and for one another, it was a cool moment."

"Cool" would soon become the week's prevailing sensibility.

The Three-Point Shootout debuted in 1986 in Dallas and supplanted the Legends Classic as the weekend's other big draw, thanks to one Larry Joe Bird.

Every rebellious act needs an ambassador to broker mainstream acceptance. The dunk was represented by Julius Erving before Michael

Jordan and Nike massaged it into a lifestyle brand. Stephen Curry—whose game has garnered the approval of old-school titans such as Elgin Baylor and Bill Walton—has turned long-distance shooting into basketball's glamour move, a social media sensation, and a respected, equal-opportunity playground move. But Larry Bird saved it from being a lark. Along with the theatrical, roller-skate-skinny Reggie Miller, Bird made the three-point shot exciting. Dick Helm, a long-time NBA assistant coach, saw both men incorporate the shot into their floor work. Helm got to see Bird work out in the Boston Garden. Bird spent ten to twelve minutes on last-second shots from all over the famed parquet floor: falling out of bounds, coming off a screen. Miller did the same thing. He practiced as if he were against the clock, instead of robotically hoisting up threes. For Bird and Miller, Helm said, taking a three-point shot at the end of the game became as normal as a layup.

Bird's participation in the inaugural shootout gave the competition legitimacy and Bird a chance to bask in his infamous competitive swagger. The frequently retold story of him walking into the locker room and asking the other participants, "Who's going to finish second?" has become associated with Bird's brash confidence. The Chicago Bulls' Kyle Macy, a participant, said Bird also predicted what position players would finish in as they entered the locker room, treatment Macy somehow escaped. "As a fellow Indiana guy," he theorized, "maybe he knew it wasn't going to affect me." Another person present in the locker room that day said Bird begged competitors to bet against him: "Who's got fifty thousand dollars that I'm not going to win this?" Bird considered Leon Wood his biggest threat. Wood mentioned that the contest's red, white, and blue balls felt slick. Bird agreed* but dug deep into his bag of psychological tricks.

---

*A common complaint about the ABA's red, white, and blue ball was its slipperiness. That inspired the title of Terry Pluto's fascinating oral history of the ABA, *Loose Balls.*

"Yeah, Leon, I can't hold them. There's no way we can shoot *these* things. Leon, if we can't make one of them, we're never gonna win."

Unlike the Slam Dunk Contest, no precedent existed for the Three-Point Shootout. Greg Jamison, the director of marketing for the Dallas Mavericks, got the idea from watching journeyman and future NBA referee Wood at a shoot-around. "He was shooting stuff literally almost from the seats and it was going in," Jamison recalled. The Mavericks were hosting 1986's All-Star Weekend. Why not put on a three-point contest? According to Jamison, the NBA liked the idea but took the credit. Welts said a three-point contest had kicked around the NBA for a couple of years before anyone followed up. "Look, it's not the end of the world," Jamison said. "The big thing is it happened, and it worked."

The latter was far from guaranteed in 1986. The format of five racks—filled with four one-point balls and an ABA-inspired "money ball" worth two points—positioned around the three-point arc was in place. Now it had to be tested. Jim Podhoretz at NBA Entertainment recalled Steve Mills of NBA Properties, who played professional ball in South America, shooting from a rack of balls at the NBA's weekly pickup game at Louis D. Brandeis High School. "It was like watching all this stuff incubate in front of you," Podhoretz said.

The more official testing occurred at halftime of Continental Basketball Association games. The CBA was "an angry league," said Steven Warshaw, a veteran CBA team executive, then business manager for the Bay City Bombardiers of Worcester, Massachusetts. It teemed with transients, misfits, and the undiscovered enduring rickety bus rides and ungodly early coach flights to disinterested crowds in Yakima, Tampa, and Grand Rapids—"horseshit little cities," Warshaw said—en route to a (possible) NBA roster spot. But it was an ideal laboratory. The Bombardiers hosted the first three-point contest, followed by another in Tampa. The NBA brain trust spent a day workshopping the contest with the participants, ironing out details like placement of the racks and time on the clock. Players had to adjust their shots to Worcester Memorial Arena's upper deck, which protruded over the three-point line. Compensation was minimal: a few basketballs and a nice meal for the participants, recalled Warshaw.

The contest in Worcester the next day was virtually the same that occurred in Dallas, Warshaw said. Former Cleveland Cavalier Stewart Granger won, earning five hundred dollars for a performance lost to time and that day's tire ads. The CBA test drive inspired little confidence. "It was borderline awful," Welts said. "It really took kind of a leap of faith—well, we'll try it and if it doesn't work we'll figure out something the next year."

What Welts didn't realize then was a CBA player's show looked a lot different than Larry Bird's. "We sort of knew with NBA All-Stars doing it in a major-league arena with the lights and the sounds and the music and the celebrities, it was going to be a far cry from our little barn with a thousand people there on a weeknight," Warshaw said.

A big-time operation operated on small favors. Stirling* had a friend in California with access to a recording studio who made an audio track featuring a sixty-second version of the theme song to *Miami Vice* to accompany the shooting. A cassette tape of the edited song was sent to contestants. "What I remember clearly is word started to get back to us that the invited competitors were putting some time in," Stirling said. "They'd stay after practice. They'd get their teammates to help them. They'd set up the racks. They'd play the music. These guys are not going to walk into Dallas and hope things go well." Macy was an exception. The Chicago Bulls guard didn't practice at all. He couldn't shoot fast enough to reach the final rack in the first round. Dale Ellis practiced without ball racks. He went to the designated spots and had

---

*Stirling wrote the lyrics to "Who's Going to Keep Me Warm" by Phil Everly, one of the Everly Brothers.

someone pass him the ball. Bird, goaded by Celtics teammates' barbs that he wasn't going to win, spent two weeks practicing.

On the floor at Reunion Arena, Stirling held his breath. "We didn't know how this thing was going to play out," Mills said.* The NBA was about to find out in front of more than sixteen thousand fans. If the players kept bricking shots, Stirling later realized, the contest would become a home run derby where nobody hit a home run. Ellis, who won in 1989, called the competition "nerve-racking." You don't have the luxury of time to find your shot and get settled. The mental toll required is extraordinary: "You've got to really concentrate on blocking everything out around you and concentrate on just the mechanics of shooting a basketball," Ellis said. Not to mention, said Macy, that the contest can fatigue a jump shooter who uses a lot of lift.

Craig Hodges of the Milwaukee Bucks went first, Stirling recalled. Hodges, who later won three straight shootouts with the Chicago Bulls, went on a tear. As each shot found twine, the crowd's energy spiked. Hodges finished with 25 points, exactly the start the nascent contest needed. Stirling looked at his colleagues. Everyone knew they had something here.

Bird won the first contest handily—in addition to the next two. "I'm the king of the three-point shooters," he said afterward. "I always thought I was, and I proved it." Leon Wood, the contest's muse and Bird's "nemesis," didn't make it past the first round.

Jack McCallum, the great NBA writer for *Sports Illustrated*, thought the NBA initially pursued the dunk contest with trepidation—the league didn't want to get mixed up in old stereotypes associated with athletic black guys. Michael Jordan, he thought, "mainstreamed" the idea of a dunk contest not becoming a carnival. Larry Bird's involve-

---

*Stirling and Mills donned ball boy uniforms and worked the contest to make sure the kids did their jobs properly.

ment in the first three three-point contests provided another seal of approval. If the game's most fundamentally sound player participated, it must be okay.

The arena was packed for the three All-Star Weekend events, and a scalper offered David Stern a five-dollar ticket for twenty.

"I hope that's a sign of the health of the NBA," Stern said.

All-Star Weekend was a huge success before Jordan and Bird arrived. The league was no longer its own worst enemy. In late January 1984, the issues that typically submarined the NBA—money woes; drugs; indifferent television coverage; labor strife—were being addressed. All-Star Weekend gave the NBA an immediate boost. Now, two out of three potential sponsors told Welts to take a hike instead of nine out of ten. The NBA had always been talked about in terms of its future. All-Star Weekend represented relevancy.

Before Stern had officially started the job, the tone was set for his administration, as well as for the NBA, Welts thought. The purpose of All-Star Weekend reverberated; now it had to be refined. Baseball had its All-Star Game, the midsummer night's classic; the NFL had the Super Bowl. But the NBA was bereft of a showcase that stayed in one place for days. Yes, the Finals pitted, in theory, the two best teams against each other, but the series ping-ponged between cities for an indeterminate amount of time. The matchup wasn't known until late May or early June. The All-Star Game eliminated those inconveniences. The site was determined well in advance, cities could properly prepare, and everything was geared to show the NBA at its very best. *Enjoy our most glorious fliers. Behold the legendary players from our storied past. Savor our most accurate shooters. And then enjoy a game featuring the world's best basketball players together.*

The All-Star Game itself mattered, especially in the early 1980s. "We understood [that] in order to expand our game, we had to bring in more people and more fans," Isiah Thomas told VanityFair.com in 2018. "There was a partnership between the players and the league and the sponsors to come to this venue, on this day, and put on a great, entertaining show, to give [the fans] something that they won't see during the course of a regular-season game." That meant, he added, that both sides had to compete.

"Every one I was ever involved in, everybody was trying to win," said Paul Westphal, who played in five All-Star Games and coached another two in 1993 and 1995. "You wouldn't step aside so some guy could get a lob and then he'll step aside so you can get a lob."

In terms of talent level, the NBA was in the middle of a fecund period. It was a time, thought analyst and coach Hubie Brown, when the NBA was at its most physical and cerebral. Players couldn't be dumb and play in the league. Bernard King's Hall of Fame career lasted from 1977 to 1993. In that span, King played against more than fifty Hall of Famers, a bulk of whom played his position. And since the age of player empowerment was but a gleam in Gloria James's eye, the players stayed with teams longer. Chemistry ripened. Teams were good for years. "The list goes on and on of great small forwards that played during that era," King said. "So, nightly, *nightly*, you had to be at a very high level. And then there were nights when you had to raise your game because that great player was on a great team."

Nearly any development in the NBA's growth as a cultural player in the 1980s and 1990s can be attributed to Jordan.* All-Star Weekend is no exception. In 1988, Jordan replicated Erving's foul-line dunk in the Slam Dunk Contest, besting Dominique Wilkins in a showdown of the era's two greatest aerial artists. That's when the events took precedence over the game, McCallum thought. Paul Gilbert, the NBA's director of production, felt a change was happening based on the number of celebrities

---

*Jordan's rise as a brand demigod and NBA influencer is covered in Chapter 8.

he spotted in Chicago. And Jordan was as big as any of them. Everyone noticed him. In April 1986, Gilbert was in Philadelphia for a first-round playoff game. Afterward, Gilbert headed to the 76ers' locker room. Stars Moses Malone, Julius Erving, and Charles Barkley retreated to the trainer's room and huddled around a little black-and-white TV to savor Jordan's playoff-record 63-point performance on Larry Bird and the Boston Celtics. Jordan and the Bulls lost in double overtime, but the legend was well under construction. "Michael Jordan was—and is—a completely different type of player from anyone I had ever seen before," Bird recalled.

Another telling anecdote from 1988's dunk contest: Gatorade executive Bill Schmidt scouted Chicago Stadium for the best points of exposure, a gamble that paid off when posters of Jordan's dunk—complete with the thirst slayer's logo prominently displayed—became an art object in hoop dreamers' bedrooms from coast to coast. Events, all with a corporate sheen, became a presence during the weekend. It's the norm today; witness the All-Star Celebrity Game presented by Ruffles. McCallum knew the affair wasn't for him, a middle-age white guy, but for kids. The All-Star Jamboree begat the Stay in School celebration, a morning affair with pop singers and athletes. Then came Jam Session, with its trivia contests and seven-foot hoops for dunking, an attraction for the people who couldn't get tickets to the actual game to enjoy the hoopla they saw at home.

Gradually, the game didn't need to be an epic contest to entice a wide audience. That purpose was served by NBA Entertainment's growing marketing savy, the Magic-Bird narrative, Jordan's individuality, and cable television's encroachment. By 1989, 50 million homes in the United States got stations beyond the dial. The fans' and players' priorities at the All-Star Game changed. "There's more hype than there is game, and the sport can't possibly live up to that," Bird wrote years later. "It's not if you win, or how you play, but how you look when you play, or where you play." Spud Webb would love for strangers to talk about other highlights of his accomplished twelve-year NBA career, but they always ask him about winning the 1986 Slam Dunk Contest. It's how the 5'6" Webb is introduced. Webb's teammate Doc Rivers said he'd never live that down. He was right.

The players who got up for the game were Nike, Reebok, and Converse. The All-Star Game's February date became a hook for sneaker companies to introduce lines, said John Horan, the founder of *Sporting Goods Intelligence* magazine, who has covered the sneaker industry for decades. The players got to show their new kicks to a nationwide audience, but Horan observed that February was when tax refunds first became available. The All-Star Game drove one of the sneaker industry's biggest months.

All-Star Weekend was no longer, as Stern said, "a celebration of our sport." It was also "a celebration of our business," said Don Stirling. "Though it took a long time to get there and a lot of blood, sweat, and tears, we were the new, shiny thing. We were the breakout artist, to take a music term. And more and more people wanted to be associated with us, and the gathering place was the All-Star Game."

Arlene Weltman said that the NBA's agreements with sponsorship clients didn't come down to money but a presence at All-Star Weekend. The first All-Star Weekends were fun, Weltman said. It was like being at a party with three thousand of your favorite people. Then it became big business. NBA employees clamored for tickets to give to their clients, who used the perks of the weekend to entice their clients. A meet-and-greet with a player was better than a dinner at Ruth's Chris. Weltman understood the value to, let's say, a shave gel manufacturer. "What that client's responsibility is, is to make sure that their product gets the best shelf space in the A&P," she explained. "If he can have three regional directors from A&P at All-Star Weekend and they can get to meet Magic Johnson, then man, he is going to get his shave gel in better position on the shelves in stores."

That the game was an exhibition contributed to a much more relaxed environment, said Dick Strup, a marketing executive with Frito-Lay and Miller Brewing Company, two NBA partners. Because it was a convivial scene—hell, even the always-competitive Michael Jordan managed to smile once or twice—Strup found it was easier to talk business.

"That's the venue I would use to take either my international guests or key distributors or key salespeople from the region where I was trying to make some difference," Strup said. "I'd invite them to that. 'Hey, Joe, you like Charles Barkley?' 'Charles, I want you to meet someone. Joe's a big fan of yours.' And, of course, Barkley being Barkley would throw me under the bus: I'm such an asshole. Why did he deal with me? Everybody loved it. It all worked out." Plus, the weekend was new and exciting. Strup was working on a deal with an English client and brought him to an All-Star Weekend. The client, a cricket player, knew nothing about basketball but he *loved* it. And he signed with Strup.

The NBA was an active partner. Bill Ginn, the national accounts manager at Sheraton from 1988 to 1993, remembered Rick Welts urging the other All-Star Weekend sponsors to talk with each other about possible business deals. The NBA wanted its sponsors to be partners, to make the league better, Ginn said.

That meant sponsors had to step up. As the official hotel of the NBA, Sheraton had reserved rooms for league employees to use for the NBA Draft in New York. However, an NBA executive arrived at the host hotel late in the evening and was turned away—not enough beds. The next day at the league office, Ginn encountered Stern, who flashed what Ginn called a "get down here look." The Sheraton employee obliged. "He takes me into an office by myself and rips me a new one from the top of the head to the bottom of my feet," he said. How can you operate a hotel like this? We want to be associated with good companies. "It was as good a takedown as I've ever seen." And Ginn represented a *sponsor*.

Ginn walked to the hotel and let the staff know. "It showed a lot of how he cared," he said. "He wanted us to be better, and that was a great message. I've never forgotten that."

For their money, sponsors were invited to become an integral part of the NBA story, said Tom Fox, who started at Gatorade in 1988 before joining the NBA in 1993. "It was very much a partnership, and David and Rick sold that: 'We will get where we're going if you help us,'" he said. "'And if you're a part of it, you'll benefit from that growth, because as we grow, you will have been in on the beginning and you'll get all the benefits of that.'" Companies could tell their story and the NBA's story with brands, which made sense to Fox. The NBA was exciting and young. Bird and Magic were around. This kid Michael Jordan was incredible. Plus, you had a wave of college superstars arriving every year. David Stern and Rick Welts inspired confidence. You didn't look at these men and think, *Ah, the NBA's problems of the past will persist*, Fox said.

The brilliance of Stern's philosophy was its frugality. He believed in OPM—Other People's Money. "Use other brands' money to tell our story," Fox said. And Gatorade and McDonald's wanted to spread that mutually beneficial story. "If you're the NBA at that point, and someone is spending their money to reach an audience you may not be reaching, and they're showcasing your star athlete or athletes and they're showing game footage at the same time—that's a dream come true," Fox explained. "We helped broaden their audience."

The concept would grow increasingly lucrative as the 1980s ended.

"They understood the brand, and they had a vision that wasn't about how much money they could collect, but how could they grow their business," said Steve Koonin, a former executive at Coca-Cola and later CEO of the Atlanta Hawks. "David Stern said something to me that I've always remembered: that his business was leverage. His business was using his brand to grow our brand, and basically have his sponsors market his brand. If you think about it, between Nike, Sprite, and several others, there was probably a quarter of a billion dollars' worth of off-court NBA advertising happening in the U.S. annually. Maybe a billion dollars' worth of advertising that put the NBA in the *Today* show and in *Friends* and on cable, when television was such an incredibly powerful ad medium. It wasn't about the games. It was about the players and the lifestyle." The players weren't uniform, Koonin said, but an "entire cast of stars who were the epitome of cool in sports."

Stern and his crew were open for business. Strup first dealt with the NBA when he was vice president of marketing at Frito-Lay and wanted to boost awareness for Fritos, a regional brand. The NBA seemed like a good option—it was on the rise, for sure—but Strup didn't know whom to call. He asked a friend in advertising, who then followed up with his friend, CBS broadcaster and Celtics legend Tommy Heinsohn, for a contact.

That was how Strup ended up cold-calling the commissioner of the NBA to ask about national exposure for a salty snack chip with a small national advertising budget.

"Come into New York and let's talk," Stern said.

Strup met David Stern in the NBA office. What was developed, with an assist from Stern and Heinsohn, was the Frito Make It and Take It sweepstakes. The winner attempted to make five shots worth $10,000 each during halftime at Game 4 of the NBA Finals; Heinsohn served as the emcee. Frito-Lay promoted the hell out of the contest, which gave Fritos an unprecedented boost, Strup said.

The NBA lacked the sex appeal to have advertisers buy time or revel in being a league sponsor with signage, said Judy Shoemaker, vice president of marketing at NBA Properties, who joined the NBA in the late 1980s. "The more we could get a sponsor to activate with some kind of promotion or marketing program with the NBA, then that broadened our reach," she explained.

One in-store Gatorade promotion—of many—featured a pop-a-shot, the arcade stalwart. The display was surrounded by Gatorade boxes. The backboard was plastered with NBA logos. And the game was functional—serving as catnip for kids, who could play it while their parents shopped. Not that there was an age limit. Gatorade had one in its office. "We played all the time," Fox said. "I was the reigning champ."

Those kinds of partnerships—like a McDonald's NBA-related Happy Meal—benefited all parties. "That would bring audience to us in a way that television alone just couldn't do it," said Bill Jemas, who became the NBA's vice president of business development and business affairs in 1988. "And then, of course, we would bring our audience to them, and we would be pretty effective in moving their needle in terms of increasing their sales."

Stern's disdain for "this is how we've always done it" meant Strup could bring his creative partners to proffer ideas. It was buoyed by Stern's desire to understand how his clients' businesses worked. When Strup headed to Miller, Stern attended a couple of the beer giant's distributor meetings. "He listened to and talked to the corporate officers and the distributors," Strup said. "He understood how beer was sold. He understood the essence of our brands. By being the way he was, he brought a lot of good imagery for me that we were partners. It paid a heck of a lot of dividends to be personally involved with the guy."

Strup felt the relationship with the NBA was personal; Stern was "like an older Jewish brother." He would ask what Strup needed, what he wanted to accomplish. That was a refreshing attitude in corporate America, where creative ideas were met with "can't do it" or "talk to our lawyer." Strup would attend a big, fancy dinner, a real tux and gown affair, and feel Stern's hand clap him on the back. After Stern met Strup's parents, he always asked how they were.

"He'd pressure me to be at meetings myself," said Jeff Goodby of

Goodby Silverstein & Partners, the NBA's longtime advertising firm. That presented a challenge for Goodby, who would take a red-eye from San Francisco to New York to make a morning meeting with Stern. Afterward, Goodby headed back to JFK and got home before family dinner. Goodby thought Stern's insistence on face-to-face meetings was smart. "Not everybody wants to have that personal relationship that pressures people to do the best job, but he would do that," Goodby said. "And people would give it back."

The NBA kept trying hardest. When Strup worked at Miller, Welts would visit him monthly. Sometimes there was no urgent need. He just wanted to see what the NBA could do to help. "It got to a point I'd say to my promotions guy, 'I can't meet with him today.' 'Well, you've got to say hi to him. He's in the building.' Rick just did it. That was the kind of guy he was. If the answer was, 'We're not doing anything different but thanks for coming,' that was okay by him. He made the attempt, and others didn't do that." That effort allowed the NBA to call upon favors from its partners, said Nancy Fitzpatrick of NBA Properties. "If we got an opportunity we hustled," she said. "All of our licensees backed us up."

The NFL, Bill Ginn thought, carried itself with such arrogance. One year, the NFL had talked to Sheraton about sponsoring the man of the year award. Sheraton made no commitment and, frankly, had zero interest. Ginn and his boss attended the league's meetings in Hawaii, where their contact introduced them to Commissioner Paul Tagliabue.

"These are the guys from Sheraton that are going to do the man of the year award," said the NFL marketing guy, whom Ginn declined to name.

Ginn was stunned.

"Oh, that's great," Tagliabue said.

Ginn instantly updated Tagliabue on the reality. Tagliabue looked at Ginn and then looked at the marketing guy.

"That was the end of *that* conversation," Ginn said.

At the NBA, the conversation never ended. If a sponsor had an idea, the NBA listened. "The one answer to any question I learned at the NBA was 'It depends,'" Fox said. The flexibility started with David Stern. "You'd make what you'd think was a good point and he'd be like, 'Yeah, but how about this? What about this?'" Fox said. "You'd be like, 'I hadn't even thought of that.'"

Russ Granik said when Stern became a businessman instead of a lawyer the NBA really took off. But he was always a student. Bill Jemas saw Stern ask questions and display humility in the face of experts confidently spouting jargon as gospel. He was never afraid to ask anyone to explain a concept in plain English.

"He never stopped learning," Jemas said. "He would learn a lot about business from negotiations and discussions with people who were prospective partners."

The beat reporters had once considered the All-Star Game an ideal time to score interviews with stars outside of their coverage area, work on features, and build relationships with sources. Roy S. Johnson met Julius Erving on a bus ride to practice. Jackie MacMullan of the *Boston Globe* could approach Charles Barkley in the locker room and grab fifteen uninterrupted minutes with the unfiltered Sir Charles. The years passed. The players' entourages swelled. The international press came out in droves for the spectacle. A Steph Curry press conference resembled the floor of the New York Stock Exchange. MacMullan, who became a Hall of Fame basketball writer and a high-profile talent at ESPN, was one voice in a wall of sound— What's your favorite band? What's your favorite color?—trying to get Kevin Love to talk about mental health. (When she bellowed if Love had ever seen a mental health counselor, everyone's head turned.) "The whole All-Star Weekend was almost like a complete waste," Jack McCallum said. "The way we had to do our job, which was to get somebody alone, try to get some time with them. That kind of a thing never really worked."

If there was one benefit to being an NBA reporter in the league's dark ages, thought Harvey Araton, who did just that in New York for the *Post* and the *Daily News*, it was the access. You could work a locker room. "The attitude of the players in baseball was still like, 'Hey, we're doing God's work here,'" he said. "There was much more of a 'Hey, son, have you ever played the game?' mentality. Basketball had none of that. There was a sense that the players intuitively understood that there was a lot of selling to do: the access, the cooperation, and the willingness of the players to really open themselves up." Fred Mitchell of the *Chicago Tribune* could grab members of the Boston Celtics as they walked out of the gym and onto the bus. Robert Parish and Larry Bird talked for as long as you wanted and were comfortable doing so. Araton not only used to stay in the same hotel as the Knicks when the team traveled; he received a list of the players' room numbers with his hotel key. He joined them on the plane and the team bus, where he had no place to hide from the target of that day's story. Traveling with the players, Ron Thomas, then with the *San Francisco Chronicle*, believed, led to better reporting. Over a Danish and orange juice at the airport, away from the sweat and din of the locker room, he had a more intimate opportunity to ask questions. It also allowed him to see how the players interacted with one another.

The NBA beat did not hold the same cachet as covering baseball or the NFL, but journalists, including women, encountered an almost unheard-of freedom. "It was just a much more open, relaxed, friendlier, media-friendly environment," said MacMullan. "I *hated* covering baseball. I *dreaded* it in the eighties. They didn't want me in there; I didn't want to be in there. There was no support for me among the MLB. In the NBA, if anybody messed with me, David Stern would know about it in an hour and they'd be held accountable."

The older, white writers gravitated toward baseball, NFL, and prime-time college ball, Thomas said. Many young African-American sportswriters like himself counted the NBA as their first pro beat. The league's media contacts—Alex Sachare, Brian McIntyre, and Terry Lyons—could not have been more welcoming, he said. The openness extended to the teams. Thomas could cover practices and interview whomever. Practices became his classroom. Thomas spent time with veteran coach Jack McMahon, a wonderful storyteller who shared his observations on the players.

"You just learned to understand things," Thomas said. That included the curious case of Purdue's Russell Cross, whom the Warriors selected with the sixth pick in the 1983 draft. He quickly fizzled. Cross was a strapping 6'10" and 215 pounds, but Magic Johnson was badly outrebounding him. Thomas was puzzled, until a coach explained it to the sportswriter: Cross had short arms. A shorter guy with unusually long arms—like the 6'9" Johnson—is a more effective rebounder because he has an additional two to three inches in height. "You needed to be sitting with a scout or an assistant coach to understand that stuff," Thomas said. "I think it helped me write better stories."

Bob Ryan, the *Boston Globe*'s vaunted NBA writer, said the best time to cover the NBA was during the 1980s. Everyone was accessible. Reporters had pregame and practice access and got to travel with the team. The games were wonderful, and the press wasn't relegated to the rafters but sat close to the court. A reporter could capture the sights and sounds—those crucial, little things that make a story sing. "The whole experience was at its absolute peak," Ryan said.

Stern set the tone for a more open relationship with the media. Kevin Sullivan, who handled the Dallas Mavericks' public relations, remembered Stern, sleeves rolled up, coffee cup in hand, shooting the breeze with the beat writers in the Mavericks' pressroom before tip-off. "He was so accessible and affable and had a good sense of humor," Ryan said. "He seemed to appreciate us and let us feel that we were somebody that should be treated well." The NBA press corps loved PR director Brian McIntyre. McIntyre had worked for the Chicago Bulls, a job he landed after four years of selling Blackhawks and Bulls programs—which he wrote and reported on during his off hours from trade magazine work—outside Chicago Stadium. Years later, McIntyre's right hand acted up in cold weather, a result of doling out change in frigid winters.*

McIntyre excelled at making the media's job easier, said Alex Sachare, his longtime colleague. Reporters could carry the NBA's messages and shape the public's impression, so it was crucial to make key figures, like Stern, available. At the very least, a PR person was always around. Sachare, a former AP basketball writer, knew from experience. It was sometimes hard to get a quote from the league office. Stern understood that a writer from a smaller paper such as *The Oregonian* would be viewed much more favorably by her editor and her readers if she talked to the commissioner on an issue instead of a spokesperson. So Stern talked. Baseball writer Steve Wulf, McCallum's *Sports Illustrated* colleague, couldn't believe how accommodating the NBA was when he did a basketball story. "I can't believe what it's like dealing with your league!" he gushed to McCallum, who heard that often from his colleagues. Thomas noticed the difference when he returned to the *San Francisco Chronicle* to cover the San Francisco 49ers. The football team's PR people hovered while he interviewed players; it was an uneasy experience.

Stern had his spats with reporters, but negative coverage did not guarantee exile. In June 1990, a story emerged about Isiah Thomas's possible involvement in a nationwide gambling operation. (Thomas

---

*McIntyre was happy to discuss his pre-NBA days for the book but declined interview requests to discuss his NBA career.

was later cleared of any wrongdoing.) McCallum didn't want to cover it; his editors at *Sports Illustrated* insisted. He spent the weekend with the NBA and Pistons PR trying to get Thomas to talk. He did. McCallum felt Isiah never quite forgave him. Lyons and McIntyre and Matt Dobek, the Pistons' longtime PR guy, did. The next time, it was business as usual. "Not to hold a grudge and to continue to be professional—it is huge," McCallum said. "You start getting this us-against-them mentality when you're the league and somebody else is a reporter, you're lost."

The players knew part of the business was in marketing the league. The writers felt a similar responsibility. Ryan started writing about the NBA for the *Boston Globe* in 1969. He was a twenty-three-year-old college basketball aficionado, but immediately knew the NBA was a far superior product. "I kind of made it a mission to preach the gospel about how good this was," he said. Ryan took that approach into the 1980s. Harvey Araton felt the players and writers were in it together. "We all loved the game," he said. "We wanted to see it do well. We were kind of the renegade, upstart league. I think a lot of writers took pride in that." As a tide of wonderful players entered the league—highlighted by the triumvirate of Bird, Magic, and Jordan—McCallum had a press pass to the league's renaissance. The secret was finally out. He noticed the change at *Sports Illustrated*, the unofficial sports publication of record, the magazine of Frank Deford and Dan Jenkins that treated sportswriting as stylish, rigorous journalism. The editors passed over pro basketball—unless a scandal surfaced—in favor of football and baseball.

Now, McCallum said, the editors conceded that Magic, Larry, and Jordan were the new heroes worthy of the *Sports Illustrated* cover, a great honor before the Internet destroyed the impact of a great weekly magazine. "It would be hard not to have felt that, because that's when it was new and fresh," McCallum said. "Not just anecdotally, but provably, that's when the league found its footing and started to zoom into the stratosphere. That's just a fact. To be covering the league then was very exciting and very rewarding: nobody would know my name if I didn't cover those guys." McCallum felt he was lifted along with them.

He was not alone.

All-Star Weekend allowed the NBA to play Dr. Frankenstein and construct the perfect corporate synergistic monster. It was now an "entertainment property," said Adrian De Groot, the longtime president of NBA Properties. That was how Stern envisioned the NBA, he added. It was no longer "just basketball."

Judy Shoemaker, another NBA Properties star, said one reason why All-Star Weekend grew longer is because of companies' willingness to sponsor events that Stern got televised, which provided constant exposure and promotional opportunities galore. "We created some opportunities for celebrities beyond singing the national anthem before the game," said Ski Austin, who organized the All-Star Game for years. "When we had the Stay in School Jamboree or the Celebrity Slam Dunk Contest or when we made autograph stages, everything was precise and controlled, so it was a safe place for them to show up and be a part of the crowd if they wanted to or to participate in things, knowing that it was a buttoned-up organization."

Larry Bird saw the NBA's evolution to an MTV league start at the All-Star Game in 1986. With all the loud music in Dallas, it was "more like a dance than a game." The Slam Dunk Contest had turned into "some kind of rap contest." He knew the NBA was trying to attract young fans and sponsors, but the NBA had gone corporate.

Bird's comment on music was accurate. All-Star Weekend morphed into a hip-hop community family reunion. *Los Angeles Times* columnist J. A. Adande memorably dubbed the NBA's in-season break "the Black Super Bowl" for a good reason. "In terms of hip-hop culture there is no bigger weekend than NBA All-Star Weekend," said Doc Wynter, the music industry veteran. "*Everybody* is there, and any town that gets it sees how people just run to this event, man. . . . It's part of what we do. People who love hip-hop love basketball." NBA All-Star Weekend started becoming the hangout in the early 1990s, because hip-hop conventions and music conventions faded away. The hip-hop artists arrived with a bang, as street teams took over swanky hotels and stuck their artists' stickers on their windows. The cities and hotels, according to Wynter, said, "Hell, no. This shit is over." The hip-hop community needed "the next big thing to do." The NFL never fully embraced hip-hop, so the Super Bowl wasn't ideal. The NBA laid out the welcome mat. That was a good thing. Because of the connection between hoops and hip-hop, Wynter said, the thrill of seeing your favorite football player in comparison to seeing your favorite basketball player or rapper.

"The panache of the NBA All-Star Weekend definitely supersedes the Super Bowl," Wynter said. "People want to go, but the NBA is different. It has to do with the activities, the All-Star Game, the dunk contest. They've done a great job of curating events that people want to participate in. Then, the parties. [Michael] Jordan has his parties. Other rappers have events. It goes to cities that people really like attending." That makes a difference. Ask anyone who had the misfortune of attending 2005's Super Bowl XXXIX in Jacksonville, Florida.

"They didn't have any hotels there," said Wynter, who hosted a party that year. The NFL brought in ships to make up the difference.

Scott Messick of NBA Entertainment said that in the swirl of work, All-Star Weekend provided a moment to appreciate the NBA's status. When the All-Star Game returned to Denver in 2005, twenty-one years after the first weekend, the scene had changed a bit. Rapper and entertainer David "D-Stroy" Melendez worked his first All-Star Weekend that year. He ate breakfast next to Denzel Washington and spotted teenagers sleeping in the hotel staircase, waiting to meet a celebrity. Hall of Fame guard Sidney Moncrief played in five straight All-Star

Games in the 1980s. When he served as an assistant coach on Don Nelson's West squad in 2002's game, players were warned that prostitutes had traveled from all over to Philadelphia, eager to get pregnant by the players. Moncrief burst out laughing when the players were told not to have their entourages carry firearms into the arena. Those concerns were never voiced when he was an All-Star.

Stern's relentless pursuit of perfection peaked at the All-Star Game. Weltman remembered one edict from Stern: I don't care if two people are taking the buses, nobody will wait more than two minutes for a bus. As All-Star Weekend's status grew, Stern's dedication to putting on the best show for the league's guests remained intense. He approved *everything*, said Bill Daugherty, who was hired by the league in 1990—even the color of the tablecloth for the owners' breakfast. At his second All-Star Game in Dallas, Steve Mills gathered the judges' scores from the Slam Dunk Contest to be tabulated. It sounded easy enough, but Stern was so upset at Mills's pace he sent Russ Granik, the NBA's deputy commissioner, to tell Mills, who played basketball at Princeton, to walk faster.

"David would get so mad about anything," Mills said. Then Stern's seat at the All-Star Game came equipped with a phone—that went directly to Mills. "I don't like this." "I don't like that." "Why are you playing this song?" "Why are you doing this?" Mills actually preferred this method of communication—Stern's issues didn't fester for hours.

"I am sure they don't teach you this at Harvard Business School," Stern told Daugherty, a graduate. "But I care about everything." So, if Stern saw Bob Lanier standing in line at a buffet, he lost his mind. The person in charge of buffets made sure there were four to eight access points for guests to chow down, and that the hotel and the caterers were on point.

"I'm going as a client, but also going as a fan," said Lynn Bloom, director of authentics and archives at Mitchell & Ness, the sports nostalgia apparel giant. "It's spectacular." All-Star Weekend is run almost like a resort vacation. They're not clients, but guests. She gets tickets for everything. Her hotel room is booked. "They literally cater to your every need," she said. "It's such a smoothly run weekend." When she leaves the hotel for the NBA's shuttle bus—provided for every event—staff members with huge signs direct her where to go. You leave feeling great about the NBA, Bloom said. That is exactly the point. All-Star Weekend was the league's opportunity to put on its best face, and everyone pitched in. "All the sponsors are there; there are thousands of guests," said the NBA's Paul Gilbert. "It's a big party where you're the host. It's multiple parties, actually. From the working side, it's like a month's worth of energy and intensity and stress in a weekend." "It was hell," Weltman said. Her husband stopped going; he couldn't stand to watch her work that hard. At the end of the night, Gilbert returned to his hotel room vibrating. The effort did not go unnoticed. "The NBA was so intent on making the weekend as special as they could," Dick Strup said, and it always came out "damn near perfect."

All-Star Weekend unfurled Stern's belief that the NBA was not a sports league. "Guys, you just don't get it," Weltman remembered Stern telling a small group of her coworkers. "You just don't get it. We're not just a sport. We're Disney." It sounded outlandish, even megalomaniacal, but not to Weltman.

Jesus, she thought, *maybe he's right.*

To Stern, the NBA's business plan was similar: home videos, theme parks/arenas, easily identifiable characters. But Stern had much in common with how Walt Disney, the boss, operated. Both wanted employees to take chances, displayed a preference for hiring talent for talent's sake, and were fully invested in their businesses. They also were invested in their customers. In talking about Epcot Center, which opened more than fifteen years after his death, Walt Disney declared that "people will be king." He told Marty Sklar, one of his lieutenants, that meeting their needs would be the starting point. Solving all the problems before they became problems was paramount. Disneyland had a "philosophy founded in a belief of people, and it answered their needs." Epcot would follow the same path.

"The nonstop entertainment model, which defined Disney, was a combination of remarkable customer service across all demographic groups," said David Schreff, who worked for the NBA after serving as vice president of the Disney Channel in the mid-1980s. "When you go to Disney World everyone is represented there. The other part is since they have long lines for a 90-second to 180-second attraction, you have to keep people entertained." That's why there were bands coming through and jugglers. Everywhere you turned, while you were waiting on line, there was some other form of entertainment. The ride or the attraction would be the culmination of that. The NBA's foray into light shows took a cue from Disney's light parades. The goal, Schreff said, was to become "the Disney of sports."

Shortly after Tom Wilson became the Pistons' president, he attended a meeting of the teams' general managers, Wilson ran into Stern, who informed him that he was not going there.

"What do you mean I'm not?" Wilson said.

"That's not where the business is going," Stern said. He wanted Wilson at the NBA's meetings on various marketing strategies. "*That's* the future of this league." Besides, Stern added, you'll learn more in here than from the GMs. "He was right," Wilson said. "He was one hundred percent right."

Stern may have learned his business style working weekend shifts at Stern's Deli, but the just-folks aura of that New York City staple belied a sophistication. Deli owners had to distinguish their higher-priced goods from the cheaper, more varied offerings in supermarkets. Loyal deli customers, wrote an industry expert in a trade publication called *Voice of the Delicatessen Industry,* view the "delicatessen as choice food, as special relishes, and does not mind if he has to pay a bit more." To stoke that loyalty, teams had to cater beyond the die-hards who could identify Granville Waiters's helipad baldness, who devoured Zander Hollander's *Complete Pro Basketball* handbooks until the spines split.

"When David came in it was just kind of like a rising tide: let's make everybody better, and ultimately, we all win," Wilson said. "And that changed almost everybody's attitude. Almost every team instantly bought into it. And then we would share halftime entertainment, and we would share promotional ideas, and we would share the crazy things that we did in our market. You started trying more things. He really drove it. He was the one person who saw the potential in the league." Before Stern, teams were involved in their own operations. He encouraged them to think bigger.

"A lot of times, the people on the sports/team side don't really understand the need for all these halftime shows," said Steve Schanwald, a longtime Chicago Bulls employee. "The need for entertainment for time-outs. They think all you need is the basketball game." Stern understood the concept of entertaining fans for two-and-a-half hours, not forty-eight minutes, Schanwald said.

To make that work, a mutual exchange of ideas had to exist. Before Stern's administration, "teams didn't talk to each other," said Paula Hanson, the NBA's director of team services, which helped share ideas with the various teams. League meetings became vital to attend, said Greg Jamison of the Mavericks, because you'd gain insights from your colleagues on what worked, whether it was halftime acts or tending to your local broadcast.

The guys on the other side of the table—agents, sponsors, TV and radio stations—had all the information on what the deals looked like, said Steve Patterson, general manager of the Houston Rockets and later the Portland Trailblazers. Teams were "always negotiating at a disadvantage." Stern made the teams understand that by sharing information they would run more effective businesses: the owners got more revenue; the players got higher salaries.

Patterson said it was "a battle" to get teams on board—Stern had to threaten to withhold Chicago's and Boston's shares of the TV money to ensure their cooperation. By the time Judy Shoemaker joined NBA Properties in 1988, information—particular marketing-related—was exchanged freely between teams. She had worked for baseball's Chicago White Sox. Major League Baseball's winter meetings were all about the players. At the NBA, ideas ruled. The biggest one was to create an experience that pleased every demographic.

"If you're going to sit on a hard, wooden bench that's got splinters sticking out of it and the hot dogs are cold and the beers are hot and there's not enough restrooms and there's no place to park and the ushers are surly and the ticket takers are unkind, and there's no elevators in the building for older people—one by one, with all of those things—you're eliminating someone wanting to come to the game unless they're just such fanatics that they'll put up with all that to go to a game," Patterson said.

What that meant to Jamison was not to have the entertainment overwhelm the actual game, but to provide in-game experiences fans would brag about to their friends afterward: Boy, the game was great. There was this amazing halftime act, and the suite was unbelievable. "Those were the things that really began to drive it," Jamison said. An increasing objective for teams, he added, was to have their guests enjoy their time out but come back with a friend.

Older fans sometimes pine for the Boston Garden and Chicago Stadium—places with alleged character—and ignore their inhospitable nature. Yes, Schanwald said, Chicago Stadium was a more intimate place to watch a basketball game than the fancy United Center. But

Schanwald, the former executive vice president of business operations for the Chicago Bulls, will always take the United Center. It was a much better environment to watch a game than Chicago Stadium, with its cramped seats, narrow aisles, and paucity of restrooms and concession stands. If a keg of beer had to be delivered to the upper level, the poor schmuck tasked with that job took the stairs. The Boston Garden with its rats and no air-conditioning and dead spots on that famed parquet floor was, said longtime referee Joey Crawford, "a total toilet." In the early 1980s, many of the buildings were tremendously outdated, Steve Patterson thought. The crowds leaned toward older males, "almost like a boxing or horse racing crowd."

The amenities for the players were not much better. Chicago Stadium's visitors' locker room, recalled longtime NBA assistant coach Dick Helm, teemed with cockroaches. Helm was joking with John "Hot Rod" Williams, the Cavs' talented sixth man, about the necessity of closing his gym bag when the 6'11" Williams spotted a critter on a concrete post. He smooshed it with his massive basketball shoe. Months later, the Cavs returned to find the visitors' locker room repainted. Helm noticed a bump. The painter had slathered over Williams's kill with a fresh coat.

The first NBA venue geared to the nonzealot customer experience was the $90 million Palace of Auburn Hills, home of the Detroit Pistons, which opened in August 1988. The difference: it was built by marketing people, observed Jon Spoelstra, the longtime Trailblazers marketing executive. It was, he said, "the first fan-friendly building." Pistons president Tom Wilson, a ferocious marketer back to his days of having to fill the Silverdome to see mediocre teams, had a lot of input into the venue. It was built, Wilson told the *Lansing State Journal*, with the average fan in mind—the Disney philosophy for the sports crowd.

"The NBA had always had great stars, but the variable is how they were marketed and packaged," said Schanwald. "The Palace of Auburn Hills and the many arenas that followed was just another block in the foundation."

It was all about the amenities: twenty-one concession stands, a lounge bar, more restrooms for women, a "state-of-the-art scoreboard" with instant replay, and "TV-quality" pictures. The seats were more spacious. The food went beyond beer and hot dogs—muffins, imported beers, vegetarian options. You could order a pizza and have it delivered to your seat. There were 180 personal suites, located on all three levels of the 21,000-seat arena. They could be leased for three to five years for anywhere between $30,000 to $120,000 a year. And they sat underneath the stands, not at the highest level, a request Wilson illustrated to the Rosetti Firm via a sketch on a napkin.

According to Wilson, $120,000 was the highest price in the country. And it was in Detroit, not exactly an entertainment mecca. "It was a little bit crazy in terms of its ambition," Wilson said. He expected the Pistons to lose $3 million the first year. Instead, he said, the team *made* between $20 million and $25 million.

Those numbers did not escape David Stern's attention. At that year's board of governors' meeting he ordered every team to head to Auburn Hills. "I want you to look at that building and understand we're not just in the basketball business anymore," Wilson recalled Stern saying. "We're in the real estate business. We're in the arena business. We're in the entertainment business. *And* we're in the basketball business."

"A lot of those things were not really big deals, then they became big deals," Jamison said. "Suddenly, you didn't dare build an arena without suites. You didn't dare have an arena without a big Jumbotron. All those things began to appear." Stern was all for it. "David used to say, 'I want every arena to be viewed as a basketball theme park,'" Harvey Benjamin, the attorney and veteran NBA employee, recalled.

The Pistons were also one of the first NBA teams to treat its players as investments. A private plane (*Roundball I*) carried the team comfortably to its destination. Players and coaches avoided the endless inconveniences of airline travel: lost bags, autograph requests, cramped seats, early flight departures. Bucks broadcaster Jon McGlocklin asked Pistons coach Chuck Daly how he swung that asset. Daly said he promised owner Bill Davidson a certain number of wins if the team got a charter; the charter, Daly reasoned, will cost what the Pistons' twelfth man costs.* It wasn't an exaggeration. Daly believed travel sapped the team's emotional, physical, and mental strength. "Not even injuries are as much a threat to a player's health and sanity as the 82-game schedule," Daly wrote in his 1990 autobiography. The plane, he thought, lengthened careers—and contributed to the team's back-to-back championships. Coach George Karl saw the team plane, next to drug testing, as the best deterrent to keep players out of trouble. "By flying to the next city right after a game," he wrote, "we arrive too late for anyone to go out."

The NBA is a league of imitation, McGlocklin said, so once the Pistons got their charter and started winning, teams followed suit. When Pat Riley began to book the Lakers in luxury hotels, the imitators came. "Why do teams do it? You do it to compete," McGlocklin said, "because you're really in the recruiting business for free agents to come to your city and play with all of your amenities. If you don't do it, you're not keeping up with the other teams." It was about time. After a glorious career at UCLA, twenty-one-year-old Bill Walton was drafted by the Portland Trailblazers in 1974. He signed a $3 million contract and "the quality of my life went down," he said.

This increased investment, 76ers general manager John Nash thought, probably drove some owners out of the league, but the NBA had someone waiting who'd be happy to pay. Success cost money. The suites and luxury seating's use as business tools fascinated Wilson. Dur-

---

*Daly credited Isiah Thomas with approaching Davidson about buying a plane.

ing the Bad Boys era, when the Palace was at its most raucous, those who had tickets near the floor would purposefully take a circuitous route to those prized seats. They made sure the crowd saw them and their client perform that "waltz." "And it was huge," he said, "because whoever was your guest felt like a million bucks." For a moment, Ed, the purchasing guy from General Motors, felt like a star. And everyone else seethed. *He's in the seats I wish I had, the seats I wish I could afford.*

Andy Dolich's lengthy career in pro sports has included stints with the Golden State Warriors, Memphis Grizzlies, and the Philadelphia 76ers. The lack of intimacy in today's arenas bothers him. Not too long ago you could talk to the person next to you at an NBA game. "The big difference to me is just the tidal wave of sound and prompting and *this is what you should do,* as opposed to I'm here with my family, with my friends, with my buddies," said Dolich. "We can figure it out. We know when to cheer." The entertainment became uniform—the same hot dog cannons, the same videos, the same scantily clad dance teams. It was hard to know what arena you were in. That wasn't a problem during the old days at Oakland–Alameda County Coliseum Arena, the Warriors' longtime home court. For years, an unofficial "weed ramp" hosted folks toking at halftime. It was a highlight—pun fully intended—well before the team's championship run in the twenty-first century. "Even if you were pissed off, you were mellow for the second half," Dolich said.

The regular folks who felt like celebrities as they trekked to their floor seats were replaced by actual celebrities. In the era of smartphones, the game became a neat backdrop to the selfie-snapping sect. "Oh, is there a basketball game going on?" Dolich scoffed. "I really don't give a shit." Wilson heard the elitist accusations on the Palace, with its suites and wine list. Ticket prices went up only $5. The Pistons could have charged an extra $15 or $20. Prices for concessions and parking were the lowest of the four Detroit sports teams. This was nothing new, Wilson thought. Lakers owner Jerry Buss, who pioneered the basketball game as an entertainment experience, priced courtside seats accordingly. In a city of millions, Buss knew he could get four thousand Los Angeles–area residents to pay to get close to the action. Once he succeeded, the other teams raised their rates.

In July 2020, the Palace of Auburn Hills was demolished, a casualty of the "greed is good" decade. Today, attending an NBA game is an investment, like vacationing in Disney World. The NBA isolated itself from the people who loved the game without the accoutrements. It wasn't just the Palace, but its location. Auburn Hills was more than thirty miles from Detroit. Those players, thought Dave Bing, the Pistons' Hall of Fame guard, were less likely to step into the city's neighborhoods and community centers. The bigger downside was fans who lived in Detroit had no easy way to reach the Palace beyond "a long, tangled commute on Interstate 75," Harvey Araton wrote in 2005. And public transportation didn't go out that far.

Madison Square Garden was known for its celebrity crowd going back to the Knicks' Walt "Clyde" Frazier and Willis Reed heyday of the early 1970s, but great seats were not reserved for the penthouse crowd and Zanzibar denizens. Regular people—a mailman, an entrepreneur—could buy a season courtside ticket and not sweat their mortgage. Michelle Musler read the New York dailies and never missed a game. As the 2000s plodded along, Musler was an old fan in a new world. She paid the $330 for a ticket—right behind the Knicks bench—not for the status. She got to know players and coaches. The new generation, Musler told Araton, felt entitled to unleash profanity on the players based on an impossible set of criteria. Or they called everyone on their contacts list to alert them that they were on TV. The prize ticket holders lacked respect, said Fred Klein, a longtime Knicks fan.

Director Spike Lee, a lifelong Knicks worshipper, inched closer to

Garden floor seats with each artistic triumph. He first bought season tickets in 1985, a year before his debut feature film, *She's Gotta Have It*, became an art-house sensation and the inspiration for an adventurous ad agency in the Pacific Northwest. When Lee finally landed on his version of sacred ground, he wasn't with fans like him, who donned their favorite player's jersey and prayed John Starks would stop shooting the goddamn ball. During the Knicks' brief resurgence in the early 1990s under coach Pat Riley, "many fans in the Garden might as well have been at Tavern on the Green or Elaine's," Lee wrote in his 1998 memoir. "It was now the chichi thing to do—go see the Knicks and be seen."

This was the cost of prohibitive ticket prices, the Knicks great and U.S. senator Bill Bradley told Lee. "The people that come to the arena now are like a studio audience," he said. "They are going to be part of that show." The Garden, Klein said, now felt like a fashion show. A true fan like Lee, who paid $2,000 per game for his two floor seats in 1998, was an outlier.

The NBA's new savvy required a different set of skills. "Generally, rather than hiring expertise in your discipline, you'd hire people who knew things that you didn't know about the real world and then let them learn your sports marketing discipline on the job," NBA veteran executive Bill Jemas said. When Jemas ran Marvel from 2000 to 2004, he did exactly that. David Schreff, the NBA's future president of global marketing and media, got a preview of the NBA's new direction when he interviewed with Bettman, Stern, Welts, and Granik—the big four—in December 1989. Everything proceeded as normal. For about five minutes. Then Schreff got a question about Disney. Then another. And another. Why did Disney do this? Why did Disney do that? Over two days. Schreff was bewildered. He was never asked one basketball-related question. And he still didn't know what the open job was.

Finally, the quartet finished. Did Schreff have any questions?

Yes, said Schreff, a lifelong Boston Celtics fan. Why, in all these hours of conversation, have none of you asked if I like basketball or if I know anything about basketball?

Schreff's interrogators gawked at him.

"We have plenty of people who get the game," Stern told Schreff. "We assume you like it enough, otherwise you wouldn't be talking to us." What was required, he said, was someone who could make the most amazing presentation to the CEO of Coca-Cola so the NBA could get a massive deal. Someone who could figure out how to build relationships around the world to help the game become a global entertainment brand. Exactly like Disney.

Schreff realized it right then. These are real businesspeople.

It was easier to use this approach when the NBA landed its Mickey Mouse. He was young. He was marketed as an individual from the moment he became a professional, a beacon to teens. He was polite and listened to his parents, a beacon to Baby Boomers desperate for someone to carry the load. He hated to lose. He loved to win. He was well-spoken but kept his opinions to himself. He scored in inconceivable, heavenly ways, but he played in-your-jock defense. He was a man without a history, someone to whom fans and boardroom warriors could affix their hopes. He arrived in 1984 spry and glorious, the flying avatar for a league that sought to peddle its past in new clothes to the world.

Michael Jordan was a mortal. In basketball shorts and in front of the camera, he spread the gospel of NBA-branded cool and all its retail-ready sacraments—especially basketball shoes—to a new flock.

THE ACCIDENTAL GOD

INTERVIEWER: Why didn't Julius Erving have the same impact as Michael Jordan?

BUTCH BEARD: TV.

Sonny Vaccaro didn't come to watch Michael Jordan play on March 29, 1982, but he inadvertently witnessed an American hero's origin story.

The University of North Carolina, Jordan's team, wore Converse. Georgetown University, the Washington, D.C., powerhouse, was who Vaccaro wanted to win the NCAA Men's Championship. After all, the Hoyas wore Nikes, the shoes he had spent years selling to college coaches with great success.

Jordan ruined it. The skinny freshman, with the eyes of a nation on him, confidently swished a jumper from the wing with fifteen seconds left to give UNC a one-point lead. The Tar Heels won when Georgetown guard Fred Brown crumbled from the pressure Jordan had shouldered. After the basket, Brown pushed the ball up court. He stopped and looked for the open man, passing the ball directly to James Worthy—who played for UNC. Worthy raced in the opposite direction toward a national championship.

But Jordan had won the game. Vaccaro never forgot what he saw.

*   *   *

Sneaker companies did not attach a player's name to a shoe, save for two notable exceptions now part of sneakerhead lore. There was the stylish Adidas Jabbar, first released in 1978, which found an audience among hoop fans and hip-hop heads in New York City.

Walt "Clyde" Frazier was the first basketball player to have his own shoe when the colorful, suede Puma Clydes strutted into stores in 1972. There was little pomp and circumstance to the arrangement. Bill Mathis, a former New York Jets halfback and a Puma rep of sorts, arranged the meeting. Frazier was offered five thousand dollars and shoes galore. He signed the sneaker deal not to enhance his already groovy legacy, but for the money.

Puma's first attempt at the shoe was a disaster, clunky and heavy. Frazier suggested some modifications. The shoes sold out in New York, Connecticut, and New York—the Knicks' tristate area of fans. They were so prized that some inventive admirers wore plastic bags over the sneakers to keep them dry. Frazier saw the impact where it mattered most—his paycheck. He got twenty-five cents per pair of shoes sold, an arrangement that landed him hundreds of thousands of dollars.

Younger basketball fans know Frazier today as the Knicks announcer who puts the *color* in color analyst with his ROYGBIV suits and rhyming, polysyllabic vocab. Decades before he was "dishing and swishing" and inadvertently teaching SAT words, Frazier was the NBA's first superstar of style and substance. "The idea of the basketball player as a style icon, Clyde absolutely created that," hip-hop journalist Nelson George said. In today's NBA, where the players' pregame amble to the locker room has become a nightly catwalk, Frazier was Twiggy with muttonchops. He didn't take his wardrobe cues from *GQ,* but women's magazines. "You see so many more different styles with the women," Frazier said.

Frazier was a star for the storied, endlessly chronicled Knicks teams that won two NBA championships in the early 1970s. But so was Bill Bradley. So was Willis Reed. Frazier stood out because of his on-court style, thought Marv Albert, the team's cherished broadcaster. If he was knocked down, no matter how hard the shot, he took his time getting up. "Cool I think is reactions, reflexes, and attitude," Frazier wrote during that time. "You got to feel out the situation. You can't be out of control. I think I'm cool—most of the time." That applied to getting hit in the chops. If the other team saw how much pain he was in, it would take advantage.

The stoicism did not apply to his fashion sense. He wore—amid nonstop mockery—wide-brimmed, velour fedoras well before Warren Beatty in *Bonnie and Clyde* turned the item into pop culture ephemera. When Knicks trainer Danny Whelan dubbed Frazier "Clyde," he didn't shrink from the moniker. Frazier embraced "sartorial splendor": the mod, perfectly tailored suits, the Rolls-Royce with WCF license plates, a bedroom dominated with silk, shag, and a nine-foot round mirror on the ceiling. He had such a rapturous work-life balance that he wrote a guidebook (*Rockin' Steady*) on how he achieved that. The shoes— which Frazier wore on the Garden floor—got you a step closer to *being Clyde*. Frazier's fame came when pro athletes didn't shroud their social lives in high-priced secrecy. He took the subway to Madison Square Garden. He inhabited a world you knew, but like Joe Namath, Frazier grabbed New York City by the haunches. John C. Jay, later Wieden + Kennedy's creative director, remembered sitting at a club in the Upper East Side on a slow Sunday night. That burgundy and antelope Rolls-Royce pulled up. Frazier scoped the room and sat down next down to a beautiful woman at the bar. Fifteen minutes later, Clyde and the lady departed to the double-parked Clydemobile.

As Puma attempted to put you in Clyde's world—and good luck with that—Nike helped turn sneakers into casual wear in the mid-1970s. After the waffle trainer—affordable, with a splash of color—was offered in blue to pair better with jeans, "we couldn't make enough," Nike cofounder Phil Knight recalled. Americans, thought John Horan, the founder of *Sporting Goods Intelligence Magazine*, started to dress less formally. Baby Boomers started to get into fitness—*The Complete Book of Running*, Jim Fixx's huge bestseller, was published in 1977. Nike, he said, grasped the changing American lifestyle. Sneaker historian Bobbito Garcia noted that sneakers as an everyday accessory sprang from 1950s American youth culture. "Casual dress became desired and its acceptability was unprecedented," Garcia wrote in his fascinating chronicle of New York City's sneaker culture, *Where'd You Get Those?* "Sneakers were no longer just gym class shoes, but the preferred choice of kids everywhere."

Around the time more Americans wore sneakers to Pathmark or to class, the footwear became an integral part of the hip-hop wardrobe. The style became "fresh out of the box"—clean. As rap worked its way onto MTV, kids did more than copy what they heard. They had constant exposure to a look, one that was relatively easy to emulate, if they weren't already doing that. "What we wear onstage is just what all the youth wear," said Darryl "DMC" McDaniels. "So dressing this way lets them know, 'Oh, he's just like me.'"

When Run-DMC sang "My Adidas" at Madison Square Garden on July 19, 1986, and asked the crowd to lift their Adidas in the air, thousands responded. It was an historic and predictable moment. After he caught Run-DMC's performance at the Garden, Adidas executive Angelo Anastasio urged company founder Horst Dassler to sign the group to a contract.*

"Almost incidentally, if you achieve that kind of prominence in American life, you're going to achieve it for whatever it is you're offi-

---

*Run-DMC famously wore Superstars, but Garcia writes that Jabbars started the hip-hop community's loyalty to Adidas.

cially doing, but also people are curious," said Bill Adler, a longtime executive at Def Jam Records and a hip-hop historian. "You do this work, and your work wins applause, then also they want to learn about the person. And among the things they're going to look at is the clothing." In this case, Adler said, it was the Superstars—Jackie Kennedy's pillbox hat for the MTV generation—and how Run-DMC rocked them without laces. Jam Master Jay, the group's DJ, started it. According to Adler, prison inmates couldn't wear sneakers with laces because they could become weaponized. After some of these men were released, they kept the look. Jay adopted this aspect of "Queens street hustler style" and inspired a pop culture moment.

Fashion trends, said Logo 7 founder Tom Shine, don't come from Scarsdale. Sneakers had always been an integral part of hip-hop culture, said Sean Williams, the sneaker historian. Music was one part. "It's graffiti, it's DJing, it's B-boying, and one of those elements that doesn't get spoken about a lot is knowledge and passing it on, and mentorship," he said.

Again, an element of rebellion was commodified and turned into fashion, like the leather jacket. As Williams said:

> Sneakers were part of the official hip-hop uniform, because they represented anti-establishment. That's why sneakers were chosen as part of the hip-hop uniform; there were so many places you couldn't go wearing sneakers. They were a marginalizing thing. You were deemed as someone less likely to succeed if you wore sneakers all of the time. You couldn't wear them in churches; you couldn't wear them in certain restaurants, you couldn't wear them in clubs. There are so many places— you couldn't wear them at work. So anything anti-establishment was going to gravitate toward that. So when hip-hop culture was being established in the '70s, they were like "Yeah, we wear sneakers; we could give a shit about going to your establishments—your churches, your

clubs, your workplace." So that's why you hear a lot of genuine hip-hop people, like myself, who say, "Hip-hop really is a lifestyle; it's really not just the music."

Years after its initial release, Frazier heard stories of rappers and break dancers asking for "Clydes" who didn't know who "Clyde" was. It would take a couple of years after Run-DMC's capitalistic triumph for hip-hop and sneakers to enjoy a mainstream marriage, a development that involved a couple of contrarian acts that immediately sprang a nation into commerce-driven cool.

Frazier wouldn't have minded one bit. He was the pioneer. When he attended an event at Puma's headquarters in Germany decades after his shoes hit the street, Frazier came onto the stage unannounced. The crowd unleashed a five-minute-long standing ovation for the man whose shoe his grandchildren were once embarrassed to wear.

The speaker (via phone) who preceded Frazier: Jay-Z, the man who had turned retro basketball jerseys into high fashion.

Converse's Mickey Bell remembers the phone call. Come work for Nike, the North Carolina–based rep said. Bell tried to let the suitor down easy. Converse owns the basketball market. We have the coaches. Everybody wants to wear our shoes.

For decades, Converse had been *the* basketball sneaker for pros and college athletes. Nike arrived with a novel idea: pay college coaches to have their teams wear Nike. Bob Cousy, the Boston Celtics superstar, wore Converse for years and was never paid a dime, said John J. O'Neil, Converse's longtime president. "Everybody wore the Converse All-Star," O'Neil said. "You didn't have to pay them." (Converse's endorsements in the 1960s ignored black ballplayers, which enraged Oscar Robertson.)

Nike had hired Vaccaro, who organized high school's Dapper Dan

Roundball Classic and the ABCD Camp, to penetrate the college ranks with utter aplomb. But the company did little promotion for basketball shoes. Its biggest endeavor, said Mike Caster, a longtime Nike marketing executive, involved posters: Moses Malone dressed like his biblical namesake with a staff and basketball; Bobby Jones, in a suit and tie, held a basketball as "the Secretary of Defense"; Nike's basketball players donned judicial robes as the Supreme Court.

"It was a great marketing ploy from Nike and it was a good brand seller for us," said George Gervin, the owner of his own classic poster where he sits on a throne of ice, a nod to his famous nickname, the "Iceman." "So many people tell me even today that they had that poster on the wall. Some people still got it."

Nike's first TV commercial, Caster said, was an abstract number that featured "somebody running primitively through the desert or high desert" for its running shoes. Other than that, "it was word of foot," Caster half-joked. "Get your product on the right guy and let the players be your ads." That's where the posters—which gave the players personality—came in.

The upstart Nike followed Converse's strategy of cultivating a stable of great basketball players, including Gervin and Artis Gilmore. One of the company's first NBA additions was Phil Chenier, the young Washington Bullets guard. When Chenier returned home to the Bay Area in the 1973 offseason, John Phillips, a Nike sales rep he knew, kept hounding him to try these new shoes. Finally, Chenier relented. They were much softer. Converse, the old standby, were tough to break in: Chenier's feet would be riddled with calluses and corns. "It took a week to break those bad boys in," Chenier said. After that, "those shoes were good for the rest of the year."

Nike was also willing to pay Chenier. Adidas couldn't match that offer. When Chenier mentioned that he might switch to Nike, the Adidas sales rep thought quickly. The client's mom was in the room. "Hey,

I've got some stuff for your family," said the rep, who stuffed some shirts and giveaways into a gym bag.

"I wasn't getting anything from Adidas," Chenier said. "Kareem [Abdul-Jabbar] was getting a paycheck. Wilt [Chamberlain] was getting a paycheck, maybe some of the other big-name players. For the most part, players weren't getting any kind of residuals from these shoe companies. For me, Nike was the first to even offer money. I thought certainly that was a step in the right direction. It became a no-brainer."

Nike provided unlimited shoes, which proved necessary. They were very comfortable, Chenier said, but couldn't handle the stopping and starting a basketball player does. After a month, he needed a new pair. The shoes improved—Nike would take molds of their players' feet—and the money was great. Chenier believes his first contract with Nike guaranteed him $1,500, or ten cents for each pair sold. He was surprised when he got a check for $3,000. Every year, Chenier got about double the guaranteed money. Every summer, its choicest clients, known as the Pro Club, and their families were treated to a resort vacation. Nike even paid for Chenier's sister to come along to serve as a babysitter.

The perks-ridden Pro Club, along with posters of its clients, was meant to send a message: "Nike was in the basketball world, and not only were we in it, we were going to be one of the leaders in the industry," said John Morgan, an executive at Nike in the 1970s and 1980s. "That's the beginning."

The Pro Club helped advertise Nike—and the NBA—across the nation. Instead of pinning their sales on one guy, Nike identified impact players from different teams and signed them. "There really wasn't a Jordan at the time, where there was one player who was an umbrella," Morgan said. There was an added benefit: players heard about the perks and wanted to be part of the Pro Club. Among them was Gervin, who went to Nike when it offered him a $150,000 shoe deal, thirty times more than what he had signed for at Adidas.

J. Walter Kennedy, left, with Cleveland Cavaliers owner Nick Mileti, celebrate the Cavs' inaugural home game in October 1970. The NBA's second commissioner, Kennedy was a decent man who had pushed the NBA to success. But by the mid-1970s, Kennedy was overwhelmed, fatigued, and ready to retire.

The appointment of Larry O'Brien, a member of John F. Kennedy's vaunted "Irish mafia," as league commissioner in 1975 brought much-needed legitimacy to the NBA. On the left is Zander Hollander, the iconic sports book editor.

3

MASTER TELEPHONE LIST OF KEY NBA PERSONNEL

(As of September, 1981)

NBA OFFICE
645 Fifth Avenue
New York, NY   10022
212/826-7000

Lawrence F. O'Brien	Commissioner
Simon P. Gourdine	Deputy Commissioner
David J. Stern	Executive Vice President, Business and Legal Affairs
Russell T. Granik	General Counsel
Joseph A. Axelson	Vice President, Operations
John W. Joyce	Director of Security
Kenneth A. Bailey	Controller
Gary B. Bettman	Assistant General Counsel
Matt Winick	Operations Coordinator
Alex Sachare	Director of Information
Janice E. Akerhielm	Executive Assistant to the Commissioner
Richard Dorfman	Director of Broadcasting
Michael G. Suscavage	Vice President of Marketing
Bob King	Vice President of Team Services
Bill Marshall	Director of Merchandising
Cecil K. Watkins	Referee Development Administrator
Darell Garretson	Chief of Officiating Staff
Connie Maroselli	Assistant to the Controller
Terry Lyons	Public Relations Assistant
Gail Davey	Secretary/Communications
Regina McDonald	Secretary/NBA Properties
Nat Broudy	Director of Office Services
Edythe Verdonck	Secretary/Controller
Nancy Progel	Secretary/Commissioner's Office
Madie Rouse	Secretary/Security
Rhea Williams	Receptionist
Noreen Reilly	Secretary/Executive Vice President
Liz Kupec	Secretary/Information
Barbara Ward	Secretary/General Counsel
Susan Stein	Secretary/Broadcasting
Judy Gamm	Secretary/Operations
Marge Kellerman	Assistant to the Controller
Lizza Parilla	Secretary/Operations

The NBA's staff in the early 1980s was so small that it fit on a single sheet of paper.

The NBA's lack of tradition meant that entertainment took precedence, especially after the ABA was absorbed into the league. Here, one of the early attractions, the San Diego Chicken, grabs a seat with the San Diego Clippers.

Kareem Abdul-Jabbar unleashes his famous sky-hook over the Cavaliers' Nate Thurmond in the final seconds of a 1975 contest. Abdul-Jabbar was a generational talent, but his churlish rapport with fans and the press—coupled with his Muslim faith—was not conducive to crossover appeal.

Blessed with a gravity-defying elegance and off-the-court eloquence, Julius Erving was the superstar the NBA craved. No matter who you were, said Paul Gilbert, one of the forefathers of NBA Entertainment, you were guaranteed a positive experience with "Doctor J."

Larry Bird (left) and Magic Johnson battle for position during Game 2 of the 1985 NBA Finals. The duo's style of play not only made their teams iconic, their rivalry provided an unbeatable narrative that attracted a new audience to the NBA.

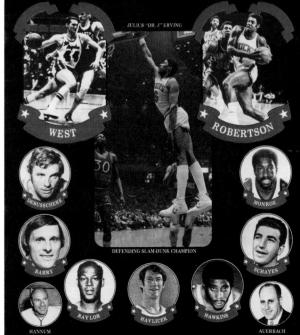

The program cover for the inaugural All-Star Weekend shows how much the NBA favored the Old-Timers Game over the Slam Dunk Contest. The enthusiasm ended quickly. The weekend's reputation as the "black Super Bowl" has endured.

9

Marvin Gaye, the day before his performance of the national anthem at the 1983 NBA All-Star Game. Next to Gaye is his temporary nemesis, Lon Rosen, the Los Angeles Lakers' director of promotions, who feared for his job after Gaye's soulful interpretation of the anthem. "That was the greatest anthem of all time!" Lakers owner Dr. Jerry Buss told Rosen. "Are you kidding me?"

Salem Sportswear's player caricature T-shirts propelled the NBA into personalized apparel, a perfect match for a business driven by star power. Electrician Bill Fickett started selling T-shirts, like this Larry Bird one, to guys on the job. When he paired with screen printers Keith Kennelly and Kyle Nagel, the NBA took notice. (Yes, the artwork improved dramatically.)

11

The Denver Nuggets were all about giving its guests a good time, whether it was throwing a circus or providing playful team posters to attendees.

12

Cable Systems Receiving WTCG-TV Atlanta
May 1979

● Full time (3,735,438)
▲ Night (1,237,586)
Full time cable plus Atlanta off-air
(4,315,438)

Ted Turner, the owner of the Atlanta Hawks and baseball's Atlanta Braves, was far savvier than the average businessman who thought it would be great fun to run a sports team. The budding cable magnate saw those two franchises as programming for markets without a home team—as indicated by these marked-up maps.

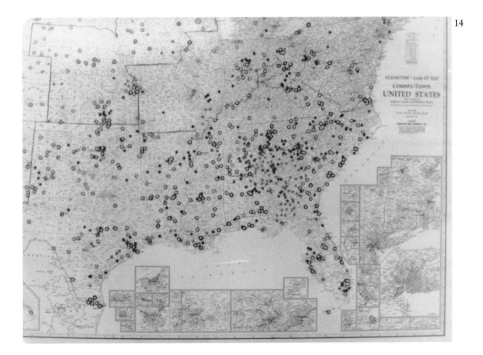

When David Stern was elected the NBA's commissioner in 1983, the longtime league employee had no public profile. But colleagues knew that the combative, brilliant Stern was the NBA's power broker—and the game's biggest fan. By the time Stern left in 2014, his "vision" for the league had reached dizzying heights.

In the early 1980s, CBS Sports turned the NBA into a relevant television property by highlighting the league's stars and overhauling its approach to game coverage. The latter included hiring fresh talent, including analyst Tommy Heinsohn and reporter Pat O'Brien (pictured between Larry Bird and Magic Johnson) to handle halftime.

The Los Angeles Lakers of the 1980s were a movie studio on hardwood. Magic Johnson was the matinee idol. Pat Riley, the coach, directed the production. And Jerry Buss (right) was the mogul whose business acumen, salesmanship, and love of action turned the Lakers into a glitzy spectacle for his guests—and TV viewers.

Poised, pretty, and precise, the Laker Girls represented the apotheosis of Jerry Buss's mingling of entertainment and sports, and provided a way for guests to enjoy the game beyond the players. "Oh, man," said actor Nathaniel Bellamy Jr., a regular attendee at the Forum. "They took it to a whole other level."

The klieg-light smile. The empirically beautiful style of play. The charisma. The sneakers. A confluence of factors made Michael Jordan the camera-ready star who turned the NBA into a pop cultural phenomenon—well before his six NBA championships.

The Air Jordan wasn't just a basketball shoe, it was a cultural identifier in a world where casual wear ruled the marketplace. This photo represents a sliver of Cory Butler's collection. He wears Jordans every day—and even got married in them.

Nike wasn't the only king of the court. In the late 1980s, Reebok emerged as a major player, thanks to innovative, popular lines such as the Reebok Pump. Here, the shoes are on Boston Celtics stars Reggie Lewis (left) and Dee Brown, pictured with Reebok mainstay Joanne Borzakian Ouellette.

The Boston Garden might have been the stage of legends, but it and other no-frills venues would soon become relics in David Stern's entertainment-for-all NBA.

Two legendary basketball scribes, Jackie MacMullan and Bob Ryan, cover the action. A big difference between the NBA and other leagues: the media were seen as an ally, not an obstacle. They got enviable access to players and coaches; the NBA got a free method to carry its narrative of ascendance.

NBC landed the NBA in November 1989. Soon the network treated the league as part of its regular programming. That included NBA commercials with stars from the network's most popular shows, including *Mad About You*. Pictured is a script written by NBA Entertainment's Gil Kerr.

Mad About You -- I Love This Game (:60)
(As of 1/27/93)

Fade up on Paul Reiser and Helen Hunt in their apartment. Helen is standing in front of a closet, there is a large wastepaper basket nearby, and it's obvious that she's been doing some spring cleaning.

                         Paul
Hey, what's going on ?

                         Helen
Paul, I think it's time to clean out this closet.

                         Paul
Now wait a minute. Let's not get drastic here.

                         Helen
         (reaches into the closet)
Take this old deflated basketball for instance.

                         Paul
That's the championship ball for the '70 Knicks! It's been signed by every member of the team!

                         Helen
Well, I think it should go. (Throws it toward the basket. It goes in. She looks pleased with herself and then reaches back into the closet.) And what about this? (Pulls out a humongous sneaker).

                         Paul
That's Bob Lanier's. Size 22! He's in the Hall of Fame!

                         Helen
Well, I think it should join him there. (Tosses it towards the basket. It goes in.) Hmm...not bad. (Reaches back into the closet.) And this! (Pulls out a gross green towel.) What is this!

NBA ENTERTAINMENT, INC. 450 Harmon Meadow Boulevard, Secaucus, NJ 07094 (201) 865-1500

NBC also allowed the NBA to air a show for kids. *NBA Inside Stuff* debuted in 1990 and was a thinly veiled, highly popular promotional vehicle. Here some NBA Entertainment staffers bask in the sun during a shoot. From left: Stephen Koontz, producer; Peter Winik, cameraman; Ken Rosen, senior producer; and Patrick Kelleher, producer.

Vlade Divac of Serbia was one of four high-profile players to go from their home country to the NBA in 1989. Before then, foreign players in the NBA were mostly an oddity. Thanks in large part to Divac's success with the Los Angeles Lakers, that perception changed. More than thirty years later, the NBA is truly a global game.

The company showed it appreciated you, Gervin said. The idea, Morgan said, was to take care of the players and their families. At one retreat, Knight announced that players could take their money and invest it in Nike. Chenier and his friend, Cleveland Cavaliers All-Star Austin Carr, both had the same thought: *Nah, just give us the money.*

A year later, after the pair reconsidered, Knight said the offer was off the table. Carr and Chenier still joke about the small fortune they declined. They were not alone. Spencer Haywood, an early Nike spokesman, was offered a percentage of the company. His agent figured Haywood wouldn't get enough up front, so he asked for cash. Haywood got $32,000 and a lifetime's supply of what-if. Only a few players and coaches, Knight said, took the stock.

By 1984, Nike couldn't sustain the endorsement model. The contracts, the trips, the royalties to Pro Club members cost the company millions of dollars a year. Nike had become saturated with NBA ballplayers. Morgan convinced Knight to sign bench players, following Converse's strategy of saturation. (Knight: "Nobody gives a shit about who sits on the end of bench. We want the guys on the floor!" Morgan: "We can get them too, Buck, just give me a checkbook.") One hundred twenty players were now under contract—or more than 50 percent of the league's players. A group of Nike executives—which included bulldog attorney Howard Slusher and the brilliant Rob Strasser—decided a few strategic signings would yield bigger results. About half of Nike's NBA player contracts expired at the end of 1984. Those contracts would not be renewed, though the players could keep wearing the shoes.

Slusher and Strasser came up with an idea to clear more room in the books. From now on, Nike would not bid on any new player contracts unless he was truly special. Also, if most of their clients found a better shoe deal, they were welcome to join it. Nike was so serious that it would *pay a small portion of that contract* to let the player go. Two agents took Strasser up on his offer. That was okay. Nike was set to reshape its image.

Alvan Adams, an inaugural member of the Pro Club and a onetime All-Star, was told that Nike was putting a good deal of effort behind one guy—Michael Jordan. Adams thought Jordan was a really good young player but didn't anticipate the career that was to come. He wasn't alone. If that's the direction Nike wanted to go in, fine. It had been a good run.

"Well, thanks for letting me be part of it," Adams said. "Can you still provide shoes?"

How Jordan landed at Nike tends to resemble *Rashomon* in sneakers. Phil Knight credits Peter Moore, who designed the first Air Jordan and was the man behind Nike's posters, along with Rob Strasser. David Falk, Jordan's longtime agent, casts his vote with Strasser, with whom he worked out the deal. Jordan says George Raveling, an assistant coach for the 1984 U.S. Olympic basketball team, spurred him to try Nike.

Sonny Vaccaro said he recommended Jordan—Sam Bowie, John Stockton, and Charles Barkley were all suggested—when Nike was deciding what incoming pro they should invest in a signature shoe. He insists that he was not intimate with Jordan's game. UNC was a Converse school, and Jordan loved Adidas. He wore them at practice. Vaccaro's biggest impression was from the 1982 NCAA championship. "The answer is one answer: that's how my mind worked," Vaccaro said. "That's what I said. I can't give you an exaggerated claim that I researched him and watched film, I knew every instinct. I didn't know shit other than he took the shot. The kid took the goddamned shot. Not James Worthy,* not the four other All-Americans.[on the floor]. That's what I'll never forget."

Jordan was a known quantity beyond that game. North Carolina lost

---

*Worthy, a client of David Falk's, signed a huge deal with New Balance, one reason why Jordan went with the super-agent.

guard Al Wood, who had enjoyed a terrific college career, to graduation in 1981. Jordan was the new wave. Gary Walters, then head coach at Providence College, attended a game at Howard Garfinkel's Five-Star Basketball Camp in the Poconos and gawked as Jordan, who had committed to UNC, annihilated his man on defense. He commanded the game with his athleticism and intensity. Walters turned to University of North Carolina assistant Roy Williams and issued a prediction: *Man, Jordan's going to make you forget about Wood in a hurry*. When Jordan left UNC after his junior year in 1984, he had earned national player of the year honors and would soon play on an Olympic team alongside future superstars Patrick Ewing and Chris Mullin. Quinn Buckner, a special assistant on that team, thought Jordan was a good player. Coach Bobby Knight, a notorious hard-ass, *loved* Jordan and advised Trailblazer general manager Stu Inman to draft the 6'6" guard. Inman said the team needed a center. "I don't care who you're thinking of drafting," Knight responded. "You need to draft this guy, because he can play any position you need him to play."

Only "nobody, including the Bulls, thought that Jordan was going to be the greatest player of all time," said Irwin Mandel, the team's longtime salary cap whiz. Jordan played in the McDonald's All-America Game in 1981, an honor for a high school player. His roommate Nigel Miguel, a future commercial actor who served as Jordan's body double, thought Jordan was the best player there. He also had the most memorable photo in *Street & Smith's* high school preseason All-America issue. Everyone else submitted a head shot from the local newspaper; Jordan, Miguel recalled, was clad in a prom tuxedo complete with tails and a white hat.

Once Nike deemed Jordan its guy, Strasser talked to Falk at Washington, D.C.–based ProServ. The two had worked together in the past. Strasser liked Falk, who he felt could secure Jordan. Nike wants to do a signature shoe, and Jordan is an option, Strasser told Falk. If you end up representing Jordan, keep us in mind. That's exactly what happened. Jordan was drafted third overall by the Chicago Bulls in 1984, the small player behind two talented big men. Inman ignored Knight's advice. The Blazers already had an All-Star shooting guard in Jim Paxson and a future star in Clyde Drexler, so the team drafted the injury-plagued Sam Bowie. The Houston Rockets wisely took the transcendent Akeem Olajuwon first overall. He was a new breed of big man, thought Alvan Adams, the Suns' center. Adams was 6'9" and lasted for thirteen seasons because he was quicker than everyone else. Olajuwon nullified that advantage. He was strong—as a college student he played pickup ball against Moses Malone—*and* fast, bestowed with a ballerina's nimbleness that left opponents dizzy. When he played during the summer, freed from coaches' restrictions, Olajuwon modeled his game after guards and small forwards not tethered to the low post. It was how he could get the ball.

As for Jordan, "there was not a huge buzz about his arrival," said Fred Mitchell, who covered the Bulls for the *Chicago Tribune.* "In fact, I think the Bulls sort of regretted the fact that they could not get a big man." It was as if the Bulls *settled* for Michael Jordan. Kevin Loughery, the Bulls' head coach, said the team was elated to get Jordan, but he was their second choice. "If we had the number-one pick," he said, "we probably would have taken Olajuwon."

Nike and Jordan's marriage was far from guaranteed. "He was heavily recruited," Mike Caster said. "Everybody wanted him." Converse thought it had a chance. "We offered him substantial funds for all of his playing years," O'Neil said. "We'd purchase an annuity on his life and pay him the same amount as long as he lived." That translated to $400,000 a year, he recalled, which impressed the Jordan party. But the company could not offer Nike's instant prestige—that is, a signature shoe. He'd be part of a roster. "We had the three top players in the league in Doctor J and Magic and Bird," O'Neil said. "The best they would be with us was number four, and with them, he'd be number one."

Reebok, eager to expand beyond the lucrative world of aerobics—one that Nike had overlooked—wanted Jordan. Badly. He was a great player, thought Gordie Nye, a marketing executive there, but the young man's character shone brighter. Jordan was polite, deferential, without a trace of edge. His personality, Nye said, was effervescent. The long-told story of Jordan struggling to make his high school team was great. "Not to make us sound prescient, because everyone was chomping at his bit, but he was special," Nye said. Reebok also offered "hookups"—clothing that matched the shoes. Jordan would not be Reebok's first NBA spokesperson. A basketball pack of random talents—a solid pro (Roy Hinson), a talented young forward (Wayman Tisdale), a defensive menace (Dennis Johnson), and the NBA's baby-faced irritant (Danny Ainge)—shared that honor. Sneaker deals for NBA players were fading, said Hinson, including his own at PRO-Keds. Hinson's agent told him about Reebok. Luckily, Hinson loved the shoes, the additional $5,000, and the company's staff. "They cared about the players," he said.

Nike was the perfect fit for Jordan. Falk and Strasser both wanted a signature shoe. The money, $500,000 a year for five years, was right. Jordan remained reluctant. In 1984, as David Halberstam observed, the idea of a shoe deal had changed little since the peak of the Pro Club. It provided some cash and some nice freebies, but it had yet to become an athlete's identity, a key component of mainstream appeal, and a source of massive wealth. A shoe, and the associated advertising, didn't serve as a method of expression.

Walt "Clyde" Frazier was the exception, not the rule. Frazier retired in 1980, right when the NBA got its first crop of camera-ready superstars. Sneaker companies enlisted their aid in hawking sneakers without taking Puma's path. Converse, the market leader for years, boasted Magic Johnson, Larry Bird, and Julius Erving as endorsers. But the sneakers weren't *theirs*. Doctor J hawked Converse All-Stars. Magic and Bird were later associated with Converse Weapons, but so were Bernard

King, Mark Aguirre, Isiah Thomas, and Kevin McHale—all legitimate stars, but not in the duo's class. Bird, Magic, and Dr. J made the NBA relevant. Yet they did not have a signature shoe until they had become the NBA's old men. The situation rankled Johnson for years. When he finally forced Converse to give him one, the Triple Double, during the 1989–90 season, Magic was in the twilight of a career that essentially ended in abrupt, world-stopping retirement.

Basketball fans might know that Bird and Magic wore Converse, but the spots said little about their personalities, the kind a suburban kid immediately possessed when they stepped into pristine, freshly laced sneakers and bounced down the aisle in a strip mall Foot Locker. That was the job of CBS Sports and NBA Entertainment. That's what Nike's posters did.

Jordan's mother, Deloris, set her son on a path of incalculable influence. Your father and I are going to be on the flight to Portland, Oregon, she told him. You better be on it.

"The strategy of what to do with him when he came in, that was Sonny, Strasser, Peter [Moore], and Falk," said Caster, then a junior-level advertising executive at Nike. "The four of them were sort of aligned: 'We're going to show him this Harley Davidson–type logo*. We're going to talk to him about a signature shoe, which we had never done. That was a massive step for us."

Nike put on a show. There was food for all; a highlight video of Jordan set to the Pointer Sisters' "Jump" played to the room. There were sketches of the shoes and apparel. In one of the sketches, the shoes were colored red and black.

"I can't wear that shoe," Jordan said. "Those are the Devil's colors."

Strasser, a bearded, barrel-bellied tornado of personality, did not

---

*Caster said the inspiration for the original Air Jordan winged logo—drawn by Peter Moore on an airplane napkin—was Harley Davidson's iconic logo.

waver. "Michael, unless you can get the Bulls to change their colors to Carolina blue," he said, "those are going to be your colors."

Nike kept courting. Jordan was given free rein at Nike's store, and left with six bags. A toy car was rolled out, a joke that left Knight ashen (we're buying this unproven player a car?) and Jordan (who really wanted a car) confused. Strasser dissipated the awkwardness by assuring Jordan that with what Nike was offering, he could buy any car he wanted. Falk thought the presentation was tremendous; Nike's top guns threw themselves at the kid.

Jordan sat expressionless during the entire presentation. Moments after the meeting, he turned to Falk. "Let's do the deal."

Falk was surprised. You didn't even crack a smile, he said.

"I had my business face on," Jordan said.

Jordan didn't drop it, according to J. B. Strasser (Rob Strasser's widow) and Laurie Becklund's *Swoosh: The Unauthorized Story of Nike and the Men Who Played There,* Falk had met with Adidas and felt the company was "completely unprepared" to handle Jordan. The young man didn't care. He called an Adidas rep he knew: come close to what Nike is matching, Jordan said, and I'm yours.

Adidas offered a $100,000 contract and no signature shoe. Jordan signed with Nike.

A year later, Adidas signed Patrick Ewing, the freshly drafted New York Knicks center and a Falk client, to a massive shoe deal. How much did Jordan and Nike inspire this signing?

"It was one hundred percent," said Dave Fogelson, the former public relations director at Adidas U.S.

The game had changed forever in a year.

Jordan aligned with Nike's rebellious ethos, Falk said. The company had a soft spot for iconoclasts dating back to Steve Prefontaine in track and field. But as Jordan's stature reached such heights that he couldn't leave his hotel room without attracting a mob, what became apparent was Nike's power as a marketing company. It could focus its attention on Jordan the brand—the inventive commercials, Tinker Hatfield's increasingly ambitious shoe designs—and let its overseas contractors deal with the glamour-free headaches of manufacturing.

The first shoe was a rush job, but there was time for some flair. "[Jordan] told me he wanted to be close to the floor," Peter Moore said. "He thought the air bag made the shoes higher," which could contribute more to a sprain. The cushioning was skived down so he'd be closer to the floor. Though the shoe was designed specifically for Jordan—it was built off a cast of his foot, said John Morgan—it was neither terribly comfortable nor based on science. "It was just simple common sense," Moore said. It did have an air cushioning system in the heel. The concept of "air" was not new at Nike—Rasheed Wallace's treasured Air Force 1s were released in 1982. But it remained a huge selling point, said future Converse president Mickey Bell, because "you didn't have to explain it to anyone. Air—people automatically associate that with cushioning, rebound effect, all this kind of stuff. That was a great, great technology." All the other shoe companies, Bell explained, had to explain theirs but, "Nike just had it."

The points of distinction, Moore said, were "the color and the fact that this guy is wearing it." The former got everyone's attention. Most basketball shoes were some combination of white and the team's colors. The first Jordans were black and red, a deliberately raised middle finger to the NBA's rules. John Morgan said Rob Strasser wanted the shoe banned.

"We knew it was going to be an issue," Caster said. "We didn't know how the NBA was going to deal with it. We really didn't care. It was great. Think about Nike. We took on everybody. We kind of had this edge about us that sort of made fun of the industry. We used advertising to do that: poke fun at stupid rules or people taking themselves too seriously."

The shoe that actually drew the NBA's attention was a modified Air Ship; the Jordans were being worked on when Jordan began his NBA career. Also, the original Air Jordan was never banned. The NBA demanded that Jordan stop wearing the shoes; Nike refused. Jordan wore the pair in his second game and was fined a thousand dollars; Nike happily paid the fee. The press covered the whole affair. It was unbelievable free advertising, an irresistible impetus for every bored suburban teenager looking for their parents to give them sixty-five dollars to make a stand.

"It was more about setting up the mind-set that Nike was this renegade company and we were going to do these things in the NBA that no one else was doing," Morgan said. "It was a little bit of shock factor."

Nike capitalized on the concocted controversy. It started with a simple commercial. The camera panned down on Jordan, who alternately massaged and dribbled a basketball in Nike gear, a man eager to jump into the game. "On September 15, Nike created a revolutionary new basketball shoe," the narrator said. "On October 18, the NBA threw them out of the game."

The camera ends at Jordan's Air Jordan–clad feet. We hear a hammer on steel once, then twice. The feet are now covered with two black boxes.

"Fortunately, the NBA can't stop you from wearing them . . . Air Jordans from Nike."

Russ Bengtson, the former editor in chief of *SLAM* who later designed an Allen Iverson sneaker for Reebok, can't remember if Jordan got him involved in Air Jordans or the other way around. "They're just forever intertwined to me," he said. "That speaks to how well Nike marketed that shoe."

The NBA's reluctance to work with Nike was a blessing, said Nike attorney Mark Thomashow, who later became the company's senior global director of business affairs/brand marketing. Jordan became a star independent of the NBA. That gave him more influence—and more flexibility—as a corporate spokesperson. "We had to take Michael, in a sense, off the NBA court" and put him in other situations, Thomashow explained. "I think that might have—no, I know that contributed—to making Michael the popular icon that he became, much more so than if we'd been able to say, 'Okay, he does that amazing stuff on the court. Let's do ads with game footage and put in some clever captions.' We were forced to find other ways to market Michael, and the stuff that we did was timeless."

Strasser showed David Stern the commercial. The commissioner thought it was funny and gave it his blessing. And he relented on the shoe ban. Air Jordan could help the league—and help Stern build a bridge with his biggest constituency.

"My kid," Stern told Strasser after the shoe ban was announced, "thinks I'm an asshole because I didn't let Jordan wear those shoes."

The first Air Jordans were released in six cities on April 1, 1985. The frenzy rivaled Cabbage Patch Kids. The Air Jordan line made $130 million its first year. "Holy shit, we weren't quite ready for that," said Morgan, who was in Korea helping to get the Air Jordans out. Five factories—which could make up to 5 million shoes a month— were making Jordans. The production would have been greater, but the air units had to be made in Exeter, New Hampshire, before being shipped to the Far East. Morgan raced to get extra molds made for the shoes.

"It was a real juggling match to get it going," Morgan said. "Of course, Strasser and Knight decided they needed to have these huge quantities like yesterday. In manufacturing, yesterday has already taken place."

For kids who didn't scour Army-Navy stores in the five boroughs for long-forgotten kicks in remainder piles, the shoes were a revelation.

"There were white sneakers and black sneakers," said Lou Nagy, Converse's director of advertising from 1984 to 1989. "The trend was conservative. Nike and Jordan created these products that had the color blocking and fashion appeal." The shoes would have been a multicolored outlier, a thrift store triumph for the fashion-savvy millennial, if Jordan had suffered Sam Bowie's injury history or had merely been a good player.

"They hit all the boxes perfectly," said Mickey Bell. "Then, of course, Michael did the rest." Bill Hazen, the Bulls' announcer during the 1984–85 season, remembers Jordan's first practice. He got the ball, beat his guy off the dribble, and dunked. The next time Jordan's team had the ball, a smaller player took over. Defensive strategy suggested that he should have been in Jordan's face, but he gave the rookie a ton of space. Jordan was so explosive, Hazen said, that the defense didn't know how much cushion to give him to stop him from the hoop. The problem with that, head coach Kevin Loughery said, was Jordan could go anywhere he wanted.

Barely anyone else was watching at the Angel Guardian gym—a couple of writers and the Bulls' coaches. Hazen turned to Loughery, who tried to hide his glee by putting his hand over his mouth. Fred Carter, an assistant coach, had a little smile on his face. "Those guys *knew*," Hazen said. It took maybe five minutes for everyone to recognize that "something of historical implication" was happening right now. It didn't matter if you knew sports, said Jon Miller, the longtime NBA executive. Michael Jordan elicited amazement from *anyone* who watched him.

As the eighties rolled on, Jordan elevated everything he was associated with. Bobbito Garcia, the sneakerheads' foremost scholar, thought the first Jordans "looked garbage. The only person who looked jazzy in them was Jordan himself, yet everyone had them and swore they were the shit." Bengtson, then growing up in Suffolk County, Long Island, loved them. The Jordans were an entry point for him, and countless other suburban white kids, into sneakers. It was like Beastie Boys' *License to Ill* or Run-DMC's *Raising Hell,* another springboard to explore black culture. "You end up learning the whole history," Bengtson said. Instead of Kurtis Blow, it's Air Force 1s and Jabbars.

"If you got into hip-hop, you would get into sneakers, and through sneakers you would maybe get into basketball," said Bengtson. They were all connected. Jordan was the hub, the first player who belonged to the hip-hop generation, thought DJ Jazzy Jeff. "Before Michael Jordan, it was Dr. J," he said. "I couldn't necessarily say Dr. J had swag, when Doc was fifteen or sixteen years older than I was, and Doc had an Afro. Michael Jordan was my peer. Michael Jordan was also the peer of the hip-hop generation." Not only was he doing something they'd never seen with a basketball, DJ Jazzy Jeff said, but he possessed style: the controversial sneakers were followed by the long shorts, the armbands, and the bald head.

The other alluring part about Jordan, said Sean Williams, the sneaker historian, was that Jordan had no nemesis save for the Pistons beating the ever-loving hell out of him every spring in the playoffs. He was a man apart. Rebellion in sports finally had a business portfolio. Jordan turned the shoes into a must-have item. He was an unabashed soloist fresh out of the box, someone that new, young fans could embrace as their own. Larry Bird and Magic Johnson were team players. When Julius Erving arrived in the NBA in 1976, he already had a storied history with the ABA. The NBA fan adopted him. Eight years later, he was an elder statesman—the Afro and goatee were shorn into respectability—whose brilliant career faded each time Jordan took off. *Esquire's* Mark Jacobson wrote that Erving was once the only man who could do what he did in the air. But by simply doing *it,* he inspired a legion of other players. Erving was great; like everyone else, he had to submit to the onslaught of time. Jordan's emergence allowed Erving to step down as the NBA's great ambassador—and resume life as a human being.

Jordan's brilliance granted the NBA a promotional freedom, said Don Sperling of NBA Entertainment. Since Jordan practically marketed himself, the NBA could promote and focus on players who resided in smaller markets. A confluence of factors fueled Jordan's popularity. Jordan arrived as cable expanded and the VCR became a household staple. And he had no agenda. Aaron Freeman, a Chicago-based black actor and political activist, said Jordan and other "model Negroes" achieved *transcendental irrelevance*. In other words, Jordan played a hero on TV. He wasn't going to stump for affordable housing or talk about the racial inequalities happening a brisk walk from Chicago Stadium. After all, Republicans bought sneakers, too. His endorsements, thought Sean Williams, were light, fun. "There's no controversy to Gatorade and Wheaties, and there's no controversy to his shoes, because the only reason why you were supposed to buy his shoes is because you wanted to be like Mike—and look at what Mike is doing," Williams said. "He really had simple parameters by which to be a great off-court persona." And Jordan excelled at it. Before his first retirement in 1993, Jordan made $30 million from endorsements and $4 million from the Bulls at his peak.

For those who saw Jordan outside a television, "there was no bullshit," said Nathaniel S. Butler, the NBA's longtime photographer. "He was Jordan *all the time*. What you see is what you get. He wasn't turning on the charm for the cameras and doing something else off-camera. He commanded that respect, and as a result, people followed. Whether it was as a player or kids running to go buy Nike and go to McDonald's, he was a leader that way."

Jordan knew the responsibility he had to the public. In a rare moment of candor, he admitted to GQ writer David Breskin that he had nightmares of robbing a bank, doing cocaine, committing an act that would tarnish people's high opinion of him. The fear of ruining his image weighed on him daily. Later in his career, when the legend was nearly complete, Jordan had wrapped a commercial for Nike underneath the Great Western Forum in Los Angeles. It was done in secret. Word got out: 250 fans greeted him. Jordan was due back at the Bulls' hotel; Nike had booked him for four hours. Time was tight, but he ventured into the crowd.

Five minutes passed.

"Mike, remember, we gotta go," said Nike's Scott Bedbury, Jordan's handler that day.

"One more second," said Jordan. He signed for another five minutes.

Bedbury finally intervened. It was Jordan's last appearance of the year for Nike. If he went over four hours on the shoot, Nike had to renegotiate with David Falk. That could cost millions of dollars. "I'm really sorry," Bedbury boomed. "We gotta go."

Jordan didn't head to the car. He scanned the crowd for thirty seconds. Then he left the frenzy he had created and returned to his sanctuary of affluent routine. Bedbury asked Jordan if he had forgotten something.

"When I can't sign an autograph for a kid, I at least want to look him in the eye," Jordan said.

He also played in the perfect market. "If I could choose any city to be predominant in my league, I'd choose Chicago," said Barry Frank, the longtime sports television executive and sports agent. Why? "Chicago really dominates the Midwest, and that whole area around Illinois for almost one thousand miles on either side, the main focus is Chicago and sports. I've always felt that the ratings were dominated by Chicago teams, and Jordan playing for Chicago certainly helped the popularity of the sport." When superstation WGN started carrying Bulls games, the audience spread wider.

"How you play on the court has nothing to do with being marketable," Falk said. Jordan was well-spoken, polite, scrubbed of anything objectionable. It was as if he had been created in a focus group. "He's a relatable size," said NBC's Bob Costas, who covered Jordan's championship run in the 1990s, which made it easier for him to star in teenagers' sports fantasies. And he had sex appeal. In the early 1990s, when Jordan became Gatorade's spokesperson, Quaker Oats held an all-employee meeting in Chicago to welcome its new corporate hero. President and COO Phil Marineau noticed that the front row was filled with women. "He had such a sparkle to him and an adorable grin," Cindy Hale, an advertising executive for Nike, recalled. "He just had a presence." It worked on Juanita Vanoy, then an administrative assistant and "the new hot woman" at Burrell Advertising, said Jimmy Smith, who started his prestigious advertising career there. "And the fellas were trying to get a date with her, but it wasn't working. Nobody was getting *anywhere*, and nobody knew why." The old story is Vanoy and Jordan met on a blind date, but Smith said Jordan made his move when he first visited Burrell. It was about a year before the news broke. The couple married in 1989 and had three children before their divorce was finalized in 2006. Jordan, who never ceased working on his game, married Cuban model Yvette Prieto, fifteen years his junior, in 2013.

While Jordan blasted off in arenas from coast to coast, Nike had galvanized a new way to sell basketball shoes. Hale called Strasser and Moore's model "one person, one concept." It incorporated the athlete, the image, the shoes, the apparel, and the product's launch. The days of tying multiple players to a shoe were nearly over. Basketball shoes would come to resemble blockbuster movies: a name or a franchise could get people excited to buy a shoe the same way Tom Cruise or *Star Wars* enticed millions to the multiplex. The massive success of Air Jordan, Hale thought, proved "that one athlete well marketed top to bottom was more valuable to the company than having X percentage of NBA players or X percentage of college players wearing your product."

After 1985, Falk said, the search for the next Jordan commenced—and hasn't stopped. The players got caught up in that too. "Today, young players come in and the first thing they're worried about is their brand," Falk said. "They don't even have a brand." Not at Nike. For Howard "H" White, the Nike stalwart and a member of Jordan's inner circle, an endorser had to offer "elements of style." Did the player get high on his dunks? Did he excite people? "'Cause if he can't move people and offer an attitude we can work with," he said, "then he just won't do much for us as an endorser."

In 1986, Converse premiered the Weapon, a high-top in several colors, most notably purple, white, and gold and white on black. The advertising campaign began with Magic Johnson being chauffeured through the sun-kissed rural splendor of French Lick, Indiana. Larry Bird waited. Magic stepped out of the limo and onto Bird's literal home court for a game of one-on-one: Larry ("the Bird shoe") versus Magic ("the Magic shoe").

"Okay, Magic," Bird barked. "Show me what you got." The command launched into Magic taking his signature push shot and the narrator gravely informing viewers to "choose your weapon."

"It wasn't viewed internally as a threat at all," said Nike's Mike Caster. "It was kind of viewed as 'nice try.'"

The Weapon sold well: 1.2 million pairs its first year and 600,000 more the next year. The numbers belied Converse's inability to generate cultural currency. Bird and Magic were marketed "almost as if they were Siamese twins," said *Boston Globe* basketball writer Bob Ryan. But the ad punctured Bird and Magic's rivalry, one that the NBA and its partners had bludgeoned the public with for years. James Worthy, Magic's teammate, said the commercials showed that Bird and Magic "weren't enemies, just two very tough guys who hate to lose." The two—gasp!—became friends at the shoot. Where was the fun in that? Converse never grasped the 1980s' defining business principle of messaging, a concept Nike started to master. The Weapon's next ad was another creative gem. A group of six All-Stars, one after the other, rapped the benefits of the Weapon—"For the kind of moves that never fail, the Weapon is the choice of Kevin McHale"—that ended with Bird bragging that he "walked away with the MVP."

The fun spot has endured as a slice of 1980s NBA pop culture. "The outtakes were just hilarious," said Bink Garrison of Quinn and Johnson, which did the ad. (Yes, he has an outtake reel.) "Larry had the worst time. He was not a natural rapper, let's put it that way." The commercial had to be shot in one take in one day. It was difficult to herd six high-profile pro athletes in one place on time, said Lou Nagy, Converse's director of advertising. Pals Isiah Thomas and Magic Johnson arrived late, because Magic wanted to get a haircut beforehand, a move that rankled the other stars.

In retrospect, the Weapon spot feels quaint—Bird and Magic shouldn't have shared the stage with anybody. Nike cast Jordan as a rebel who created art in the air, later represented with the now-ubiquitous Jumpman logo. Air Jordans went beyond being a sneaker. The issue with the Weapon rap ad, journalist Nicholas Smith observed years later, was the players asked you to buy a shoe without offering a hint into their personalities, an ineffective sales tactic. McHale's sharp wit was absent, though he was a surprisingly smooth MC. Ditto Magic's gregarious charm or Bernard King's game face or Mark Aguirre's giant ass. There was another bothersome issue, Sean Williams pointed out: the Weapons came in team colors. "They're forcing you, based on which pair you buy, to choose an allegiance to a team," he said.

The Weapon ads were memorable—and provided a retreat from the industry's focus on print, long considered the best way for shoe dogs to savor the goods. "We went beyond the shoe to the people who wore the shoe and what that means," Garrison explained. "And not just Converse. The whole category started doing much, much better advertising. When you have to move beyond a photograph of your product to what your products stands for, that's what branding is supposed to do."

Image was not the only thing Converse couldn't nail down. "One of the big mistakes I think Converse made over the years was that we were a manufacturing company," Converse's Mickey Bell said. "In essence, 'This is what we can manufacture, thus, consumer, this is what you will wear.' Nike was a marketing company: 'Consumer, tell me what you want to wear, and we'll go have someone around the world make it.'" Converse was limited by its manufacturing mind-set, Bell thought. It spent years perfecting a leather sneaker made in Lumberton, North Carolina, home of the Chuck Taylors. "If Lumberton can make the shoe," Bell said of the reasoning, "we will introduce it." Nike had no such sentimentality. Converse, Magic Johnson felt, was stuck in the 1960s and 1970s. "They think the Chuck Taylor days are still here," Johnson said. In 1992.

"When you have four or five factories around the country that are hand-making canvas All-Stars three shifts a day and can't keep up with the orders, it's very difficult to shut it down and say we're going to do something new and different," said Roger Morningstar, who worked in various capacities at Converse from 1976 to 1996. Converse, he said, "kind of morphed" into making basketball shoes. For years, it made military footwear and wader boots.

"It was a new time," Morningstar said, "and we just didn't read those signs. We owned the basketball business and over a fifteen-, maybe twenty-year period we just got passed by."

The Weapons were colorful but bulky, a stark contrast to Jordan's new kicks. As Nike's ads concentrated on Jordan's athletic talents—and the young man kept skirting the laws of gravity eight months a year— the differences became critical.

"The thing about Air Jordan and those original shoes was the shoe matched the advertising," said Mark Richardson, who worked on Converse's advertising for years at Ingalls, Quinn & Johnson and Houston Efler. "The whole story was completely new and different—the aerodynamics and flying through the air and the light weight." Into the 1990s, Converse's younger spokesmen "were still wearing these Cons that looked like boots. There was a disconnect. The product development wasn't there." Converse became associated with "big guys in the middle" who needed cushioning and more material for a softer landing. The faster players, the leapers—the sexy leading men—were associated with Nike.

Before Jordan soared into the public's consciousness, said D'Wayne Edwards, a shoe designer for L.A. Gear and Nike, basketball shoes were made for big men, because that's who dominated the game. Bird and Magic were 6'9"; Kareem was 7'2". Julius Erving checked in at a relatively puny 6'7". Because Jordan clocked in at an easier-to-comprehend 6'6", Edwards said, the shoes were adjusted for smaller guys. The Tinker Hatfield–designed Air Jordan IIIs were made for Jordan, mid-cut and an ounce lighter. "We were saying that basketball players need to be faster, need to be in better shape, and need to think about training and strength," Hatfield said.

Aesthetics mattered. After the inaugural Air Jordan, Edwards said, the line didn't look like basketball shoes. The swooshless Air Jordan II, designed by Bruce Kilgore and crafted in Italy, marked the first time a basketball shoe entered the fashion world. "It started getting more and more exotic with the prints, the materials, and the textures," Edwards said. The Air Jordan III, the first effort from longtime Jordan designer Hatfield, had the elephant-print pattern and the Jumpman logo. The jump toward sophistication and luxury was not accidental. Hatfield first spent time with Jordan at the high-end men's store Bigsby & Kruthers in Chicago, where Jordan was consulting with employees on custom-made suits. "I should point out that his ability to contribute to design was obvious to me from the get-go," Hatfield said. Jordan's sense of style helped transition basketball shoes into fashion, Phil Knight thought.

The Air Jordan III hit people on a different level, thought sneaker designer Jeff Staple. He got a pair in sixth grade. The first day Staple wore them, he walked in late to his social studies class. Everybody's eyes—even the teacher's—bolted to his feet. Every sneaker up to that point, Staple thought, was a reiteration of the Chuck Taylor, the old canvas standby that became hipster chic. "The Air Jordan III was really like a left turn in footwear design," he said.

"Once you become a cultural phenomenon that leapt off the court and it became part of everyday dress, that started to creep into music, in fashion, and hip-hop," Edwards said. "Once that starts to happen, then that influences kids around the world." Hip-hop is all about self-expression, he added, including clothes. When kids began wearing basketball sneakers with jeans and a sweatshirt, they "became a personal identity statement. *This is who I am. I'm able to afford these $100 Jordans and you can't.*" Sneakers, Edwards added, became a cultural status symbol.

Clothing designers capitalized on this concept, said MC Serch, the rapper and sneakerhead. More suburban kids could rock the hip-hop look—product hit the market quickly and beyond the city. It helped, Edwards said, that suburban kids had more shopping options than inner-city kids. "The element of colorizing your clothes to match your Jordans became really simple because a lot of the street designers were already ahead of the game matching gear," Serch said. You didn't have to buy Nike or Jordan gear to complement your Jordans or an Adidas sweat suit to match your Superstars. It kept swelling: Ecko Unlimited, FuBu, Tommy Hilfiger. It hasn't stopped. "Athletes—specifically basketball players and designers and hip-hop culture—continue to create new tipping points and new credibility and new acceptance," Serch said.

"The one thing that consumer appeal did was it suddenly created this need for your sneakers to look good with jeans or to look good on the street," said Paul Litchfield, a design legend at Reebok for nearly thirty years. Basketball shoes were once designed to match uniforms. The shoes' bold design might feature a red, gray, or blue stripe. Smart sneaker companies, Litchfield said, concerned themselves with performance *and* fashion.

DJ Jazzy Jeff became a spokesman for Starter in the early 1990s. His love of sports apparel extended into aesthetics. He didn't wear a St. Louis Cardinals cap because he loved the team, Jeff told Brad Beckerman, the son of Starter founder David Beckerman. He loved the *colors*. They went with his sneakers and shirt. "They never understood that there was a fashion element," Jeff said, "because they were a sports apparel company."*

NBA teams got on board. Logos and color schemes needed to sizzle. The expansion Miami Heat's logo had different shadings on its flame, per the instruction of Lewis Schaffel, the team's managing partner. "It was almost impossible to reproduce," said David Axelson, who joined the Heat's front office after a stint with the Kansas City/Sacramento Kings. Meetings were devoted to the team's look, so it could pop and people would buy caps, T-shirts, and jackets. "It was just a nightmare," he said. Appearance also mattered to the Charlotte Hornets, another expansion franchise. Its use of teal and a kid-friendly dribbling hornet logo defined the franchise for years. The team's sweet candy-striper-meets-zoot-suit uniforms—with pleated shorts—were designed by Alexander Julian; the league didn't know how to make them. Jim Hen-

---

*The fashion element took off in the late 1990s when Outkast's Big Boi appeared in Goodie Mob's "Black Ice (Sky High)" video in a Nolan Ryan Houston Astros rainbow jersey. Sports jerseys from the 1980s started gaining popularity with rappers, said former Mitchell & Ness owner Peter Capolino, because they grew up in that era. Andy Hyman, the owner of the late Distant Replays retro jersey store in Atlanta, said NBA jerseys fit the hip-hop aesthetic. It wasn't about the player as much as how the jersey looked.

son's daughter, Cheryl, created the team's mascot. "We knew we weren't going to win, so we had to turn it into entertainment," said Spencer Stolpen, who was involved in the franchise's early days and later served as team president. "And we had a twenty-three-thousand-seat arena, which scared the hell out of the NBA. That being empty would look horrible." Something else had to keep people's attention. When Allan Bristow coached the Charlotte Hornets in the early 1990s, he sometimes brought owner George Shinn to scout college basketball games. Bristow studied the players; Shinn jotted notes on the team's entertainment during time-outs.

The Hornets' style "had a big impact on 'fashion' as it relates to our total mix," said Bill Marshall, the NBA Properties' stalwart. No pro team featured those kinds of colors, so consumers who might not have known the first thing about the Charlotte Hornets flocked to the gear. Marshall believed that popular players on winning teams drove merchandise sales. Sales of Hornets-related gear, he said, slowed down after four years. Overseas buyers had a different motivation. "We're selling colors," James Warshaw, president of Sports Specialties, told the *Los Angeles Times* in 1990. "We're in the fashion business, and our overseas marketing is ahead of our domestic marketing in that. It's the fashion element. It's the whole understanding that you don't have to be a fan of this team to wear the cap because this is matching with an outfit."

When Harvey Benjamin spent 1990 in Paris for the NBA, he'd see teenagers wearing NBA apparel. Benjamin's French was lousy. Thankfully, most of the youths knew some English, so he was able to ask if the kid wearing a Jordan jersey was an NBA fan. Regardless of the item, "the answer almost always was how much the person liked the team or the personality—and rarely about the sport," Benjamin said. The same applied to a kid who wore a Yankees cap or a University of Michigan sweatshirt.

The sports fandom Benjamin encountered was driven by images and personalities. It had become, he said, "an American cultural logo."

The Air Jordan III also kept Jordan at Nike.

Rob Strasser and Peter Moore had formed a start-up shoe company and wanted Jordan. Nike had one shot to impress its star endorser. On the day of the meeting to present the shoe, Jordan kept everyone waiting—including his parents and Phil Knight—for four hours, Hatfield said. He arrived, finally, wearing a scowl. Strasser and Moore were Jordan's main contacts at Nike, the men who had created the shoe and his image. But Nike had Jordan under written contract. "There was reason for him to believe that Rob and Peter were the reason for the success of the line," Knight said. Their departure had left the cupboard bare, and Knight saw the Air Jordan III as a way back.

"Show me what you got," Jordan said.

Knight had tried to convince Jordan that Hatfield was a fine designer, someone he could trust. Between that meeting and this presentation, ten days later, Hatfield had to design a shoe to win over a disgruntled star client now separated from the men who had built his reputation. Jordan was late because he had been out golfing with Strasser and Moore. "He was basically going to tell Nike that he was leaving," Hatfield said.

Nike was in a battle for Jordan's emotions, Knight recalled years later. Hatfield was oblivious to the drama. He was focused on his presentation, and the room was in a downward spiral. Knight barely muttered an introduction before summoning his designer to please the man who defined Nike and controlled its future.

"Take it away, Tinker!"

Hatfield unveiled the shoe with its black floater and wrinkled soft leather, the one that turned a whole classroom of sixth graders covetous. It was a mid-cut, designed to be worn right out of the box, without a breaking-in period. Jordan, Knight recalled, "lit up" when he held the shoe. "In ten minutes, he was laughing, looking at the shoe, and he was asking questions," Hatfield said. "His outward demeanor had completely changed."

Later, when they were firmly established as creative partners and friends, Hatfield asked Jordan why he stayed at Nike. After the meeting, Jordan recounted, James Jordan caught up to his son in the parking lot and laid into him. "Don't you ever disrespect me, Mr. Knight, and your mom like that."

Michael Jordan then asked the question most twentysomethings— including the ones admired worldwide as a paragon of cool and athletic perfection—occasionally need answered by their parents.

"What should I do?"

"Son, I think you should stay with Nike, because it's guaranteed money, and they've proven they can do the work."

Hatfield and Jordan grew more inventive, incorporating "design flavor"— drawing upon cars or fighter planes or Afropop Worldwide—into a performance shoe. The shoes had a narrative, Hatfield said, and Jordan "had confidence in the way we could tell the stories and get everything out there." The shoes became a way for fans to get closer to a man who lacked the luxury of vulnerability. When people asked Hatfield his inspiration, he had an easy answer. "You need to start from a place of authenticity," he said. "You need to start from a place that's special and people can either remember or grasp. Regardless of anything else that's happened all along the way, including the six championships and the huge business success that exists today, it's him. It's the man." Jordan and Hatfield worked one-on-one. David Falk participated in meetings and made recommendations on product design—until Hatfield told Jordan to ban him.

The duo wanted the design and aesthetics of each new shoe to be innovative. Hatfield ignored the marketing briefs and feedback from focus groups. Then the prototype arrived. Hatfield would visit with sales people, marketing people, and others who didn't *know*. The shoe, they said, was too different, too crazy. That was the point. Hatfield and Jordan knew they could move the market to new places. And they did.

Every year, Hatfield listened to the objections. He always had the same response. He removed a piece of paper from his back pocket. "All right, who wants to call Michael Jordan and tell him we're not doing this shoe? Here's his number. Any takers?"

Nobody, Hatfield said, took him up on the offer.

Mark Richardson tried to get Converse to change course. His agency would arrive with shoe designs to reflect the changing market. The Converse folks would show enthusiasm and then release a shoe that looked like the Weapon.

Paul Litchfield said there was nothing wrong with Converse's approach of making basketball shoes for basketball players, except "they missed the boat on being cool." The leadership, Morningstar thought, was older, set in its ways. It lacked a rabble-rouser like Phil Knight or Rob Strasser. Bird and Johnson, said John O'Neil, a longtime Converse executive and John J. O'Neil's son, suffered through it. When the pair wanted a royalty on the kids' version of the Weapon, the Revolver, chairman Richard B. Loynd refused. Converse was the leader in basketball shoes, so there was no need to follow Nike's lead. Johnson refused to wear next year's Weapon. That move shredded Converse's sales and credibility. Magic vented his frustration to the press. That is when Converse started to lose ground.*

---

*The cover to *When the Game Was Ours*, Johnson's 2009 memoir with Larry Bird, features a game shot of Johnson and Bird. The Converse stars on Bird's sneakers are visible; the ones on Johnson's are whited out. Were relations so strained that such a move was required? "No comment," replied Johnson's longtime agent, the usually loquacious Lon Rosen, via email. Johnson, through Rosen, declined to be interviewed for the book.

"It was the most—I don't know how strongly I can word it— 'frustrating' is one. 'Stupid' is another," O'Neil said. "It was just unreasonable."

Loynd, said O'Neil, believed in one way—his own. That attitude interfered with business, including Converse's status as the official shoe of the NBA. John O'Neil wanted more from the designation. Could the NBA help players without shoe deals wear Converse? The league refused. The honor meant little as the product was not a standard part of the game, like the Spalding game ball. In the late 1980s, Converse was renegotiating the contract. O'Neil and his colleague took their time. Since the NBA was preoccupied with the Players Association, Converse could get more perks. Loynd thought negotiations were too slow, so he covertly signed a new deal with David Stern.

"We were headed toward a better deal for us," said O'Neil, who saw Loynd's style up close. They once met with a regional retail chain in New Jersey. The chain's head buyer requested some changes regarding a program—O'Neil thinks it was related to Bird and Magic. Loynd got up, sat on the conference room table in front of the client, pointed his finger at him, and scolded the dumfounded host: That's not what we do. That's not what we're going to do. We're the leader in basketball. This is the way it's going to be.

Holy shit, John O'Neil thought, *this is a great way to sell a program.* Converse left with maybe 10 percent of the business it should have gotten.

"He was the toughest guy we ever presented to in my agency life," said Richardson. "He was the meanest, most caustic guy ever." The Converse execs embraced ideas and collaboration. "You'd present it to Dick Loynd and he'd stand up like a bull at the end of the table, with steam coming out of his nostrils, sneering and screaming at us," Richardson added. He understood. Loynd was there to improve the business's financial health. "He was so demanding," said John J. O'Neil,

Converse's president, who argued with Loynd frequently. "He expected results that weren't really possible."

Loynd denied the incidents with the retailer and the NBA, but he did address his management style. "Back in the day, my friends used to say I had a very big engine. I did a lot of different things, and I never did them half-time," he said. Loynd admitted he may have been overly involved. He worked sixteen-hour days. "I think that's where some of this came from."

Bill Davenport and Jim Riswold built their reputation—and several others'—killing time at the movies.

About Last Night . . . , based on David Mamet's acidic and observant play, *Sexual Perversity in Chicago*, and directed by Ed Zwick, is the epitome of a mediocre movie. "You've a right to wonder why anyone would want to work so hard—with such an expenditure of imagination—to transform a play with such a distinctive voice into a movie that sounds like any number of others," wrote Vincent Canby in the *New York Times*. But in the summer of 1986, a bubbly romance starring two members of the short-lived Brat Pack was an obvious to-do that carried an unforeseen cultural impact.

Riswold and Davenport, coworkers at Portland, Oregon–based ad agency Wieden + Kennedy, were in Los Angeles to edit a Jordan spot for Nike. They decided to catch *About Last Night . . .* . Riswold deemed it "terrible." The highlight came in the coming attractions, long before Rob Lowe and Demi Moore's stylized romantic travails.

"Tube socks! Tube socks! Three for five dollars! Three for five dollars! Three for five dollars!" a slight, young African-American man bellowed to a procession of disinterested pedestrians. Then he turned to the audience, all puckish confidence.

"Hi, I'm Spike Lee and when I'm not directing, I do this. It pays the rent, puts food on the table, butter on my whole wheat bread. Anyway, I have this new comedy coming out, this very funny film: *She's Gotta Have It.* Check this out." Then the proper preview, illustrating a New York City love rectangle between the gorgeous graphic artist Nola Darling (Tracy Camilla Johns) and three very different suitors. The film was shot in sultry black and white and featured not a trace of Hollywood slickness, including expensively coiffed white folks and Sheena Easton tunes. Everybody on-screen looked and acted like a real person. It was the opposite of the high-concept misery Riswold and Davenport were doomed to endure.

Lee returned in vivid color.

"So, you're bugging out, right? *Yougonnagoyougonnagoyougonnago?* If you don't, I'll still be here on this corner."

This is somebody worth seeing, Riswold thought.

The admen answered the young filmmaker's plea and saw his debut feature back in Portland. Lee played one of the men vying for Nola's affections. Mars Blackmon was a motormouthed, bespectacled city kid who worshipped at the altar of Michael Jordan and Nola. It was a close race as to who was more important.

Then, said Riswold, came the "wonderful, serendipitous stubbing of the toe." In a memorable scene, Mars has sex with his dream woman in his Air Jordans. Riswold said he and Davenport turned to each other and said, "You'd better be thinking what I'm thinking." Davenport, in particular, loved *She's Gotta Have It*. It was so different and new. Mars Blackmon popped from the screen. Davenport said Riswold saw the opportunity to unite Blackmon with his basketball infatuation. The idea was too much damn fun to pass up, especially if the hip, young director with that unapologetic style worked behind the camera.

Davenport hounded Riswold, a brilliant and prolific talent, to see if he had written the script for the commercial. In the middle of the night. The next morning at work. Then an hour later. "Once it's on paper," said Davenport, who didn't recall this follow-up, "you can react to it and you can make sure everyone is one the same page."

"Shut up!" Riswold finally said. "I'm trying to write the script!"

Wieden + Kennedy had Nike as a client; Jordan was a layup. Lee was a different story. Davenport took a shot.* He picked up his office phone and dialed 718-555-1212, information for Brooklyn. He asked for Spike Lee. Soon Davenport was speaking to the future director of *Do the Right Thing, Malcolm X,* and *Black KKKlansman.* Davenport couldn't believe his luck and gave Lee the pitch.

"Bullshit," Lee replied. "Who is this?"

Davenport finally convinced the auteur he wasn't a film school classmate pulling an awful prank. It sounded great to Lee, who had craved this kind of exposure since graduating from film school. The lifelong Knicks fan would star and direct the commercial (a rarity for African-Americans back then), take home a $50,000 paycheck, *and* work with Jordan. This was sweet vindication. Nike gave Lee a Jordan poster—which hung in Mars's bedroom—for the film. That was it. The director had to buy two pairs of Air Jordans out of his own pocket. Now he was poised to be the face of its ad campaign alongside one of America's most popular athletes. That's the way it had to be. Lee owned the rights to the Mars Blackmon character, Davenport said, and nobody knew Mars better than the guy who created him and played him.

Nike couldn't have asked for a better partner. Lee knew sneakers represented more than footwear. They defined a person. DJ Clark Kent believed Lee created sneaker culture. Nike played a memorable role in *She's Gotta Have It.* The kicks received another stage two years later in *Do the Right Thing,* Lee's brilliant drama about racial tensions boiling over on a scorching day in a Brooklyn neighborhood. When Buggin'

---

*The books *Playing for Keeps* and *Best Seat in the House* have Riswold calling Lee, who declined to be interviewed for this book.

Out's white, pristine Jordans—108 American dollars, with tax—are scuffed by an indifferent bicyclist, a passel of Bed-Stuy allies deem them "fucked up" and ready for the trash. A brief, potent argument on racial politics ensues.

"Yo, what you want to live in a black neighborhood for anyway, man?" the black Buggin' Out (Giancarlo Esposito) tells the white man (John Savage), who owns a brownstone. "Mother fuck, gentrification."

"As I understand, it is a free country, a man can live wherever he wants," says the building owner, who sports a Larry Bird shirtsey.

Buggin' Out is nonplussed. "Free country? Man, I should fuck you up for saying that stupid shit alone."

At that point, Kent said, the Jordans became a character.*

Riswold and Davenport didn't feel like they were about to enter risky territory. For one thing, Davenport said, Nike had total faith. "Nike ads back then weren't as iconic or held to such high esteem and regard as they are now because we were just starting out," Davenport said. Phil Knight was so averse to research and marketing that Scott Bedbury, Nike's worldwide advertising director from 1987 to 1994, was warned not to mention either to Knight. Bedbury finally asked his boss why. "Marketing?" Knight scoffed. "That's what *other* companies do. We don't do that here." What Knight abhorred was traditional advertising, which Wieden + Kennedy avoided. Both parties believed that didn't work anymore.

Riswold's scripts, featuring Mars expounding on various topics, were terrific. Davenport could visualize Lee saying the lines as Mars. Riswold gave Mars and Jordan dialogue that sounded comfortable, not a thinly disguised sales pitch. And it told a story.

"Jim is the mastermind behind that, hands down" Davenport said.

---

*In 2016, Nike released the Air Jordan 2 "Radio Raheem," a tribute to *Do the Right Thing*'s boom-box-toting martyr.

"It's not all that hard," Riswold said. "It really isn't. My sisters know how stupid I am. Advertising is very, very simple. It's just populated by people who have very little to do but to make it difficult."

Wieden + Kennedy had reservations. "We were doing Honda scooter commercials at the same time with Lou Reed and Grace Jones," Riswold said. "There were questions: Are we pop culturing Nike? Are we turning them into Honda?" But Riswold said agency heads David Kennedy and Dan Wieden saw how excited he and Davenport were about the pairing. And if they fucked up, Riswold half-joked, they'd only lose their jobs.

With the script having garnered the right people's approval, the shooting began. Jordan was clearly the alpha male with nothing to prove. "He was immediately friendly," Lee wrote, "but in a challenging kind of way." The first time the two met, Jordan said, "Spike Lee." Lee interpreted that sparse greeting as a challenge. *Show me what you've got.* Jordan knew. About a year before the commercials aired, Knight and Jordan were out at dinner, when Jordan unleashed *"Pleasebaby-pleasebabypleasebabybabybabyplease."* He said it another two or three times.

"What the hell is that?" Knight asked.

That was Mars Blackmon's signature line from *She's Gotta Have It*, which Jordan loved.*

Davenport witnessed Lee and Jordan grow comfortable with each other. There were no problems. Lee was not like most commercial directors, men with outsize egos. He worked with a small, diverse crew devoid of hangers-on and company men. Like *She's Gotta Have It*, the shoot was a low-tech, simple affair. It worked.

"We knew with the first shot we had something magical," Riswold said.

---

*Knight said he relayed Jordan's love of the film to Weiden + Kennedy, who then talked to Jordan and created the spot.

Davenport thought the first spot, which ran in 1988, was perfect. Mars Blackmon came across as authentic and believable, Davenport said. Mars was the proxy for every basketball fan—"and a better actor," Riswold said. The motormouth brought Jordan down to earth, made him human, a perfect retort to the otherworldly athleticism. Riswold's script took the burden off Jordan to act. Jordan's assignment was to express disapproval or approval, have fun, and dunk. He could joke at his untouchable image without risking anything. Jordan and Lee, Riswold thought, made each other look good.

"In order to have effective advertising rather than traditional advertising, you really need to know who the subject was," Knight said. "And so we want to know who Michael was, and Michael really liked this character, so what we were showing was that something he really believed in. And that's sort of been the cornerstone ever since."

"Nike was very fortunate to have had Wieden + Kennedy as its ad agency, because Wieden understood pop culture, it understood Nike, and it understood Nike's messaging, and it understood how to get to that part of the athlete that the consumer wasn't seeing," Nike's Mark Thomashow said.

Riswold saw the footage from the shoot. When everything was put together, he entered Dan Wieden's office.

"Wieden," Riswold said, "all I can tell you is, we're blessed."

Hip-hop, according to Russell Simmons, is an attitude. The Jordan-Blackmon ads brought that to a mainstream audience. Jordan's and Lee's lack of passion for rap was irrelevant; the spots embraced the culture. They were unabashedly hip and unabashedly black with not a trace of coddling—goofy raps that started with "My name is . . ."; cute kids with baseball caps turned askew—to pacify white viewers.

"Mars Blackmon was a hip-hop kid," said Def Jam's Bill Adler. "He

had it both ways. He was a hip-hop kid literally looking up to this basketball star. So, in effect, that one commercial embodied the meeting
of basketball and hip-hop."

When John C. Jay first saw the Mars-Jordan spot, he thought, *I don't
know what that is, but that's not advertising.* Jay, who later became a marketing star at Wieden + Kennedy, realized years later what made the
ads so special. It wasn't about selling something, but a series of moments—in politics, American history, sports, and shoes.

"Everything came together and that was what made it so powerful," he said. "It was unlike anything else on television." Scott Bedbury
didn't realize how profound the spots were until he got a letter from a
woman asking who that darling little black boy with Jordan was. Riswold once told Bedbury that good advertising was about presenting
two ends of a rope and never tying them together. You could see whatever you wanted in the ads. The joke at Nike, Thomashow said, was it
would be great if an ad featured a shot of a shoe. Riswold finally com-
plied. "Okay, I've put a hundred different shoes in that ad. Don't bug
me anymore about shoe shots in ads," he said.

Reebok's Gordie Nye compared Nike to another cutting-edge
company, Apple. Competing with that spirit was close to impossible.
Reebok focused on endorsers interested in community involvement,
said Joanne Borzakian Ouellette, Reebok's beloved athlete wrangler.
That gave Reebok a more intimate connection with the towns where
the players plied their trade. The company's foray into outdoor basketball came from John Morgan, who knew it was suicidal to battle Nike
on the basketball court. Reebok's Blacktop line was a success, though
founder and CEO Paul Fireman was dubious.

"Is this going to create an image problem with us with the inner-city
kids?" Fireman asked Morgan.

"No, Paul, blacktop is the surface they play on," Morgan said.

Between 1989 and 1994, said Sean Williams, Reebok killed Nike.

"Reebok was running the sneaker industry," he said. "They had the Blacktop line, they had Shaq" In a time when shoes got lighter, Paul Litchfield, who designed perhaps Reebok's greatest basketball shoe, the Pump, said buyers wanted variety. A sneaker made for everybody pleased no one. Plus, basketball players were getting bigger and faster.*

"We were the cool article of gear or stuff that identified people," he said. "These days it's all about mobile phones and electronics and what kind of apps you have. Back in the day it was sneakers."

Morgan and Nye thought Reebok suffered from "Nike envy." (Litchfield disagreed: "We never tried to make a shoe that was like somebody else's or purposely different than somebody." "Fireman had a big jones to be like Phil Knight," Morgan said. "For sure.")** Fireman did get a chance to sign another illuminating talent. One day, Nye found a decidedly noncorporate dude wearing a cowboy hat and a big brass belt buckle waiting to meet him. "He looked like Crocodile Dundee," Nye recalled. Nicholas Rodgers carried a brown shopping bag and removed a high-heel shoe, which he made and sold out of the back of his van at discos in Montreal. Nye was telling Rodgers to visit Rockport, when he tapped the heel against Nye's desk. The heel lit up.

Nye wanted in. Reebok incorporated that technology into two sneaker lines, including a children's shoe, according to Peter Foley, who held a variety of product development and marketing positions at Reebok during the 1980s and 1990s. Months later, Nye presented samples of "Foot Lights" to Fireman. "It's not technology," he told Nye. "It's a toy." Litchfield said production was "ramping up" when Reebok's run-

---

*When John Morgan left Nike for Reebok, he brought along Celtics guard Dennis Johnson. He wore the Pump in 1989, which boasted a dense polyurethane midsole. "These fucking things are like friggin' army boots," Johnson informed Morgan. "They're really comfortable, but they're heavy."

**Fireman did not respond to multiple interview requests made through his representatives.

ning team nixed the shoe as "gimmicky." Soon after, Nye left for L.A. Gear, which picked up the shoe. He estimated the battery-operated shoe made $550 million in sales its first year.

What differentiated Nike from the pack was that it dealt in athletes, said Gary Way, the NBA attorney. It has always exerted its creativity outside the control of professional sports and its assets. That strategy occasionally made people uncomfortable, as witnessed by Nike's 2019 advertisement with Colin Kaepernick. It was fitting that Jordan, the original swoosh-branded irritant, established a truce between Nike and the NBA.

Nineteen eighty-eight is a crucial year in the creation of Jordan the sports hero–unassailable brand. The Air Jordan III premiered as well as the Mars Blackmon Nike ads. His on-court greatness bloomed. He won the NBA's Most Valuable Player Award and the Defensive Player of the Year Award, a rare double honor. The showman hadn't left. In the All-Star Game, the league's advertising showcase, he won the MVP and the Slam Dunk Contest.

What made Jordan perfect for an increasingly plugged-in world was that his career could be summarized. "You need moments," Bob Costas said. "You need moments that people remember. Jordan had these moments." The Shot against Cleveland in 1989. His "switch-hands" move against the Lakers in the 1991 Finals. The shrug after his three-point barrage against Portland in the 1992 Finals. The Slam Dunk Contest in 1988 provided another one—Jordan in mid-flight as he took off from the free-throw line. "The whole idea of Jordan and flight really was cemented through that image," said Way.

Nike wanted to use that shot for a poster, but Converse stood in its way. One of the few perks of being the official shoe of the NBA, Way said, was other shoe companies couldn't use NBA footage, photography, or the trademark. Into the picture entered Mark Thomashow, the veteran Nike marketing executive. He lobbied Way, his future colleague, to exempt Nike from the restriction. "You have this amazing moment," Thomashow told Way. "You have all this buzz around this kid and this particular moment, and you're not leveraging it, and it's going to die basically if no one's able to do anything with it." That made sense to Way. NBA Properties' job was to cater to its fans, and they clamored for Michael Jordan–related products. Gary Bettman persuaded Converse to waive its exclusivity one time. To a new crop of kids, Jordan flying in his red Bulls uniform, Way said, was Farrah Fawcett smiling in that red bathing suit.

"That began the process of the NBA looking at the wisdom of being locked into an official shoe sponsorship with Converse," Way said. Giving the footwear brands opportunities to highlight the players, while paying NBA Properties for the privilege, he explained, "was a much better model in terms of exposing players and promoting players than the captive model for just having an official shoe."

Converse is now owned by Nike. It no longer makes basketball shoes, save for the occasional reissue. Its dominance in basketball is a faint memory.

Relations between the NBA and Nike didn't thaw right then. Thomashow thought the NBA harbored resentment over the initial Air Jordan release. One day, Thomashow was in his office in Beaverton when the phone rang.

We know Charles Barkley is filming a Nike commercial in New York, Gary Bettman said. Thomashow had no idea.

"If you mention Philadelphia or the 76ers, we will sue you," Bettman said.*

The relationship between the NBA and Nike works today, Way

---

*When John Gaffney of CBS-Fox Video spent a wild night with Pistons forward John Salley, Bettman called as Gaffney nursed a hangover. "John, it's Gary Bettman. If you ever leave one of my players at a strip club again, I will cut your balls off and feed them to you. Do we understand each other?"

said, because both sides know they can succeed without the other. There was a common interest, said Scott Bedbury: Nike and the NBA wanted to export the game. The NBA's rise as a cultural force was directly tied to a now-antiquated device that boggled the minds of Generation X kids and began the transition into a world where we can be entertained anytime, anywhere.

What Jordan did for footwear, he was set to do for the VCR.

LET'S GO TO
THE VIDEOTAPE!

This here's the future. Videotape tells the truth.

—FLOYD GONDOLLI (PHILIP BAKER HALL), *BOOGIE NIGHTS*

For young Dave Zirin, the three-block walk to Video Connection on New York City's Upper West Side was as big a thrill as going to the movies. He'd enter to the smell of popcorn and a store full of possibilities. The pilgrimage was indeed rare; he'd also have to rent the VCR—a major expense at the time. He'd head over to the NBA tapes. He loved the year-in-review ones, because they contained exotic talents such as Phoenix's Walter Davis in Phoenix or Sacramento's Reggie Theus.

The VCR saved bored, housebound children of the 1980s. No longer were they confined to cable TV or Mom's willingness to drive them to the movies. The NBA took a while to find this audience. Its limited offerings during the mid-1980s featured mostly a yearly wrap-up and that season's All-Star Game. By the late 1980s, George Krieger, the president and CEO of CBS/Fox Video, felt the NBA needed to extend its marketing creativity in home video. There was nothing with teams or star players or the flashy highlights. As Krieger told John Gaffney, director of sports marketing at CBS/Fox Video,

"Why can't we make videos for the kids that want to watch them instead of the guy sitting around with the light beer? That guy is not buying home videos."

Krieger had a valid point. As the 1980s progressed, home video sales skyrocketed because tapes were cheaper to produce. That meant lower retail prices, an enticement for kids—or their parents—to buy instead of rent. Krieger was a New Jersey Nets season ticket holder whose eleven-year-old son was a giant hoops fan. NBA pictures hung all around his bedroom, so Krieger "had a nice little test market to eat dinner with every night." CBS/Fox Video laid out possibilities during a meeting with the NBA: bloopers, great endings, dunks, and a video on Michael Jordan, the NBA's biggest name. Stern, "the extreme executive producer," agreed and offered more ideas.

(Don Sperling, the *pater familias* of NBA Entertainment, said Krieger helped shape NBA's home video business and got the league to recognize the audience desire for home videos featuring NBA videos, but he draws the line that NBA Entertainment needed to be told to make a video on one of the world's biggest stars. Krieger disagreed. There was no doubt NBA Entertainment could make those videos. It needed to be nudged in the right direction.)

CBS/Fox Video had to ask a player's agent to get permission to do an individual video. Jordan was represented by David Falk, one of the NBA's most powerful men, who knew the video could fold in Jordan's sponsors. It also helped that Jordan was a friend of NBA Entertainment. "He let us in to see how hard he worked," said Stephen Koontz, a producer at NBA Entertainment. "He was proud of the work. He didn't want people to think he was just this beautiful, privileged uber-athlete. He was all about every dimension of the process. He wasn't fickle. He wasn't surly like a lot of guys I won't mention. He came to know us and trust us."

"He could be an asshole to people in a ball-busting way, but because he was so popular, he could have been the biggest asshole on the planet and gotten away with it, and he wasn't," said NBA Entertainment's Patrick Kelleher, who worked with Jordan at his zenith. "Patrick Ewing was a bigger asshole"—and he didn't have half of Jordan's public profile.

Michael Jordan: Come Fly with Me (1989), the NBA's first "hero, superstar-driven tape," validated Krieger's theory. Six hundred thousand units were initially shipped out, and the retail and rental markets went bananas. *Sports Illustrated* started offering an edited version of the tape to entice new subscribers.

Given the video's popularity and impact, "I often joke that it's been downhill for me ever since," said David Check, who was assigned to the project after a mere seven months at NBA Entertainment. "I'm not quite sure we knew the magnitude of what we were doing at the time," he added. "We just dove into it with a lot of passion and lot of long hours, which tend to go together, but we didn't care. I think we loved it because we were drawn to the subject matter, and why wouldn't you be?" Check and David Gavant, who led the project, stayed up four days straight to reach the deadline for CBS/Fox Video. Gavant, running on adrenaline, could have stayed up another day.*

Two more Jordan videos followed—*Michael Jordan's Playground* and *Michael Jordan: Air Time*. Each tape was a smash and the predecessors were repackaged. That led to more sales as the years passed. The success was part of the NBA's blueprint. Stern's ability as a marketer and promoter, legendary Chicago Bulls head coach Phil Jackson thought, attracted the masses to the game. Stars were everywhere. CBS took notice. John Kosner sent a memo to *NBA on CBS* executive producer Ted Shaker with another of his "dopey ideas." Instead of marketing Detroit versus Atlanta, he advised, let's use head shots of Dominique Wilkins

---

*David Gavant loved Stern's insistence on "clean feeds" of NBA games. A specific cable from the production truck went into the NBA's record decks in every arena. Otherwise, *Come Fly with Me* would have been the "history of television graphics" on every shot.

and Isiah Thomas. "And we began to market that relentlessly," Kosner said. "The NBA would get criticized in certain camps for promoting players versus teams. We were trying to light the match."

"Jordan was the big one," said Charlie Bloom, a senior producer for NBA Entertainment at the time. He set NBA Entertainment's home video direction. "We started going down the line," Don Sperling said. "Is there room for a Barkley? Is there room for a Ewing?"

Heidi Palarz, another NBA Entertainment veteran, said the appeal of *Michael Jordan: Come Fly with Me* was fans got to know the players "outside of what they had seen from just watching the game." That trend culminated with the 1990 premiere of television's *NBA Inside Stuff*, where fans could accompany Chris Mullin as he sharpened his buzz cut or shop at FAO Schwarz with the perpetually scowling Ewing. The individual approach worked because the players were as good as the hype, said Butch Beard, the player and coach. There was another benefit, thought Len Elmore, who has been around professional and college basketball as a player, agent, and broadcaster for almost fifty years. It took attention away from all the other ills the NBA suffered.

Social activism was not part of the black athlete's public persona in the 1980s. Dr. Harry Edwards, the sociologist who organized John Carlos and Tommie Smith's historic raised-fist protest in the 1968 Summer Olympics, said the "activist dimension of racial perception" had begun to fade by 1972. Martin Luther King was assassinated in 1968. The Black Power movement had "virtually collapsed." The Black Panthers' leaders—including Eldridge Cleaver and Bobby Seale—were running for public office.

Plus, Edwards said, there was protest fatigue, paving the way for a less purpose-driven era. The Baby Boomers, those kids who took to the streets and turned Larry O'Brien into a political irrelevancy, quit activism "in the early 1970s," essayist Joe Queenan wrote. "They got all tired from Vietnam and Nixon and the Kennedys and all those race riots and decided that they needed a break. The break never ended." This permanent vacation, Queenan claimed, started on April 21, 1971, the day singer-songwriter Carole King's easy-listening gem *Tapestry* was released. To date, the album has sold 25 million copies.

Starting in the mid-1970s, Edwards told Howard Bryant, black athletes lacked a defining movement or ideology to get behind. With no more Jim Crow or riots, black athletes mistakenly thought they didn't have to speak out. Therefore, a talented, corporate cipher like O. J. Simpson could serve as the voice of the black athlete for mainstream America. "The specter of black athletes who were *not* delivering a racial message was the fallback position, the default position of American society," Edwards said. "They had gone through Muhammad Ali, Smith and Carlos, Bill Russell, and Jim Brown and a straight-up, almost uncensored expression of what they felt about race and so forth in American society. All great athletes, world-class athletes, but they had that protest edge, that edge of militancy."

Every time Russell laced up his sneakers, he played for the black race, civil rights activist Al Sharpton thought. Even though the Boston Celtics were riddled with white players—for years, a white "quota" for teams was the worst-kept secret in the NBA—his outspokenness and aloofness with fans didn't endear him to ticket holders. The string of championships did little to satiate fans. Russell returned to his Reading, Massachusetts, home one night to find that vandals had ransacked his house and shat in his bed. When Michael Burns, who worked for the Celtics in the late 1960s before heading to the league office, sold group tickets, one out of three clients bitched about Russell's attitude. "It was a pain in the neck," he said. "It just caused lower ticket sales."

As the activist mind-set faded, whites got some not-at-all-needed comfort at the arenas and in their living rooms. The black athlete was finally shutting up and playing the goddamn game. As Edwards explained it, "I can't escape the fact of black athletic dominance, but at least I don't have to look at message sports or messenger athletes in terms of the race issue in American society." There was no change in the average white sports fan's "disposition toward race," Edwards clarified: blacks could dominate if their form of expression was how they put a ball into a basket or ran with a football. That philosophy lingers to this day. LeBron James and Colin Kaepernick get lambasted for having the temerity to comment and act out on the inequalities they see as young black men. Bryant called this effect "greenwashing." Black players who make millions of dollars a year, who play a game "I'd play for free," give up their right to complain. They cease to exist as black men in the eyes of white sports fans.

Stern, Edwards thought, expressed the personalities of great players without any racial messaging. The players knew this, too. You never heard Magic Johnson talk about race or Larry Bird reference "white folks who were in the lower echelons of society." Players who brought up race faced consequences. Isiah Thomas's 1987 rejoinder that if three-time MVP Bird were black "he'd be just another good guy" made national headlines. Thomas held a press conference in Detroit to apologize—and then flew to the NBA Finals in Los Angeles to hold *another* press conference with Bird, whose mother loved Thomas's game. The *Chicago Tribune* reported that Thomas was worried about the damage his comment, which he claimed was made in jest, would have on his image.

"That's the bad thing," Thomas told reporters. "Everything I stand for as a basketball player, everything I stand for as a human being, I still stand for. I didn't do anything wrong, but I don't know if the media can take back what it's done."

Image mattered to Stern. When Lakers star James Worthy was arrested for solicitation of prostitution in 1990, he paid a visit to Stern's New York City office and got a refresher course. "James," Stern said loud enough for John Gaffney of CBS/Fox Video to hear, "the NBA is *not** about stay in school, say no to drugs, and suck my dick." In 2005, Stern was widely criticized for instituting a league-wide dress code. He expressed his frustration to ex–Nike executive Scott Bedbury. "You manufacture brands. You deal in shoes. You deal in products. You deal in leather. I deal in people. They're so much harder to handle."

Stern also had to live up to expectations. Advertising legend Jeff Goodby, who helped create memorable campaigns for the NBA, saw it in action. In 2007, Stern invited Goodby and his son, Nathaniel, to a Warriors playoff game. Goodby offered to buy a bucket of popcorn for his host. Stern declined. "They know I'm here," he said. "Get the biggest one."

The tub arrived. "You have to hold it," Stern informed Goodby.

"Why?"

"If the TV shows that I have a big popcorn on my lap, I'll look like an idiot," Stern said. "You have to hold my popcorn."

The public's jangled nerves might have been better assuaged if Thomas had committed himself to playing the role of humorous rabble-rouser. Years later, when Charles Barkley proclaimed, "I am not a role model" in a Nike commercial, it sounded rebellious, but Edwards knew it reaffirmed what a great many white Americans already believed. *I didn't want you near my kids anyway, pal.* Besides, it was an image that Barkley honed, starting when he was a college student. "He had his own raucous style to sell," veteran sportswriter Filip Bondy concluded. Barkley and the media-savvy Jordan came out of the 1984 NBA draft.

---

*Worthy could not be reached for comment.

David Stern's brilliance, Edwards said, was that he read the "trade winds of history in the post–civil rights era," Edwards said. "We were not post-racial. We were post–civil rights. But David Stern was able to market these athletes and the NBA as individual personalities as if we *were* in a post-racial era, when really we were post-militancy, post–civil rights." As long as there was no reference to actual social change and militancy, the NBA machine moved on.

All those details paved the way for Michael Jordan's arrival and his subsequent takeoff, picking up where Simpson—a symbol, writer Howard Bryant observed, of long-promised equality and whites' generosity in opening the door—stopped.

"Twenty years after the Civil Rights Act—we're talking the peak of the Reagan revolution; we're talking about the Reagan backlash to Great Society programs, affirmative action; 1970s civil rights protest movements—Jordan emerges as this figure who can illustrate racial progress without any reminders about racism," said David Leonard, the basketball author and academic. "He could represent acceptance in his exceptionalism. He became evidence of the exception that he was a breath of fresh air, that he was unlike the players of the 1970s. In many ways it fed into a narrative that what needed to change was not white fans of the NBA or society as a whole or our laws or our culture, but we just needed more Michael Jordans. That added to his power, that added to his cultural significance, that added to his greatness. In some ways, they fed off one another."

Or as John Gaffney, the CBS/Fox Video marketing executive, put it, Jordan was Bruce Springsteen with a jump shot.

The NBA's marketing savvy served as a balm for the threatened white consumer but isolated players who lacked entertainment value. Outstanding was no longer good enough. You had to have sizzle. Remember Alex English? "You don't hear nothing about him," said George Gervin, a longtime opponent.

English, the leading scorer of the 1980s, got 2,000 points a year for the Denver Nuggets—"Do you know how *hard* that *is*?" Gervin said—via a methodical, efficient midrange game. But English's brilliant game lacked a hook. "It wasn't attractive," explained Gervin, forever associated with the finger roll. "Attraction sells, and effectiveness is all right. That's what it came to. It's attractive to shoot a three. It's attractive to dunk. It's unattractive to lay it up." The understated, graceful English saw the same thing. The 1980s was when the NBA had the most *stars*. Earl Monroe placed a lot of the blame on ESPN, which he said showed nothing but dunks on its highlight reels. That changed the way the game was played because all the kids emulated what they saw on TV.

"I'm not so flashy, not so boisterous. I'm low-key. My job is to do the job I'm supposed to do," English said during his playing days. "There are people who don't see it. But they aren't paying attention." English always felt like he was a singer or dancer performing onstage. In the off-season, he punctuated his runs with ballet dancer leaps. If English—who published several books of poetry and starred in the somber 1987 no-nukes fairy tale *Amazing Grace and Chuck*—was Paul Simon, then Michael Jordan was Michael Jackson. Both men were phenomena that rattled the idea of traditional idols because they rewired our fantasies. *Sometimes I dream / That he is me.* While one teenager executed a bumpy moonwalk at a high school dance, another stuck their tongue out en route to a Nerf hoop fastened their bedroom door. (Many did both.) Years later, Jon Miller of NBA Entertainment knew the NBA had broken through when Michael Jackson's business manager, Sandy Gallin, called him. Jackson wanted to premiere his new music video at halftime of an NBA game. And in the video for "Jam," released in June 1992, the cultural icons' worlds collided. Over eight minutes, Jordan tried to dance like Jackson; Jackson tried to play basketball like Jordan. Both looked robotic and uncomfortable. The humor jarred a nation of young dreamers. Wait a second—these guys are human?

The NBA's big money didn't come from "true fans." They didn't need to be seduced. *Dazzling Dunks & Basketball Bloopers** (1989) moved more than one million copies. That special, and its sequel, were hosted by smooth, sardonic announcer Marv Albert and Frank Layden, the gregarious former Utah Jazz coach, who found himself internationally known for reasons outside his vocation. A teacher in Israel used the video to teach her students English. When he visited London to watch a Niagara University basketball game, Layden was not identified as an alumnus or the 1988 NBA Coach of the Year but as "the Blooper Man." The influence came with a cost. Layden became better known as a jolly cutup who kissed Morgana than a successful basketball coach and executive. Years later, he had some regrets. If he knew his reputation as a coach would have taken a backseat, Layden "would have taken a more serious approach to things." In September 1997, Albert pled guilty to assault and battery charges, which stemmed from Albert throwing his longtime lover onto a hotel room bed, biting her back, and forcing her to perform oral sex.

The pull of marketing was too strong. "We had gotten onto something that worked, and in particular worked across a wider swath of age groups," Krieger said. "We could pick up the eight-year-olds along with the twenty-eight-year-olds who were like, 'Can you believe these dunks? Can you believe he made this shot at the buzzer?'"

Gavant has lost track of how many people have told him *Michael Jordan: Come Fly with Me* changed their childhoods by turning them on to Jordan and basketball. *Michael Jordan's Playground* (1991) was flagrantly geared to kids, which Krieger said was the NBA's modus operandi. The

---

*Because the NFL was associated with "bloopers," the NBA wanted to avoid any connection, Don Sperling said. Hence, the longer title.

happy idea came from a sad set of circumstances. John Gaffney's mother had recently died, leaving him parentless and in a deep depression. On his lunch breaks, he'd take a long walk from Forty-Sixth Street to a playground on Sixth Street in Greenwich Village, where the black kids always played ball like Jordan. Their tongues were out; they talked trash. *That's it,* Gaffney thought. *The next video should take Jordan out of the arena and put him on the blacktop.* In the finished product, Jordan, decked head to toe in his signature gear, drops in on an insecure teenager (Tyrin Turner, shooting a Spalding NBA basketball) eager to make his high school team. Of course, there were tons of highlights and interviews attesting to Jordan's greatness, plus an appearance from rappers Kid 'n Play to keep it real.

Krieger said Falk saw value in another video for his star client at minimum cost: two or three days of shooting. Jordan made the most of it. Part of the shoot took place in a gym, and Jordan practiced during the downtime, slapping his right arm anytime he went in for a layup. The sound reverberated throughout the gym, Gaffney recalled.

The synergy between rap and basketball had a few hairline fractures. Christopher "Play" Martin had to be briefed by his partner, Christopher "Kid" Reid, on Jordan's importance. "I didn't really care," Martin said. When he finally met Jordan, Martin acted like he understood exactly how big a deal this was.

Jordan saw right through him. "You don't even know who I am."

"Thank you," Martin said. "No, I don't."

Martin became friendly with Jordan and other NBA stars. There was one advantage for the players, Martin said. When he called them, it wasn't for tickets. Martin went to the games for "party reasons and women reasons." He never regretted it.

As more stars got the good kind of direct-to-video treatment, not the Eric Roberts kind, some were left in the cold. A representative for Isiah Thomas called the NBA: the Detroit Pistons superstar wanted to make a tape of his own. The NBA and CBS/Fox Video said no way.

NBA Entertainment, Krieger said, relented out of political strategy. At the time, Thomas was heavily involved with the Players Association. "Nobody bought it," Krieger said. "He was not a very popular player. He felt slighted, because Magic [Thomas's longtime friend and rival] had one and he didn't get a home video. Research showed no one was going to buy it—and the research was right."*

Gaffney got phone calls from agents. "So many athletes were all over that," he said. They wanted to go beyond their sport. Jordan had done it, right? But he was a phenomenon, the divine combination of timing and ability and aesthetics. The cultural impact couldn't be passed along. He was an unassailable archetype that resonated through generations for a thousand different reasons. There have been a million beautiful blondes—some even caught the public's eye for a moment or two—but only one was Marilyn Monroe. What Monroe did for billowy white dresses and "Happy Birthday," Jordan did for the slam dunk and basketball sneak—not so fast. When they "cost more than one hundred dollars," Falk explained, "they call them shoes. These aren't, like, PF Flyers or Keds or canvas Cons."

The NBA couldn't be about Jordan, not in David Stern's equal-opportunity business model—where Salem Sportswear had to scour the Sacramento Kings' paltry roster for another T-shirt subject, where every team deserved to play on national television. Krieger said Gaffney had the idea to marry popular music with the highlights. So the NBA worked out a deal with Music Corporation of America to use its artists' songs. "People picked their own music, and then NBA Entertainment made a music video to attach to the music," Krieger said. The result was *Superstars* (1989), billed as "a fusion of music and sports like never before." Charles Barkley's freight train play was appropriately paired with Scandal's "The Warrior." Akeem Olajuwon's nimble moves were set to

---

*A representative for Thomas did not respond to emails seeking comment.

Kool Mo Dee's "How You Like Me Now?"—and a few puzzling scenes of "The Dream" in a recording studio. Jordan's acrobatics were set to Berlin's "Take My Breath Away," the synth-heavy somnolent serenade for *Top Gun*'s shadow-saturated sex scene. Barkley had commodified rebellion, essayist Nelson George wrote, and had become a beloved national spokesman in the process. The NBA, like rap and MTV, had followed suit. It was *neither* hip nor profitable to be square.

"The *Superstars* video was all about the MTV generation," Gaffney said. The goal, Krieger said, was to get some of the segments on the network. There was another benefit, thought NBA Entertainment's Patrick Kelleher: pairing fast-paced music to the highlights allowed the NBA to differentiate itself from the pack. "I think that's one of the reasons that our stuff got so popular," he said, "because it was a little bit different in terms of our expectation and editing and style." Andy Thompson—the brother of Lakers center Mychal and the uncle of basketball star Klay—excelled at that merger, Kelleher thought. Nowhere was that flair more on display than at the 1990 All-Star Game. He electrified players and coaches walking on the floor, employing funky editing tricks, handheld camerawork, and player highlights that worked on both TV and the Miami Arena's Jumbotron. A mash-up featuring Janet Jackson's "Rhythm Nation" served as the main theme. "I remember when I watched that for the first time, I was like, 'Wow, this is what MTV is doing,'" Kelleher said. "MTV had taken shows and incorporated popular music into it in a way that people hadn't before, and [had] done a great job of it." The year before the All-Stars were introduced in a series of personalized raps set to their highlights. *On the court / Patrick Ewing / See what he's doing / Nobody's booing.*

Superstars, thought Cory Butler,* a child of the 1980s who be-

---

*Butler is married to Sondra Murphy, the Mitchell & Ness employee and Salem Sportswear devotee.

came a die-hard NBA fan, served as an introduction to the players. He spent part of his childhood in Binghamton, a central New York city of fifty thousand with no local pro team, and scant opportunities to see players out west like Olajuwon or Karl Malone. The NBA tapes were easily available highlight reels that offered a taste of the players' personalities. They were 100 percent geared toward kids, said Butler, who had every tape. "Players took on these personalities, and I think people gravitated toward the perception that was created for these guys," Butler said.

Dazzling dunks and fantastic finishes could not ease the game's physical nature. Sometimes it would turn violent. After Kermit Washington's near-fatal cold-cocking of Rudy Tomjanovich in 1977, fights still happened, said referee Joey Crawford—even if Crawford had prior knowledge. Before a December 1984 game between the Washington Bullets and the Atlanta Hawks, bruising Bullets center Jeff Ruland approached Crawford.

"Listen, I don't like Scott Hastings," Ruland said, referring to Atlanta's center.

"Yeah, what do you want me to do about it?" Crawford said.

"I'm going to punch him in the face."

"Jeff, don't do that," Crawford warned. "I'll throw your ass out."

The game went on without a fist meeting face. In the fourth quarter, Bullets guard Gus Williams took a three-point shot. Crawford got in position—and saw Ruland punch Hastings in the head.

"Jeff, you fucker!"

"In our primes, we were already men," said Terry Cummings, the Milwaukee Bucks All-Star forward. Since most of the players—black and white—didn't come from privileged backgrounds, "we were fighting to maintain. In the eighties, you were not guaranteed a job no matter what your name was. You had to come to camp every year and compete for your spot." That meant "laying wood"—putting a forearm in a chest, using your body to get better position—was an equalizer. A player who drove to the hoop needed to learn a lesson. "Back then," Ruland said, "you would forearm-shiver a guy so he wouldn't come back that way again." A head coach from that era said many teams imposed fines in the postseason if a player allowed their opponent to score a layup instead of taking the charge—or fouling them.

In the final years of the 1980s, physical play was best represented by the Detroit Pistons, an aggressive, scrappy team defined by a ferocious defense that occasionally led to bench-clearing altercations. The "Bad Boys" got away with it for two reasons. First, the game wasn't called as tightly as today, and Detroit took advantage. "We were always taught as refs, we didn't want anybody to get thrown out," said Crawford, who refereed from 1977 to 2016. "That's the way we officiated back then. I think we could have done a better job, but in defense of our staff and in defense of the league, we didn't have the rules to back us up." Second, the team, coached by the personable Chuck Daly, brought NBA Entertainment into its inner sanctum.

"All those guys," said Don Sperling, the longtime NBA Entertainment leader, "loved what we were doing. They loved being on camera."

NBA Entertainment practically lived with the Pistons during their championship years, said senior producer Mike Antinoro. "We became part of what they were doing," he said. "They understood we were part of their family; we weren't going to do anything to embarrass them. But they also understood the role we helped play in growing the league. It was a mutual respect." Without the Pistons' cooperation, NBA Entertainment, Sperling said, wouldn't have been as successful and it would have been unable to gain the trust and access of the other NBA teams.

NBA Entertainment wasn't a network or outside media but "the good guys," Antinoro said.

The Pistons also played a crucial role in the NBA Entertainment story line. This was not a glamorous team with a widely popular star, Sperling said, but "a Midwest, blue-collar team" that regular joes could cheer for. "Everything is like a Hollywood script," he said. The Pistons served as the perfect villain—and relished the role. Its video rundown of the 1987–88 season was titled, aptly, *Bad Boys*. "If we're going to be the bad boys, then we've got to act like bad boys," Isiah Thomas crowed after a montage of the Pistons hitting, bumping, and trash-talking their opponents. "We can use this reputation in two ways. Either we can use it to our advantage or it's going to hinder us severely." Bill Laimbeer, the Pistons' maligned center, advised the team to wear that reputation as a badge of honor, like the down-and-dirty Oakland Raiders of Jack Tatum and Gene Upshaw.

"David was very protective of the image of the league at that time," said John Gaffney of CBS/Fox Video. "David was not happy about that whole Bad Boys thing."

Stern would spend his thirty years as commissioner doing his utmost to curb fighting, instituting a kind of point system for extreme fouls that ultimately resulted in suspension. "One of my bad mistakes—greenlighting that [video]," he said years later. Sperling said Stern (jokingly) blamed him. "I pushed and promoted, and he didn't want to do it," he said. Calling the video *Bad Boys* was controversial, but it sold and signified a remarkable turnaround for the NBA's public image. A style of play that would have caused stentorian anchormen to deliver stolid commentaries and op-ed writers to parse racial dynamics in eight hundred words ten years ago was now an effective marketing tactic.

Tom Wilson, the Pistons president, said much of the Bad Boys' success went beyond their style of play. What connected the Pistons to fans, Wilson thought, was local news. Most people back then watched the three syndicated network stations, and the Pistons were on the sports roundup twice a night, every night. The team had big personalities. And it won—a lot. The Pistons became like a part of the family to many Detroit-area residents. When that happened, the team could "get away with anything—good or bad," Wilson said.

The Pistons didn't really fight *that* much. Longtime referee Ed T. Rush deemed Detroit's reputation a marketing tactic. The team got into maybe ten dustups in an eighty-two-game season that featured playoff games. Yes, Dennis Rodman boasted in *Bad Boys* that the Pistons were like a hockey team—the fans wanted to see them fight, but Sperling saw a group of good guys with clean off-court lives. The Rodman best known to the public—the enfant terrible who dated Madonna, wore a wedding dress to a book signing, and dyed his hair like a Haight-Ashbury Easter egg—was years away. On the court, they wanted to win, which meant not getting ejected from games. It was all about *portraying* enforcers and tough guys, though Laimbeer and Rick Mahorn took a more Method approach.* That made the Pistons ideal villains. The Pistons' two NBA championships in 1989 and 1990 enhanced that image.

It wasn't kids who got hooked on the human highlight reels. When he covered the Italian League for a book, journalist Jim Patton grew close to fellow expatriate Mike D'Antoni, a star in Italy after a short-lived NBA career. D'Antoni and his wife, Laurel, let Patton stay in their Milan apartment. The author had Thanksgiving dinner along with former NBA players and their family members. D'Antoni brought out *Superstars*. Many of the players watched the tape. Then they watched

---

* "Bill tried to hurt you," Larry Bird told Bill Simmons during the latter's Grantland days. In the 1988 playoffs, Mahorn kept stepping on the foot Kevin McHale had broken the year before. "We're trying to win the game, and if you've got screws in your foot, hey, it's on you," Mahorn told the *Boston Herald* in 2008.

it again. And again. Patton wished everyone would leave so he could sleep, but he understood the fascination. These men probably watched these great players over and over for the same reason Patton kept re-reading *Light in August*.

Referees also relied on videotape. When Rush worked in the ABA, he had to head to a TV truck to see something. Darell Garretson, the supervisor of NBA officials, had referees bring a VHS player to the arena and plug it into the truck to record the game. Then the refs would take the VHS player back to the hotel to watch the footage.

"There was a sophistication of everything that was done," said Rush, who cited footwork technique as a big example. "That was all because of video."

Video also turned refereeing into a stable profession, Joey Crawford thought. Referees had to beat the tape, because it never lied. Crawford remembered one playoff game where his crew bombed. "Make sure you get to that hotel and you go over that tape and you call me when you're done," Garretson said.

Two hours later Crawford called Garretson.

"How were you?" Garretson said.

"We suck," Crawford said.

"I had you guys down for about fifteen mistakes," Garretson said.

"If you weren't an objective person, and you didn't take that in the proper context, that tape, you weren't going anywhere," Crawford said. "It shows you where you were wrong, why you were wrong. It was a game-changer. Video for us really, really improved everything we were trying to accomplish."

Videotape and Garretson's system for how the referees worked a game—if this is where the ball is, you go here—were invaluable resources. When Crawford started, "you were refereeing by the seat of your pants, by philosophies," he said. "It was insane, because one night you would be with Richie Powers, and the next night you would be with Earl Strom. And you had to ref the way they reffed." Garretson's system eliminated those differences, and video let a referee know if they were following the system. Minus years of tweaks, "that's exactly what we do today," said Crawford.

The casual NBA fan doesn't hear much about Garretson's impact. Stern and Garretson kept these developments private. Crawford has a theory why. For all of Garretson's basketball brilliance, he offended everyone he met. "When you walked away from a conversation with Darell Garretson," Crawford said, "you went, 'I hate that motherfucker.'"

Crawford saw that when Garretson addressed NBA coaches on rule changes. A group of referees attended, but Garretson made it clear that any input from Crawford, Hue Hollins, and the future whistle-toting luminaries would not be welcome when they entered the gym. "Everybody keep your fucking mouth shut when we're in here," Garretson said. "I'm the only one talking."

At the end, the coaches were up to speed on illegal defenses, but "everybody in the stands wanted to fucking kill him," Crawford recalled. Anyone who asked a question was rebuffed with extreme prejudice. "It was almost beneath him," he said. "It was just the strangest thing."

The NBA could afford to have one less goodwill ambassador. The VCR served as an unbeatable marketing tool. That magnificent boxy machine, coupled with a burgeoning slate of international TV programs, brought the NBA to the world.

When he is a teenager in Serbia, NBA tapes pass among Vlade Divac's basketball friends. Though by the time he got one, its quality had been obliterated by repeated viewings—that tape had toured the country's basketball population—Divac revels in how Pete Maravich plays with a freedom he's never known or how Jerry West or Wilt Chamberlain are built for basketball. Divac, a pro player as a teen, will head to America as the newest member of the Los Angeles Lakers, the successor to Kareem Abdul-Jabbar, in 1989. He's drafted by West, the team's astute general manager.

Leigh Ellis, an eleven-year-old from Australia, watches his first NBA game: a recording of the 1987 NBA All-Star Game passed along by his brother. Ripe with stars—Isiah, Jordan, Magic, Bird, Kareem—the game goes into overtime after Rolando Blackman of the Dallas Mavericks cans two free throws with no time left. Ellis is hooked. Afterward, he grows desperate to secure any NBA information. When the Australian Broadcasting Company airs a weekly NBA game, he hits record and watches the contests over and over again. A few years later, he'll record *NBA Inside Stuff*. Or watch the show by himself at 5 a.m. on Saturday. He touts the NBA to any kid who will listen. Years later, Ellis heads to America. He'll cohost a popular cable television show, *The Starters*, and talk to the same men who fueled his love. He'll shoot a couple of free throws in front of Blackman, reenacting the scene that created the life contemporaries covet.

After Joe Bryant's middling NBA career ends, he takes his family to Italy to ply his trade. Bryant's young son can't stay up late to watch NBA games. He relies on his grandparents back in the United States to send him tapes of the games, living and dying with the postman's daily visits. Father and son break down the small, almost imperceptible details that lead to easily understandable greatness. Kobe watches the headliners—Jordan, Bird, Magic, 'Nique. He adds their pieces to his game, like a great DJ sampling the best beats to create a better song.

The Lakers trade Vlade Divac for Kobe Bryant in 1996. Kobe, a seventeen-year-old Jordan acolyte and basketball prodigy, becomes another one-word superstar. Divac resumes a superb Hall of Fame career. The young man who learned English by watching *The Flintstones* will later become the general manager of the Sacramento Kings, a new version of the American dream fulfilled.

Divac and Bryant's crossing was not accidental. Stern had once trumpeted the NBA as America's Game. That would no longer suffice.

IMPORTS AND EXPORTS

The McDonald's Open was an exhibition game in the same way that *The Godfather* is a movie or the Grand Canyon is a crater. And Del Harris, in his first season as the Milwaukee Bucks' head coach, knew it.

The Bucks were the lone American team in the inaugural competition. This was not hooping for diplomacy and conditioning, far from an ideal scenario for Harris. The tournament took place during training camp for NBA teams. He had only five or six practices to get the Bucks into shape with two stars absent (Ricky Pierce was in a contract dispute; Sidney Moncrief was injured). Harris was tasked with winning a tournament rife with international implications during the final days of the Cold War, no less. Today's opponent was the excellent Russian national team anchored by the brilliant Arvydas Sabonis, but Americans didn't acknowledge Europeans as being legitimate players. When the Bucks beat Italy's Tracer Milano, led by former NBA scoring champ Bob McAdoo, by only twelve points, rumblings surfaced that the Soviets might have a chance. Losing this game, Harris thought, would be like losing the Olympics.

That afternoon, Harris didn't have to apologize to David Stern, Ronald Reagan, and Rocky Balboa. First, Sabonis sat out with an injured Achilles' tendon. The Bucks, led by the long-forgotten Jerry "Ice" Reynolds, rolled. The lead swelled to forty points after three quarters. The NBA remained in an enviable position. "You could tell after it was over that the league was very happy with it," Bucks center Jack Sikma said. "They saw that this was a tremendous way to grow the game. I was happy in one respect: the competitiveness was there in each game, and it exposed the fan in the U.S. to just where international basketball was at the time."

That pressure didn't subside in future contests. When the Denver Nuggets played in the 1989 McDonald's Open in Rome, David Stern visited the team's locker room for a talk, remembered All-Star guard Lafayette "Fat" Lever.

"You guys are doing a great job," Stern said. "This is a fantastic trip. It's time to go out and play—and you guys better not lose." Lever got the point. For the NBA to grow, its teams had to beat international competition and show that it was the best basketball league in the world.

This was business. The storied Dream Team of the 1992 Summer Olympics concluded a plan that started years before Charles Barkley elbowed an Angolan and Michael Jordan coyly shielded the Reebok logo on his Olympic warm-up jacket. Millions of Americans had too much fun to see the machinery behind the spectacle.

Basketball coaches and players had spent decades teaching the game to the world's citizens or playing in exhibitions. Bill Russell embarked on a State Department–sponsored tour of Africa in 1959, a restorative experience. Armed with a basketball and a few words, he saw kids enraptured by their introduction to the game. He felt like a magician. Russell, along with Oscar Robertson and Bob Cousy, later toured behind the Iron Curtain in the summer of 1963. In 1979 the Washington Bullets played two exhibition games in China, whose citizens had been introduced to the game via U.S. missionaries in the late nineteenth century.

"We had just normalized relations with China," John Thomson, then counselor for cultural affairs at the U.S. embassy in China, told the *Washington Post* in 2009. "It was a big deal that the team was coming. It was part of the opening up of China."

Agent and Players Association head Larry Fleisher, who loved to travel, organized overseas trips every summer with players as a way to build camaraderie. They'd play games to offset the travel costs, said his son, Marc. One was to China in 1982 for three games. The year before, Marc was there with his client, singer Donny Osmond, who was performing with the Shanghai symphony. Marc Fleisher knocked on the door of the Chinese Basketball Federation and talked to officials about bringing NBA talent over. The Chinese agreed, and ESPN bought the rights. There was a problem: no camera operators knew how to film a basketball game, so the younger Fleisher taught a Chinese cameraman a few words of English—*close-up*—and hoped for the best. "It's one of the worst productions probably ever," Marc Fleisher boasted.

Diplomacy and international fun didn't sell. The members of the Dream Team of the 1992 Summer Olympics didn't turn into celebrities *after* the games. They *arrived* as gods and saw their reputations swell, a perfect illustration of how wide the NBA had spread beyond North America.

"In a world where we all began to realize that nascent technology was taking us outside our borders, David recognized something that nobody else did: there were facilities everywhere in the world where you could play basketball," said Rick White, the former president and CEO of Major League Baseball Properties, who knew Stern. Hockey, White said, didn't have the territorial reach of basketball. Baseball had an odd-shaped playing field, an uneasy fit for buildings or a soccer pitch. Basketball fit into more spaces than a football field. A basketball hoop could go pretty much anywhere, not much equipment was required, and you needed ten people for a game. Fewer worked, too. Three-on-three half-court. Twenty-one. One-on-one. Bliss could be achieved alone, chasing the purity of the swish, intoxicated by the pitter-patter of a ball on asphalt or dirt or hardwood. Not to be overlooked, said Akeem Olajuwon, who first learned the game in Nigeria before his fabulous NBA career, the game was flat-out cool. Olajuwon was initially captivated by how someone could dribble the ball between their legs and behind their back without looking at it.

The NBA needed a platform to sell itself to the world. The McDonald's Open, arranged by Stern and Boris Stankovic, the secretary-general of FIBA (the International Basketball Federation), the governing body for world basketball, pitted NBA teams against international teams in an array of locales. It was "a huge step for the league," said Kim Bohuny, the NBA's longtime international czar. "Because now the head of the NBA and the head of FIBA not only had a warm personal friendship but a great business relationship. Our two leagues have made a commitment to promote the game."

The McDonald's Open established the NBA's international presence and started a relationship with a golden corporate sponsor. McDonald's Europe initiated an agreement with European basketball in the mid-1980s, said Judy Shoemaker, who represented McDonald's when she worked at Frankel & Company, the renowned Chicago-based marketing firm. In Europe, pro basketball was presented much like soccer—a playing field surrounded by advertising, which McDonald's Europe loved. It urged corporate headquarters to get involved with American basketball, thinking it might be a good synergistic opportunity. The NBA made the most sense, said Shoemaker, as college basketball was fraught with complications involving the institutions and the amateur athletes. McDonald's reached out to the NBA to discuss possibilities. One option: a European team would come to the United States or an NBA team would cross the pond.

"The first piece was, get Europe involved and get it on television in Europe, and process it from there," Shoemaker said. The Milwaukee game didn't get a lot of attention or ratings in the United States—but that was secondary. The game got great ratings in Europe. McDonald's was thrilled. "Quite frankly," Shoemaker said, "that led to the next step on trajectory—the first NBA preseason games in Europe." The first three or four years, she said, were all McDonald's.

It was appropriate that Del Harris was here. A basketball lifer, Harris had been exposed to a world of hoops in thirty years, including seven summers coaching in Puerto Rico. The United States' loss to the Soviet Union in the 1972 Summer Olympics may have shocked the world, but Harris knew the Europeans were ready. Wayne Embry, an All-Star center before his lengthy career as a general manager in Milwaukee and Cleveland, was part of another goodwill cavalcade in the late 1960s. In Belgrade, the game was stopped because it was so competitive, he said. Fans threw coins on the court. Jeff Ruland got the same treatment when he played in Barcelona instead of joining the Washington Bullets in 1980. Only the coins were hot. In Rome, a lady hit him over the head with an umbrella. "Oh, it was great," Ruland said.

The USSR's gold medal victory over the U.S. men's basketball team—then all college players—in the 1972 Olympics was defined by its controversial ending(s). Dan Peterson, who enjoyed a lengthy, influential career coaching in Italy, knew the better team won. The USSR led by more than ten points most of the game and outplayed the Americans save for a desperate rally at the end. "Vladimir Kondrashin outcoached Hank Iba, though you cannot say that or people get upset," Peterson said. "Telling it the way it is comes with a price."

A mere twelve years earlier, Peterson said, a U.S. men's team featuring Hall of Famers Jerry West, Oscar Robertson, Jerry Lucas, and Walt Bellamy steamrolled the competition. The gold medal no longer was preordained to the Americans. The United States boycotted the 1980 Summer Olympics held in Moscow, which may have been fortunate. "Trust me," Peterson said. "They would have had a very tough time winning the gold against Yugoslavia, the USSR, and Italy." In 1988, the USSR got another gold medal. The United States settled for a bronze. What was bad for the United States' morale promoted basketball elsewhere. The fate of a country's national basketball team drove the game's popularity, observed Walt Szczerbiak, who enjoyed a starry career as a player and basketball executive in Spain. When that country earned the silver medal in the 1984 Olympics, Szczerbiak saw interest in the game spike.

The Bullets easily beat the Chinese competition in 1979. Larry Fleisher's barnstormers featured Bob Lanier, David Thompson, and Kareem Abdul-Jabbar. Marc Fleisher thought the games would be a breeze, a nice distraction between loading up on cheap souvenirs, sightseeing, and knocking back Moutais. It was not. "The Chinese didn't miss," Fleisher said. "It was absolutely fascinating."

The foreign leagues appealed to U.S. players, said Rich Kaner, the longtime international scout who worked with the Atlanta Hawks. Here was an option if an NBA team lacked interest or offered scant minutes. The play could be very good: Spain, Italy, and Belgium had competitive leagues. The American influx was mutually beneficial, Kaner said. As the foreign players kept facing more talented Americans, their play improved. And former NBA players got to feel like stars. Mike D'Antoni had an uneventful four-year career in the ABA and NBA. Playing for Tracer Milano was better in every way. "I'm running the team, it all depends on me," he said late in his playing career. "It's almost like I'm Michael Jordan. It's fun going into a game knowing you can dominate."

The talent gap inadvertently closed, thanks to college basketball coaches. Today's international basketball clinics feature members of the NBA family, Bohuny said. Before then, college coaches—Bobby Knight, Lou Carnesecca, Dean Smith—taught the game. "What happened is back in the sixties and seventies, a lot of college coaches here would invite foreign coaches to come in to watch practices," Harris said. "At the same time, the Europeans—not the Asians—and the South Americans were hungry to know about basketball. In those days, you didn't have the television." These coaches learned the game through magazine articles by American coaches and clinics or camps, where the attendees got a treat. When Harris attended clinics in America, coaches hesitated to share substantive strategies. After all, they might see you down the road. That pressure didn't exist overseas. "You never worried about giving away any secrets," Harris said.

Attendees took the clinics seriously. In 1989, Dick Helm and his longtime boss, Cleveland Cavaliers coach Lenny Wilkens, ran one in Granada, Spain, for four hundred young players on about twenty courts. The players were so focused on shooting, "they'd beg you to see if they were doing it correctly." The European players, Helm thought, were desperate to hone their fundamentals. American players tried to beat with you their athleticism. The Europeans were getting better, and there were more of them, Szczerbiak said. Europe had replenished its population after the casualties of World War II and other battles. The new generation had access to better nutrition. When Szcbzerbiak, a George Washington University star, came to Spain in the 1970s, he could only find evaporated milk.

Though there was hometown pride, the appeal of the NBA was international. That was confirmed when the McDonald's Open, led by the Boston Celtics, visited Madrid in 1988. What stuck with Nathaniel S. Butler, the longtime NBA photographer, wasn't that the Spaniards knew Bird; they knew *everything* about him. "That was just the most mind-blowing experience, because I didn't know how big the NBA was or if it was big at all in Europe," said Andrew D. Bernstein, another NBA Photos icon. "Driving into the arena, the first day, it was raining. And there were, I don't know, five hundred to six hundred fans standing outside all in Larry Bird jerseys—fathers and sons and grandfathers."

The spread of cable brought American culture with it, but Stern thought more was possible. For years, the NBA used sports agencies to sell their games overseas. Sandy Brown did that at ProServ. Stern thought the league could eliminate the middleman, so the NBA hired Brown in 1989. "He was the first one to do it," said Brown. Mere weeks into his time at the NBA, Brown had to travel to MIPCOM, the big programming convention in Cannes, France. Before the trip, Stern spent two invaluable hours preaching the gospel—"the NBA according to David Stern"—to the young employee. The game is global, he told Brown. We're selling the greatest athletes in the world, and we can slice and dice this content any which way. No one should be beholden to one particular form of content.

"I will never forget that as long as I live," Brown said.

Brown had a good trip, but the second year was a barrage of meetings, about one every half hour, over three or four days. "It's like anything else: you tell enough people about a certain thing and tell it in a certain matter, and people are going to drink the Kool-Aid," Brown said, "and we had them drinking the Kool-Aid." As of 2018, NBA games and programming were available in 215 countries and territories in fifty languages.

What drove demand internationally, besides enthusiasm and customer service, was customization, Brown said. The NBA didn't give the world one game a week and call it a day. It offered an international highlight show that provided a magnificent option for advertisers like Nike with global reach. It offered the opportunity for programming featuring voice-overs in the market's native language. The game's popularity overseas came from the same source as the United States: the players. Viewers wanted to see the personalities, led by Michael Jordan, and hear what they had to say.

According to David Schreff, Stern's "number-one word"—or three—"at the time was global, global, global. We had to make sure that the teams, who, of course, are the shareholders after all, were successful in adopting and adapting both the Disney model, while at the same time, making sure that the international television—the capability for our athletes to shine across two hundred–plus television markets—was there. All of this was done in parallel." By the Dream Team's arrival, Schreff said, "we were ready."

International professional players—Olajuwon, Jamaica's Patrick Ewing, and Germany's Detlef Schrempf starred at American colleges—came into the NBA in dribs and drabs. One of the first drafted by the NBA was Dino Meneghin, a twenty-year-old, 6'9" banger from Real Madrid. The pick was a low-risk proposition for Atlanta Hawks general manager Marty Blake, who later became the NBA's scouting director. Meneghin was the Hawks' eleventh pick. He never got a phone call and Atlanta's owners forbade Blake to sign a European. In a career that ended in 1994, Meneghin, basketball's George Burns, never played in the NBA.

"He was a great rebounder, a great defensive player," Blake said. "Anybody who said he wouldn't have been a great power forward in the NBA doesn't know what he's talking about." Del Harris agreed: "Dino Meneghin could have played here anytime."

Eastern Europe had the most NBA-caliber talent. National teams visited the United States regularly for exhibitions. "They would come every year and a lot of college and pro scouts were saying, 'In Eastern Europe, there is so much talent. How can we have access to it?'" said Bohuny, whose involvement in international basketball goes back more than thirty years. The USSR's much-publicized centralized system contributed to athletic dominance. "You had sports schools in every province that were well-funded, well-coached," Bohuny said. "It was very systematic. They would go to the primary schools and they would look for the best athletes, and they would do tests." Giving a kid a bone density test to see if he'd grow tall was done to bring glory to Russia.

Thus the Atlanta Hawks' 1988 trip to the Soviet Union became a major plot point in the NBA's expansion plan cum intercontinental love story. The trip came about because Hawks owner Ted Turner had a good relationship with Soviet officials. The Goodwill Games, an ersatz Olympics that Turner created, launched in Moscow in 1986. The Hawks and some Soviets had practiced with each other and played semipro teams across the United States the year before, an arrangement bereft of international incidents. The Hawks also kept a keen eye abroad. The team drafted Eastern European stars Sabonis and Alexander Volkov and courted Sarunas Marciulionis, a future Hall of Famer.

Stan Kasten, the Hawks' longtime general manager, didn't bow to isolationist thinking. "There was nothing about our humble, little continent that could dictate that physical specimens born here were the only people who could play basketball," he said. Plus, "we had the right colors," Atlanta Hawks head coach Mike Fratello quipped, referring to the team's red uniforms.

The 1987 Soviets-Hawks squad, organized through the proper channels, was another way to thaw the ground for an Eastern Europe–NBA pipeline, said Bohuny, then manager of research for the Goodwill Games. In talking to the Soviet Olympic Committee, Bohuny felt the Soviets were ready to lift its ban restricting movement to the United States. "It didn't make sense for their athletes not to have the chance to make money," she said. The decision had to come from a higher power.

What worked in the Russian players' favor was their coach, Aleksandr Gomelsky, had accepted a coaching job in Western Europe. He wanted the same freedom for his players. Bohuny talked to players and coaches on the Russian team; the agreement was clear: if the USSR basketball team won the gold medal in the 1988 Summer Olympics, Gomelsky would make sure his players could play abroad.

Volkov, a star Russian player, dreamed of the NBA, but kept silent for fear of embarrassing himself. It sounded so ridiculous. Volkov's first trip to the United States took place in 1983 for a tournament against AAU teams. Because of sanctions, the flight couldn't land in the United States. The plane trip went from Russia (two stops later) to Montreal to Boston to New York City. It was incomprehensibly dark when the Russian team arrived at a Holiday Inn. They were half-past-dead. But there was a plus. The Soviet teens got to sample the forbidden cuisine of the East: McDonald's complete with Cokes. "It was a big deal for us," Volkov said. Then they turned on the TV. There it was. NBA basketball.

"We forgot about sleeping," Volkov said.

Volkov was transfixed. "I thought I came to another planet," he remembered. The style of play, the raucous crowds, the refereeing. Who knows when he'd ever see this again, let alone face Bird and Magic, the two players he immediately identified as his favorites.

"If someone told me I would play against them, and guard them, and score against them, I would not believe them," Volkov said.

The three games were held in the middle of the summer, and initially the Hawks players were not thrilled to make a long, amenities-free off-season trip. It was mostly "patchwork summer league–type guys," said Kasten. Veteran forward Kevin Willis was ordered by Turner to go; superstar Dominique Wilkins suffered a twelve-hour wait in Moscow after a missed connection. By the third game, Jack McCallum, who covered the spectacle for *Sports Illustrated*, noted that the Hawks resembled "a club in a hurry to get home."

With Volkov, Marciulionis, and Sabonis, the national team boasted "three legit NBA players and NBA players right then, not as far as 'They're going to be drafted in three, four years down the line. They're going to be able to compete,'" said Lee Douglas, an Atlanta Hawks executive. The three games were decided by five total points; the Russians won the final contest.

"I scored thirty-seven points, and the game was broadcast live on TBS," Volkov said. "When you score thirty-seven points against an NBA team and that game is broadcast live in the United States, you start to feel something different after that game."

With the NBA making its intentions with Eastern Europe clear, the first domino had fallen. The Soviets secured their mobility by winning gold in the 1988 Olympics, and glasnost-sponsored talent mixed with good old-fashioned history altered the NBA's ethnic makeup forever. But pushing jet-lagged NBA players to the limit on the Soviets' turf was a compromised victory. The foreign players—the ones not groomed at American colleges—had to succeed on the NBA's terms. The first wave of high-profile imports arrived in 1989. Russian national teammates Volkov, who headed to Atlanta, Marciulionis, Serbian center Vlade Divac, and Croatian shooting guard Drazen Petrovic made NBA rosters. Out of the quartet, Divac had the biggest immediate impact as a key contributor for the Magic Johnson–Pat Riley Lakers, the NBA's glitziest franchise.

Divac, a first-round draft pick, didn't feel pressure. If he stumbled, he'd return to Europe and resume his pro career. Divac spotted the differences when he faced the Celtics in the McDonald's Open a year earlier. NBA players were in better shape. When he came to the NBA, the game's physicality and fast pace surprised him. The style of basketball he and his former teammates played compared to the NBA were "two different sports."

Luckily, Divac "came to the best organization in the entire sports world. The Lakers, they really took the time and focused on my development to make me an NBA player." Divac felt like he belonged in the NBA by midseason. His stellar play provided a huge boost to the international player's NBA reputation, Sandy Brown thought. Not that Divac had an option: "Playing with Magic and all those guys, there's no way you can't succeed," he said. "They'll make you be part of it." NBA scouts stepped up their presence beyond the fifty states. Eric Fleisher, who represented Divac and a crop of Lakers, knew the criticisms. The European players weren't tough enough or serious enough— they smoked cigarettes!—to thrive in the NBA. They couldn't speak English, so they couldn't bond with their teammates. Part of Divac's success, Fleisher believed, was that he quickly adapted to life in America, and in Los Angeles no less. Marciulionis meanwhile deflated the notion of the soft European player. "He was more physical than any guard in the league," said Chris Mullin, Marciulionis's All-Star teammate at the Golden State Warriors. He recalled Scottie Pippen and Michael Jordan, two exceptional defenders, arguing one game over who *wouldn't* cover the pesky, bulldozing Lithuanian. When Petrovic* hit the weight room and turned into a sharpshooting star for the resurgent New Jersey Nets, the image further improved.

"We opened all of Eastern Europe to the NBA, which had a major impact," Bohuny said. Once more talent from Europe arrived, she said, every team had scouts in Europe and all over the world. At the start of the 2019–20 season, the NBA had 108 players from 38 countries or

---

*Petrovic reached the cusp of stardom, making the All-NBA third-team in 1993. That June, the twenty-eight-year-old died in a car accident on a rain-soaked autobahn en route to a game in Munich. Petrovic, according to his biographer Todd Spehr, was a passenger and likely asleep when the speeding Volkswagen Golf slammed into a stopped truck.

foreign territories. Victor de la Serna, the Spanish basketball journalist, said that today's NBA foreign player does not have to dominate international competition for years. An NBA drafting an unproven foreign talent is now normal.

Today NBA teams have an infrastructure in place to help foreign players adjust to life in America. That did not exist in 1989. Head coach Mike Fratello tutored Volkov on "basketball language" and slowed down his speech so Volkov could understand English. Fratello was always available to help and made him aware of that offer. The coach became like a father to Volkov. "He invited me to Christmas at his house," he said. "If I had some problem not in basketball, but in life, he always came to my house to help me. His wife took care of my wife. And I became part of his family, basically, up to now." Volkov and his wife, Alla, grew to love Atlanta. It became a second homeland. Their oldest daughter, Anastasia, attended Auburn. Volkov became a huge football fan, who went "crazy" when the New England Patriots overcame a twenty-five-point deficit to beat his Atlanta Falcons in Super Bowl LI.

Like Volkov, Divac got help from his new team. Mychal Thompson invited Divac into his home; Mark McNamara taught his young teammate English; A. C. Green, a born-again Christian who remained a virgin until his 2002 marriage, helped him navigate the NBA lifestyle.

The European players' arrival in America resonated across the ocean. Bohuny noticed that with Marciulionis, a Lithuanian. "Everyone in his homeland, any game they could see, any article they could read, there was a tremendous sense of pride," Bohuny said. But it was also a hook. Schreff didn't understand Stern's strategy in turning the NBA into a global entertainment brand until he asked why the NBA was enamored with Detlef Schrempf. He's an All-Star, but not a superstar. We're building a game of the week that's for a key television network in Germany, Stern responded, and a lot of games feature Schrempf.

"I understood how these scouting and recruiting of international athletes was playing to that overall integrated marketing and media models," Schreff said. Jordan was an attraction anywhere, but sending games featuring teammate Toni Kukoc to Croatia proved an effective way to build an international fan base. Around the world, everyone wants the hometown boy to do good. Reinis Lācis, a twenty-five-year-old basketball journalist from Latvia, said people stayed up late to watch Andris Biedriņš play for the Golden State Warriors, who debuted in 2004. He paved the way for Kristaps Porzingis, who is now arguably the country's most popular athlete.

The highlight shows, *Inside Stuff*, the advertising partnerships—everything was tied toward attracting a key demographic. "That's how we built it," Schreff said. "I think it was pretty clear at the time we were never going to conquer—not that we needed to—soccer as the global sport because they had a big head start overall. But we said, 'Let's focus on age thirty or less or better yet, twenty-five or less, and let's work there, because the kids will want us eventually, perhaps maybe not more than soccer, but maybe as much.' And lo and behold, twenty years later, what do you see? Basketball and soccer are neck and neck—not in overall audience—but with the younger audience as far as participation and interest."

Steve Koonin, the former Turner Sports and Coca-Cola executive, saw Stern use the NBA and its players to enter the international market before the game itself. Marketing and advertising whet that consumer's appetite. Stern, he thought, invented "virtual consumption." Ninety-nine percent of NBA fans outside North America will never set foot inside an arena. But they'll buy merchandise, watch games on TV, play video games, and now subscribe to digital NBA packages. "All of the ancillary elements around the game allow you to take the game global," Koonin said.

The international scene impacted the NBA beyond imported talent. Dan Peterson hosted NBA coaches in Italy, including Pat Riley, who bonded with Peterson over pasta and basketball. Mike D'Antoni took Peterson's lessons to America and fielded successful teams in Phoenix and Houston built around ball-dominant guards Steve Nash and James Harden. Whether you call it entertaining or a scourge, the Euro Step, a sidestepping variation on the traditional two-step trip to the hoop, "was normal in Europe, especially in Yugoslavia," said Vlade Durovic, who played and coached throughout Europe and used the move himself in the 1960s. It is now as big a part of the current NBA experience as T-shirt cannons and Red Panda.

And there was another, less publicized import. NBA Properties' Judy Shoemaker was in Madrid for the 1988 McDonald's Open when she met with a representative from Dorna.

"I want to show you something," the rep said. "You're with the NBA, right?"

It was a sign that spun through advertisers. That equipment would provide arenas with a ridiculous amount of ad space. Shoemaker loved the idea and shared it with the NBA. Stern and Welts didn't jump right away, so Shoemaker took it to her old boss and mentor Bud Frankel, who successfully negotiated with Dorna. By the early 1990s, those rotating signs proved inescapable at NBA games, and offered a glimpse into the NBA's business philosophy. Welts and Stern, Shoemaker said, didn't want the NBA to resemble European soccer, which was surrounded by advertisers. They wanted to give sponsors recognition without becoming too commercial. "You have to have some sensibility about it," Shoemaker said. "You can't line the whole basketball court with signs." The technology got massaged into the NBA experience.

That fine-tuned passion would soon turn the NBA into a game for the world. But in 1989, the NBA had important business to settle at home.

The league's contract with CBS was set to expire. Stern's patience already had.

READY FOR PRIME TIME

First came the jubilation; then came the wake.

The Detroit Pistons' victory over the Portland Trailblazers in five games for thier second straight championship, set off a raucous, champagne-soaked celebration, punctuated with references to MC Hammer's rap smash "U Can't Touch This." It marked the end of two nascent dynasties, not counting Hammer, who had "2 Legit 2 Quit" and a gig hosting *Saturday Night Live* left in him. Dampened by injuries, age, and Michael Jordan's emergence as a player who trusted his teammates and his coaches, the Bad Boys were done.

CBS knew its fate. The previous November, it had been outbid to carry the NBA by NBC. Game 5 of the 1990 Finals would be the last NBA game CBS televised. The news devastated Mike Burks, lead producer for *The NBA on CBS*. "It had been our life for so long, and then it's gone," he said. Burks was there when few cared about pro basketball. He had put all his energy into the NBA, and watched it grow into something that excited people. Now it was over, like a marriage where one day one spouse coldly announces to the dedicated, stunned other that it's time to move on. What was he supposed to do now?

The Pistons' victory party gave way to an after-party that stretched into the next day. "Everybody's feeling their pain, congratulating and thanking each other not just for the series, but the long ten years," Burks said. Away from the emotional fray, he hung out with Pistons stars Joe Dumars and Isiah Thomas, two of his favorites. He put his hand on their shoulders.

"I'm going to miss you guys," Burks told the men.

It was five in the morning. The day's first light was emerging.

By 1989, the NBA had achieved a milestone deemed absurd less than a decade ago: it was a desirable television property. A large part of that came from the work of CBS Sports. Its coverage had given life and verve to NBA games. They had become attractions worthy of the TV-savvy superstars. The NBA and CBS folks got along great. David Stern built the league around the endless marketing of a dynamic class of players.

The NBA was ready to be the star of a network's sports programming.

CBS was reluctant. NCAA men's basketball proved its Nielsen power after the highly watched 1979 championship game that spawned the Bird-Magic narrative. Van Gordon Sauter, then the president of CBS Sports, wanted to push into college sports. NCAA basketball was a top priority. In March 1981, Sauter landed the rights for the NCAA Tournament, a three-year, $48 million deal. The door opened after NBC, college basketball's home, wanted to put some tournament games on during prime time. Walter Byers, the NCAA's executive director, refused—then offered a one-year deal for the tournament at a higher price. The NBC negotiators responded by walking out.

"I viewed them as entirely different entities," Sauter said. "One was not taller, faster, more spectacular than the other. They were just different products. College basketball had a cachet. It had a large following, but I never thought NBC was doing that well with the games in terms of the production and the promotion. We worked very hard at that. We caught that sport as it began to really emerge as a powerhouse."

Advertisers knew the games were being watched by young males, making college basketball "an incredibly valuable product," Sauter said. There was an excitement the sport possessed that the NBA lacked. "You sold magic as much as you sold the numbers," Sauter said. Look at the 1981 NBA All-Star Game in Cleveland. He was there. It was pretty good; the press covered it with gusto. The crowd cheered when appropriate. But "it didn't have any of that energy that drove college basketball," Sauter said. "That energy was a bonus to the ratings."

NCAA games had a certain appeal to advertisers, said Joe Abruzzese, the veteran ad executive at CBS. For example, if Georgetown was playing, an advertiser thought it would reach Georgetown alums—who were more affluent than the audience watching an NBA game.

Because the network had the NCAA and NBA television rights, CBS "owned basketball," said Len DeLuca, vice president of program planning at CBS Sports in 1989. "Period." The NCAA Tournament became a ratings powerhouse. "We gradually increased our coverage," said Neal Pilson, then president of CBS Sports. "We got rid of ESPN, so that we ended up doing every game. By the late 1980s, we had a terrific property in the NCAA Tournament and the NBA was doing very well for us as well."

Stern fumed. Forget that the NBA playoffs ruled CBS in May and June. He loathed losing three weeks of televised games to the NCAA Tournament. The NBA had been cooperative. To sweeten CBS's coverage and improve ratings in the early 1980s, the NBA had scaled back its cable television coverage. To no longer be the victims of May sweeps, the NBA had started its season later, which gave CBS riveting live programming with Magic and Bird. Cable understood the value of the NBA. When Ted Turner launched TNT in October 1988, NBA games—along with movies Turner owned from the MGM–United Artists library—were the attractions for a channel that started with 30 million subscribers. Both were "fuel for the growth of TNT," said Arthur Sando, the vice president of marketing and communications for Turner Broadcasting System.

Nothing sat well with Stern, an "extreme advocate for the NBA and its properties," said Jay Rosenstein, then vice president of programming at CBS Sports. He once was saddled with showing Stern CBS's new promotional campaign for the NBA Finals. The promo ran. Stern looked at Rosenstein, looked at his staff—"They were all kind of afraid of him, because he could do a dance," Rosenstein recalled—and delivered his verdict.

"The ball they're using for this, it's not an NBA ball," Stern said.

Stern had led the NBA's rise as a business and cultural power by abhorring complacency in anyone—his employees, his corporate partners, himself. He wasn't going to back off now, not with the NBA's network television exposure stagnating.

He made his move.

"Pilson, you're going to have to choose between us and the NCAA basketball tournament," Stern said. "We don't want to go dark for three weeks in March and play second fiddle while you guys run around the country trumpeting the NCAA basketball tournament."

"Jesus, David," Pilson said. "This gives you great promotion."

"No, it doesn't," Stern said. "You don't promote us within the tournament."

The NCAA prohibited CBS from doing that, Pilson said. The NBA and NCAA had a "binding distrust of each other," DeLuca said. "Walter Byers was a brilliant leader but had a blind spot about professional basketball." NCAA basketball did offer continuity: a basketball fan could track a college basketball star on Saturday afternoons and March Madness for four years right into the NBA. All on CBS. Pilson didn't want to lose the NBA.

Numbers led to the decision. In 1989, CBS retained its deal with the NCAA for $1.06 billion over four years. "The consensus within the company—particularly from the affiliate relations department—[was] we may have twenty or twenty-five affiliates who love the NBA," Pilson said, "but we have two hundred affiliates who love the college game because the college game reaches out to states and parts of the country that the NBA doesn't reach." Plus, said Rosenstein, the single-elimination aspect of the tournament made every game dramatic and engaged the whole country. Those hooks—plus the fact that the NCAA Tournament's ratings were "far higher" than the NBA's—made it a dream product for the sales team.

It was in CBS's best interest to prioritize NCAA basketball. "David, we will make you an offer," Pilson told Stern. "We're not willing to just walk away. But we're not giving up the tournament."

Stern had almost walked away from CBS. ABC, which saw past "Roone's Revenge" to the $15 million CBS cleared annually from the NBA, made a play in 1985. Jim Spence, the senior vice president of ABC Sports, negotiated with Stern and NBA officials and felt he was close to a deal.

"It wasn't so much CBS's coverage," Spence said. "David was very attracted to the point that ABC Sports did not have basketball. CBS had the NCAA contract, and obviously that was a major commitment on the part of CBS Sports, and so necessarily a lot of their efforts were put toward NCAA basketball, whereas if the NBA came to ABC Sports that was our only basketball package." Spence said that the network was committed to put NBA games on late Sunday afternoons from the start of the regular season through the playoffs. It would put its top people like Keith Jackson on the broadcasts and promote the games to death. The price was right, thought Roone Arledge, who still ruled ABC Sports: 160 games over four years for $160 million.

"If any deal was a sure thing," Arledge wrote, "this was it."

ABC's new owner, the economical Capital Cities, was less enamored. It was not keen on the escalating rights fees for sports, more so since they feared a big payday for the NBA would drive the NFL's rights fees. Spence scoffed at that notion. The NFL and NBA were separate entities, he said. The NFL commanded a fortune compared to the NBA. To think "that the NFL was going to be impacted by what the NBA did is ridiculous." Then there was the revival of an old issue. The increased money, Cap Cities thought, would lead to increased drug use among NBA players. Spence thought a broadcast company concerning itself with a sport's drug policy was absurd. That was the NBA's domain, and Spence knew how aggressive the league policy was. Cap Cities' pretzel logic twisted on. Right before Christmas 1985, Arledge brought the deal to his boss, ABC president Frank Pierce, who sent it to Cap Cities' Tom Murphy and Dan Burke. The result came back later that afternoon: a hard, nonnegotiable no.

"What?!" Arledge said. Pierce had expected instant approval.

Murphy, Pierce explained, wanted to "send a message": ABC "won't be taken for granted anymore" when it started coming in second on bids.

"If Capital Cities had not have taken over ABC, I would have been able to close that deal with Stern very, very quickly," Spence said. He asked Stern, whom he respected, for more time to talk sense into everyone, including Arledge. "I felt personally so strong that this was the right thing for ABC Sports," Spence said. He finally had to deliver the reality to Stern, "one of my real regrets" of his time at ABC Sports. CBS reclaimed the television rights for the NBA for $176 million through the 1989–90 season and earned a reprieve it could not sustain.

*   *   *

"With the acquisition of baseball, CBS Sports secures its position as the undisputed leader in network sports programming," Pilson said in December 1988. "No other network can claim the range and depth of coverage of major sporting events worldwide." Jon Miller, then senior vice president of programming at NBC Sports, thought CBS overbid by $500 million. "They were desperately looking for some programming," he said. "They had an affiliate body that was going through some unrest, and they had not really made any kind of strives in prime time."

The four-year deal was borderline comical: $1.1 billion for twelve regular season games, the League Championship Series, the All-Star Game, and the World Series starting in 1990. Thirty-four games total—and that was if all the postseason series went the distance.

CBS now covered every athletic competition short of Duck Duck Goose. NBC, which shared Major League Baseball with ABC, now had a giant sports programming gap. The network's prime-time schedule was loaded with scripted hits—*The Cosby Show, L.A. Law*, and *Cheers*. (A show about nothing would premiere in July 1989.) With sports, NBC lacked "a cornerstone franchise," said Ed Markey, vice president of sports press for NBC Sports.

Stern felt undervalued at CBS. NBC needed a sports property beyond sharing the NFL. Unlike Arledge and Spence at ABC a few years earlier, nobody was telling Dick Ebersol, the new president of NBC Sports, no. It was corporate kismet.

What worked in NBC's favor, Markey thought, was that the anticipated change in the NBA's power structure devalued the product to some. The Lakers, Celtics, and Pistons featured aging stars. The young contenders hailed from smaller markets: Salt Lake City, Portland, Oregon, and Cleveland. But those teams had great players—John Stockton and Karl Malone; Brad Daugherty and Mark Price; Clyde Drexler. That appealed to Ebersol, who believed stars drove any television program, Markey said. Ed Desser, the NBA's director of broadcasting, diagnosed CBS with "incumbent disorder." It knew the NBA only as a bridge between college, the NFL, and quote-unquote important sports.

"David wanted us to do more," Pilson said. "More games, more cameras, more promotions. He felt CBS didn't promote the NBA." CBS might have ruled network sports, but its crown was festooned with jewels: tennis, college basketball, the Masters, figure skating, and now baseball. The network lacked free hours to give the NBA more coverage, Jay Rosenstein said. And it wasn't as if CBS had a cable network to deposit extra games.

NBC, Desser said, had the advantage of looking at the NBA with a fresh perspective. It could offer the treatment Stern craved. "Now that CBS had baseball," said Jon Miller of NBC Sports, "they would never be able to do what we would for the NBA." At CBS, he added, the idea was to protect *60 Minutes*, a longtime Sunday evening staple. NBC had no sacred cow to fence in; no sports behemoth to placate; the NBA would be "front and center."

The interest of NBC—ABC was also an active bidder, said the NBA's vice president of broadcasting, John Kosner—emboldened Stern. "David took that opportunity to push it from being a completely sports discussion into a sports and entertainment discussion," said Jon Miller, vice president of programming at NBA Entertainment. Stern recognized that Ebersol, who had an entertainment background (he was executive producer on *Saturday Night Live* during Eddie Murphy's heyday), would understand that logic. He did, and brought in Brandon Tartikoff, the head of NBC Entertainment. Stern could get prime-time coverage. He could get a kid's show, which CBS had filmed with announcer James Brown. "David recognized that NBC Sports' hunger to have the property could be translated and expanded to meet his strategic vision," Miller added.

The NBA's contract was inspired by Bryan Burns, the head of

broadcasting at Major League Baseball. Instead of waiting for the network to make an offer, MLB offered packages to bid on. That led to the billion-dollar CBS contract. "We were intrigued at this idea of creating a model contract," Kosner said. "You would have to agree together on the money, but there were all these things that we wanted. It was a masterpiece of detail." One of the conditions was the winning network would produce a studio show in an actual studio, not in front of a wall of monitors, not from courtside.

That kind of contract always upsets the incumbent, Kosner said. That applied to CBS, which had followed baseball's demands. "It was like, 'Okay, we've been in business a long time,'" he said. "'We doubled your rights fee the last time. What do you mean you want so much more?' The reason we wanted so much more is we thought we had earned it." It was the NBA's time, but Kosner thought some at CBS considered the network the NBA's savior. "You know the experience you have," he explained, "where you meet people and their view of you is when they knew you as a kid, but you're an adult now?"

The NBA was all grown up. Ratings for the NBA's games on television increased 21 percent during the 1980s; pro football's and baseball's ratings *dipped* 14 percent and 21 percent, respectively. Average NBA game attendance increased by 42.6 percent. The annual NBA take from its network and cable TV contracts reached $175 million by the decade's end. Gross revenues, which included the sweet plum of NBA-licensed merchandise, would swell from $110 million in 1980 to $1.25 billion in 1990.

David Stern called Ted Shaker, the executive producer of CBS Sports.

"We're going to NBC," Stern told Shaker. "We have to keep moving forward, and they blew you out of the water." NBC's agreement with the NBA, finalized in November 1989, was for $600 million over four years.

Rosenstein recalled CBS offering $525 million. Kosner remembered the bid being between $300 million and $400 million, nowhere close to what ABC and NBC were willing to pay. "When they gave us that $600 million number, we knew we couldn't get there," Rosenstein said. After he delivered CBS's formal offer, Gary Bettman or Russ Granik said, "Well, we have a lot of work to do." That's when Rosenstein knew NBC was waiting.

NBC employees, Ed Markey recalled, discovered their new acquisition when they saw NBA hats hung with care on their office doorknobs. CBS Sports reporter Pat O'Brien was on an airport pay phone when announcer Dick Stockton walked by and delivered the news. "It was like losing my left arm," he said. "Oh, everybody was crushed," said reporter Lesley Visser. There was little changeover at CBS Sports and the NBA teams, she recalled. These men and women became your family.

"I fucking hated it," Shaker said.

Stern was privately triumphant. The NBA was now the star of a Big 3 network's sports coverage. That gave the NBA power. Jim Drucker, the former commissioner of the Continental Basketball Association and then a consultant for the minor league, visited Stern shortly after the NBC deal. What Stern loved most was the half-hour Saturday morning kid's show, which became *NBA Inside Stuff*. Drucker asked why. It's a guaranteed deal, Stern said. NBC can cancel *The Cosby Show* anytime, but *Inside Stuff* was immovable.

"It's going to put us on prime time for children," Stern told a stunned Drucker. "And I'm going to recruit the next generation of NBA fans by giving a program to them, so they'll have their parents take them to games and buy NBA T-shirts."

Desser was more reserved. Late 1989 into early 1990 was devoted to determining what Shaker had created with the NBA television coverage and sharing those assets with NBC to ensure a smooth transition.

What Desser didn't expect was "how Dick Ebersol was going to turbocharge the next wave of the NBA."

NBC had 600 million reasons to cut costs but opened its wallet. It started at the first meeting. For most games, CBS used three or four replay sources. Desser looked at the equipment complement and did a double-take: NBC wanted to use eight—for a regular season game.

"Under Dick's leadership, there was no property that was more important in our arsenal than the NBA, because we would have it exclusively," NBC's Jon Miller said. "We weren't sharing it like we were the AFC package or golf at that time. The NBA was going to be ours and ours alone. So we put everything into it: our best talent, our best producers, our best directors, our best programming time, our best promotional windows, you name it. That was the commitment that he made, and I think we more than lived up to it."

Holy shit, Desser thought. *This is a whole new ball game, folks.*

POSTGAME

The guys I talk to now, they say, "Ah, man. We miss you, Pat. We miss the fraternity. People were looking out for each other."

—PAT O'BRIEN, FORMER CBS SPORTS REPORTER

The good old days mean nothing to me.

—JOEY CRAWFORD, NBA REFEREE, 1977 TO 2016

POSTGAME

IT'S MY GAME NOW

June 2, 1991, Chicago

Journalists, Harvey Araton said, weren't ready to abandon the Lakers-Magic-Celtic-Bird narrative. Game 1 of the 1991 Finals—Magic versus Michael—stalled the inevitable for a day. Johnson got the ball as the last seconds of the fourth quarter raced away. He backed Jordan toward the basket. Center Bill Cartwright came to help Jordan. Magic saw the embryonic double team and whipped the ball over to Sam Perkins, who had enough time to drain a three-pointer with fourteen seconds left. The Lakers led 92 to 91. Jordan had a chance to win the game, but his jump shot rattled in and out with 2.7 seconds to play.

Araton watched on NBC at his friend's daughter's birthday party. Not bound by the journalistic impartiality required by his new employer, the *New York Times*, an ebullient Araton issued a prediction after Perkins's shot rattled through the net.

"Fucking Jordan will never beat Magic!"

Decades later, Araton had a different take. "Talk about clinging to a story line."

The next one would dazzle, too. Jordan and *The NBA on NBC* enjoyed a symbiotic relationship. NBC caught Jordan right as spiritual, cerebral coach Phil Jackson's team-first teachings took hold. The Lakers' Game 1 victory marked the last great moment of Magic Johnson's career as an NBA player. The Bulls, led by a wiser, older Jordan, won the last four games of the 1991 NBA Finals—and dominated a healthy chunk of the decade. The championships legitimized Jordan, but the first one humanized him, thought Howard "H" White, a longtime Nike employee and a member of Jordan's inner circle. The nation saw Jordan battered by the Detroit Pistons, his longtime rival, dig deeper and reach his goal. NBC chronicled the legend from start to finish as part of Ebersol and Stern's grand entertainment experience.

And that included the Dream Team. NBC's endless coverage of the star-studded men's basketball team in the 1992 Summer Olympics was more than a basketball fantasy come to life—*what if the NBA's best players faced the world?*—it was Stern's grandest marketing coup. The games, all artistic massacres, enchanted the globe. "We take a lot of research detail from our international players," the NBA's Kim Bohuny told Jack McCallum in his excellent book, 2012's *Dream Team*. "I can't begin to tell you how many say they started watching basketball at the '92 Olympics."

The most frequent comparison to the Dream Team's presence in Barcelona is the Beatles during its shaggy-haired, teeny-bopper heyday: pure pandemonium and pheromones. "It was bigger than the Beatles on some level, because the Beatles didn't have as many marketing people behind them, and I don't mean that in a pejorative sense," said David Schreff, the NBA's former president of global marketing and media. There was ample time before the Olympics— the first ten players were announced in September 1991—"to plan, fine-tune, figure out the event, and build up the marketing/media/ publicity machine, that of course culminated in Barcelona," Schreff said. The NBA also assembled a roster of sponsors worthy of the team's stars—McDonald's, Coca-Cola, IBM,* AT&T, FedEx, and Kellogg's.

The presence of NBA players in advertising went from athletic wear to consumer products, said Steve Koonin, a former Coca-Cola executive. "That's a massive, massive shift."

"One way we thought would help us stand out against our competitors was through the use of sports marketing," said Mary Reiling Spencer, an AT&T sponsorship and marketing executive. The Dream Team had big names with big talent working together for a big cause. It was too good an opportunity to pass up—not just for customers looking to choose a long-distance provider. AT&T's corporate clients were titans in the business world, Reiling said. Yet when presented with the opportunity to meet Michael Jordan or Larry Bird in an intimate setting, these important men and women were starstruck. Some turned shy and would wait for an intermediary to make the introduction. The players never disappointed. "They were as cordial as can be," said Reiling, who later worked for the NBA. "They knew that the people in that room supported them from a sponsorship perspective, that it was their investment, if you will, in helping promote this new opportunity."

It was irresistible theater: one part rock concert, one part goodwill tour, "and absolutely calculated," Schreff said. "David and Russ and Gary and Rick knew that if we did it right, it would exceed all expectations, and it did." Jim Drucker, the former Continental Basketball Association commissioner, said Stern didn't want NBA players in the Olympics for American pride. "He wanted all the great foreign players to be able to play in the NBA without losing their Olympic eligibility, so that he could sell NBA television rights to TV networks all over

---

*When Schreff told Stern he had secured IBM as the NBA's computing partner, Stern shook Schreff's hand—and pulled him in for a kiss on the cheek. "It was a good kiss," Schreff said.

the world." Stern now had an opening to sell NBA merchandise worldwide. All because someone from Spain or Portugal or Lithuania played in the NBA. Drucker was in awe of Stern's logic.

Of course, Jordan was the star of the Dream Team. He famously reminded his iconic teammates, Larry Bird and Magic Johnson, that their time was up. "This is my game now," Jordan said. NBC Sports was ready. If Ebersol saw sports as a weekly event, then viewers got unbeatable real-life drama for eight months. It usually centered on Jordan. Every season a challenger tried to knock the king from his throne, and almost every year Patrick Ewing or Reggie Miller or Clyde Drexler met the harsh soil of mortality. People tuned in. Game 6 of the 1998 Finals, Jordan's last championship, attracted 72 million viewers. NBC was there for all of it.

The loss of the NBA was unpleasant for CBS and for Neal Pilson, then president of CBS Sports. Stern never let him forget about what slipped away. Baseball, CBS's big investment that cleared the way for NBC's acquisition of the NBA, struck out. The idea, said Joe Abruzzese, a longtime sales executive at CBS, was that the network could sell baseball—specifically the World Series—like a limited-run prime-time series. But the idea backfired. There were a lot of short series. Even in cramming advertising spots, CBS lost money.

The qualities that gave Jordan the ethereal glow of an athletic deity reached everyone, including millions who couldn't afford to see a basketball game. There were basketball cards, videotapes, cable television, *Inside Stuff,* and oh-so-many commercials that presented Jordan as the perfect representative of Stern's all-entertainment NBA. After all, how much do you know about Mickey Mouse? Today, Phil Knight admits most people know Michael Jordan as a brand. He is so removed from the realities of everyday life that as president, Barack Obama viewed Jordan's on-court performance as a role model for leadership. A multiple-level Jordan Brand store now stands in Chicago, complete with a basketball court. To Sonny Vaccaro, who knew Jordan before he became a commodity, the store sounded like a museum.

From the start, NBC Sports was enamored with the NBA. Both parties had weekly lunch meetings to discuss that week's games and beyond. "It was truly something that no one had ever done," said Gil Kerr with NBA Entertainment.

Stern and Ebersol developed a deep rapport, though with the former's nature, that came with qualifiers. "There was no margin for failure or disappointment," said Jon Miller, now president of NBC Sports. "You were not going to let David Stern down because you did not want to be on the other end of that phone call." Stern, said Gregg Winik, one of Barry's sons and another NBA Entertainment mainstay, liked to establish tension in any discussion. He sought to portray himself as someone to be reckoned with. Stern, Winik recalled, arrived at one meeting, grabbed a sandwich, and expressed his dissatisfaction with NBC's pregame show to the responsible party. "So, Mr. Fucking Executive Producer," Stern barked, "what do you have planned for this week?" Executive producers at networks were like gods, Winik thought, and Stern had open-handedly smacked one right in the face. "I didn't know if I fell off my chair or shit my pants," Winik recalled.

Ebersol, handsome in a Newport yacht captain kind of way, loved stories and doing the impossible, said David Gavant, an executive at NBA Entertainment. He found a kindred spirit in Stern, the scrappy kid from Teaneck. "They were both brilliant minds, that's what really attracted them to each other," Gavant added. They talked—or jousted—on the phone incessantly, and even vacationed together. Once Ebersol made the mistake of wearing an overcoat like "something from *The Nutcracker*'s costume department," Gavant recalled. Stern ribbed him about the unfortunate choice. For two years. Stern showed his appreciation for others by busting their balls. This long-term derision was practically an engagement ring.

The changes started well before Marv Albert's first barb at Mike Fratello. Jim Burnette, head of sports sales for NBC, wanted to change how the NBA was sold to potential advertisers. CBS offered the NBA two automobile sponsors. Burnette wanted to get eight exclusive automobile advertisers—or one quarter exclusivity every other game. "What that meant was instead of two automotives in every game," the NBA's John Kosner said, "if you're Mitsubishi, you'd get the first quarter of the first game and the last quarter of the last game." That plan also prevented competitors from colliding into each other.

NBC, said Ed Desser, realized the NBA had been sold at a discount. Spring was when league action peaked: the regular season segued into the playoffs and the NBA Finals. That was also a big car-buying season, a pull for the NBA's young, urban demographic. Desser believed this pattern had been established without provocation. NBC sought to reprice the market—which it ultimately did. "It's much more difficult for the incumbent to do that," Kosner said.

NBC televised the Super Bowl in 1990. Burnette traveled to New Orleans determined to get car companies signed.

"And he did it," Kosner said. "The most amazing thing was about a week after the Super Bowl, there was a terrible recession that hit, and everything got scrambled. I remember thinking to myself that as great as our plan was, as fantastic as the prospects were, if Jim Burnette did not have the presence of mind to come up with a strategy and aggressively go early to lock it up, history might have been different."

Instead, NBC got a $400 million base to launch the NBA package, which became geared toward a general audience. The NBA was off. As part of its NBC deal, the league got to run more promos, including in prime-time. That required something beyond Stern's adored "It's Fantastic" spots. The NBA hired noted advertising firm Goodby, Berlin & Silverstein to come up with ideas. According to the NBA's Judy Shoemaker, the genesis for the new campaign came from Jon Steel, then the firm's director of planning.

Because Stern, Russ Granik, and Gary Bettman were lawyers, Steel took a rational route. He presented a plan that emerged from nationwide focus groups. "It's Fantastic" was fine, Steel said, but it spoke only to the fans. If the NBA wanted to become more popular, it had to approach people who watched the Finals (maybe) or who had never seen an NBA game. Think of the NBA's audience as concentric circles, Steel advised: the further you radiated from the center—the true fans—the less familiarity people had with the NBA. The league needed to bring those outsiders in.

Steel, a Golden State Warriors fan, wasn't a minute into his presentation when Stern interrupted: "What's this? They've got a Limey talking to me about basketball."

"Well, David, I do know the difference between Moses Malone, Karl Malone, and Bugsy Malone," Steel said. "Maybe that qualifies me to talk to you."

"I Love This Game," Shoemaker said, showed how basketball "permeates everybody's life, even if they don't know it," like tossing a wad of paper toward a wastebasket. The campaign attracted new fans and sparked a new element of the NBA brand conversation. The players would sell themselves, Stern thought. It was time to sell *the game* to a prime-time audience. That was vital. Magic Johnson and Larry Bird were nearing retirement, and Jordan had shed his ingénue status.

Ebersol had a different focus, one that was no less effective. "From a TV perspective, the star power was the fuel for a television series," said Ed Markey, a veteran in NBC Sports' PR department. "That's the way they viewed the NBA—as a television series, week to week, leading to a culmination at the end." That notion, Markey added, "was driven by stars, and the NBA had them. And there were going to be more coming." Michael Jordan topped the marquee, but there was Charles Barkley in Philadelphia and later Phoenix, Reggie Miller in Indiana, Larry Johnson in Charlotte, and Orlando's dynamic big man, Shaquille O'Neal—who premiered in 1992 as a full-fledged marketing, rapping force. Year after year, great young players arrived like blockbuster movies or hot holiday toys.

"Coming up next, Allen Iverson and Shaquille O'Neal," said CBS Sports announcer Dick Stockton, referencing NBC's promotional style. "What does that mean? Are they playing each other?"

It became all about the new stars, said NBC Sports' Jon Miller. Once you identified them, "you made sure you saw these guys' faces, you heard their voices." *Inside Stuff* played a huge role. The show was NBC's "thirty-minute promotional opportunity" to highlight the players, Miller said. NBC gave the NBA carte blanche to use any copyrighted music. "It was a luxury to use those lyrical bridges," said Stephen Koontz, the NBA Entertainment producer. "You could segue from segment to segment" and hook multiple generations.

In the 1990s, the NBA, finally, sat at a network's grown-ups table. Characters from NBC shows extolled the game in spots. Jerry Seinfeld riffed on the head fake while watching a game with Elaine Benes; in a spot written by Gil Kerr, Paul Buchman of *Mad About You* dove into the closet to retrieve a series of NBA artifacts, much to the chagrin of his wife, Jamie; the ladies of *Friends* lamented the demise of players in short shorts—but . . . hello, John Stockton?!—while Phoebe Buffay cradled a pristine NBA basketball so the league logo faced the camera.

The promos and the shows merged. "The NBA then was so much a part of pop culture that you'd be watching *Seinfeld* or *Friends* or *ER* or Jay Leno, and promos for the NBA would be running during those programs," said Bob Costas, an announcer and host during *The NBA on*

NBC's run. "Even if you were just a mainstream casual fan, if you were a grandmother from Omaha who didn't know a pick-and-roll from a free throw, you knew who Michael Jordan was. You knew who Charles Barkley was. They were part of the zeitgeist."

A ten-second spot promoting that weekend's game during one of NBC's hit shows drew higher ratings than the game itself, Gavant said.

It was, indeed, a whole new ball game.

The lack of complacency remained.

Bill Daugherty, the former senior vice president of business development, started at the NBA in 1990. Yet, he said, somehow Stern had "everybody coming to work thinking we're going out of business next week." Rick Welts's mantra was "change is good," recalled Kim McBride, an NBA employee from 1990 to 2004. Into the 1990s, part of the NBA's apparently endless gilded age, Welts, then the president of NBA Properties, wanted to re-create the NBA every eighteen months. As the NBA ballooned in size and scope in the 1990s, the corporate culture changed, thought Nancy Fitzpatrick, part of the NBA's old guard. It was more "uptight" and "a little more cutthroat." There was no choice. With a larger number of employees, "things had to change. They needed to be a little more black-and-white, less gray."

Reflection got holstered, Daugherty said, save for one time: the 1997 All-Star Game in Cleveland, a three-day celebration of the league's fiftieth anniversary. "I've never seen our group as happy and self-satisfied just hanging around," he said. The present and the past met in peace. The crowd teemed with legends. The dancing girls and fireworks were sidelined. At halftime, the NBA's fifty greatest players, a flesh-and-blood reminder of the league's evolution, assembled on court. Jordan stood—drenched in sweat, a gift for the present and a fable for the future—with Bird, Magic, Kareem, Moses, and Doctor J. The men who made the NBA. Daugherty's older colleagues, the men and women who gave everything to fulfill Stern's vision of more, who joined the relentless pursuit of perfection, who persisted when nobody believed in them save for each other, exhaled. Paula Hanson, Don Sperling, Brian McIntyre. Steve Mills, Bill Marshall, Leah Wilcox. The men and women who made the NBA.

ACKNOWLEDGMENTS

I never spoke with David Stern. He declined multiple interview requests, including one I made about six weeks before his death. I interviewed some 315 people for this book, many of whom worked for or with Stern. With a few (vitriolic) exceptions, these men and women loved David Stern. It wasn't for his business acumen and inability to tolerate bullshit.

For many former NBA employees who had moved out and on with their professional lives, January 1, 2020, was the day Dad died.

I felt for *them*, because these men and women brought David Stern and his vision to life. I am beyond grateful for the time they spent answering my questions and follow-up questions and, well, follow-ups to my follow-ups. Paul Gilbert ("Didn't we talk about this already?"), Don Sperling, Don Stirling (who *insisted* on follow-up interviews), Judy Shoemaker, Gary Way, and Jon Miller ("That's all I got, Pete.") sat for multiple in-depth interviews. All were terrific. Rick Welts, who has indulged my nostalgic diversions for *years*, and Steve Mills took time from controlling the destinies of billion-dollar franchises to vividly describe life as peons in building the NBA dynasty. Bill Marshall never hesitated in providing a comment or a phone number. Stephen

ACKNOWLEDGMENTS

Koontz, aside from providing referrals, helped me crack the mystery of "Thorough Bread." Bill Jemas helped me understand the salary cap. Rob Millman, who still works at the NBA, detailed his conversion to Stern's vision.

Without Larry O'Brien, there would be no David Stern and no NBA as the world knows it today. To help re-create O'Brien's second career, I am in debt to his son, Larry O'Brien III, who was one of the first people I called. Within a few days, a package arrived with documents and a biographical DVD, essentially a Larry O'Brien starter kit. That would have been enough. Then he let me read his father's unpublished history of his time at the NBA. That was an invaluable resource, in addition to fielding my incessant follow-up emails and phone calls. I'm beyond grateful to Larry and his assistant, the downright decent Marie Quinlan, for hosting me in Washington, D.C., for two days in July 2018. Nick Curran, Joseph A. Califano, John G. Stewart, Jan Akerhielm, Ed Desser, Alex Sachare, Harvey Benjamin, and Ted Van Dyk detailed a great man's overlooked later years. They don't make people as dignified and dedicated as Patricia Gourdine anymore, nor do they make storytellers like Mike Suscavage and Michael Burns either.

In constructing the Larry O'Brien–led NBA, a special thank-you to Barbara Ward, who spent hours recalling her days as a young Katharine Gibbs graduate in the big city with color and candor. She's 100 percent Jersey, the highest compliment this erstwhile Aberdeen boy can provide.

Nike declined to make anyone at the company available to speak after Michael Jordan declined to participate. This was expected. Nike is a world that few strangers are allowed to enter. During reporting, I dropped Mark Thomashow, the retired Nike executive, a line. I didn't know him and had no agenda beyond securing an interview. We talked on FaceTime. Even after expressing consternation about the Walt Frazier Puma poster on my office wall, he decided to participate—and convince others to do likewise.

"I have a pretty good batting average," Mark said.

Mark was Ted Williams hitting a beach ball off a tee. If you see a source associated with Nike's rise in this book, including Tinker Hatfield, Phil Knight (who talked twice), and Bill Davenport, it's likely because Mark vouched for me. If I ever have a second child, Thomashow Croatto is officially in committee.

Though I enjoy rap—"Parents Just Don't Understand" was my jam in the summer of '88—I needed an education. Ryan Flanders introduced me to Kenny Keil, who introduced me to Patrick A. Reed, a hip-hop historian who was beyond helpful in sharing his contacts and knowledge. Thanks to Eric Aiese, one of my favorite people on the planet, and Daniel Sozomenu, a friend dating back to my bad goatee days, for the music history tutorial.

There's no way I could have written about the NBA's time on CBS without Ted Shaker. His enthusiasm for the project was unflagging. Thank you as well to Dick Stockton (who *sang* me *The NBA on CBS* theme song), Suzanne Smith, Bob Stenner, Mike Burks, Len DeLuca, Lesley Visser (I was seventeen when the Boston Garden closed, Lesley! And a Knicks fan!), Jay Rosenstein, John Kosner, and Pat O'Brien. When it came to cable television's early days on the national and regional side, Tony Acone, Kay Koplovitz, Jim Zrake, Jody Shapiro, and especially Bob Sieber provided enlightening insight.

For those who helped in ways big and bigger, thanks galore (in no particular order) to Bill Fickett, Phil Chenier, Mark Eaton, John Gaffney, Bobbito Garcia, John A. Walsh, Del Harris (a true gentleman), Charles Grantham, Doug Adkins (a class act), Rich Kaner, Lon Rosen (the earliest advocate), George Krieger, Susan Hagar, Colleen Miller (the pride of the CBA), Joe Cohen, Geoff Belinfante, Sean Williams, Cameron Ballard, Raymond Ridder, Nick O'Hayre, Dan Schoenberg,

ACKNOWLEDGMENTS

Lisa McKillips, Scott Bedbury, Kenny Mauer, Stan Kasten, Jimmy Smith, Donna Orender (who took a call as the Sacramento airport literally crumbled around her), Jon McGlocklin, Jade-Li English, John O'Neil, Marc Fleisher, Andy Dolich, Tim Frank, Bill Hofheimer, Steve Patterson, Tom Wilson, Alexander Volkov, Russ Bengtson, Pam Greaney, Peter Vecsey, Charley Rosen, Ed Markey, Nathaniel S. Butler, Hugh Dodson, Sondra Murphy, Jennifer Keishin Armstrong, and Joanne Borzakian Ouellette.

Thank you to anyone who provided a phone number, answered an email, or talked to me on or off the record. Every conversation led to clarity. And, boy howdy, did I need it. To quote Sonny Vaccaro: "You're writing *War and Peace* here." Thanks to Sonny as well.

Being a freelance writer can be lonely, but not when you have allies aplenty: a Bobby Jones finger-point to Seimond London, Jancee Dunn, Patrick J. Sauer, Jen A. Miller, Will Leitch, Adam J. Criblez, Howie Kahn, Ryan Jones, Todd Spehr, Vince Guerrieri, Lindsay Champion, Brian Hiatt, John Thorn, Alan Siegel, Molly Sullivan French, Greg Hanlon, Alex Belth, Sam Borden, Trina McKenna, and Kent Babb. Jeff Pearlman remains a mentor despite his best judgment. Jonathan Eig didn't know me at all, but spent a half hour dissecting a sample chapter, an incomprehensible act of kindness. I do know Erik Malinowski, author of the definitive book on the modern-day Golden State Warriors, *Beta Ball*. He provided insight on the beautiful monotony of book writing.

A nice chunk of this book came about because of previous articles I've written. For their patience, guidance, and employers' money, I want to thank Ming Wong, Ben Osborne, Adam Figman, Sarah Larimer, David Roth, and James Montgomery. I also want to give a hearty shout-out to Lauren Roberts, the editor in chief of the late, great BiblioBuffet. She gave me a column reviewing sports books that made me think deeper about the games people play, but she helped me find confidence I had lost.

I wouldn't be a sports fan at all if the Zailskis hadn't introduced that joy into my life when I was six years old. Thanks to Coach, Aunt Linda, Chris, and Amy.

And I wouldn't be a writer without Dr. Bob Cole (RIP), Professor Kim Pearson, Dr. Jo Carney, and Professor Barry Novick at the College of New Jersey.

I had finished my story for Grantland on Marvin Gaye's national anthem, and I was texting with Lon Rosen, a key source and a constant help since. Sounds you like got a book here, he wrote.

That was in February 2013.

Mark Rotella, my friend and a veteran author, shared my enthusiasm. He counseled me on how to write a proposal, offered suggestions, and introduced me to his agent. His confidence sustained me. The American Society of Journalists and Authors hosts an indispensable annual conference. I pitched my idea to several agents there. John Bowers at the Bent Agency took a shot.

Then John, who was wonderful, left. Thankfully, Louise Fury stepped in. She had unerring faith in my idea and didn't treat me like a hand-me-down. She was *relentless*, and it resulted in a deal that gave me the freedom to focus on writing, researching, and pestering strangers from coast to coast. Louise also whipped the proposal into shape with help from her husband, Shawn, who wrote a great book on the history of the jump shot, *Rise and Fire*. He also wrote a fascinating article for VICE Sports on the rise of NBA Entertainment and graciously shared his contacts and his terrific one-on-one interview with David Stern. His enthusiasm and support kept me aloft.

Todd Hunter at Atria originally championed this book. Then Todd, who was wonderful, left. Rakesh Satyal took over, a daunting prospect for a ham-and-egger such as myself. Have you read Rakesh's novel, *No*

ACKNOWLEDGMENTS

One Can Pronounce My Name? I worried for nothing. He urged me to have each chapter serve as a word in a sentence, a simple piece of advice that improved the narrative tenfold and spared readers a painful first-person aside involving the 1992 Summer Olympics. He gave me space to be myself, while providing thoughtful commentary throughout. That Rakesh reviewed what I wrote made me work harder. Part of it was his unquestioned ability as a writer; the other part was he wasn't a sports fan. Loan Le, an associate editor and Rakesh's lieutenant, was a calm and steady presence as the book inched closer to reality. This book is better because of their care.

I'm most thankful of all to my family, starting with my parents, Dot and Lou. And not because they bought the books.

Mom, a former editor at McCormick-Mathers Publishing Company, taught me how to write by editing each paper, every movie review, every wobbly short story. She cared about every word and taught me to care about the little things. Those lessons apply to life as well, and I had the best teacher. Because of her, I am a halfway decent writer and (I hope) a better person.

Dad's gestures are small but pack a wallop. In 2006, when I was stuck at a torturous magazine gig, he took me out to dinner and yanked me toward sanity. "This job is making you miserable and everyone around you miserable." In 2009, when I was spiraling into an unemployable liberal arts cliché, he looked at me and said, "If you were doing something wrong, I'd tell you." A talented craftsman, he let me tag along as an untrained assistant and paid me $100 a day—which I desperately needed—to fall asleep in his Subaru Forester and hand him the wrong tools. When his longtime friend Stuart Barish mentioned that his next-door neighbor worked for the *New*

York Times, Dad launched into publicist mode. A ferocious reader, he urged me to expand my literary horizons beyond *The Pete Rose Scrapbook.* He's my hero.

I have one brother, and I'm thankful every day that it's Dave Croatto. He's been there through everything and has gotten me through all of it. When I hemmed and hawed about leaving that toxic trade magazine gig in 2006, he pushed me out the door. "I will pay you $10,000 if you leave," he told me. Dave didn't do that. He simply paid my cell phone bill for two years—and never asked for a dime. He treated me to lunches and gave me countless pep talks. Most important, he had the good sense to marry Darcy Savit Croatto, the sister I never had.

That's enough good fortune for any person. But in July 2008, I met a pretty, whip-smart brunette who reeked of presence and teemed with decency. She was a doctoral student with boundless potential. In a month, thanks to the Great Recession, I was eating instant oatmeal for dinner and crying in frustration. Yet she stuck around. This book does not get written without my wife, Laura Amoriello. She is my best friend, my confidante, and the person who inspires me every day. I love you, Laura.

I love you, too, Livvy. Thanks for the hugs, the inquiries about my "white book," the office visits, and for being as curious and spirited and hilarious as Mom. You're truly fantastic.

Dryden, NY
2-3-20

BIBLIOGRAPHY

Below is a partial list of books that inspired and informed this work. Each one can be read and savored at your leisure.

Araton, Harvey. *Crashing the Borders: How Basketball Won the World and Lost its Souls at Home.* New York: Free Press, 2005.

Bird, Larry, and Earvin "Magic" Johnson with Jackie MacMullan. *When the Game Was Ours.* New York: Houghton Mifflin Harcourt, 2009.

Boyd, Todd. *Young, Black, Rich, & Famous: The Rise of the NBA, the Hip-Hop Invasion, and the Transformation of American Culture.* New York: Doubleday, 2003.

Charnas, Dan. *The Big Payback: The History of the Business of Hip-Hop.* New York: New American Library, 2010.

Colás, Yago. *Ball Don't Lie! Myth, Genealogy, and Invention in the Cultures of Basketball.* Philadelphia: Temple University Press, 2016

Garcia, Bobbito. *Where'd You Get Those? New York City's Sneaker Culture, 1960–1987.* New York: Testify Books, 2003.

George, Nelson. *Hip-hop America.* New York: Penguin Books, 2005.

Halberstam, David. *The Breaks of the Game.* New York: Alfred A. Knopf, 1981.

————. *Playing for Keeps: Michael Jordan and the World He Made*. New York: Random House, 1999.

Klosterman, Chuck. *Sex, Drugs, and Cocoa Puffs: A Low Culture Manifesto*. New York: Scribner, 2003.

Koppett, Leonard. *24 Seconds to Shoot: An Informal History of the National Basketball Association*. New York: The Macmillan Co., 1968.

Mahler, Jonathan. *Ladies and Gentlemen, the Bronx Is Burning: 1977, Baseball, Politics, and the Battle for the Soul of a City*. New York: Picador, 2006.

McCallum, Jack. *Dream Team: How Michael, Magic, Larry, Charles, and the Greatest Team of All Time Conquered the World and Changed the Game of Basketball Forever*. New York: Ballantine Books, 2012.

Pearlman, Jeff. *Showtime: Magic, Kareem, Riley, and the Los Angeles Lakers Dynasty of the 1980s*. New York: Gotham Books, 2013.

Pluto, Terry. *Loose Balls: The Short, Wild Life of the American Basketball Association*. New York: Simon & Schuster Paperbacks, 2007.

Simmons, Bill. *The Book of Basketball: The NBA According to the Sports Guy*. New York: Ballantine Books/ESPN Books, 2009.

Stauth, Cameron. *The Franchise: Building a Winner with the World Champion Detroit Pistons, Basketball's Bad Boys*. New York: William Morrow and Co., Inc., 1990.

Weinreb, Michael. *Bigger than the Game: Bo, Boz, the Punky QB, and How the '80s Created the Modern Athlete*. New York: Gotham Books, 2010.

INTERVIEWS

For this book, I talked to more than three hundred people. Here is a list of sources who are either quoted directly (via original reporting or unused material from previous stories) or whose observations and remembrances buttressed or clarified my reporting and research.

To all who helped—thank you.

(Asterisk denotes online correspondence.)

Joe Abruzzese	Pete Babcock	Russ Bengtson
Tony Acone	Rick Barry	Harvey Benjamin
Alvan Adams	Elgin Baylor	Andrew D. Bernstein
Doug Adkins	Butch Beard	Bob Bestor
Bill Adler	David Beckerman	Charlie Bloom
Jan Akerhielm	Scott Bedbury	Lynn Bloom
David Allred	Geoff Belinfante	Kurtis Blow
Mike Antinoro	Mickey Bell	Kim Bohuny
Harvey Araton	Nathaniel Bellamy,	Steve Bornstein
Ski Austin	Jr.	Junior Bridgeman
David Axelson	Allyson Bellink*	Allan Bristow

INTERVIEWS

Hubie Brown

Larry Brown

Marc Brown

Michele Brown

Sandy Brown

Howard Bryant

Quinn Buckner

Mike Burks

Michael Burns

Jeanie Buss

Cory Butler

Nathaniel S. Butler

Peter Capolino

Dyan Cannon

Donna Caravaggio

Ron Carter

Don Casey

Mike Caster

David Check

Phil Chenier

Al Coburn

Joe Cohen

Jerry Colangelo

Wayne Cooper

Bob Costas

Dave Cowens

Joey Crawford

Terry Cummings

Nick Curran

Margaret Cusack

Bob Dandridge

Bill Daugherty

Bill Davenport

Adrian De Groot

Victor de la Serna

Len DeLuca

Ed Desser

Vlade Divac

DJ Jazzy Jeff

Andy Dolich

Rich Dorfman

Eddie Doucette

Lee Douglas

Jim Drucker

David DuPree

Theodore
   Duquette*

Mark Eaton

D'Wayne Edwards,

Dr. Harry Edwards

Dale Ellis

Leigh Ellis

Len Elmore

Wayne Embry

Alex English

Julius Erving

David Falk

Joyce Feigenbaum

Bill Fickett

Danny Finocchio*

Nancy Fitzpatrick

Eric Fleisher

Marc Fleisher

Dave Fogelson

Jim Foley

Peter Foley*

Tom Fox

Barry Frank

Mike Fratello

Ed Frazier

Walt "Clyde" Frazier

David Fredman

John Gaffney

Bink Garrison

David Gavant

George Gervin

Ted Giannoulas

Paul Gilbert

Artis Gilmore

Bill Ginn

Jeff Goodby

Patricia Gourdine

Peter Gourdine

Michael Granberry

Charles Grantham

Peter Gruenberger

Susan Hagar

Cindy Hale

Paula Hanson

Del Harris

Grant Harrison

Gary Hart

Tinker Hatfield

Bill Hazen

Tommy Heinsohn

Dick Helm

Roy Hinson

Jonathan Hock

Tom Hohensee

Dave Hollander

John Horan

Andy Hyman

Dan Issel

Marty Jacobson

Phil Jackson*

Greg Jamison

John C. Jay

Bill Jemas

Lisa Johnson

Marques Johnson

Roy S. Johnson

James "Jimmy"
  Jones

Rich Kaner

Stan Kasten

Patrick Kelleher

Bartan Kennedy

Keith Kennelly

Gil Kerr

Sandy Knapp

Billy Knight

Phil Knight

Steve Koonin

Stephen Koontz

Kay Koplovitz

John Kosner

George Krieger

Reinis Lācis

Rex Lardner

Frank Layden

Bobby "Slick"
  Leonard

David Leonard

Nancy Leonard

Lafayette "Fat" Lever

Paul Litchfield

Kevin Loughery

Richard B. Loynd

Jackie MacMullan

Kyle Macy

Robin Mahkorn

Irwin Mandel

Phil Marineau

Ed Markey

Bill Marshall

Christopher "Play"
  Martin

Amanda Mayo

MC Serch

Kim McBride

Jack McCallum

Jon McGlocklin

Brian McIntyre

David "D-Stroy"
  Melendez

Barry Mendelson

Scott Messick

Nigel Miguel

Jon Miller (NBA)

Jon Miller (NBC
  Sports)

Rob Millman

Steve Mills

Matt Mirchin

Fred Mitchell

Steve Mix

Sidney Moncrief

Peter Moore

John Morgan

Roger Morningstar

Sondra Murphy*

Brent Musburger

Betty Myers

Jim Nagel

INTERVIEWS

Kyle Nagel

Lou Nagy

John Nash

Swen Nater

Don Nelson

Gordie Nye

Pat O'Brien

John J. O'Neil

John O'Neil

Akeem Olajuwon

Donna Orender

Joanne Borzakian
  Ouellette

Heidi Palarz

Steve Patterson

Dan Peterson*

Neal Pilson

Donald Pitt

Jim Podhoretz

Ruth Pointer

Jim Quinn

Bill Rasmussen

Mark Richardson

Pat Riley

Jim Riswold

Oscar Robertson

Charley Rosen

Lon Rosen

Jay Rosenstein

Jeff Ruland

Ed T. Rush

Bob Ryan

Alex Sachare

Jerry Sachs

Arthur Sando

Van Gordon Sauter

Steve Schanwald

David Schreff

Nancy Welts Schulte

Ted Shaker

Jody Shapiro

Tom Shine

Judy Shoemaker

Bob Sieber

Jack Sikma

Herb Simon

Jimmy Smith

Suzanne Smith

Paul Snyder

Norm Sonju

Todd Spehr*

Jim Spence

Mary Reiling
  Spencer

Don Sperling

Jon Spoelstra

Jack Stanfield

Jon Steel

Bob Stein

Bob Stenner

Bill Stephney

John G. Stewart

Don Stirling

Dick Stockton

Spencer Stolpen

Dick Strup

Robert Stutman

Kevin Sullivan

Rick Sund

Mike Suscavage

Walt Szczerbiak

Reggie Theus

Isiah Thomas

Ron Thomas

Mark Thomashow

Bob Thompson

Sonny Vaccaro

Ted Van Dyk

Peter Vecsey

Doug Vennard

Lesley Visser

Alexander Volkov

Frank Vuono

John A. Walsh

Gary Walters

Barbara Ward

Steven Warshaw

Julie Ann Wasti

Gary Way

Spud Webb

Jon Weiss

Arlene Weltman

Rick Welts

Ken Wesley

Paul Westphal

Howard "H" White

Rick White

Steve White

Bob Whitsitt

Pat Williams

Sean Williams

Tom Wilson

Matt Winick

Gregg Winik

Doc Wynter

Annie Yee*

Dave Zirin

Jim Zrake

NOTES

Many quotes from Larry O'Brien's time with the NBA, from his courtship to his retirement, come from an unpublished memoir, which I was granted access to by Larry O'Brien III. Any quote or statement from that document is noted by "LOB Memoir."

Though a list of complete interviews is provided in a few instances, I occasionally denote original interviews with "AI."

Basketball Reference, Newspapers.com, and YouTube proved invaluable help in confirming dates, locations, descriptions, and statistics.

INTRODUCTION: OUR GAME

1 The description of Derek Fisher's dance number and his quote: *Dancing with the Stars*, "Derek and Sharna's—Salsa—Dancing with the Stars," September 18, 2017, https://www.youtube.com/watch?v=d1sfKGZHx_E&t=16s. (The dance sequence must be seen to be believed.)

2 "... Nearly 11 million people." Joel Otterson, "TV Ratings: *Dancing with the Stars* Returns Down, Still Tops Monday," Variety.com, September 19, 2017, https://variety.com/2017/tv/news/dancing-with-the-stars-premiere-rat ings-1202563575/.

2 "James Michener portrayed the frustration . . ." James A. Michener, *Sports in America* (New York: Random House, 1976), page 171.

3 "Lon Rosen, then the Lakers' director of promotions . . ." Pete Croatto, "The All-Star Anthem," *Grantland*, February 16, 2013, https://grantland.com/features/the -marvin-gaye-national-anthem/.

4 "We're Disney," AI, Arlene Weltman.

CHAPTER 1: THE POLITICIAN, THE DOCTOR, AND THE BRAT

5 The account of Larry O'Brien in his office and the quotes come from the Associated Press article: Alex Sachare, "What's ahead? . . . NBA Commissioner

O'Brien has a five-year answer for that question," *Hattiesburg American*, March 6, 1977.

6 "The former bartender had begun 'The O'Brien Manual . . .'" Lawrence F. O'Brien, *No Final Victories: A Life in Politics from John F. Kennedy to Watergate* (Garden City, NY: Doubleday & Co., Inc., 1974), page 12.

7 "Its burden is that every vote counts . . ." Theodore H. White, *The Making of the President 1960* (New York: Antheum House, Inc., 1988), pages 102–3.

7 "At the 1960 Democratic National Convention . . ." No author, "The Nation," *Time*, September 1, 1961, page 13.

7 "In the White House, O'Brien enjoyed 'the all-out backing of the President himself.' The understanding on Capitol Hill was that anybody who wanted to run policy by the president had to speak with O'Brien first." Ibid.

7 "Out to pasture . . ." Robert A. Caro, *The Years of Lyndon Johnson: The Passage of Power* (New York: Vintage Books, 2013), page 181.

7 "Kennedy, like every president before or since . . ." Doris Kearns Goodwin, *Lyndon Johnson and the American Dream* (New York: St. Martin's Griffin, 1991), page 163.

7 "'No good politician . . .'" Ibid., page 165.

7 "Johnson 'detested every minute . . .'" Ibid.

7–8 O'Brien's White House accomplishments: Albin Krebs, "Lawrence F. O'Brien, Democrat, Dies at 73," *New York Times*, September 29, 1990.

8 "O'Brien, who knew that his boss . . ." O'Brien, *No Final Victories*, pages 225, 229.

8 "Some liberals saw little difference . . ." Ibid., page 262.

8 "This was after McGovern had asked O'Brien . . ." Ibid., pages 314–15.

8 "'The three worst months' . . ." Ibid., page 319.

8 "'You're identified as a politician, and we feel we should stay away from a political image.'" Ibid., page 322.

8 "He didn't have the support of moderates and big labor. The loathing on the floor . . ." Joseph A. Califano, *Inside: A Public and Private Life* (New York: Public-Affairs, 2004), page 263.

9 "'Larry O'Brien used to be important; now it was these kids.'" Nora Ephron, "The Making of Theodore H. White," *Esquire*, August 1975. (The piece can be found in Ephron's wonderful anthology, *The Most of Nora Ephron*.)

9 "The party he had dedicated his heart and soul to since he passed out flyers and organized car pools . . ." O'Brien, *No Final Victories*, page 8.

9 "Nixon considered O'Brien . . ." Krebs, "Lawrence F. O'Brien, Democrat, Dies at 73."

9 "O'Brien had no specific plans . . ." LOB Memoir.

9 "'You are left with memories and scrapbooks, but little provision for your later life,'" O'Brien, *No Final Victories*, page 359.

9 "Then J. Walter Kennedy called." LOB Memoir.

9 O'Brien's recollections of playing basketball as a child and his love for the Celtics: O'Brien, *No Final Victories*, page 41.

10 "His love of the sport made O'Brien an anomaly with the Kennedys . . ." LOB Memoir.

10 O'Brien's recollections of Kennedy's desire to retire and his reluctance to take his position: Ibid.

10 "That notorious event was preceded by three separate audits . . ." O'Brien, *No Final Victories*, pages 345, 349.

10 "The NBA had a national television contract . . ." Leonard Koppett, *24 Seconds to Shoot: An Informal History of the National Basketball Association* (New York: The Macmillan Co., 1968), page 151.

11 "He possessed . . ." Howard Cosell, *Cosell* (Chicago: Playboy Press, 1973), page 383.

12 Cosell's recollections on Kennedy's job performance and distress: Ibid., page 384.

12 "Kennedy 'let himself be controlled and manipulated' . . ." Jim Spence with Dave Diles, *Up Close and Personal: The Inside Story of Network Television Sports* (New York City: Antheum Publishers, 1988), page 190.

12 "Renewal seemed inevitable . . ." The owners' logic for rejecting ABC's deal comes from author interviews with Michael Burns, Jim Spence, and from *Up Close and Personal*, pages 190–91.

13 "As part of its agreement with ABC . . ." Roone Arledge, *Roone: A Memoir* (New York: HarperCollins, 2003), page 141.

13 ". . . Cooke already had a commitment from CBS without the restrictions" and the description of the meeting to back out of the ABC deal: Ibid, page 141.

13 "One clause was particularly ingenious." Ibid.

14 "Not to Lakers owner Jack Kent Cooke . . ." Ibid.

14 "'It was as severe a chastising as I've ever seen Arledge receive,'" Spence with Diles, *Up Close and Personal*, page 194.

14 "'An unapologetic ratings grabber' . . . The idea came from Barry Frank . . ." Arledge, *Roone: A Memoir*, page 141.

14 "Franchises eked out a living. In 1970, three out of the fourteen teams . . ." David Wolf, *Foul! The Connie Hawkins Story* (New York: Warner Paperback Library, 1972), page 364.

14 "Kennedy was a notorious spendthrift . . ." Howard Berk, *When My Boss Calls, Get the Name* (New York: iUniverse, Inc., 2008), pages 91–92.

15 "'It was utter chaos.'" Dan Shaughnessy, "Teamwork Could Be the Issue in Cozy Club Called 'The Owners,'" *Philadelphia Inquirer*, May 2, 1982.

15–16 Details and quotes regarding O'Brien's courtship by the NBA: LOB Memoir.

17 "'No league executive had a job description . . .'" Nick Curran, "Eight Fabulous Days When the Warriors Won It All," *The Ultimate Sports Guide: A Reference Guide Serving San Francisco and Northern California: 2014 Spring/Summer Baseball Edition*, page 84.

17 "O'Brien discovered that the staff of 16 was one of many issues that plagued the NBA." LOB Memoir.

17 "His one professional foray outside politics . . ." Ibid.

17–18 Details of the McGinnis signing and punishment: Sam Goldaper, "The Next Move Is Up to McGinnis," *New York Times*, June 7, 1975 and Associated Press and United Press International, "O'Brien Voids McGinnis Signing," *Indianapolis Star*, June 6, 1975.

18 "'They would have been faced with extinction.'" Bill Livingston, "Court King: In Naming Stern, NBA Has Smooth Succession in Top Job," *Philadelphia Inquirer*, January 29, 1984.

18 Information on the Oscar Robertson Rule: "Oscar Robertson Rule," www.oscar robertson.com/oscar-robertson-rule, accessed March 7, 2019.

19 "The ABA never had a national television contract . . ." Terry Pluto, *Loose Balls: The Short, Wild Life of the American Basketball Association* (New York: Simon & Schuster Paperbacks, 2007), page 48.

20 "The ABA's founder, Dennis Murphy, wanted to merge with the NBA within three years." Ibid., page 421.

20 "The league was down to seven teams . . ." Ibid., page 427.

20 "The ABA made the first move on April 16, 1976 . . ." LOB Memoir.

21 Wussler comments on NBA and $5 million boost: Sam Goldaper, "NBA Gets Merger 'Spur,' " *New York Times*, May 25, 1976.

21 "That 'never could happen if the four ABA survivors insisted on keeping Kentucky, Virginia, and St. Louis' players. If that were the case, then all bets were off.' " LOB Memoir.

21 O'Brien's decision to hold meeting and the quote, "I told them [the ABA] the deal of yesterday was the deal of now, and I had to ask my board to vote on it by 9 a.m." Bob Logan, "All Parties in Merger Laud O'Brien's Role." *Chicago Tribune*, June 18, 1976.

21 " 'I had tried to put across some of the facts of life . . .' " LOB Memoir.

22 " 'The difference between a good negotiator and a bad negotiator . . .' " Pluto, *Loose Balls*, page 429.

22 Account of Thursday's ABA–NBA meeting, featuring "Up or down?" Frank De-ford, "One Last Hurrah in Hyannis," *Sports Illustrated*, June 28, 1976, https://vault .si.com/vault/1976/06/28/one-last-hurrah-in-hyannis.

22 " 'Larry made it work . . .' " Logan, "All Parties in Merger Laud O'Brien's Role."

23 " 'They pulled a massacre on us.' " Dana Hunsinger Benbow, "How Slick Leonard Saved the Pacers with a 1977 Telethon," *Indianapolis Star*, February 17, 2016.

23 " 'What we . . . did was save the business.' " Logan, "All Parties in Merger Laud O'Brien's Role."

23 "The jump shot was considered exotic back in the 1950s . . ." Bill Russell and Tay-lor Branch, *Second Wind: The Memoirs of an Opinionated Man* (New York: Random House, 1979), pages 63–64.

23 " 'He did stuff nobody had thought of yet.' " John McNamara with Andrea Cham-blee and David Elfin, *The Capital of Basketball: A History of DC Area High School Hoops* (Washington, D.C.: Georgetown University Press, 2019), page 33.

23 ". . . Derived from the jazz and R&B he heard in his head . . ." Earl Monroe with Quincy Trope, *Earl the Pearl: My Story* (New York: Rodale, 2013), pages 61 and 62.

23 ". . . 'who went beyond the level of sports as sport to the realm of sports as art.' " Woody Allen, "A Fan's Notes on Earl Monroe," *Sport Magazine*, November 1977, http://reprints.longform.org/a-fans-notes-on-earl-monroe, accessed October 22, 2019.

23 ". . . the 'paradigm shift in the pro game of basketball,' " Monroe with Trope, *Earl the Pearl: My Story*, page 361.

24 " 'It's kind of a misnomer . . .' " Gary M. Pomerantz, *The Last Pass: Cousy, Russell, the Celtics and What Matters in the End* (New York: Penguin Press, 2018), page 57.

24 "Hawkins's' college and pro career were derailed by an imaginary betting scandal,

an overzealous New York DA's office, knee surgery, and partying." Details confirmed in Wolf's *Foul!* and Steve Aschburner, "Connie Hawkins' 'Interrupted' Career Will Forever be Remembered Fondly Among His Peers," NBA.com, October 10, 2017.

24 "By the early 1960s, the pain in Baylor's knees was so bad he was chauffeured to home games." Mark Heisler, "A Road Well Traveled," *Los Angeles Times*, November 16, 1997.

24 ". . . Parroted what black players had done, only Pistol's results appeared labored and studied." Charley Rosen, *Sugar: Micheal Ray Richardson, Eighties Excess, and the NBA* (Lincoln, NE: University of Nebraska Press, 2018), page 78.

24 "'The white establishment has an uncomfortable feeling . . .'" Pete Axthelm, *The City Game: Basketball in New York from the World Champion Knicks to the World of the Playgrounds* (New York: Harper's Magazine Press, 1970), page 127.

25 "'It was absolutely a way to get out of the ghetto . . .'" Jon Entine, *Taboo: Why Black Athletes Dominate Sports and Why We're Afraid to Talk About It* (New York: Public Affairs, 2000), pages 198 and 199.

25 "'Basketball served as the foundation of which social workers and reformers built huge intellectual and bureaucratic structures . . .'" Elliot J. Gorn and Walter Goldstein, *A Brief History of American Sport* (New York: Hill and Wang, 1993), pages 174–75.

25 "'Then, in the 1940s, blacks entered the southern and northern cities.'" Yago Colás, *Ball Don't Lie! Myth, Genealogy, and Invention in the Cultures of Basketball* (Philadelphia: Temple University Press, 2016), page 63.

27 "Erving, Bill Russell thought, was beautiful . . ." Russell and Branch, *Second Wind*, page 98.

27 "'Writers aren't supposed to idolize, only report . . .'" Woody Paige, "How Dr. J Will Dissect the NBA," *The Complete Handbook of Pro Basketball*, 1977 edition, edited by Zander Hollander (New York: Signet, 1976), pages 7 and 8.

28 "'I look around and see a bunch of guys . . .'" Curry Kirkpatrick, "A Season for All Men," *Sports Illustrated*, October 25, 1976, https://vault.si.com/vault/1976/10/25/a-season-for-all-men.

30 ". . . teams based their playbooks on power basketball . . ." This and Phil Jackson's other observations on the latter-day NBA game: Phil Jackson and Hugh Delehanty, *Sacred Hoops: Spiritual Lessons of a Hardwood Warrior* (New York: Hyperion, 1995), page 85.

30 "For one thing, the idea had a long precedent." Shawn Fury, *Rise and Fire: The Origins, Science, and Evolution of the Jump Shot—and How it Transformed Basketball Forever* (New York: Flatiron Books, New York), pages 269–71.

30 "Warriors owner Franklin Mieuli called the new shot 'a panic move' destined to 'destroy the team concept . . .'" United Press, "Mieuli Calls the Three-pointer a Copout," *Oakland Tribune*, July 23, 1979.

30 "Sure, Mieuli had flouted tradition . . ." Fury, *Rise and Fire*, page 122.

31 Eddie Gottlieb's letter outlining his objections to the shot were obtained from a former NBA team executive who requested anonymity.

31 "The Celtics wouldn't feature cheerleaders until after Auerbach's 2006 death." Kate Darnton, "Go-go Dancing All over Red's Grave," *Boston Globe*, February 17, 2008.

32 "In the early 1950s, all kinds of amendments were discussed . . ." Koppett, *24 Seconds to Shoot*, page 82.

32 "Larry Bird loved using it to break the opposition's spirit late in games." Larry Bird with Bob Ryan, *Drive: The Story of My Life* (New York: Bantam Books, 1990), page 225.

32 "In the 1979–80 season . . ." Three-point statistics for that year and 2016–17 come from Basketball Reference, https://www.basketball-reference.com/leagues /NBA_1980.html and https://www.basketball-reference.com/leagues/NBA _2017.html, respectively.

32 " 'It makes it tougher to cover that much room defensively on the court.' " Fury, *Rise and Fire*, pages 274–75.

33 "As time went on, the center's role as an inside force changed." Brian Fleurantin, "A Look at the 'End' and the Evolution of NBA Big Men," Nets Daily, February 15, 2016, https://www.netsdaily.com/2016/2/15/8856445/a-look-at-the-end-and -evolution-of-nba-big-men.

35 Magic Johnson's conversation with Abdul-Jabbar and the ensuing anecdote: Larry Bird and Earvin "Magic" Johnson, with Jackie MacMullan, *When the Game Was Ours* (New York: Houghton Mifflin Harcourt, 2009), pages 209–10.

37 " 'I would have eaten his shit.' " Robert Huber, "Julius Erving Doesn't Want to be a Hero Anymore," *Philadelphia Magazine*, August 23, 2008, https://www.phillymag .com/news/2008/04/23/julius-erving-doesnt-want-to-be-a-hero-anymore/12/.

37 "The flawed man in the larger world emerged later." Ibid.

38 "O'Brien considered the ABA's absorption into the NBA a top-ten career highlight." Logan, "All Parties in Merger Laud O'Brien's Role."

38 "The NBA was no match for working in the White House for a young, war hero president." LOB Memoir. (O'Brien makes it very clear in his account of working for the NBA that nothing compared to working in the White House.)

38 "Hobnobbing with the political elite at his Washington, D.C., home . . ." Caro, *The Years of Lyndon Johnson: The Passage of Power*, page 180.

39 "The first day on the job . . ." Berk, *When My Boss Calls, Get the Name?*, page 92.

39 " 'I figured you couldn't even talk to *him* . . .' " Bird with Ryan, *Drive: The Story of My Life*, page 287.

40 Observations on O'Brien's workplace and off-the-clock anecdotes: Berk, *When My Boss Calls, Get the Name*, page 93.

41 "On the recommendation of his son, Larry III . . ." LOB Memoir.

41 ". . . played ball well into adulthood . . ." Barry Cooper, "Stern Story with a Happy Ending," *Orlando Sentinel*, June 2, 1987.

41 "He could get good seats with a fifty-cent student card and a tip to the usher . . ." David Halberstam, *Playing for Keeps: Michael Jordan and the World He Made* (New York: Random House, 1999), page 122.

42 "Stern's early duties at Proskauer . . ." Halberstam, Ibid., pages 123–24.

42 ". . . He was murdered in 1975 in an apparent mob hit." Erick Konisberg, "Double Dribbling," *New York Times*, March 3, 2002.

42 " 'If there was one lesson he was learning . . .' " Halberstam, *Playing for Keeps: Michael Jordan and the World He Made*, page 124.

43 ". . . A title Stern insisted on having." LOB Memoir.

43 " 'Well, you schmuck . . . how can you put your life in the hands of one client?' " Harvey Araton, *Crashing the Borders: How Basketball Won the World and Lost Its Soul at Home* (Free Press, New York: 2005), page 12.

43 "O'Brien deemed the hire a necessity." LOB Memoir.

43 "He had lobbied the owners hard . . ." LOB Memoir.

44 " 'Si Gourdine is very efficient, he follows through . . .' " Mike Farber, "Eager Gourdine Is Left in Role of Bridesmaid," *Record* (Hackensack, NJ), February 20, 1977.

44 ". . . Who made more money than the veteran NBA executive." LOB Memoir.

44 "Patricia had a hefty binder as evidence . . ." (I had to lug it on the train ride back from New York City to suburban New Jersey.)

45 " 'There were never any barriers against me . . .' " Richard Goldstein, "Simon P. Gourdine, Pioneer in Sports Management, Dies at 72," *New York Times*, August 20, 2012.

45 "The start of Stern's rise to power coincided with a period he later called the 'dark ages.' " John Feinstein, *The Punch: One Night, Two Lives, and the Fight that Changed Basketball Forever* (New York: Little, Brown and Co, 2003), page 21.

45 " 'The league had a number of players . . . ' " LOB Memoir.

46 "Major League Baseball's drug issues . . ." Associated Press, "Pittsburgh Cocaine Trial: Baseball's Second Biggest Scandal: One Year Later," *Los Angeles Times*, September 21, 1986.

46 ". . . the *Los Angeles Times* reported that up to 75 percent of NBA players used cocaine." Chris Cobbs, "NBA and Cocaine: Nothing to Snort At," *Los Angeles Times*, August 19, 1980.

47 ". . . 80 percent of the league used cocaine in the 1979–80 season." Jeff Pearlman, *Showtime: Magic, Kareem, Riley, and the Los Angeles Lakers Dynasty of the 1980s* (New York: Gotham Books, 2013), page 79.

47 " 'Oh yeah . . . it was everywhere.' " Ibid.

47 " 'So much coke is snorted in the NBA . . .' " Russell and Branch, *Second Wind*, page 102.

47 " 'If someone chose to, they could have concluded that 100 percent of the black players were involved with drugs . . .' " Jane Gross, "Gourdine Reflects on NBA," *New York Times*, June 27, 1981.

47 " 'The talk among the players was that if a guy was being promoted as part of the NBA's marketing program . . .' " Rosen, *Sugar*, page 65.

47 "The rise of cocaine . . ." Lewis Cole, *Too Young to Die: The Death of Len Bias* (New York: Pantheon Books 1989), pages 130–31.

47 "A wealthy user . . ." Ibid., page 134.

48 "The rise of crack . . ." Ibid., page 150.

48 "As more blacks entered the league . . ." Kareem Abdul-Jabbar and Peter Knobler, *Giant Steps* (New York: Bantam Books, 1983), page 293. (Despite Abdul-Jabbar's curt personality, *Giants Steps* is a forthright and first-rate memoir.)

48 " 'Most guys can take it . . .' " Ibid., page 294.

48 " 'I didn't feel I was worth very much . . .' " Jackie MacMullan, "Why Sinking Phoenix May Find It Hard to Rise Again; Gervin and Thompson: From Shame to Fame; Charlotte Waits on Karl," *Sports Illustrated*, May 6, 1996, https://vault.si.com/

NOTES

vault/1996/05/06/why-sinking-phoenix-may-find-it-hard-to-rise-again-gervin
-and-thompson-from-shame-to-fame-charlotte-waits-on-karl.

48 "'With so many games, it gave your body energy when you were feeling down . . .'"
Pearlman, *Showtime*, page 80.

48 "'That first hit felt like the best thing that could ever to happen to me. I was invisible and invincible.'" Rosen, *Sugar*, page 35.

49 "Haywood compared his first time . . ." Pearlman, *Showtime*, page 82.

49 "Richardson spent the next seven years . . ." Rosen, *Sugar*, page 35.

49 "Drug use was not a black problem . . ." Ibid., page 65.

49 "Rosen supplied Steve Patterson . . ." Ibid., page 28.

49 "'It seemed so harmless . . .'" David Thompson with Sean Stormes and Marshall
Terrill, *Skywalker: The Remarkable and Inspiring Story of Legendary Basketball
Player David Thompson* (New York: Sports Publishing, LLC, 2003), page 171.

49 "In 1981, 16 of the league's 23 teams lost money. Four were on the block . . ." Bren-
ton Welling, Jonathan Tapsini, Dan Cook, and bureau report, "Basketball: Business
Is Booming—The NBA Has More Going for It than Pat Ewing," *Business Week*,
October 28, 1985, page 73.

49 "Forty percent of the teams depended on its $800,000 check from CBS . . ." David
Halberstam, *The Breaks of the Game* (New York: Alfred A. Knopf, 1981), page
187.

52 "'This is not a dying sport.'" Associated Press, "O'Brien Forecasts Worldwide
Competition," *Poughkeepsie Journal*, April 25, 1979.

53 "'What I remember most about Larry's early years . . .'" Bob Schron and Kevin
Stevens, *The Bird Era: A History of the Boston Celtics* (Boston: Quinlan Press, 1988),
page 81.

53 "As college basketball writer Seth Davis observed . . ." Seth Davis, *When March
Went Mad: The Game That Transformed Basketball* (New York: Times Books,
2009), page 247.

53 "When NBC put together its college basketball schedule for that season, Indiana
State wasn't on it." AI, Rex Lardner.

54 "The summer after his senior year, Bird was student-teaching at West Vigo High
School," Davis, *When March Went Mad*, page 233.

CHAPTER 2: THE PLAYERS GET THEIR CLOSE-UP

55 "On the heels of improperly paying tennis players . . ." Les Brown, "Robert Wussler,
President of CBS Sports, Resigns," *New York Times*, March 16, 1978.

56 "Jack Kent Cooke, unhappy with CBS Sports, had already crawled back to ABC . . ."
Jim Spence with Dave Diles, *Up Close and Personal: The Inside Story of Network Television Sports* (New York: Antheneum Publishers, 1988), pages 194–95.

56 "'We were never given the opportunity to determine whether we were ready for
prime time.'" LOB Memoir.

57 ". . . Spent hours confronting his backyard hoop . . ." Pete Croatto, "Jumpman,
Jumpman, Jumpman," *SLAM*, February 2016, https://www.slamonline.com/nba
/larry-nance-dunk-contest-slam/.

58 "... The NBA's $88 million contract was hardly good news ..." Jack Craig, "Network Cutback Brings Alibis from Both Sides," *Philadelphia Inquirer*, May 4, 1982.

58 "CBS aired fewer regular season games ..." Florida Today wires, "Television Ratings Bounce Skyward for NBA Viewers," *Florida Today*, February 1, 1986.

59 "'The self-depreciating role of blacks as comic relief...'" Knolly Moses, "The Black Image on Television: Who Controls It?" *Black Enterprise*, September 1979, page 33.

59 "Media experts George Gerbner and Larry Gross suggested to Moses ..." Ibid., page 40.

63 "At the time, he claimed that Shaker and Neal Pilson ..." Steve Nidetz, "Musburger Charges 2 CBS Execs 'Conspired to Get Me,'" *Chicago Tribune*, April 6, 1990.

64 "More important, so did David Stern ..." Ron Thomas, *They Cleared the Lane: the NBA's Black Pioneers* (Lincoln, NE: University of Nebraska Press, 2002), page 241.

65 "If anyone wasn't in step with the NBA's 'relentless pursuit of perfection'..." Shawn Fury interview with David Stern transcript, provided by Fury. (Despite sources interceding on my behalf, I could never wrangle Stern for an interview. I bombarded Stern with emails until he responded with a polite decline. I tried one last time. "Again, if you have any questions, don't hesitate to ask," I wrote. "If you want to reach out to my parents to inquire why I'm a persistent pain in the ass. Feel free. I'm sure they can provide some perspective." His response: "Good luck with the publication. I do not need parent explanation or validation—but appreciate the offer." David Stern died six weeks later.)

66 "'Larry is a very nice person, but sometimes he just forgets about other people ...'" Diane K. Shah, "The Bird and the B's: Basketball, Boston, and Big Bucks," *Inside Sports*, October 1979, page 63.

67 "'Hey, Jack. Later on you wanna blow us?'" Jack McCallum, *Dream Team: How Michael, Magic, Larry, Charles, and the Greatest Team of All Time Conquered the World and Changed the Game of Basketball Forever* (New York: Ballantine Books, 2012), page xxv.

67 "Johnson visited his barbershop ..." Bird and Johnson with MacMullan, *When the Game Was Ours*, pages 101–2.

67 "Bird played a white man's game ..." Charles P. Pierce, "The Brother from Another Planet," *Esquire*, February 1992. (Retrieved from Pierce's outstanding collection, *Sports Guy*.)

68 "Bird and Johnson made fundamentals and teamwork..." Ibid.

68 "'Dad pointed out everything down to the smallest detail ...'" Earvin "Magic" Johnson and Roy S. Johnson, *Magic's Touch* (Reading, Mass.: Addison-Wesley Johnson Publishing Company, Inc., 1989), page 7.

68 "What made him so special ..." Roland Lazenby, *The Show: The Inside Story of the Spectacular Los Angeles Lakers in the Words of Those Who Lived It* (New York: McGraw-Hill, 2006), page 190.

69 "'I began to feel physically ill ...'" Leigh Montville, "The Tube That Won't Let You Up," *Boston Globe*, April 3, 1981.

69 "Koplovitz explained the setup years later ..." Kay Koplovitz, "How Muhammed Ali, Joe Frazier, and Satellites Changed TV History," MediaVillage, September 30,

2015, https://www.mediavillage.com/article/how-muhammed-ali-joe-frazier-and
-satellites-changed-the-course-of-television-history/.

70 "In 1977, federal district court in Washington, D.C. . . ." No author, "The Rise of
Cable Television," Encyclopedia.com, accessed November 13, 2019, https://www
.encyclopedia.com/arts/news-wires-white-papers-and-books/rise-cable-television.

70 "Satellites allowed channels to spread . . ." Ted Turner with Bill Burke, *Call Me Ted*
(New York: Grand Central Publishing, 2008), page 128.

72 "USA paid $400,000 for the first year in a three-year deal . . ." John Ourand,
"Cable Vision: TV pioneer Kay Koplovitz saw the future of sports networks,"
Sports Business Journal, March 6, 2018, https://www.bizjournals.com/newyork
/news/2018/03/06/cable-vision-tv-pioneer-kay-koplovitz-saw-future.html.

74 "Meanwhile in Atlanta . . ." Turner with Burke, *Call Me Ted*, pages 129 and 131.

75 "WTCG, rebranded as 'SuperStation TBS'. . ." Ibid., page 134.

76 ". . . His purchase of the Lakers involved the Chrysler Building." Jeff Pearlman,
Showtime: Magic, Kareem, Riley, and the Los Angeles Lakers Dynasty of the 1980s
(New York: Gotham Books, 2013), page 9.

CHAPTER 3: SETTING UP THE BUSINESS PLAN

83 "That was why Suscavage witnessed Stepien toss softballs from the Terminal Tower . . ." Associated Press, "Look Out Below for Flying Softballs," *News-
Messenger* (Fremont, OH), June 25, 1980.

83 "The owners, David Stern observed, needed to be protected from themselves."
Brenton Welling, Jonathan Tapsini, Dan Cook, and bureau report, "Basketball:
Business Is Booming—The NBA Has More Going for It than Pat Ewing," *Business
Week*, October 28, 1985, page 78.

85 "The association voted to strike on April 2 . . ." NBA documents provided by Larry
O'Brien III.

85 "Many owners, O'Brien recalled later, dreaded a strike. If the strike lasted . . ." LOB
Memoir.

85 " 'I never doubted . . . that eventually, somehow, somewhere, common sense would
prevail." LOB Memoir.

87 " '. . . the prospect of profitability means that basketball franchises . . ." Welling,
et al., "Basketball Business is Booming," page 74.

87 " 'If I had bought a factory or a shopping center or even T-bills . . .' " Ibid., page 74.

88 "Four years later, he sold the Nuggets for $65 million." Associated Press, "Nuggets
are Purchased by Black Investors," *New York Times*, July 11, 1989.

88 ". . . Schlenker reportedly paid $20 million." Welling, et al., "Basketball Business is
Booming," page 74.

88 (Another sign of the NBA's health: In April 1987, when the league announced the
addition of four new teams, each one was charged an entrance fee of $32.5 million.
For the NBA, observed Bob Ryan and Terry Pluto in *48 Minutes: A Night in the Life
of the NBA*, that meant "a quick $130 million in found revenue.")

88 " 'We're trying to be responsible to the people who, in turn, enjoy our sport, attend our sport, and view our sport . . . There's a credibility factor.' " *Face the Nation*,

"Anti-drug efforts in sports in 1983," February 5, 2016, https://www.youtube.com /watch?v=pytRLmqe_OQ.

88 "Robert Reid said his teammates . . ." Jonathan Abrams, "The Greatest Team That Never Was," *Grantland*, November 8, 2012, https://grantland.com/features/an -oral-history-hakeem-olajuwon-ralph-sampson-1980s-houston-rockets/.

88 "Darryl Dawkins said Micheal Ray Richardson . . ." Charley Rosen, *Sugar: Micheal Ray Richardson, Eighties Excess, and the NBA* (Lincoln, NE: University of Nebraska Press, 2018), pages 67–68.

88 "In *Sugar*, Charley Rosen reported that Phoenix Suns star Walter Davis . . ." Ibid., page 67.

88 "In fact, Russ Granik . . ." Ian Thomsen, *The Soul of Basketball: The Epic Showdown Between LeBron, Kobe, Doc, and Dirk That Saved the NBA* (Boston: Houghton Mifflin Harcourt, 2018), page 55.

88 "That decision, which Stern hated to enact . . ." Rosen, *Sugar*, page 130.

89 "At the McDonald's Open in 1997 . . ." Ibid., page 127.

91 " 'Fleisher was 'a genuinely honest man . . .' " Howard Cosell with Shelby Whitfield, *What's Wrong with Sports?* (New York: Simon and Schuster, 1991), pages 204 and 205.

92 "He felt a twinge of jealousy when Stern left for the NBA . . ." Jonathon Gatehouse, *The Instigator: How Gary Bettman Remade the NHL and Changed the Game Forever* (Chicago: Triumph Books, 2012), page 18.

CHAPTER 4: GETTING READY FOR STAR TIME

97 " 'We asserted that we could do it whether we could or couldn't and we did.' " David Stern interview with Shawn Fury; transcript provided by Fury.

97 "In addition to securing old games from ABC . . ." Ibid.

97 " '. . . Things that any normal sports league should do . . .' " Ibid.

101 ". . . to give the 'NBA the dignity I thought it deserved.' " Ibid.

104 " 'The best promotion for us . . .' " Ibid.

105 " 'I was becoming obsessed with the fact . . .' " Ibid.

106 ". . . Aside form too-cool-for-anything Jack Nicholson . . ." Paul Gilbert, "He Loved this Game," *New York Times*, June 11, 2006.

106 "That was used for a blooper-ridden spot." Ibid.

107 " '. . . In pursuit of a greater good.' " Stern interview with Fury.

107 " 'We enjoyed each other's company.' " Ibid.

109 "*Episodic Micromanagement is Underrated . . .*" Ibid.

115 " 'It's just not who I am, period.' " Rob Tornoe, "Jerry West Doesn't Want to Be on the NBA Logo Anymore," *Philadelphia Inquirer*, April 8 2017.

120 "Shawn Kemp credited the Costacos Brothers' . . ." Amy K. Nelson, "Poster Boys," SBNation, February 5, 2013, https://www.sbnation.com/longform /2013/2/5/3951634/costacos-brothers-sports-posters-oral-history.

120 " 'The poster made you cool . . . You didn't make the poster cool.' " Ibid.

120 Most of the material on the Salem Sportswear section of this chapter comes from my oral history for Rolling Stone.com, "Big Heads, Bad Boys, and Bird: How Salem

Sportswear Changed the Game Forever," which was published on May 13, 2016. I am indebted to *Rolling Stone* for allowing me to use the article as material for the book. In the name of conserving space—and your sanity—I am referencing what was *not* used from the article, https://www.rollingstone.com/culture/culture-sports/big-heads-bad-boys-and-bird-how-salem-sportswear-changed-the-game-forever-189867/.

120 "'I'm a capitalist at heart . . .'" AI, Bill Fickett.

121 "'I'll tell you a small story I heard from Keith.'" AI, Doug Vennard.

123 "'The NBA was a family business and so was Salem.'" AI, Nancy Fitzpatrick.

123 "'Salem had such an incredible influence . . .'" AI, Danny Finocchio.

124 "She owns a dead-stock Salem shirt." AI, Sondra Murphy.

124 "'Everything now is so robotic . . .'" AI, Sondra Murphy.

125 "Stark, a former ditch digger . . ." Bill Madden, "Daily News cartoonist Bruce Stark dies after battle with emphysema," New York *Daily News*, December 31, 2012.

126 "'You have to put exposure on it . . .'" AI, Bill Marshall.

126 "The organizers at Live Aid asked Alex English . . ." AI, Don Sperling.

126 "An estimated 100,000 music fans . . ." Deb Kiner, "Live Aid Concerts Held Simultaneously in Philadelphia and London in 1985," PennLive.com, July 13, 2008, https://www.pennlive.com/life/2018/07/live_aid_concerts_held_simulta.html.

127 "'We'd read the sports pages like other businesses would read the sports pages.'" AI, Al Coburn.

127 "'Every day, he said, is a hot market. Nobody did it better than Salem . . .'" AI, Jon Weiss.

128 "'All those orders are already in . . .'" AI, Kyle Nagel.

128 "The big stores—Foot Locker, Sports Authority—needed the shirts the next day. Stores always under-ordered." AI, Kyle Nagel.

128 "In 1993, the Chicago Bulls and the Phoenix Suns played in the Finals . . ." AI, Al Coburn.

128 "' . . . I didn't sleep the night before.'" AI, Al Coburn.

129 "'You had so much invested in the games . . .'" AI, Keith Kennelly.

129 "One day Kyle's son called his grandfather 'Dad.'" AI, Jim Nagel.

129 "As a bonus, Fickett met his fashion inspiration and sports hero." AI, Bill Fickett.

129 ". . . Fruit of the Loom bought Salem at the worst time." AI, Bill Fickett.

129 "'As the leagues got bigger, better, smarter, more mature . . .'" AI, Matt Mirchin.

130 "Fruit of the Loom kept its old business model . . ." AI, Marc Brown.

130 "Flying by the seat of their pants . . ." AI, Jon Weiss.

CHAPTER 5: OH SHIT . . . HERE WE GO

131 This chapter is based on my 2013 article for *Grantland*, "The All-Star Anthem." I want to thank ESPN for allowing me to use it here.

131 "Lon Rosen, the Los Angeles Lakers' young director of promotions . . ." Pete Croatto, "The All-Star Anthem," *Grantland*, February 16, 2013, https://grantland.com/features/the-marvin-gaye-national-anthem/.

131 "Rosen knew that plenty of people . . ." Ibid.

131 "Marvin Gaye had been one of Rosen's musical heroes . . ." Ibid.

132 "At the run-through the day before . . ." Ibid.

132 "Halftime rolled around . . ." Ibid.

132 " 'That was the greatest anthem of all time . . .' " Ibid.

132 "Fergie's memorable portrayal . . ." ESPN, "Fergie Sings the National Anthem at the NBA All-Star Game," February 19, 2018, https://www.youtube.com /watch?v=CMA2iF6RuXk. (Getting this description right was one of the book's great challenges. I'm not sure if I nailed it. Send your suggestions to pscroatto@gmail.com.)

133 "When Irvin Molotsky talked to Zimmerman . . ." Irvin Molotsky, *The Flag, the Poet, and the Song: The Story of the Star-Spangled Banner* (New York: Dutton, 2001), page 12.

133 "Ronald Reagan's election to the White House . . ." Todd Boyd, *Young, Black, Rich, & Famous: The Rise of the NBA, the Hip-Hop Invasion, and the Transformation of American Culture* (New York: Doubleday, 2003), page 45.

134 "In private, he jokingly referred to himself as 'Ron-bo.' " Michael Weinreb, *Bigger than the Game: Bo, Boz, the Punky QB, and How the '80s Created the Modern Athlete* (New York: Gotham Books, 2010), page 12.

134 "One of Buss's earliest memories was waiting in food lines in Depression-era Wyoming." Scott Ostler and Steve Springer, *Winnin' Times: The Magical Journey of the Los Angeles Lakers* (New York: Collier Books, 1988), page 17.

134 "His life was defined by hard work . . ." Ibid., page 20.

134 "Thankfully, Buss returned and found an ally . . ." Ibid., pages 21–23.

134 "his fortune came from real estate . . ." Jeff Pearlman, *Showtime: Magic, Kareem, Riley, and the Los Angeles Lakers Dynasty of the 1980s* (New York: Gotham Books, 2013), page 23.

134 "A voracious partier . . ." Ibid., page 24.

135 "Corporate sponsorships for arenas were a bit of a to-do . . ." Andrea Adelson, "The Media Business: Great Western's Name on Los Angeles Forum," *New York Times*, December 7, 1988.

135 "A couple of years earlier, Buss hosted his successful head coach . . ." Pat Riley, *Showtime: Inside the Lakers' Breakthrough Season* (New York: Warner Books, 1988), pages 29–30.

136 "He brought in members of USC's marching band . . ." Pearlman, *Showtime*, 69.

136 "He turned the Forum Club . . ." Ibid., 200.

136 " 'If you couldn't get laid at the Forum Club . . .' " Ibid., 203.

136 "He agreed to have USC and UCLA coeds for a cheerleading squad." Ibid., 69.

136 " 'What I am better at anyone than anyone I've ever met . . .' " Ostler and Springer, *Winnin' Times*, page 34.

136 "The marketing . . . was on the floor." Roland Lazenby, *The Show: The Inside Story of the Spectacular Los Angeles Lakers in the Words of Those Who Lived It* (New York: McGraw-Hill, 2006), page 275.

136 "Abdul inadvertently played hit maker . . ." Amy Wallace, "Paula Abdul," *Los Angeles*, August 9, 2011, http://www.lamag.com/lastory/paula-abdul1/.

137 " 'I knew I was being packaged by CBS and everybody else in the media.' " Chuck

Klosterman, *Sex, Drugs, and Cocoa Puffs: A Low Culture Manifesto* (New York: Scribner, 2003), page 102.

138 "'There was no doubt that in the '80s I got totally full myself.'" Ian Thomsen, *The Soul of Basketball: The Epic Showdown Between LeBron, Kobe, Doc, and Dirk That Saved the NBA* (Boston: Houghton Mifflin Harcourt, 2018), page 16.

138 "Magic wasn't called 'Buck' because of his spirited play . . ." Pearlman, *Showtime*, page 114.

138 "'The best real estate . . . can be sold at any price.'" Roland Lazenby, *The Show: The Inside Story of the Spectacular Los Angeles Lakers in the Words of Those Who Lived It* (New York: McGraw-Hill, 2006), page 184.

140 "'It was this thing that was out there that you were probably never going to touch . . .'" Pete Croatto, "Full Court Press," Court Basketball, accessed November 5, 2019, http://courtbasketball.com/article/full-court-press/.

140 "Pop star Lionel Richie, deep into his reign . . ." Croatto, "The All-Star Anthem," *Grantland*.

141 "Once Gaye was booked, there wasn't a lot of time to prepare . . ." Ibid.

141 "CBS Sports' Ted Shaker was stunned for the opposite reason . . ." Ibid.

141 "'We all kind of went, 'Wow.'" Ibid.

141 "'I remember that night and the following day . . .'" Ibid.

141 "Whether you loved it or hated it . . ." Ibid.

142 "The last singer to give the anthem a stylistic, high-profile twist . . ." Ibid.

142 "The Tigers' switchboard lit up with objections . . ." Ibid.

142 "'I made history and nothing can besmirch that . . .'" Ibid.

143 "Nearly fifteen years later . . ." Ibid.

143 "Afterward, Banks made a copy." Ibid.

143 "'We just did what we did.'" Ibid.

143 "No one with the Lakers . . ." Ibid.

143 "The simple two-part beat . . ." Ibid.

143 "*Ah, shit, man . . .*" Ibid.

143 "'*This is kind of groovy, kind of funky . . .*'" Ibid.

143 "'If you are listening, and if you have any ear for music at all . . .'" Ibid.

144 "As Gaye neared the climax . . ." Ibid.

144 "By 'wave,' the crowd was *clapping* to the beat . . ." Ibid.

144 "The players didn't want to leave." Steve Nidetz, "Singletary, CBS Weigh Options on Pro Football Analysis," *Chicago Tribune*, February 22, 1993.

144 ". . . Mayo said she heard them . . ." Croatto, "The All-Star Anthem."

144 "'I just never heard anything so good . . .'" Ibid.

145 "'When you introduce someone to do the national anthem . . .'" Ibid.

145 "'In a way, Marvin is trying to copy something I did,'" Ibid.

145 "Legendary New York sports columnist . . ." Dick Young, "A Pro by Any Other Name," *Pensacola Journal*, February 26, 1983.

145 "Stan Hochman of the *Philadelphia Daily News* . . ." Stan Hochman, "NBA Stars Make Their Game Shine," *Philadelphia Daily News*, February 14, 1983.

145 "Gaye didn't care . . ." David Ritz, *Divided Soul: The Life of Marvin Gaye* (Cambridge, MA: Da Capo Press, 1991), page 313.

146 "On April 1, 1984, Gaye and his father, Marvin Gay Sr. . . ." Ibid., pages 332–33.

146 "After Larry O'Brien seethed . . ." Croatto, "The All-Star Anthem."

146 "As the flashy, funky version . . ." Ibid.

CHAPTER 6: FINDING A SOUNDTRACK, GAINING A CULTURE

147 "'Rap is likely . . .'" Dan Charnas, *The Big Payback: The History of the Business of Hip-Hop* (New York: American Library, 2010), page 58.

147 "Rock pretends it's still rebellious . . ." Bill Watterson, *Calvin & Hobbes*, March 11, 1992, https://www.gocomics.com/calvinandhobbes/1992/03/11.

147 "Music essayist Rob Sheffield suggested 1982 . . ." Rob Sheffield, *Talking to Girls about Duran Duran: One Young Man's Quest for True Love and a Cooler Haircut* (New York: Dutton, 2010), page 60.

148 "'I guess for a lot of the white mainstream public . . .'" Firehouse SoundLabs, "The Hip Hop Years Part 1," January 6, 2011, https://www.youtube.com/watch?v=Lh rSlOa2bsA&feature=youtu.be. (Note: as of March 2020, the video has been removed.)

149 "'The people at the top had all come from radio stations . . .'" Rob Tanenbaum and Craig Marks, *I Want My MTV: The Uncensored Story of the Music Video Revolution* (New York: Plume, 2012), page 139.

149 "The video for 'Billie Jean' wasn't approved for rotation until March 1983." Ibid., page 141.

149 "'It's a way of programming black music to white youth . . .'" Ibid., page 139.

149 "It was the most widely accepted music there is . . ." Stephen Gayle, "Solar Empire Strikes Gold," *Black Enterprise*, July 1982, page 40.

149 "As George Carlin famously illustrated in the premiere episode of *Saturday Night Live* . . ." *Saturday Night Live*, "Monologue George Carlin," October 24, 2013, https://www.youtube.com/watch?v=5ebyLkCaAL0.

150 "Rap . . . was teenage music." Tanenbaum and Marks, *I Want My MTV*, page 244.

150 "Rap stars, Simmons thought, were rebellious . . ." Russell Simmons with Nelson George, *Life and Def: Sex, Drugs, Money + God* (New York: Three Rivers Press, 2001), page 7.

151 "City kids heard the lyrics and found them relatable . . ." Chris Broussard, "Walk This Way," *ESPN the Magazine*, accessed November 7, 2019, https://www.espn .com/espn/magazine/archives/news/story?page=magazine-20050228-article25.

151 "When parents started to think rock and roll was okay for their kids, it became a 'museum piece.'" Simmons with George, *Life and Def*, page 8.

151 "'There is no future in rock and roll . . .'" Joe Hagan, *Sticky Fingers: The Life and Times of Jann Wenner and Rolling Stone Magazine* (New York: Alfred A. Knopf, 2017), page 386.

151 "'The territory we're in . . . the thing that no one else is touching . . .'" Ibid.

151 "If all Americans . . . in labor and management, who make steel or cars or shoes or textiles . . ." Marc Dolan, "How Ronald Reagan Changed Bruce Springsteen's Politics," *Politico*, June 4, 2014, https://www.politico.com/magazine/story/2014/06 /bruce-springsteen-ronald-reagan-107448_Page2.html.

NOTES

151 "Music journalist and essayist Nelson George . . ." Nelson George, *Hip-hop America* (New York: Penguin Books, 2005), pages 59–60.

152 ". . . The idea that only 500,000 African Americans . . ." Ibid.

152 "The first national rap tour . . ." Charnas, *The Big Payback*, page 78.

152 "Hip-hop, Afrika Bambaataa said, was derived from an abundance of musical sources . . ." Craig Werner, *A Change Is Gonna Come: Music, Race, & the Soul of America* (New York: Plume, 1998), page 239.

152 " 'Rock Box,' the first rap video to land on MTV in 1984 . . ." Charnas, *The Big Payback*, page 115.

152 "In 2017, Israel Horovitz was dismissed . . ." Jessica Bennett, "Nine Women Accuse Israel Horovitz, Playwright and Mentor of Sexual Misconduct," *New York Times*, November 30, 2017.

152 "The remake, by the way, charted higher than the original single . . ." Charnas, *The Big Payback*, page 162.

153 ". . . The first rap album to hit number one . . ." Ibid., 166.

153 "Some white listeners and black listeners . . ." Charnas, *The Big Payback*, 161; George, *Hip-hop America*, 66.

153 "The message was clear: rap was no longer just a fad . . ." Simmons with George, *Life and Def*, page 70.

153 "Because Run DMC was indifferent toward the rock audience . . ." Ibid.

153 "George thought the ethos of rock translated beautifully to rap . . ." George, *Hip-hop America*, page 68.

153 "It's a superficial and frequently hypocritical form of rebellion . . ." Ibid.

153 ". . . Def Jam's records were structured more like pop songs . . ." Charnas, *The Big Payback*, 202.

153 " '. . . refined like sugar . . .' " Jeff Chang, *Can't Stop, Won't Stop: A History of Hip-Hop Culture* (New York: Picador, 2005), pages 132–34.

154 "Russell Simmons knew rap had gone mainstream in the late 1980s . . ." Simmons with George, *Life and Def*, page 165.

154 "Created by a white production assistant . . ." Chang, *Can't Stop, Won't Stop*, pages 418–19.

154 "Millions of subscribers . . ." Vincente Fernandez, "A Decade of MTV: Music Video Channel Keeps Tempo as Audience Grows," *Baltimore Evening Sun*, July 15, 1991.

154 ". . . has sold more than 100 million copies worldwide since its release." Colin Stutz, "Michael Jackson's 'Thriller' Becomes First-Ever 30 Times Multi-Platinum Album: Exclusive," Billboard.com, December 16, 2015, https://www.billboard.com/articles/columns/pop/6812781/michael-jackson-thriller-30x-multi-platinum-album.

155 ". . . Topping the Nielsen ratings for . . ." *Encyclopedia Britannica* entry for *The Cosby Show*, accessed November 14, 2019, https://www.britannica.com/topic/The-Cosby-Show.

155 "Murphy's *Beverly Hills Cop* made $234 million domestically . . ." No author, "Domestic Box Office for 1984," accessed October 16, 2019, boxofficemojo.com/year/1984/.

155 "They watched the videos and thought . . ." Chang, *Can't Stop, Won't Stop*, page 419.

156 "This was how companies started to differentiate themselves . . ." John Leland, *Hip: The History* (New York: Harper Perennial, 2005), pages 301–2.

156 "The look that defined Run-DMC . . ." Broussard, "Walk This Way," ESPN.com.

158 "'Like anything that grows so powerful, rap lost its innocence long ago.'" Robert A. Ford, Jr., "Two Turntables & A Microphone," from Ashley Kahn, Holly George-Warren, Shawn Dahl, *Rolling Stone: The '70s* (New York: Little, Brown and Company, 1998), page 285.

CHAPTER 7: MAKING A SUPER BOWL

161 "The banquet's special guest in 1983 was 57-year-old comedian and *Mork & Mindy* alumnus . . ." Larry Bird and Earvin "Magic" Johnson, with Jackie MacMullan, *When the Game Was Ours* (New York: Houghton Mifflin Harcourt, 2009), pages 93–94. (Jonathan Winters was also Julius Erving's costar in the 1978 movie *The Fish That Saved Pittsburgh*, playing two equally unfunny roles.)

161 "When O'Brien started as commissioner . . ." LOB Memoir.

161 "By comparison, when Bill Cosby performed at the All-Star Game . . ." Howard Berk, *When My Boss Calls, Get the Name* (New York: iUniverse, Inc., 2008), page 104.

162 "The 1964 All-Star Game was considered the NBA's showcase event . . ." Leonard Koppett, *24 Seconds to Shoot: An Informal History of the National Basketball Association* (New York: The Macmillan Co., 1968), page 151.

162 "Then, hours before tip-off, the players . . ." Tommy Heinsohn with Joe Fitzgerald, *Give 'Em the Hook* (New York: Pocket Books, New York, 1988), page 251; Elgin Baylor and Alan Eisenstock, *Hang Time: My Life in Basketball* (Boston: Houghton Mifflin Harcourt, 2018), page 229.

162 "Finally, with assurances from commissioner . . ." Koppett, *24 Seconds to Shoot*, pages 152–53.

164 "CBS had aired a Slam Dunk Contest featuring NBA players . . ." Adam J. Criblez, *Tall Tales and Short Shorts: Dr. J, Pistol Pete, & the Birth of the Modern NBA* (Lanham, MD: Rowan & Littlefield, 2017), pages 190–91.

164 "The young executive was watching TV in his Manhattan apartment . . ." Pete Croatto, "Old Man Game," SLAM.com, February 15, 2017, https://www.slamonline.com/nba/legends-classic-all-star-weekend/.

165 "But as Pat Williams said, nobody knew who Pete Rozelle was . . ." Phil Jasner, "Stern Next NBA Commissioner," *Philadelphia Daily News*, November 16, 1983.

166 ". . . The new home of the team Stern and his father had walked a mile up Eighth Ave . . ." Associated Press, "Stern Gets NBA Job," *Argus-Leader* (Sioux City, SD), November 16, 1983.

166 "'The fans want to see the players, not the commissioner . . .'" Don Markus, "NBA Picks O'Brien Aide to Head League," *Record* (Hackensack, NJ), November 16, 1983.

167 "Okay, but it can't cost a nickel or embarrass the league . . ." Pete Croatto, "Jumpman, Jumpman, Jumpman," *SLAM*, February 9, 2016, https://www.slamonline.com/nba/larry-nance-dunk-contest-slam/.

167 "Stern and Russ Granik had his complete confidence . . ." LOB Memoir.

167 "Marketing and promoting the league, he said, were the new priorities." Bill Travers, "NBA Appoints Stern," *New York Daily News*, November 16, 1983.

167 "O'Brien's headline in his 1990 *New York Times* obituary . . ." Albin Krebs, "Lawrence F. O'Brien, Democrat, Dies at 73," *New York Times*, September 29, 1990.

168 "Early on, presidential candidate Jimmy Carter . . ." Berk, *When My Boss Calls, Get the Name*, pages 95–96.

168 "That June, O'Brien walked to the Boston Garden for Game 7 of the NBA Finals . . ." LOB Memoir.

169 "Tickets to the Slam Dunk Contest . . ." David Halberstam, *Playing for Keeps: Michael Jordan and the World He Made* (New York: Random House, 1999), page 125.

169 "The average cost of a movie ticket at the time was $3.35." Charles Stockdale, "Cost of a Movie Ticket the Year You Were Born," MSN Money, August 11, 2017, https://www.msn.com/en-us/money/personalfinance/cost-of-a-movie-ticket -the-year-you-were-born/ar-AApSYNq#image=AApT1ft%7C34.

169 "Every time a player went in the air, so did Welts's career prospects . . ." and other remembrances from the 1984 Slam Dunk Contest: Croatto, "Jumpman, Jumpman, Jumpman."

169 "'The movements, the defiance of gravity . . .'" Anthony Cotton, "That was Some Kind of Jam Session," *Sports Illustrated*, page 26, February 6, 1984.

170 "Welts's first discovery . . ." Croatto, "Old Man's Game," SLAM.com.

170 "'Your mind is telling you . . .'" 1avardac (NBA Entertainment), "1984 Old-Timers Game Highlights," August 19, 2017, https://www.youtube.com/watch ?v=nuEXo7gNk6k.

170 "Injured players getting wheeled off the court . . ." Croatto, "Old Man's Game."

170 "Stern later said the league couldn't get insurance to cover the game . . ." David Stern interview with Shawn Fury; transcript provided by Fury.

171 "According to McIntyre, All-Star Weekend was the first day . . ." Croatto, Ibid.

172 "In the Brown Palace lobby . . ." Croatto, Ibid.

172 "'It was a fascinating bit of history . . .'" Croatto, Ibid.

173 "'Yeah, Leon, I can't hold them . . .'" Larry Bird with Bob Ryan, *Drive: The Story of My Life* (New York: Bantam Books, 1990), page 222.

176 "'I'm the king of the three-point shooters . . .'" Wire reports, "This Spud's for You," *Statesman Journal* (Salem, OR), February 9, 1986.

177 "The arena was packed . . ." Ibid.

177 "'I hope that's a sign of the health of the NBA.'" Ibid.

177 "'We understood [that] in order to expand our game . . .'" David Gendelman, "A Brief History of the NBA All-Star Game's Slide into Competitive Farce," Vanity Fair.com, February 15, 2018. https://www.vanityfair.com/style/2018/02/a-brief -history-of-how-the-nba-all-star-games-slid-into-competitive-farce.

179 "Gatorade executive Bill Schmidt scouted . . ." Darren Rovell, *First in Thirst: How Gatorade Turned the Science of Sweat into a Cultural Phenomenon* (New York: AMACOM, 2006), pages 100–101.

179 "By 1989, 50 million homes in the United States . . ." Bill Carter, "With America Well Wired, Cable Industry Is Changing," *New York Times*, July 9, 1989.

179 "'There's more hype than there is game, and the sport can't possibly live up to

that.'" Larry Bird with Jackie MacMullan, *Bird Watching: On Playing and Watching the Game I Love* (New York: Warner Books, 1999), page 273.

186 "Russ Granik said when Stern became a businessman . . ." Brenton Welling, Jonathan Tapsini, Dan Cook, and bureau reports, "Basketball: Business Is Booming—The NBA Has More Going for It than Pat Ewing," *Business Week*, October 28, 1985, page 78.

191 "Larry Bird saw the NBA's evolution to an MTV league start at the All-Star Game . . ." Bird with MacMullan, *Bird Watching*, page 274.

191 ". . . J. A. Adande memorably dubbed the NBA's in-season break 'the Black Super Bowl' . . ." Bill Simmons, "Welcome to the Black Super Bowl," ESPN .com, accessed on April 25, 2019, http://www.espn.com/espn/page2/story ?page=simmons/060220.

194 "To Stern, the NBA's business plan was similar . . ." Walter LaFeber, *Michael Jordan and the New Global Capitalism* (New York: W.W. Norton & Co., 1999), page 64.

194 "But Stern had much in common with how Walt Disney, the boss . . ." Marty Sklar, *Dream It! Do IT: My Half-Century Creating Disney's Magic Kingdom* (New York: Disney Editions, 2013), page 47.

194 "He told Marty Sklar, one of his lieutenants . . ." Ibid., page 130.

195 "Deli owners had to distinguish their higher-priced goods . . ." Ted Merwin, *Pastrami on Rye: An Overstuffed History of the Jewish Deli* (New York: New York University Press, 2015), page 86.

198 "It was built, Wilson told *The Lansing State Journal*, with the average fan in mind . . ." John D. Gonzalez, "There's Gold in Them Thar' (Auburn) Hills," August 11, 1988.

199 "It was all about the amenities . . ." Ibid.

200 "'Not even injuries are as much a threat.'" Chuck Daly with Joe Falls, *Daly Life: 'Every Step a Struggle': Memoirs of a Champion Coach* (Grand Rapids, MI: Masters Press, 1990), 103–5.

200 "George Karl, the longtime coach, saw the team plane . . ." George Karl with Curt Sampson, *Furious George: My Forty Years Surviving NBA Divas, Clueless GMs, and Poor Shot Selection* (New York: HarperCollins, 2017), page 34.

200 "'The quality of my life went down . . .'" Pete Croatto, "Grateful, Not Dead," HOOP.com, April 11, 2016, https://hoop.nba.com/nba_hoop_featured/grate ful-not-dead/.

202 "It wasn't just the Palace, but its location . . ." Harvey Araton, *Crashing the Borders: How Basketball Won the World and Lost Its Soul at Home* (Free Press, New York: 2005), pages 36–37.

202 "Regular people—a mailman, an entrepreneur—could buy a season courtside ticket . . ." Ibid., pages 36–40.

202 "He first bought season tickets in 1985 . . . When Lee finally landed on his version of sacred ground . . ." Spike Lee with Ralph Wiley, *Best Seat in the House* (New York: Three Rivers Press, 1997), page 208.

203 "'The people that come to the arena now . . .'" Ibid., page 211.

203 "The Garden, Klein said, now felt like a fashion show . . . Araton, *Crashing the Borders*, page 39.

203 "A true fan like Lee, who paid $2,000 per game . . ." Ibid., page 179.

CHAPTER 8: THE ACCIDENTAL GOD

206 "They were so prized . . ." Bobbito Garcia, *Where'd You Get Those? New York City's Sneaker Culture, 1960–1987* (New York: Testify Books, 2003), page 86. (Release dates for the Adidas Jabbar and Clydes were confirmed via this indispensable guide.)

206 "'The idea of the basketball player as a style icon . . .'" Jackie MacMullan, Rafe Bartholomew, and Dan Klores, *Basketball: A Love Story* (New York: Crown Archetype, 2018), page 254.

207 "Frazier stood out because of his on-court style . . ." Ibid., page 250.

207 "'Cool I think is reactions, reflexes, and attitude . . .'" Walt Frazier and Ira Berkow, *Rockin' Steady: A Guide to Basketball & Cool* (Englewood Cliffs, NJ: Prentice Hall, Inc., 1974), page 20. (The book is worth a gander for the beyond-groovy artwork and photographs.)

207 "He wore—amid nonstop mockery—wide-brimmed, velour fedoras . . ." Ibid., page 14.

207 "Frazier embraced 'sartorial splendor' . . ." MacMullan, Bartholomew, and Klores, *Basketball: A Love Story*, page 254.

207 ". . . a bedroom dominated with silk, shag . . ." Frazier and Berkow, *Rockin' Steady*, page 140.

208 "'We couldn't make enough.'" Phil Knight, *Shoe Dog* (New York: Scribner, 2016), page 284.

208 "'Casual dress became desired and its accessibility was unprecedented . . .'" Garcia, *Where'd You Get Those?*, page 9.

208 Account of Run-DMC's love of Adidas, cultural impact, and its deal with the company from Nicholas Smith, *Kicks: The Great American Story of Sneakers* (New York: Crown, 2018), pages 153–55.

208 "Run-DMC famously wore Superstars . . ." Garcia, *Where'd You Get Those?* page 64.

210 "Converse's endorsements in the 1960s ignored black ballplayers . . ." Oscar Robertson, *The Big O: My Life, My Times, My Game* (New York: Rodale, 2003), page 215.

213 "His agent figured Haywood wouldn't get enough up front . . ." Spencer Haywood with Scott Ostler, *Spencer Haywood: The Rise, the Fall, the Recovery* (New York: Amistad Press, 1992), page 273.

213 "By 1984, Nike couldn't sustain the endorsement model . . ." The account of Nike's bloated corporate structure and its plan to cut back: J. B. Strasser and Laurie Becklund, *Swoosh: The Unauthorized Story of Nike and the Men Who Played There* (New York: Harcourt Brace Jovanovich, 1991), pages 534–35, page 538.

214 "How Jordan landed at Nike's tends to resemble *Rashomon* in sneakers." Josh Peter, "Error Jordan: Key Figures Still Argue over Who's Responsible for Jordan Deal," *USA Today*, September 13, 2015.

214 "Worthy, a client of David Falk's . . ." Strasser and Becklund, *Swoosh*, page 539.

215 "Once Nike deemed Jordan its guy . . ." Ibid., pages 538–39.

217 "Falk and Strasser both wanted a signature shoe . . ." Ibid., page 534.

217 ". . . The idea of a shoe deal had changed little since the peak of the Pro Club . . ."

David Halberstam, *Playing for Keeps: Michael Jordan and the World He Made* (New York: Random House, 1999), page 184.

218 "Jordan's mother, Deloris, set her son on a path of incalculable influence . . ." Strasser and Becklund, *Swoosh*, page 545.

218 "Nike put on a show . . ." "I can't wear that shoe . . ." "Strasser, a bearded, barrel-bellied . . ." Ibid., pages 544–45.

219 "Nike kept courting . . ." Halberstam, *Playing for Keeps*, page 144.

219 "Jordan sat expressionless . . ." and . . . "I had my business face on," Ibid., page 145.

219 "Jordan didn't drop it . . ." Strasser and Becklund, *Swoosh*, page 547.

221 "The NBA demanded that Jordan stop wearing the shoes . . ." Ibid., page 568.

221 "It started with a simple commercial . . ." BLAZEHOOPS (Chiat/Day), "Air Jordan 1 Commercial: Banned! (1985)," October 3, 2010, https://www.youtube.com/watch?v=f5QbV-wnhtY.

222 " 'Strasser showed David Stern the commercial . . .' " and " 'My kid . . . thinks I'm an asshole . . .' " Strasser and Becklund, *Swoosh*, page 565.

222 "The first Air Jordans . . . The frenzy rivaled Cabbage Patch Kids." Brendan Dunne, "Proof That Air Jordans Have Been Selling Out for 30 Years," Sole Collector, June 17, 2015, https://solecollector.com/news/2015/06/air-jordans-selling-out-1985.

222 "The Air Jordan line made $130 million its first year . . ." Russ Bengtson, "Birth of an Original: The Air Jordan 1," Complex.com, June 21, 2013, https://www.complex.com/sneakers/2013/01/birth-of-an-original-the-air-jordan-1.

223 ". . . 'looked garbage' . . ." Garcia, *Where'd You Get Those?*, page 13.

224 "*Esquire*'s Mark Jacobson wrote that Erving was once the only man . . ." Mark Jacobson, "The Passion of Doctor J," *Esquire*, February 1985. Anthologized in Mark Jacobson, *Teenage Hipster in the Modern Word* (New York: Black Cat, 2005).

224 "Jordan's emergence allowed Erving to step down . . ." Jim Naughton, *Taking to the Air: The Rise of Michael Jordan* (New York: Warner Books, 1992), page 140.

225 ". . . achieved *transcendental irrelevance* . . ." Ibid., page 206.

225 "Before his first retirement in 1993 . . ." Stephen Fox, *Big Leagues: Professional Baseball, Football, and Basketball in National Memory* (New York: William Morrow and Co., Inc., 1994), page 433.

225 "In a rare moment of candor . . ." David Breskin, "Michael Jordan, In His Own Orbit," *GQ*, March 1989, http://davidbreskin.com/magazines/2-profiles/michael-jordan/.

228 ". . . An endorser had to offer 'elements of style' . . ." Donald Katz, *Just Do It: The Nike Spirit in the Corporate World* (Holbrook, Mass.: Abrams Media Corporation, 1994), page 221.

228 Description of the Magic vs. Bird commercial: Internet Lurker, "Converse Commercial with Larry Bird and Magic Johnson," February 10, 2008, https://www.youtube.com/watch?v=tJEa2c_939o.

228 "The Weapon sold well . . ." Larry Bird and Earvin "Magic" Johnson, with Jackie MacMullan, *When the Game Was Ours* (New York: Houghton Mifflin Harcourt, 2009), page 188. (I have a reissue pair of Magic Weapons. How Magic played in these buttery plinths is a puzzlement.)

228 ". . . 'weren't enemies, just two very tough guys who hated to lose.'" Ibid.

229 Description of the rapping Converse commercial: Nice Kicks (Quinn and Johnson), "Converse Weapon Commercial," February 15, 2010, https://www.youtube.com/watch?v=BM4r369jnnU.

229 "The issue with the Weapon rap ad . . ." Smith, *Kicks*, page 182.

230 "Converse, Magic Johnson felt, was still stuck in the 1960s and 1970s . . ." *Boston Globe*, "Magic Johnson to Leave Converse; Basketball Star Dissatisfied with Shoe Pact," *Baltimore Sun*, July 29, 1992.

231 "The swoosh-less Air Jordan II . . ." Ben Osborne (ed.), *Slam Kicks: Basketball Sneakers That Changed the Game* (New York: Universe Publishing, 2013), page 101.

231 ". . . had the elephant print pattern and the Jumpman logo . . ." Ibid., page 104.

232 "The Air Jordan III hit people on a different level . . ." Rodrigo Corral, Alex French, and Howie Kahn, *Sneakers* (New York: Razorbill/Penguin Random House, 2017), pages 49 and 52.

234 "'We're selling colors . . .'" James S. Granelli, "James H. Warshaw: Merchandising's Big Leaguers: Sports Specialties' Caps Have Made Fans Worldwide," *Los Angeles Times*, September 17, 1990.

235 "Rob Strasser and Peter Moore . . . wanted Jordan . . ." Mark Vancil (ed.), *Driven from Within* (New York: Atria Books, 2005), pages 59–60.

235 "Jordan was late because he had been out golfing with Strasser and Moore," Ibid., page 63.

239 "'You've a right to wonder . . .'" Vincent Canby, "Film: Mamet Adaptation 'About Last Night,'" *New York Times*, July 1, 1986.

240 My description of the trailer for *She's Gotta Have It*: YouTube Movies (Spike Lee), "She's Gotta Have It—Trailer," April 10, 2014, https://www.youtube.com/watch?v=Pd9oTGr_1DA.

241 "Davenport finally convinced the auteur he wasn't a film school classmate pulling an awful prank . . ." Halberstam, *Playing for Keeps*, page 181.

241 "Nike only gave Lee a Jordan poster . . ." Ibid., 179.

241 "DJ Clark Kent believed Lee created sneaker culture . . ." Corral, French, Kahn, *Sneakers*, page 64.

242 The Jordans scene from *Do the Right Thing*. Movieclips (Spike Lee), "Do the Right Thing (4/10) Movie CLIP—Your Jordans are F***ed Up!" July 27, 2011, https://www.youtube.com/watch?v=jc6_XgtOQgI.

242 "At that point, Kent said, the Jordans became a character." Corral, French, Kahn, *Sneakers*, page 64.

243 "'He was immediately friendly . . .'" Lee with Wiley, *Best Seat in the House*, page 136.

244 "Hip-hop, according to Russell Simmons, is an attitude . . ." Russell Simmons with Nelson George, *Life and Def: Sex, Drugs, Money + God* (New York: Three Rivers Press, 2001), page 5.

245 "'It wasn't about selling something, but a series of moments . . .'" Corral, French, Kahn, *Sneakers*, page 179.

245 "'Everything came together and that was what made it so powerful . . .'" Ibid.

CHAPTER 9: LET'S GO TO THE VIDEOTAPE!

251 The quote from *Boogie Nights*: Dylan R. (Paul Thomas Anderson), "*Boogie Nights*: Jack Horner vs. Floyd Gondolli," September 6, 2007, https://www.youtube.com /watch?v=cH0kOWNtLFo. (I probably could have written this from memory. Lock and load, Jack!)

255 "... 'in the early 1970s. ... They all got tired from Vietnam and Nixon and the Kennedys ...'" Joe Queenan, *Balsamic Dreams: A Short but Self-Important History of the Baby Boomer Generation* (New York: Picador USA, 2001), page 72.

255 "Therefore, a talented, corporate cipher like O. J. Simpson ..." Howard Bryant, *The Heritage: Black Athletes, A Divided America, and the Politics of Patriotism* (Boston: Beacon Press, 2018), page 65.

255 "Every time Russell laced up his sneakers ..." Jackie MacMullan, Rafe Bartholomew, and Dan Klores, *Basketball: A Love Story* (New York: Crown Archetype, 2018), page 59.

255 "Russell returned to his Reading, Massachusetts, home one night ..." Bryant, *The Heritage*, page 44.

256 "Bryant called this effect 'greenwashing.'" Ibid., page 85.

256 "Thomas held a press conference in Detroit to apologize ..." Bob Sakamoto, "Apology by 'Hurt' Thomas Satisfies Bird," *Chicago Tribune*, June 4, 1987.

256 "'That's the bad thing ...'" Ibid.

257 "Besides, it was an image that Barkley honed ..." Filip Bondy, *Tip-Off: How the 1984 NBA Draft Changed Basketball Forever* (Boston: Da Capo Press, 2007), page 231.

258 "All those details paved the way for Michael Jordan's arrival ..." Bryant, *The Heritage*, page 52.

259 "Earl Monroe placed a lot of the blame on ESPN ..." Earl Monroe with Quincy Trope, *Earl the Pearl: My Story* (New York: Rodale, 2013), page 368.

259 "'I'm not so flashy, not so boisterous ..." NBA.com staff, "Legends Profile: Alex English," NBA History, accessed on April 19, 2019, https://www.nba.com/his tory/legends/profiles/alex-english.

260 "In September 1997, Albert pled guilty ..." Brian Lowry and Miles Corwin, "Marv Albert Pleads Guilty to Sex Case, Is Fired by NBC," *Los Angeles Times*, September 26, 1997.

260 Description of *Michael Jordan's Playground*: Santiago73 (NBA Entertainment), "*Michael Jordan's Playground*," April 6, 2015, https://www.youtube.com/watch?v= _k9Jw7rDWwU.

263 Description of *Superstars*: Santiago73 (NBA Entertainment), "NBA Superstars," September 24, 2017, https://www.youtube.com/watch?v=UwjBd9qpK8Q.

263 "Barkley had commodified rebellion ..." Nelson George, *Hip-hop America* (New York: Penguin Books, 2005), page 148.

263 The 1990 All-Star Game introductions: Tyler Phelps (NBA/NBA Entertainment), "NBA All-Star Introduction (1990), February 12, 2015, https://www.youtube .com/watch?v=Vl7tgHDV_r8&t=333s.

263 The 1989 All-Star rap-infused introductions: Marcusnr1 (NBA/NBA Entertain-

ment), "NBA All-Star Rap 1989," August 28, 2008, https://www.youtube.com /watch?v=r-qH_HMj0FQ&t=145s.

266 " 'If we're going to be the bad boys . . .' " Vintage NBA Games (NBA Entertainment), "1987–1988 Detroit Pistons Bad Boys NBA Championship Documentary," February 9, 2019, https://www.youtube.com/watch?v=rIHXgU5YpyI. (With the bounty of retro NBA footage on YouTube, it's a small miracle that I have written anything since 2006.)

267 "It wasn't just the kids who got hooked on the human highlight reels . . ." Jim Patton, *Il Basket d'Italia: A Season in Italy with Great Food, Good Friends, and Some Very Tall Americans* (New York: Simon & Schuster, 1994), pages 116–17.

267 " 'Bill tried to hurt you . . .' " Sick Beats (Grantland/ESPN), "Larry Bird Explains Why He Dislikes Bill Laimbeer," May 18, 2019, https://www.youtube.com /watch?v=NVAwV880RMo.

267 "In the 1988 playoffs, Mahorn kept stepping on the foot . . ." Steve Bulpett, "Mahorn Recalls Rivalry," *Boston Herald*, May 31, 2018.

270 "Bryant's young son can't stay up late to watch the NBA games." Roland Lazenby, *Showboat: The Life of Kobe Bryant* (New York: Little, Brown and Co., 2016), page 87.

271 "The young man who learned English by watching *The Flintstones* . . ." Sam Smith, "All in All, A Memorable Season," *Chicago Tribune*, April 21, 1992.

CHAPTER 10: IMPORTS AND EXPORTS

274 "Bill Russell embarked on a State Department-sponsored . . ." Bill Russell and Taylor Branch, *Second Wind: The Memoirs of an Opinionated Man* (New York: Random House, 1979), pages 90–91.

274 "Russell, along with Oscar Robertson . . ." Oscar Robertson, *The Big O: My Life, My Times, My Game* (New York: Rodale, 2003), page 170.

275 ". . . whose citizens had been introduced to the game via U.S. missionaries in the late 19th century." hamslam (NBA.com), "Washington Bullets Visit China in 1979," October 17, 2007, https://www.youtube.com/watch?time_continue=12&v= _b00bS0iTXM&feature=emb_logo.

275 " 'We had just normalized relations with China . . .' " J. Freedom du Lac, "As Wizards Prepare to Visit China, Team Remembers its Historical 1979 Visit," *Washington Post*, September 13, 2009.

278 " 'I'm running the team, it all depends on me . . .' " Jim Patton, *Il Basket d'Italia: A Season in Italy with Great Food, Good friends, and Some Very Tall Americans* (New York: Simon & Schuster, 1994), page 115.

280 "As of 2018, NBA games and programming were available . . ." Stat provided by the NBA.

281 "The pick was a low-risk proposition . . ." Patton, *Il Basket d'Italia*, pages 45–46.

281 " 'He was . . . a great rebounder, a great defensive player . . .' " Ibid.

282 "The trip came about because Hawks owner Ted Turner had a good relationship with Soviet officials . . ." Jeremy Woo, "Many Shoot, Few Make: Inside the NBA's First Journey to Russia," SI.com, July 25, 2017, https://www.si.com /nba/2017/07/25/nba-russia-soviet-union-atlanta-hawks-1988-trip.

283 "The three games were held in the middle of the summer . . ." Ibid.

283 "Veteran forward Kevin Willis was ordered by Turner to go . . ." Ibid.

284 "By the third game, Jack McCallum . . ." Ibid.

285 "'He was more physical than any guard in the league . . .'" Andrew Sharp, "Pandora's Box," *Sports Illustrated,* January 15, 2018, pages 63 and 68.

285 "At the start of the 2019–20 season, the NBA had 108 players from 38 countries or foreign territories." Official NBA release, October 22, 2019, https://www.nba.com/article/2019/10/22/nba-rosters-feature-108-international-players-2019-20.

285 "Petrovic reached the cusp of stardom . . ." Todd Spehr, "The Tragic Death of Drazen Petrovic," SI.com, March 29, 2015, https://www.si.com/nba/2015/03/29/drazen-petrovic-nets-book-excerpt-car-accident-death.

286 "Like Volkov . . ." Andrew Sharp, "Coming to America," SI.com, accessed June 3, 2019, https://www.si.com/longform/2018/nba-international-oral-history/index.html.

288 "Dan Peterson hosted NBA coaches in Italy . . ." Ben Cohen, "The Coach Who Changed the NBA from Italy," *Wall Street Journal,* November 14, 2018.

288 ". . . 'normal in Europe, especially in Yugoslavia.'" Jordan Brenner, "The Two Steps That Changed the NBA," *ESPN the Magazine,* November 2018, page 16.

CHAPTER 11: READY FOR PRIME TIME

289 Details of the Pistons' championship celebration: Santiago73 (NBA Entertainment), "1989–90 Detroit Pistons: *Pure Pistons,*" June 7, 2016, https://www.youtube.com/watch?v=5Ge-pcsVqTU.

290 "In March 1981, Sauer landed the rights . . ." Gene Quinn, "NBC Ran Afoul of NCAA," *Philadelphia Daily News,* March 6, 1981.

293 "ABC, which saw past 'Roone's Revenge' . . ." Roone Arledge, *Roone: A Memoir* (New York: HarperCollins, 2003), page 312.

294 "The price was right . . ." Ibid., page 315.

294 "'If any deal was a sure thing . . . this was it.'" Ibid.

294 "It was not keen on the escalating rights fees . . ." Jim Spence with Dave Diles, *Up Close and Personal: The Inside Story of Network Television Sports* (New York City: Antheum Publishers, 1988), page 196.

294 "The increased money, Cap Cities thought . . ." Ibid.

294 "Just before Christmas 1985, Arledge brought the deal to his boss . . ." Arledge, *Roone,* page 315.

294 "He asked Stern, whom he respected, for more time . . ." Spence with Diles, *Up Close and Personal,* pages 196 to 197.

295 "'With the acquisition of baseball . . .'" Jim Sarni, "CBS Pays $1.1 Billion for Exclusive Baseball," *South Florida Sun-Sentinel,* December 15, 1988.

295 "The four-year deal was borderline comical . . ." Ibid.

297 "The NBA was all grown up . . ." Stephen Fox, *Big Leagues: Professional Baseball, Football, and Basketball in National Memory* (New York: William Morrow & Co., 1994), page 433.

NOTES

CHAPTER 12: IT'S MY GAME NOW

304 " 'We take a lot of research detail . . .' " Jack McCallum, *Dream Team: How Michael, Magic, Larry, Charles, and the Greatest Team of All Time Conquered the World and Changed the Game of Basketball Forever* (New York: Ballantine Books, 2012), page 313.

306 " 'This is my game now.' " Ibid., page 258.

306 "Game 6 of the 1998 Finals . . ." "NBC Sports History," https://www.nbcsports .com/our-history#decade_8, accessed on June 14, 2019.

306 "He is so removed from the realities of everyday life . . ." Bill Simmons, "President Obama and Bill Simmons: The *GQ* Interview," *GQ*, December 2015, https:// www.gq.com/story/president-obama-bill-simmons-interview-gq-men-of-the -year.

307 "A multiple-level Jordan Brand store . . ." Brendan Dunne, "Get a Look Inside the Air Jordan Store in Chicago," Sole Collector, October 24, 2015, https://solecollector .com/news/2015/10/air-jordan-store-32-south-state-chicago.

308 "Instead, NBC got a $400 million base to launch . . ." Ben Grossman, " 'Everybody Knows Jimmy'," *Broadcast & Cable*, November 30, 2017, https://www.broadcast ingcable.com/news/jim-burnette-everyone-knows-jimmy-77388.

310 "Jerry Seinfeld riffed on the head fake . . ." TheClassicSports (NBC), "May 1992—*Seinfeld* NBA-themed Promo," April 17, 2014, https://www.youtube.com /watch?v=Cn-nD8u58v0.

310 ". . . Paul Buchman of *Mad About You* . . ." Details from the *Mad About You* NBA spot comes from Gil Kerr's script.

310 ". . . the ladies of *Friends* lamented the demise . . ." Jean-Sebastien Blondel (NBA/ NBC), "I Love This Game—Rachel, Monica and Phoebe from *F.R.I.E.N.D.S.*," January 17, 2010, https://www.youtube.com/watch?v=5xJt-F-uu_0.

PHOTO CREDITS

INDEX

INDEX

INDEX

INDEX

INDEX

INDEX

ABOUT THE AUTHOR

Pete Croatto's reporting, interviews, and essays have appeared in the *New York Times, Victory Journal, Grantland, VICE Sports, The A.V. Club*, RollingStone.com, *SLAM, Columbia Journalism Review*, and many other publications. This is his first book. He lives outside Ithaca, New York, with his wife and daughter. You can follow him on Twitter, @PeteCroatto.